THE PRICE SYSTEM AND RESOURCE ALLOCATION

The Price System and Resource Allocation

RICHARD H. LEFTWICH

OKLAHOMA STATE UNIVERSITY

Third Edition

HOLT, RINEHART AND WINSTON
NEW YORK   CHICAGO   SAN FRANCISCO   TORONTO   LONDON

July, 1966

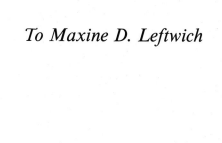

To Maxine D. Leftwich

Preface to the Third Edition

THE ADDITION OF A CHAPTER introducing linear programming techniques is the most important differentiating feature of this edition. These have become so much a part of the accepted tools and techniques of price theory that it seems desirable to introduce them at a rather early stage in the economics curriculum. I am indebted to Professors James A. Martin and Frank Steindl of Oklahoma State University, to Professor Thomas H. Naylor of Duke University, and especially to Professor Helen Raffel of the University of Pennsylvania for their incisive critiques of the drafts of the linear programming chapter. However they cannot be held responsible for its inadequacies.

The rest of the book has been subjected to a "clean up" job. The material covered is the same as before, but I hope the innumerable small changes in wording, organization, and the like, will make the book a little more helpful to neophytes in price theory.

R.H.L.

Stillwater, Oklahoma
November 1965

Preface to the First Edition

THIS BOOK IS DESIGNED to accomplish a twofold purpose. Primarily it is intended as an undergraduate price theory textbook. In this respect, instructors may find it useful for the price theory section of some basic principles courses, as well as for the usual price theory courses at the junior-senior level. Secondarily, I hope that it will provide a satisfactory review of the major principles of price theory and resource allocation for graduate students in economics.

The frame of reference for the book is a stable free enterprise economy. The operation of the price system in guiding and directing resources toward more efficient use can be seen with greater clarity in a stable economy than in one characterized by economic fluctuations. Also a clear understanding of the price theory principles evolving from a stable economy logically precedes the study of price theory principles in a dynamic economy.

Coverage of the book is selective rather than exhaustive. It concentrates on the fundamental principles of price theory. Refinements, ramifications, and highly sophisticated topics are omitted in the belief that these properly belong in advanced courses in price theory. No claim is made for originality. The analysis developed is the property of economists in general. The aim has been for clarity of exposition at a level that upper-division undergraduates can be reasonably expected to attain.

Emphasis is placed on economic efficiency throughout because the concept of economy is in a large measure a concept of efficiency. In this respect more than usual attention is focused on resource pricing, employment, and allocation. Our central problem is that of securing the highest possible level of want satisfaction — both present and future — with available resources and techniques.

With regard to the method of exposition, liberal use is made of graphic analysis. No knowledge of mathematics beyond algebra and plane geometry is required; however, some knowledge of more advanced

ix

mathematics will prove helpful. The basic mathematical relations necessary for understanding price theory are introduced as they are needed to progress through the book. The selected readings at the end of each chapter are limited in number. They are selected to provide students with the best classic and contemporary treatments of particular topics.

I owe a debt of gratitude to many who have contributed to the preparation of the manuscript. Especial thanks are due Professor Rudolph W. Trenton of Oklahoma State University and Professor Howard R. Bowen of Williams College, both of whom have read the entire manuscript through its several drafts and have continuously offered encouragement, as well as innumerable helpful suggestions. Thanks are due also to Professor Elliot Zupnick of the College of the City of New York, who reviewed the entire manuscript at a late stage and made many valuable criticisms. Large parts of the manuscript were read by Professors Joseph J. Klos and Eugene L. Swearingen of Oklahoma State University, and I profited materially from their suggestions. I did not always heed the good advice offered; consequently I must take full responsibility for the shortcomings of the book. The typing burden was borne patiently and cheerfully by Mrs. Claudette Voyles with some assistance from Mr. Kenton Ross.

R.H.L.

Stillwater, Oklahoma
April 14, 1955

Contents

THE PRICE SYSTEM AND
RESOURCE ALLOCATION

Introduction | 1

THE PRINCIPLES OF PRICE theory and resource allocation as they are developed in this book represent a part of the economics of a free enterprise system. A free enterprise economy is characterized by a large measure of individual freedom over a wide range of economic choices. Within a broad framework of legal and social sanctions, consumers are free to choose among a variety of commodity offerings; enterprisers and potential enterprisers, singly and in groups, are free to enter into or exit from the businesses of their choice; and resource owners are free to place their resources in employment wherever employment can be found. In the market places of the economy, exchanges will occur voluntarily whenever and wherever they will be of mutual benefit to the parties concerned. Both profits and losses will occur as enterprisers correctly anticipate consumer desires or fail to read correctly the signs of the economic zodiac.

The price system plays a key role in guiding and organizing economic activity and as such is of vital concern to us all. We are the participating members of a substantially free enterprise economy. We consume its milk and honey, its automobiles, and its entertainment. We own and operate its farms, its filling stations, its factories, and its gold mines. We own and command its capital and its labor. We need to know how the price system works.

In this chapter we shall survey the nature of economic activity and the place of price theory in the scheme of economic thinking. Chapters 2 and 3 will set the stage for the detailed exposition of price theory which begins with Chapter 4.

ECONOMIC ACTIVITY

The boundaries marking off economics from other disciplines or fields of knowledge are hard to draw; however, general agreement exists

＊ incapable of being satisfied or appeased

with regard to its main contents. Economics is concerned with man's well-being. It encompasses the social relationships or social organization involved in allocating scarce resources among alternative human wants and in using those resources toward the end of satisfying wants as fully as possible. The key elements of economic activity are (1) human wants, (2) resources, and (3) techniques of production. These will be discussed in turn.

Human Wants

Human wants are the mainsprings of economic activity. They are the ends toward which economic activity is directed. They constitute the driving force or the motivating power of the economy. Wants have two characteristics — they are varied, and in the aggregate over time they are insatiable.＊Insatiability does not necessarily imply that an individual's desire for particular commodities is unlimited. The quantities of particular goods consumed per week which contribute to one's well-being conceivably may be finite. It is with respect to commodities in the aggregate that wants are unlimited — and this occurs partly because of the wide variety of wants that individuals can conjure up.

ORIGINS OF WANTS • The insatiability of wants in the aggregate will become more evident if we consider some of the ways in which wants arise. First of all, wants arise for what the human organism must have in order to continue functioning. The desire for food is the most obvious case in point. In intemperate climates two other desires usually arise from necessity. These are the desire for shelter and the desire for clothing. One or the other or both of these must be fulfilled in some degree if the human organism is to survive the rigors of low temperatures or the extreme heat of the tropics.

Wants arise, too, from the culture within which we live, for every society dictates certain requisites for "the good life" — certain standards of housing and food consumption, patronization of the arts, and possession and consumption of such items as automobiles, charcoal broilers, television sets, and high-fidelity and stereo record players. Our status in society is thought to depend to a considerable extent upon our levels of consumption. Consequently many wants are generated in the process of attempting to improve one's status.

The satisfying of our biological and cultural needs requires a wide variety of goods. Individual tastes vary. Some people like roast beef, some like ham, and some like mutton. Over time the same individual wants to satisfy his hunger with different foods. Tastes in clothing differ and different social occasions call for different modes of dress, Age differences, climatic differences, social differences, educational differences, and a host of other factors give rise to variety in the goods desired by society in general.

Finally, wants are generated by the activity necessary to satisfy other wants, or want-satisfying activity may be said to create new wants. No better illustration of new wants arising from activity directed toward satisfying an old want can be found than that of a student pursuing a university education. The process of attending a university opens entirely new areas of potential desires which heretofore he had not known existed — intellectual desires, cultural desires, and many more. The generation of new wants in the process of endeavoring to satisfy old wants plays an important role in the vast expansibility of human desires.

The foregoing sources from which wants arise do not represent an exhaustive classification. Wants may arise from other sources. However, those listed will serve the purpose of illustrating the possibility of their infinite expansion in scope over time and the impossibility of an economy's ever saturating all wants of all people.

WANT SATISFACTION AND LEVELS OF LIVING • The level of want satisfaction achieved in a given economic society is hard to measure. Ordinarily it is expressed in terms of per capita income — sometimes gross and sometimes net, depending upon the availability of data. However there may be a great dispersion around the average and the average income figure may be misleading. Nevertheless, per capita income appears to be one of the most acceptable measures of the performance of an economy available.

Sometimes people judge the performance of an economy on the basis of whether per capita incomes are at a "satisfactory" level. The implication is that if the level is below "satisfactory" something ought to be done about it — that everyone is entitled to a "satisfactory" level of living. Judgments of these kinds are not very valuable from the point of view of economic analysis.

In the first place, the level of living "satisfactory" to a society is entirely relative to the historical time under consideration. A level of living with which most people in the United States would have been quite happy fifty years ago would not be satisfactory today. What is satisfactory today will not be satisfactory fifty years hence. As the economy's capacity to produce increases, the concept of what constitutes a "satisfactory" living level shifts upward. The insatiability of human wants, together with secular increases in productive capacity, leads to an ever-changing concept of what constitutes a "satisfactory" living level.

Second, the concept of what constitutes a "satisfactory" living level varies among different geographic areas. A level of living high enough to make most Asiastics content for the present will not be high enough for most Europeans or Americans. People become accustomed to certain living levels. A "satisfactory" living level for them then becomes one just a little higher than what they currently have.

From the standpoint of efficient operation the performance of an economy should not be judged on the basis of whether or not it provides a "satisfactory" level of living. Rather, it should be judged on the basis of whether or not it provides the highest level of living that its resources and techniques will permit, making due allowance for some part of current production to be set aside to augment future productive capacity. One can ask no more of the economy. It should not be expected to provide much less. To the extent that some part of current production is used to augment future productive capacity, the level of living which the economy can provide will grow continuously.

Resources

The level of want satisfaction which an economy can achieve is limited partly by the quantities and qualities of its known resources. Resources are the means available for producing goods which in turn are used to satisfy wants. Hundreds of different kinds of resources exist in the economy. Among these are labor of all kinds, raw materials of all kinds, land, machinery, buildings, semifinished materials, fuel, power, transportation, and the like.

CLASSIFICATION OF RESOURCES • Resources can be classified conveniently into two categories: (1) labor or human resources, and (2) capital or nonhuman resources. Labor resources consist of labor power or the capacity for human effort — both of mind and of muscle — used in producing goods. The term *capital* can be misleading since it is used in several different ways not only by noneconomists but by economists as well. We shall use the term to include all nonhuman resources that can contribute toward placing goods in the hands of the ultimate consumer. Specific examples are buildings, machinery, land, available mineral resources, raw materials, semifinished materials, business inventories, and any other nonhuman tangible items used in the productive process.[1]

---

[1] In a philosophic sense inventories of goods in the hands of ultimate consumers constitute capital, also, since it is the satisfaction yielded by goods rather than the goods themselves which consumers desire. Thus such goods are still means of satisfying ultimate ends or desires of consumers; i.e., they have yet to produce the want satisfaction they are supposed to produce. However, we shall not cut it this fine. Goods in the hands of the ultimate consumer will be called consumer goods rather than capital — and this will avoid some complexities.

We need particularly to guard against confusing capital and money. Money is not capital as we use the term in this book. Money as such produces nothing. It is primarily a medium of exchange — a technique facilitating exchange of goods and services and resources. This implies that the values of capital items, labor, and consumer goods and services are measured in terms of the monetary unit.

The significance of the foregoing classification of resources should not be overestimated. It is more descriptive than analytical. Within each category there are many different kinds of resources, and the differences between two kinds falling within the same classification may be more significant analytically than the differences between two kinds with one in each of the separate classifications. Consider, for example, a human ditch digger and an accountant. Both fall under the descriptive classification of labor. However, from an analytical point of view, the human ditch digger is more closely related to a mechanical ditch digger, which would fall under the descriptive classification of capital, than he is to the accountant.

CHARACTERISTICS OF RESOURCES • Resources have three essential characteristics. First, most resources are limited in quantity. Second, they are versatile. Third, they can be combined in varying proportions to produce a given commodity. These will be considered in turn.

Most resources are scarce in the sense that they are limited in quantity relative to desires for the products which they can produce. These are called economic resources. Some resources, such as the air used in an internal-combustion engine, are so abundant that they can be had for the taking. These are called free resources since they command no price. Were all resources free there would be no limitation on the extent to which wants could be satisfied, and hence no economic problem. Levels of living could soar to infinite heights. Free resources are of no significance for economic analysis and will be disregarded. We are interested in economic resources. The scarcity of economic resources makes necessary the picking and choosing of which wants are to be satisfied and in what degree. Here is the economic problem in a nutshell.

The population of an economy sets an upper limit on the quantities of labor resources available. Various factors, such as education, custom, general state of health, and age distribution, determine the actual proportion of the population which can be considered the labor force. Over a short period of time the total labor force cannot be expanded indefinitely, but over a longer period of time it may be more variable as population has time to change and as changes occur in the factors determining the actual labor force.

Generally, the total capital equipment of the economy is expanding over time, but this expansion occurs slowly. The amount that an economy can add to its total stock of capital equipment in a year's time without seriously restricting current consumption is a fairly small proportion of its existing capital. Therefore, over a short period of time, the quantity of capital available to produce goods is limited.

(2) The versatility of resources refers to their capacity to be put to different uses. In general, any given kind of resource can be used in the production of a wide variety of goods. Common labor can be used in the production of almost every conceivable good. The more highly skilled or specialized a resource becomes, however, the more limited are its uses. There are fewer alternative jobs for skilled machinists than for common laborers. There are still fewer alternative jobs for the brain surgeon, or the ballet dancer, or the big-league baseball player. Nevertheless, even with a high degree of resource specialization, supplies of one kind of specialized resource can be developed over time at the expense of the supplies of other kinds. Individuals can be trained as physicians rather than as dentists. More bricklayers can be developed at the expense of the quantity of carpenters. More tractors and fewer combines can be produced. The resources of the economy are quite fluid with respect to the forms they can take and the kinds of goods they can produce. The longer the period of time under consideration, the greater their fluidity or versatility.

(3) Possibilities of combining resources in various proportions to produce a given good usually exist. Few, if any, goods require rigid proportions of resources. The possibility exists generally of substituting some kinds of labor for capital, or for other kinds of labor, and vice versa. This characteristic of resources is closely related to the second — the characteristic of versatility. Together they make it possible for the economy to switch its productive capacity from one line of production to another. Thus, the productive capacity of the economy can be geared to the changing character of human wants. Resources can be transferred into industries producing goods that consumers want most and out of industries producing goods that consumers want least.

Techniques of Production

Techniques of production, together with quantities and qualities of resources in existence, limit the level of want satisfaction an economy can achieve. Techniques of production are the know-how and the physical means of transforming resources into want-satisfying form. The nature of techniques available to enterprisers is generally considered to lie largely outside the province of economic theory and in the province of engineering. However, the simultaneous choice of goods to be produced, quantities to be produced, and techniques to be used fall within the scope of economics. Economists usually assume that for the production of any commodity a given range of techniques is available and that for any quantity produced of the commodity the least-cost techniques will be used.

PRICE THEORY

Although price theory plays a key role in economic analysis it is not the whole show. To establish the frame of reference for the book and to guard against misunderstandings we shall discuss the place of price theory in the general scheme of economic theory. Then we shall consider its relationships to the real world.

Price Theory and the Economics Discipline

The place of price theory in the study of economics is important but its position must be kept in proper perspective. Price theory and national income theory provide the basic tools of economic analysis and are used in the special subject areas such as monetary theory, international trade, public finance, labor economics, agricultural economics, welfare economics, and so on. They are used for at least three purposes. First, they are used as a means of understanding how the economy operates and whether or not it operates efficiently. Second, they are used for purposes of prediction — to predict the impact on the economy of various kinds of changes in the many kinds of data confronting decision-making units. Third, they are used as a basis for prescribing policy measures to mold or modify economic activity along the lines thought to be desirable.

We should consider the study of price theory as the process of building up one part — a very essential part — of our analytical tool kit. But the kit is not complete when it contains only the tools of price theory. Although we are not explicitly concerned with them in this book, the national income tools of analysis are important, too. The basic concepts or principles of price theory and national income theory are further developed, and in some degree synthesized, as they are applied to the special subject areas within the field of economics as a whole.

Price theory, or *microeconomics*, is concerned with the economic activities of such individual economic units as consumers, resource owners, and business firms. It is concerned with the flow of goods and services from business firms to consumers, the composition of the flow, and the evaluation or pricing of the component parts of the flow. It is concerned, too, with the flow of productive resources (or their services) from resource owners to business firms, with their evaluation, and with their allocation among alternative uses. Price theory usually assumes a stable economy — one free from major fluctuations up or down — and reasonably full employment of resources. We shall use these assumptions throughout — not because fluctuations and unemployment are unimportant, but because the structure of price theory can be established in a more unequivocal and a simpler way when these two assumptions are made.

National income theory, or *macroeconomics*, treats the economic system as a whole rather than the individual economic units of which it is composed. The particular goods and services making up the flow from business firms to consumers are not integral parts of the analysis, nor are the individual productive resources or services flowing from resource owners to business firms. The value of the over-all flow of goods (net national product) and value of the over-all flow of resources (national income) receive the focus of attention. Price index numbers or general price level concepts replace the individual prices of microeconomics. National income theory concentrates on the causes of change in aggregate money flows, the aggregate flow of goods and services, and the general employment level of resources. Prescription of cures for economic fluctuations and for unemployment of resources follows logically from the determination of their causes. Macroeconomics has much to say about the nature of economic growth and the conditions necessary for secular expansion of productive capacity and national income.

Although we shall not discuss national income theory, price theory and national income theory are closely related and supplement each other extensively. For example, the assumptions that the economy is stable and that reasonably full employment of resources exist are really assumptions regarding the state of the economy viewed from the vantage point of national income theory. A given state of economic affairs defined with respect to national income theory forms the framework within which we shall develop price theory.

Price Theory and the Real World

Price theory is rather abstract. We may as well face this point at the outset. Difficulties will be encountered in this respect, but if we recognize the nature of the difficulties they will seem less formidable. Primarily, we shall find that price theory does not give us a description of the real world as it is. It will not tell us why a price differential of two cents per gallon for gasoline exists between Oklahoma City and Cleveland on any given date. However, it should help us understand the real world. It should show us in general how the price(s) of gasoline is established and the role that gasoline prices play in the over-all operation of the economy.

Price theory is abstract because it does not and cannot encompass all the economic data of the real world. To take into consideration all the data and factors that influence economic decisions of consumers, resource owners, and business firms would involve minute description and analysis of every economic unit in existence and, of course, would be an impossible task. Consequently, we single out what appear to be the most relevant data and from these we build up an over-all theory of how the price system operates. We concentrate on the data and principles that seem to be most important in motivating most economic units. In eliminating less important data and in building up a logical theoretical structure we lose some contact with reality. But we gain in our understanding of the over-all operation of the economy because we reduce to manageable proportions the factors to be considered. We may lose sight of individual trees but we gain more understanding and a better view of the forest as a whole.

The theoretical structure to be established should show the directions in which economic units tend to move and should explain the more important reasons why they tend to move in those directions. It should be a set of logically consistent approximations with regard to how the economy operates. The theoretical structure will show economic units acting precisely and (we hope) clearly. The real activities of economic units are less precise and frequently not entirely clear. The abstraction and precision of theory is essential to clear thinking and to policy making in the real world but we should guard against its unqualified application to the real world. We should make theory our tool and not our master.

SUMMARY

Economic activity revolves about three key elements: (1) human wants which are varied and insatiable; (2) resources which are limited, versatile, and capable of being combined in varying proportions to produce a given commodity; (3) techniques for utilizing resources to produce goods and services which satisfy wants. Not only should resources and techniques be used to produce goods which satisfy wants; they should be used also to produce the quantities of those goods which contribute most to aggregate want satisfaction. The goal of economic activity is a level of want satisfaction (level of living) as high as the economy can provide. To achieve this goal the best possible techniques must be used, resources must be fully employed, and resources must be properly allocated or distributed among the alternative wants of consumers.

At the outset the relationship of price theory to the over-all discipline of economics and the relationship of price theory to the real world should be understood. Price theory is an essential part of the economist's tool kit and is used, together with national income theory, in the special subject areas of economics. Rather than explaining in detail the activities of economic units in the real world, it establishes general principles concerning their activities on the basis of what appear to be the most important economic data. Activities of economic units of the real world approximate or tend toward those of theory. But loss in the way of detailed contact with the real world means gain in the understanding of the main forces at work.

SUGGESTED READINGS

FRIEDMAN, MILTON. "The Methodology of Positive Economics," *Essays in Positive Economics*. Chicago: The University of Chicago Press, 1953, 3–43.

LANGE, OSCAR. "The Scope and Method of Economics," *Review of Economic Studies,* XIII (1945–1946), 19–32.

MARSHALL, ALFRED. *Principles of Economics*. 8th ed.; London: Macmillan & Co., Ltd., 1920, bk. III, chap. II.

SCITOVSKY, TIBOR. *Welfare and Competition.* Chicago: Richard D. Irwin, Inc., 1951, chap. I.

The Organization of an Economic System[1] | 2

THE PURPOSE OF THIS CHAPTER is to give us a brief look at the economy as a whole before we study its details. If we can develop a preliminary working concept of the economy as a whole, then we can fit the details as we come to them into their proper places and can put them into proper perspective. We shall consider first a simple model of an economic system. Next, we shall discuss the functions of an economic system with special reference to the ways in which a free enterprise economy performs them.

A SIMPLIFIED MODEL

The widely used "circular flow" diagram of Figure 2–1 furnishes a highly simplified model of an economic system. It classifies economic units as (1) households and (2) business firms. These interact in two sets of markets: (1) markets for consumer goods and services, and (2) resource markets. Households, business firms, consumer goods markets, and resource markets are the component parts of a free enterprise economy. They form the core around which price theory is built.

Households include all individual and family units of the economy and are the consumers of the economy's product output. With minor exceptions they also own the economy's resources. Exceptions include some of the aged and infirm with no family connections, but quantitatively these are few enough to be safely disregarded in the analysis.

Business firms form a more limited group engaged in the buying and hiring of resources and the production and sale of goods and services. They include single proprietorships, partnerships, and corporations at all levels of the productive process. In some cases — notably in fam-

[1] This chapter is based on Frank H. Knight, "Social Economic Organization," in Harry D. Gideonse and others, eds., *Contemporary Society: Syllabus and Selected Readings* (4th ed.; Chicago: The University of Chicago Press, 1935), pp. 125–137.

ily units — the same economic unit functions both as a firm and as a household. The family farm is a case in point. For analytical purposes we shall assume that a clear distinction can be made between the function of the farm as a firm and the function of the family as a household. Each activity will be classified under its appropriate heading.

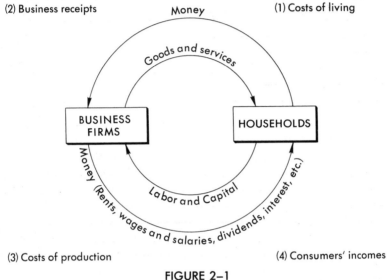

FIGURE 2–1

The upper half of the diagram constitutes the markets for consumer goods and services. Households as consumers and business firms as sellers interact within the markets. Goods and services flow from business firms to consumers and a reverse flow of money from consumers to business firms occurs. Prices of goods and services form the connecting link between the two flows. The value of the flow of goods and services will be equal to the reverse money flow.

The lower half of the diagram constitutes the markets for resources. The services of labor and capital in their many forms flow from resource owners (households) to business firms. The reverse flow of money in payment for them occurs in such forms as wages, salaries, rents, dividends, interest, and so on, depending upon the contractual arrangements under which they are delivered. These are resource prices valuing the services of resources and forming the connecting link between the two flows. In money terms, the two flows are equal.

Money circulates continuously from households to business firms and back to households again. The sale of goods and services places money at the disposal of business firms for the purchase of resource services to continue production. The sale or hire of the services of resources places money at the disposal of resource owners for the purchase of goods and services.[2] The money flow takes on four familiar aspects as it makes a complete circuit. It is costs of living of consumers at point (1) in Figure 2–1 as it leaves consumers' hands. It is business receipts for business firms at point (2). Aggregate costs of living and aggregate business receipts are the same thing looked at from two different viewpoints. At point (3) the money flow becomes costs of production, while at point (4) it is consumers' incomes. Aggregate costs of production and aggregate consumers' incomes are also the same thing considered from two different viewpoints.

If the economy is a stationary one — neither expanding nor contracting — the flow of money of the upper half of Figure 2–1 will equal the flow of money of the lower half. The aggregate value of goods and services will equal the aggregate value of resource services. Consumers spend all their incomes — no saving occurs. Likewise, business firms pay out all money received to resource owners and there is no business saving.[3] No net investment occurs. In the production of goods and services, capital equipment wears out or depreciates. Some resource services are used to take care of replacement or depreciation — but this is in reality a part of the cost of producing the goods which caused the depreciation to occur in the first place.

The model can be expanded and made as complex as we want to make it.[4] We can expand it to explain a growing economy or we can expand it to explain a contracting economy. We can expand it to take government economic activities into account. We can use the model and modifications of it to explain national income analysis. But for our purposes the simple model as presented will suffice.

We shall be concerned with the two sets of markets and the inter-

---

[2] In some instances, the money flow may be circumvented completely by direct exchange of resource services for goods, or "income in kind" to resource owners. To the extent that this occurs the money flows in each half of the diagram will be less than the value of goods and services and the value of resource services. However, since the bulk of exchange in a free enterprise economy will involve money and prices, we shall leave barter exchanges out of consideration.

[3] Profits made by business firms flow into the hands of resource owners in the form of dividends to stockholders or high prices paid to owners of other resources.

[4] For an excellent somewhat different view of the economy as a whole see Milton Gilbert and George Jazi, "National Product and Income Statistics as an Aid in Economic Problems," *Dun's Review,* LII (February 1944), 9–11, 30–38, reprinted in *Readings in the Theory of Income Distribution* (Philadelphia: The Blakiston Company, 1946), pp. 44–57.

actions which occur within each of them. In product markets the composition of the flow of goods and services, prices of each, and outputs of each will be of interest to us. Similarly, in resource markets, the prices, employment levels, and allocations of resources will be considered.

THE FUNCTIONS OF AN ECONOMIC SYSTEM

Regardless of its type, every economic system must somehow perform five closely related functions. It must determine (1) what is to be produced, (2) how production is to be organized, (3) how the products are to be distributed, (4) how goods are to be rationed over very short-run periods during which their supplies are fixed, and (5) how the productive capacity of the economy is to be maintained and expanded. Different types of economic systems perform the five functions in different ways.

Determination of What Is to Be Produced

The determination of what is to be produced in the economy is primarily a problem of determining which wants of consumers in the aggregate are most important and in what degree they are to be satisfied. Should the amount of steel currently available be used for the production of automobiles, or tanks, or refrigerators, or for the erection of sports arenas? Or should it be used to provide some of each? Since the resources of the economy are scarce, all wants cannot be fully satisfied. The problem is a social one of picking and choosing from the unlimited scope of wants those most important to the society as a whole. Essentially, the economy must set up a system of values for different goods and services that is acceptable to the group and reflects the relative desires of the group for goods and services that the economy can produce.

Value is measured in terms of price in the free enterprise economy and the valuation process is accomplished by consumers themselves as they spend their incomes. Consumers are confronted with a wide range of choices with regard to the goods they can buy. The dollar values they place on each of the various goods depend upon how urgently consumers as a group desire each relative to other goods, their willingness and ability to back up desire with dollars, and the supplies of the goods available. The more urgently certain goods are desired, and the more willing consumers are to back up desire with dollars, the higher will be their prices. The less strong the desire for certain goods the lower will be their prices. The greater the supply of any particular good available the lower will be its price. Any one unit of the good will be of less importance to the consumer when the supply is great than when the supply is small. The more bread we have to eat per week the smaller the value per loaf will be to us. Conversely, the smaller the supply of any particular commodity the higher consumers will value any one unit of it. Thus the ways in which consumers spend their incomes establish an array of prices or a price structure in the economy that reflects the comparative values of different goods and services to the consuming public.

Changes in consumer tastes and preferences modify the ways in which consumers spend their incomes. This in turn changes the structure of prices. Goods toward which consumers' desires shift go up in price while those away from which desires shift decline in price. The price structure or the value structure of goods and services changes then to reflect changes in consumers' tastes and preferences.

The foregoing analysis tells us how goods actually are valued by means of a system of prices. It does not tell us how goods *ought* to be valued. The latter problem is an ethical one and lies largely outside the scope of price theory. A consumer with a larger income will exert more influence on the value structure than will a consumer with a lower income. Conceivably, biscuits for rich people's dogs may be placed higher in the scale of values than milk for poor people's children, provided there are enough rich people casting their dollar votes in this direction and there are not enough poor people able to spend dollars for milk. The price system in this case, though working perfectly, may lead to social consequences that we consider undesirable and attempt to rectify through the political process. Income redistribution through social security and the progressive income tax furnish examples.

Organization of Production

Concurrent with the establishment of what is to be produced, an economic system must determine how resources are to be organized to produce the desired goods in the proper quantities. Organization of production involves (1) preventing resources from entering industries producing goods that consumers want least, and channeling them into the industries producing goods that consumers want most, and (2) efficient use of resources by individual firms. These will be considered in turn.

The price system in a free enterprise economy operates to organize production. Firms producing goods and services that consumers want most receive the highest prices relative to costs and will be the most profitable. Firms producing goods and services that consumers want least incur losses. The more profitable firms can and do offer higher prices for resources in order to expand. Those incurring losses are not willing to pay as much for resources. Resource owners want to sell their resources to firms offering the highest prices. Therefore, there is a constant channeling of resources away from firms producing goods and services that consumers want least and into the firms producing goods and services that consumers want most. Resources are moving constantly from lower-paying to higher-paying uses or out of less important into more important uses.

The term *efficiency* in economics differs slightly from the use of the term in physics or mechanics. However, in both contexts it involves the ratio of an output to an input. With regard to mechanical efficiency we know that a steam engine is inefficient because it fails to transform a large part of the heat energy of its fuel into power. Mechanically, an internal-combustion engine is more efficient. However, if fuel for steam engines is cheap and fuel for internal-combustion engines is expensive, cheaper power may be obtained from the steam engine. This brings us to the concept of economic efficiency which is also a ratio of output to input. The economic efficiency of a particular productive process is the ratio of useful product output to useful input of resources. The usefulness of product output, or its value to society, is measured in dollar terms. Likewise, the usefulness or value of resource input is measured in terms of dollars. Thus, the steam engine, which is less efficient mechanically, may be more efficient economically than an internal-combustion engine provided it furnishes cheaper power for a particular productive process.

The incentive for efficient production is the quest for profits. The more efficient the firm, given price of the product, the greater the profits will be. To rephrase the definition of efficiency in the preceding paragraph, it is measured in terms of the value of product output per unit input of resource value. The greater the dollar value of product output per dollar's worth of resource input, the greater is economic efficiency. This can be put the other way around. The less the dollar value of resource input needed per dollar's worth of product output, the greater is economic efficiency. Measurement of economic efficiency requires that values be placed on goods and services. It requires further that values be placed on resources of different types and on the same type of resource in different uses. Resources are valued according to their contributions to the production of goods and services.

Economic efficiency within the firm involves problems of selecting the combinations of resources to use and the techniques to use in the production process. The choice of techniques to use will depend upon relative resource prices and the quantity of product to be produced. The aim of the firm is to produce whatever output it produces as cheaply (efficiently) as it can. Thus if labor is relatively expensive and capital is relatively cheap, the firm will want to use techniques making use of much capital and little labor. If capital is relatively expensive and labor is relatively cheap, the most efficient techniques are those using little capital and much labor. The techniques to use for most efficient operation will differ with differing product outputs, also. Mass production methods and complicated machines cannot be used efficiently for small outputs, but for large outputs they can be very efficient.

Product Distribution

Distribution of the product is accomplished by the price system in a free enterprise economy simultaneously with the determination of what is to be produced and the organization of production. Product distribution depends upon personal income distribution. Those with larger incomes obtain larger shares of the economy's output than do those with smaller incomes.

The income of an individual depends upon two things: (1) the quantities of different resources that he can put into the productive process, and (2) the prices that he receives for them. If labor power is the only resource owned by an individual, his monthly income is determined by the number of man-hours he works per month multiplied by the hourly wage rate he receives. If, in addition, he owns and rents out land, the amount of land rented out multiplied by the monthly rental per acre will be his income from land. Income from labor added to income from land is his total monthly income. The example can be expanded to as many different resources as an individual owns.

Income distribution thus depends upon the distribution of resource ownership in the economy and whether or not individuals place their resources in employments producing goods that consumers want most (that is, where the highest prices are offered for resources). Low individual incomes result from small quantities of resources owned and/or the placing of resources owned in employments contributing little to consumer satisfaction. High individual incomes result from large quantities of resources owned and/or the placing of resources owned in employments where they contribute much to consumer satisfaction. Thus income differences may result from improper channeling of certain resources into the productive process by certain individuals and from differences in resource ownership among individuals.

Income differences that arise from improper channeling of certain resources into the productive process tend to be self-correcting. Suppose a number of individuals are capable of doing the same amount of labor per week in a certain skill category and are employed in the making of two different products. The value of product turned out by the first group is much higher than the value of product turned out by the second. Since society values the work of the first group higher than it values that of the second, the first group of workers will receive greater individual incomes. When workers of the second group perceive the income differential some move to the higher-paying employment. The increased supply of the first commodity lowers consumers' valuation of it while the decreased supply of the second commodity raises consumers' valuation of it. This in turn lowers the incomes of the first (but now larger) group of workers and raises the incomes of the second (but now smaller) group of workers. When the income differential between the two groups has disappeared, worker movements from the second to the first group cease. The self-correcting mechanism may, however, be prevented from accomplishing its task by ignorance on the part of the workers of the second group or by institutional barriers which prevent them from moving. In such cases the income differentials become chronic.

A large part of the income differentials arising from differences in resource ownership will not be self-correcting. The major sources of differences in resource ownership are discussed in Chapter 15. They can be classified under differences in labor power owned and differences in kinds and quantities of capital owned. Differences in labor power owned by different individuals stem from differences in physical and mental inheritance and from differences in opportunities to acquire specific types of training. Differences in kinds and quantities of capital owned come from many sources. These include initial differences in labor resources owned, differences in material inheritance, fortuitous circumstances, fraud, and differences in propensities to accumulate.

In the event society believes that income differences should be smaller, modifications can be imposed upon the free enterprise economy without materially affecting the operation of the price system. Society, through the government, may levy progressive income taxes and make expenditures for welfare purposes. It may subsidize low-income groups in various ways. Redistribution of income will, however, affect the wants to be satisfied by economic activity by changing the effective pattern of social desires for goods and services. Reduction of high incomes makes the individuals who are hurt become less effective in the market place. Augmentation of low incomes makes those who are helped become more effective in the market place. The price system will reorganize production to conform with the new pattern of effective desires for goods and services.

Rationing in the Very Short Run

An economic system must make some provision for rationing commodities over the time period during which the supplies of these cannot be changed. This time period is called the very short run. Suppose that wheat were harvested all over the country in the same month each year. From one year to the next the supply of wheat available for consumption would be fixed, assuming there is no carry-over from one year to the next. The very short run for wheat in such a case would be one year. The economy must ration the fixed supply in two ways. First, it must allocate the supply among the different consumers of the economy. Second, it must stretch the given supply over the time period from one harvest to the next.

In a free enterprise economy, price will be the device that allocates the fixed supply among different consumers. Shortages will cause price to increase, decreasing the amount that each consumer is willing to buy. Price will continue to increase until all consumers together are just willing to take the fixed supply. Surpluses will cause price to decrease, increasing the amount consumers are willing to buy until they take the entire supply off the market.

Price will also be the device for rationing the good over time. If the entire supply were dumped in consumers' hands immediately after harvest, price would be driven low. At the low price, consumption would proceed at a rapid pace. As the next harvest approaches, the disappearance of most of the commodity in the first part of the period leaves very small supplies for the latter part of the period. Consequently, price would be high in the latter part of the very short-run period.

Speculation plays an important role in smoothing out the consumption of the good over time. Knowing that price will tend to be low early in the period and high late in the period, speculators will buy up a large part of the supply early in the period expecting to sell it later at higher prices, thus realizing a net gain on their investment in the product. Their purchases will raise price in the early part of the period above what it would otherwise have been thus slowing the rate at which the product is consumed at that time. Their sales in the latter part of the period will reduce price below what it would otherwise have been and will provide greater quantities of the product for consumption in the latter part of the period. The actions of speculators modify the price rise that would have taken place over the very short-run period and bring about a more even flow of the product to consumers over time.

Economic Maintenance and Growth

Every economy in the modern world is expected to maintain and expand its productive capacity. Maintenance refers to keeping the productive power of the economic machine intact through provision for depreciation. Expansion refers to continuous increase in the kinds and quantities of the economy's resources, together with continuous improvement in techniques of production.

Labor power can be increased through population increases and through development and improvement of skills by means of training and education. Development and improvement of skills in a free enterprise economy are motivated largely through the price mechanism — the prospects of higher pay for more highly skilled and more productive work. The extent to which skills can be developed and improved is conditioned by training and educational opportunities together with physical and mental abilities.

Capital accumulation depends upon a variety of complex economic motives and much debate centers about their relative importances. For capital accumulation to occur some resources must be diverted from the production of current consumer goods and put to work producing capital goods in excess of the amount needed to offset depreciation. In a free enterprise economy this process occurs partly in response to the mechanism of price and profit; however, there is much disagreement which we can hardly dispel here with regard to the precise way in which the mechanism works.

Improvements in productive techniques make possible the production of greater outputs with given quantities of resources. The motives behind the search for and the discovery of inventions and improvements are not always easy to find. The inventor may invent because he finds that type of activity interesting. Frequently, improvements in techniques are the by-product of scholarship intended primarily to advance knowledge. However, a large part of the improvements in productive techniques is a direct result of the quest for profits. This is well illustrated by the increasing flow of fruitful results coming from the growing research departments of large corporations.

The role of the price mechanism and its degree of importance in providing for economic maintenance and growth are not clear. Certainly prices and profit prospects are an important element in determining whether or not maintenance and growth occur. But the area of economic maintenance and growth is virtually an applied subject area in itself. Consequently, we shall be concerned mainly with the first four functions as they are performed in a free enterprise economy.

SUMMARY

Our purpose in this chapter has been to obtain a picture of the economic system as a whole and to gain some appreciation of how the price mechanism guides and directs a free enterprise economy. First of all we set up a simple economic model of a free enterprise economy. Economic units were classified into two groups: (1) households, and (2) business firms. They interact in the markets for consumer goods and services and in resource markets. Households as resource owners sell the services of their resources to business firms. Incomes received are used to buy goods from business firms. Business firms receive income from the sale of goods to consumers. Business incomes in turn are used to buy resources from resource owners.

Second, we listed five basic functions of an economic system and discussed the ways in which a free enterprise economy performs those functions. A system of prices is the main organizing force. Prices determine what is to be produced. Prices organize production. Prices play a major role in distribution of the product. Prices serve to ration a particular good over its very short-run period during which the supply of the good is fixed. They are also an element in providing for economic maintenance and growth.

SUGGESTED READINGS

KNIGHT, FRANK H. "Social Economic Organization," *Contemporary Society: Syllabus and Selected Readings.* Edited by Harry D. Gideonse and others. 4th ed.; Chicago: The University of Chicago Press, 1935, pp. 125–137.

STIGLER, GEORGE J. *The Theory of Price.* Rev. ed.; New York: The Macmillan Company, 1925, chap. I.

Demand, Supply, and Market Price under Pure Competition

3

IN THIS CHAPTER we shall review certain general ideas or concepts essential for the development of price theory principles. It is difficult to move ahead in price theory without making reference to the concept of pure competition; consequently in the first section we shall discuss it rather thoroughly. We shall then turn to discussions of demand and supply of a commodity — neither of which require the concept of pure competition. But analysis of market price determination through the forces of demand and supply does rest squarely on purely competitive assumptions. The purely competitive concept is not necessary for the section on elasticity.

PURE COMPETITION

The term *competition* is used rather ambiguously in economic literature as well as in ordinary conversation. Its common denotation is rivalry. But used along with the word *pure* in economics it carries a different meaning. We shall look first at the conditions necessary for the existence of pure competition and then at its role in economic analysis.

The Necessary Conditions for Pure Competition

HOMOGENEITY OF THE PRODUCT • The first requisite for pure competition is that all sellers of a particular kind of product sell homogeneous units of the product. The product sold by seller A is identical to that sold by seller B. The important consequence of this is that buyers have no reason for preferring the output of any one seller over that of any other seller of the product.

SMALLNESS OF EACH BUYER OR SELLER RELATIVE TO THE MARKET • Each buyer and each seller of the product involved must be so small in relation to the entire market for the product that he cannot influence the price of whatever it is he is buying or selling. On the selling side, the individual seller supplies such a small proportion of the total supply that if he drops out of the market altogether, total supply will not be decreased enough to cause any rise in price. Or if the individual seller supplies as much as he can produce, total supply will not be increased enough to cause price to fall. An example is provided by the individual seller of most farm products. On the buying side, any single buyer takes such a small proportion of the total amount placed on the market that he is unable to influence its price. As consumers we are in this position with respect to most of the items we buy. As individuals we have no impact on the price of bread, meat, milk, safety pins, and so on. The main idea involved here is that of insignificance of any one individual buyer or seller of the product.

ABSENCE OF ARTIFICIAL RESTRAINTS • A third condition necessary for the existence of pure competition is that no artificial restrictions be placed on demands for, supplies of, and prices of goods and resources. Prices must be free to move wherever they will in response to changing conditions of demand and supply. There must be no governmental price fixing, nor any institutional fixing or administering of price by producers' associations, labor unions, or other private agencies. There must be no supply restriction enforced by the government or by organized producer groups. Control of demand through governmental rationing must be nonexistent.

MOBILITY • A fourth requirement is that mobility of goods and services and of resources exist in the economy. New firms must be free to enter any desired industry, and resources must be free to move among alternative uses to those where they desire employment. Goods and services can be sold wherever they command the highest price. Resources can find employment in their highest paid uses.

"Pure" and "Perfect" Competition

Economists sometimes distinguish between "pure" and "perfect" competition. The distinction between them is one of degree. The four conditions listed above are usually considered necessary for pure competition to exist. Perfect competition requires that one more condition be met.

The additional requirement is that all economic units possess complete knowledge of the economy. All discrepancies in prices quoted by sellers will be known immediately and buyers will buy at the lowest prices. This, of course, forces sellers charging higher prices to lower their prices immediately. If different purchasers offer different prices for whatever they purchase, sellers will know this immediately and will sell to the highest bidders. The low bidders must of necessity raise their price offers. In the market for any particular product or resource, a single price will prevail. Examples of perfect competition are very rare, but stock transactions on the New York Stock Exchange may almost approximate these conditions. The terms of stock transactions are flashed on the Exchange Board as soon as they are concluded. The information is then distributed via the ticker tape to interested parties all over the country. Under conditions of perfect competition, adjustments of the economy to disturbances in the conditions of demand and supply will be instantaneous. Under conditions of pure competition, it will take longer for adjustments to occur because of incomplete knowledge on the part of individual economic units.

Thus competition in economics is impersonal in its nature. There is no reason for enmity to develop between two wheat farmers over the effect that either one has on the market since neither has any effect whatever. One simply does the best he can with what he has. He is not out to get or defeat the other fellow. By way of contrast, intense rivalry may exist between two automobile agencies or between two filling stations in the same city. One seller's actions influence the market of the other; consequently, pure competition does not exist in this case.

Pure Competition in Economic Analysis

Few economists insist that thoroughgoing pure competition characterizes the economy of the United States, nor do they claim that it ever has. The question arises, then, as to why we should study the principles of pure competition at all. Three important answers may be given. First of all, the principles of pure competition furnish us with a simple and logical starting point for economic analysis. Second, a large measure of competition does exist in the United States today, although perhaps not in pure form. Third, the theory of pure competition provides a "norm" against which the actual performance of the economy can be checked or evaluated.

With regard to the first answer, an analogy can be drawn with the study of mechanics. No one questions the procedure of starting a study of mechanics leaving friction out of consideration. This, too, is unrealistic since friction inevitably occurs in the real world. Assuming away friction allows a clear statement of mechanical principles. Friction is then introduced and taken into account. Competitive economic theory occupies about the same role in economics analysis as do frictionless principles in the study of mechanics. Once we understand how the frictionless (competitive) economy works, we can observe the effects of friction (imperfect competition and restraints of various sorts) and take them into account. To study the theory of pure competition does not mean that one must believe that the real world is one of pure competition, nor does it preclude the very legitimate study of imperfect competition. It brings out fundamental cause and effect relationships which are also found in imperfect competition. It is simply the logical place to start if one is to understand the principles of imperfect competition and their applications as well as those of pure competition.

With regard to the second answer, a quantitative study made by Professor Stigler shows the substantial amount of competition which does exist in the United States.[1] Enough competition exists and enough economic units behave *as though* they operate in purely competitive markets for the theory of pure competition to give us valid answers to a great many economic problems.

Third, economic models set up on the basis of pure competition furnish us with a "norm" or "ideal" situation against which we can appraise the actual operation of the economic system. As we shall see later, *if* pure competition could and did exist throughout the entire economy, we would secure the fullest measure of economic efficiency, given the distribution of income. The want satisfaction obtained in the economy would be as great as its techniques and limited resources would allow. The purely competitive model frequently is used in this way as the basis for public regulation of imperfectly competitive situations. Presumably it underlies the philosophy and enforcement of the Sherman Antitrust Act of 1890 as amended, government regulation of public utilities, and many other public policy measures.

DEMAND

Demand for a good is defined as the various quantities of it that consumers will take off the market at all possible alternative prices, other things being equal. The quantity that consumers will take will be affected by a number of circumstances, the most important ones being (1) the price of the good, (2) consumers' tastes and preferences, (3) the number of consumers under consideration, (4) consumers' incomes, (5) the prices of related goods, and (6) the range of goods available to consumers.

Demand Schedules and Demand Curves

The definition of demand singles out for consideration the relation-

---

[1] George J. Stigler, "Competition in the United States," *Five Lectures on Economic Problems* (New York: The Macmillan Company, 1949), pp. 46–65.

ship between possible alternative prices of the good and the quantities of it that consumers will take. The other circumstances are assumed to remain constant for purposes of defining a given state of demand. Usually we think of quantity taken as varying inversely with price. The higher the price of the good the less consumers will take and the lower the price of the good the greater the quantity consumers will take, other things being equal or constant. Some exceptions may occur, in which quantity taken varies directly with price, but these exceptions must be few.

Demand refers to an entire demand schedule or demand curve. A demand schedule lists the different quantities of the commodity that consumers will take opposite the various alternative prices of the good.

TABLE 3–1

PRICE (p_x)	QUANTITY (X per U.T.)
$10	1
9	2
8	3
7	4
6	5
5	6
4	7
3	8
2	9
1	10

A hypothetical demand schedule is shown in Table 3–1. Product X is the commodity. Prices are listed under p_x and quantities taken are listed under X per unit of time. A demand curve is a demand schedule plotted on an ordinary graph. A demand curve is shown in Figure 3–1. The vertical axis of the graph measures price per unit. The horizontal axis measures quantity of the good per unit of time. Note that the inverse relationship between price and quantity sold makes the demand curve slope downward to the right.

Quantities referred to in Table 3–1 or in Figure 3–1 have no meaning unless they are stated in terms of a given time period. The quantities may be set up on a weekly basis, a monthly basis, or even a yearly basis. It means nothing at all to say, "At a price of five dollars per unit, six units of product will be taken by consumers." The statement becomes meaningful when we say, "At a price of five dollars per unit, six units of product *per week (or month, or whatever the time period happens to be)*

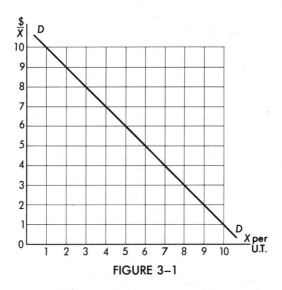

FIGURE 3–1

will be taken by consumers." Hence, we must always remember that we are dealing not merely with quantities, but with quantities per unit of time. They are rates of purchase, such as 500,000 cars per month or 60,000,000 bushels of wheat per month.

The demand curve is a maximum concept. It represents the maximum quantities per unit of time that consumers will take at various prices. At given prices they would always be willing to take smaller amounts if smaller amounts were all they could get, but they cannot be induced to take more than those shown by the demand curve. The demand curve can be viewed also as showing the maximum prices which consumers will pay for different quantities per unit of time. They will pay no more but can easily be induced to pay less for each of the various quantities.

A Change in Demand versus a Movement along a Given Demand Curve

A clear distinction must be drawn between a *movement along* a given demand curve and a *change* in demand. A movement along a given demand curve is a change in quantity taken resulting from a change in price of the good itself when all the other circumstances influencing the quantity taken remain unchanged. In Figure 3–2, a decrease in price from p to p_1 increases quantity taken from X to X_1. This should not be called a change in demand since it occurs on a single demand curve and the term *demand* refers to that entire demand curve. In defining demand we assume that the underlying demand circumstances remain constant

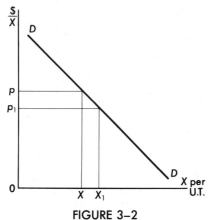

FIGURE 3–2

while we change the price of the commodity and observe what happens to the quantity taken.

When the circumstances held constant in defining a given state of

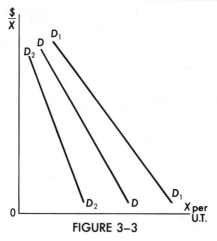

FIGURE 3–3

demand change, the demand curve itself will change. Thus, in Figure 3–3, an increase in consumer incomes will shift the demand curve to the right from DD to D_1D_1. With higher incomes, consumers will usually be willing to increase their rate of purchase at each alternative price. A shift in consumer tastes and preferences toward commodity X will have the same results. So, also, will an increase in the number of consumers in the group. An increase in the range of goods available to consumers may cause them to allocate less of their incomes to commodity X, thus shifting the demand curve to the left to position D_2D_2 in Figure 3–3.

The effect of changes in the prices of related goods on the demand for X depends upon the nature of the relationship. If a related good is a *competitive* or *substitute* good, an increase in its price will cause the demand curve for X to shift to the right as consumers turn from the now relatively higher priced substitute to X. Suppose that X is beef and that the price of pork rises. Consumers shift from pork to beef, thus increasing the demand for beef. If the related good is a *complementary* good, an increase in its price will decrease its sales and cause a shift to the left in the demand curve for X. Less X is demanded at each possible price because of the decrease in sales of the complementary good. In this case suppose that X is milk and that the price of cereal rises enough to curtail cereal consumption. The smaller quantity of cereal consumed causes demand for milk to decrease; that is, the demand curve for milk will shift to the left.

SUPPLY

Supply of a good is defined as the various quantities of the good that sellers will place on the market at all possible alternative prices, other things equal. It is the relationship between prices and quantities per unit of time that sellers are willing to sell. The same distinction is made between a supply schedule and a supply curve that is made between a demand schedule and a demand curve. Usually the supply curve will be upward sloping to the right, since a higher price will induce sellers to place more of the good on the market and may induce additional sellers

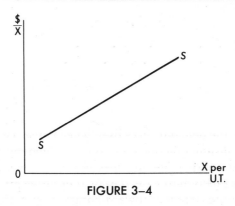

FIGURE 3–4

to come into the field. A hypothetical supply curve is shown in Figure 3–4.

The supply curve shows the maximum quantities per unit of time that sellers will place on the market at various prices. At any given price they will be willing to supply less, but they cannot be induced to supply more. From the point of view of quantities supplied, the curve shows the minimum prices that will induce suppliers to place the various quantities on the market. Suppliers will be willing to accept a higher price for a given quantity, but they will not supply that quantity for a lower price.

MARKET PRICE

The demand curve and supply curve for a certain commodity can be used on a single diagram to show us the forces determining its market price. The demand curve shows what consumers are willing to do, while the supply curve shows what sellers are willing to do. <u>Consumer demand is assumed to be independent of the activities of sellers. Similarly, the supply curve is assumed to be in no way dependent upon consumers' activities.</u> Consumers are assumed to operate independently of each other, as are sellers, also.

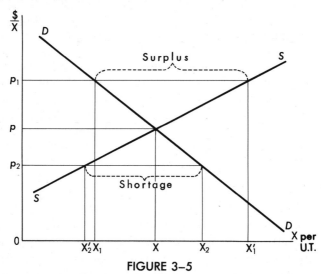

FIGURE 3–5

Market Price Determination

Market price determination is illustrated in Figure 3–5. At a price of p_1 consumers are willing to take quantity X_1 per unit of time. However, suppliers will bring quantity X_1' per unit of time to the market, so that a surplus is accumulating. The surplus accumulated for each time period is equal to the difference between X_1' and X_1. Each seller believes that if he undercuts other sellers a little he can dispose of his surplus. Thus an incentive exists for sellers to shade their prices and cut back the quantity supplied. Price will be driven down by the sellers, quantities supplied will decrease, and quantities consumed will increase. Eventually price will drop to p and consumers will be willing to take exactly the amount that sellers want to place on the market at that price.

Suppose now that sellers initially establish a price of p_2. At this price consumers want quantity X_2 per unit of time. Sellers will place on the market quantity X_2' per unit of time. This time a shortage occurs equal to the difference between X_2 and X_2' per time period. Faced by a shortage consumers bid against each other for the available supply and will continue to do so as long as the shortage exists. When the price has been driven up to p by consumers, the shortage will have disappeared and buyers will be taking the quantity which sellers want to sell.

Price p is called the *equilibrium price.* Given the conditions of demand and supply for commodity X, it is the price that if attained will be maintained. If price deviates from p, forces are set in motion to bring it back to that level. A price above the equilibrium price brings about a surplus which induces sellers to undercut each other, driving price back down to its equilibrium level. A price below the equilibrium level results in a shortage which causes consumers to bid the price back up to equilibrium. At the high price of p_1 so much of the good is placed on the market that consumers' valuation of it is less than that price. At price p_2 the quantity placed on the market is so small that its value to consumers is greater than its price. At the equilibrium price p the quantity placed on the market is such that price and consumers' valuation of the good are the same. Equilibrium prices are those prices correctly valuing the quantities of commodities placed on the market.

Changes in Demand and Supply

Changes in demand for a commodity, given its supply curve, will bring about changes in its price and the quantity exchanged. In Figure 3–6 an increase in demand from DD to D_1D_1 will increase price from p to p_1. When demand increases, a shortage exists at the old price of p. Therefore, consumers bid up the price to p_1. Sellers are induced to place more on the market and quantity exchanged increases to X_1. Suppose now that D_1D_1 is the original demand curve, p_1 is the original price, and X_1 is the original quantity. A decrease in demand from D_1D_1 to DD brings about a surplus at the original price of p_1. The surplus induces sellers to undercut each other, driving price down to p and reducing the quantity exchanged to X.

Similarly, changes in supply, given the demand curve, will bring about changes in price and quantity taken. In Figure 3–7 suppose the introduction of a new productive technique increases supply from SS to

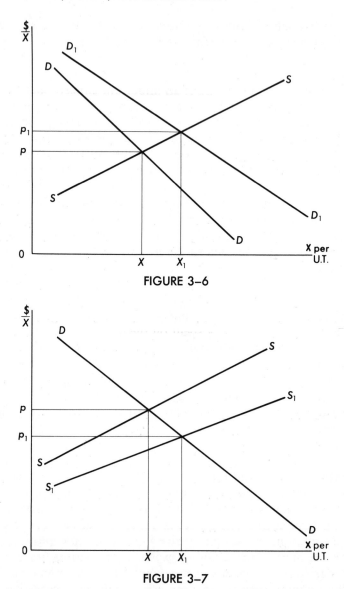

FIGURE 3-6

FIGURE 3-7

S_1S_1. A surplus exists at the old price of p. Sellers will undercut each other to get rid of their surpluses and price will fall to p_1. Quantity exchanged will increase to X_1. Now if we consider S_1S_1 as the original supply curve, p_1 as the original price, and X_1 as the original quantity, we can observe the effects of a decrease in supply. Suppose resource price increases decrease supply from S_1S_1 to SS. At the original price p_1 a shortage exists after the supply decrease. Consumers will bid price up to price p. Quantity exchanged will decrease to X.

ELASTICITY

Price elasticity of demand is an important concept met frequently in economic analysis. It refers to the responsiveness of the quantity of a product that consumers are willing to take to changes in its price, given the demand curve for the product. If quantity taken is quite responsive to price changes, a decrease in price may increase the total amount of money spent on the commodity. If quantity taken is not responsive to price changes, a decrease in price may decrease total expenditures on the commodity. These are points of direct importance to sellers. Two additional elasticity concepts will be considered, also, in this section. These are cross elasticity of demand and elasticity of supply. As we proceed through the book we shall discover more uses for elasticity measurements.

In this section we shall consider first the technical aspects of measuring elasticity of demand. Then we shall observe the relationships between elasticity of demand, price and quantity changes, and changes in the total amount of money spent on the good. Next, we shall discuss the major factors influencing elasticity of demand. Cross elasticity of demand and elasticity of supply will follow in that order.

Measurement of Elasticity

It may appear initially that the slope of the demand curve is a sufficient measure of the responsiveness of quantity taken to price changes. The slope of a small segment of a demand curve can be obtained by observing how much quantity taken will change when price goes up or down by a certain amount. For example, if a 10-cents decrease in the price of potatoes causes a 100-bushel increase in quantity taken, the slope of that portion of the demand curve is $-10/100$ or $-1/10$. Suppose we redraw the demand curve, measuring price in dollars instead of cents. The slope of the same segment of the demand curve is now $(-1/10)/100$ or $-1/1000$. A shift from cents to dollars in measuring price causes a drastic decrease in the downward slope of the demand curve even though there has been no real change in the demand curve itself. Suppose we redraw the demand curve, again measuring price in dollars and quantity taken in pecks. The slope of the same segment of the curve now becomes $(1/10)/400$ or $1/4000$. Slope of the demand curve is a very unreliable indicator of how responsive quantity taken is to changes in price.

There is an additional disadvantage to the use of slope as a measure of how responsive quantity taken is to changes in price. Suppose we

want to compare the demand curve for wheat with the demand curve
for automobiles. We want to know in which case quantity taken will re-
spond the more to a change in price. Comparative slopes of the two
demand curves tell us nothing in this respect. A one-dollar drop in the
price of wheat may increase quantity taken by 20 million bushels per
month. A one-dollar decrease in the price of automobiles may increase
quantity taken by five automobiles per month. But this does not mean
that the quantity taken of wheat is more responsive to changes in its
price than is the quantity taken of automobiles to changes in automobile
prices. A one-dollar change in the price of wheat is a tremendous change.
A one-dollar change in the price of an automobile is of little consequence.
Further, a unit of wheat and a unit of automobile are completely different
concepts and there is no basis for comparing one with the other.

The great British economist Alfred Marshall defined elasticity as
the percentage change in quantity taken divided by the percentage change
in price *when the price change is small*.[2] In terms of algebra, the elasticity
definition appears as

$$\varepsilon = \frac{\Delta x/x}{(-\Delta p)/p}$$

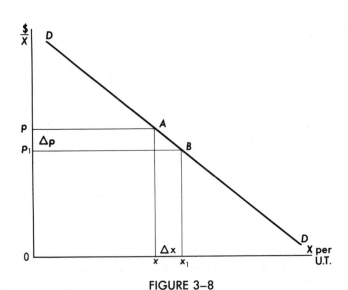

FIGURE 3–8

[2] Alfred Marshall, *Principles of Economics* (8th ed.; London: Macmillan & Co., Ltd.,
1920), bk. III, chap. IV.

The formula can be visualized by reference to the movement from A to B in Figure 3–8. The change in quantity from x to x_1 is Δx. The change in price from p to p_1 is Δp. The number or coefficient denoting elasticity is obtained by dividing a percentage by a percentage and is a pure number independent of such units of measurement as bushels, pecks, or dollars. Elasticity will be the same between given points on a demand curve for wheat regardless of whether price is measured in dollars or cents and regardless of whether quantity is measured in bushels or pecks. When elasticity is computed between two separate points on the demand curve, the concept is called *arc elasticity*. Elasticity computed at a single point on the curve for an infinitesimal change in price is *point elasticity*. We shall discuss the two concepts in turn.

ARC ELASTICITY • Suppose we want to compute elasticity of demand between A and B on Figure 3–8 and the coordinates of the two points are as follows:

	p (cents)	x (bushels)
At point A	100	1,000,000
At point B	90	1,200,000

If we move from point A to point B, substituting the appropriate numbers in the elasticity formula, we find that

$$\varepsilon = \frac{\dfrac{200,000}{1,000,000}}{\dfrac{-10}{100}} = \frac{200,000}{1,000,000} \times \frac{100}{-10} = -2$$

However, if we move in the opposite direction from point B to point A, then

$$\varepsilon = \frac{\dfrac{-200,000}{1,200,000}}{\dfrac{10}{90}} = \frac{-200,000}{1,200,000} \times \frac{90}{10} = -1.5$$

The percentage changes in quantity and price are different, depending upon the initial price and quantity from which we start. The different starting points lead us to different values of the elasticity coefficient.

The computations just completed show us that arc elasticity between two different points on a demand curve must be an approximation. The farther apart the points between which arc elasticity is calculated, the greater will be the discrepancy between the two coefficients of elasticity obtained, and the less reliable either will be. If arc elasticity is to be meaningful it must be computed between points on the demand curve which are close together.

To avoid the discrepancies in arc elasticity which occur when the computations are made alternatively, starting first with point A and then with point B, a modification of the basic elasticity formula can be used. With reference to Figure 3–8, suppose elasticity is calculated as follows:

$$\varepsilon = \frac{\Delta x / x}{- \Delta p / p_1}$$

where p_1 is the lower of the two prices and x is the lower of the two quantities. Now if we compute elasticity between A and B we find that

$$\varepsilon = \frac{200{,}000}{1{,}000{,}000} \div \frac{-10}{90} = \frac{200{,}000}{1{,}000{,}000} \times \frac{90}{-10} = -1.8$$

The modified formula provides a very usable average between the two results obtained with the basic formula.[3]

The demand elasticity coefficient will be negative in sign since price and quantity change in opposite directions. However, when economists speak of the magnitude of elasticity, they ignore the minus sign. Thus, they say an elasticity of minus one is greater than an elasticity of minus one-half, and an elasticity of minus two is greater than an elasticity of minus one.

POINT ELASTICITY • The concept of point elasticity is more precise than that of arc elasticity. If the two points between which arc elasticity is measured are moved closer and closer together, they merge into a single point. Point elasticity is simply arc elasticity when the distance between the two points approaches zero. Elasticity at the point can be measured

---

[3] A more complicated arc elasticity formula frequently used is

$$\varepsilon = \frac{x - x_1}{x + x_1} \div \frac{p - p_1}{p + p_1}$$

Elasticity computed with this formula between points A and B in Figure 3–8 is -1.7. This formula, too, strikes an average between the coefficients arrived at by means of the basic formula when we work first from A to B and then work in reverse from B to A. See George J. Stigler, *The Theory of Price* (rev. ed.; New York: The Macmillan Company, 1952), pp. 35–36.

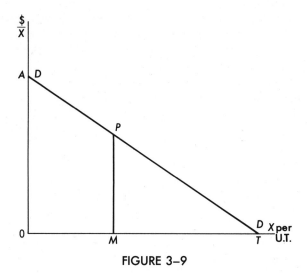

FIGURE 3–9

by a simple geometric method. Figure 3–9 shows a straight line (linear) demand curve. If we want to measure elasticity at point P, we start with the basic elasticity formula:

$$\varepsilon = -\frac{\Delta x/x}{\Delta p/p} = -\frac{\Delta x}{x} \times \frac{p}{\Delta p}$$

This can be rearranged to read

$$\varepsilon = -\frac{\Delta x}{\Delta p} \times \frac{p}{x}$$

On the demand curve, $\Delta p/\Delta x$ from point P or any other point measures the slope of the demand curve. Geometrically, the slope of the demand curve is MP/MT. Therefore, $\Delta p/\Delta x = MP/MT$, or, inverting both fractions, $\Delta x/\Delta p = MT/MP$. Price at point P is MP and quantity at that point is OM. Thus, at point P

$$\varepsilon = \frac{MT}{MP} \times \frac{MP}{OM} = \frac{MT}{OM}$$

Three categories of elasticity with respect to its numerical magnitude are important. When elasticity is greater than one, demand is said to be *elastic*. When elasticity equals one, it is said to have *unitary* elasticity. When elasticity is less than one, demand is said to be *inelastic*.

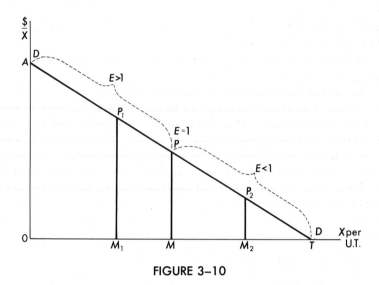

FIGURE 3–10

These categories are illustrated in Figure 3–10. Assume point P is located so that $OM = MT$. Since elasticity of demand at point P equals MT/OM, elasticity is unitary at that point. Consider any point farther up the demand curve — point P_1, for example. Since M_1T is greater than OM_1, elasticity at point P_1 is greater than one. The farther up the demand curve we move, the greater elasticity becomes, until, as we approach

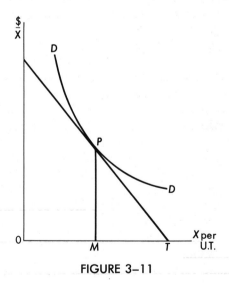

FIGURE 3–11

point *A*, elasticity approaches infinity (∞). Moving down the demand curve to the right from point *P*, we can see that elasticity is less than one and becomes progressively smaller the farther we move. As we approach point *T*, elasticity approaches zero.

The geometric technique for measuring point elasticity can be extended to apply to points on a curved demand curve. Suppose elasticity is to be measured at point *P* on the demand curve in Figure 3–11. First, draw a tangent to the demand curve at point *P* and extend it so that it cuts the quantity axis at point *T*. At point *P* the demand curve and the tangent coincide and have the same slopes; therefore, their elasticities must be the same at that point. Measurement of elasticity can proceed as before. Drop a perpendicular from *P* to *OT* and call its intersection with the quantity axis point *M*. Elasticity of demand at point *P* is equal to *MT/OM*.

Elasticity and Total Money Outlays

Of foremost importance to sellers are the relationships among price changes, elasticity, and the total amount of money spent for a given commodity. The total amount spent can be viewed either as total consumers' outlay (*TCO*) or total business receipts (*TR*) for the commodity. Total business receipts are found by multiplying quantity sold by the price per unit at which it is sold.

Suppose now that for a certain small price decrease, demand for a commodity is elastic — the percentage increase in quantity sold will exceed the percentage decrease in price. Since the increase in quantity sold is proportionally greater than the decrease in price, such a price decrease will increase total business receipts. Similarly, if demand were inelastic for such a price decrease, the increase in quantity sold would be proportionally less than the price decrease and total receipts would decline. If elasticity were unitary, the proportional increase in quantity sold would equal the proportional decrease in price and total receipts would remain unchanged. For price increases the effects on total receipts will be just the opposite.

The foregoing results can be summarized on the linear demand curve of Figure 3–12 where *OM* = *MT*. As we move down the demand curve from *A* toward *P*, elasticity of demand is decreasing but exceeds one. Hence, *TR* will be increasing. As we move down the demand curve from *P* toward *T*, elasticity continues to decrease but is less than one. Decreases occur in *TR*. It follows that at point *P*, where elasticity is unitary, *TR* is maximum.

When a demand curve is a rectangular hyperbola, elasticity of de-

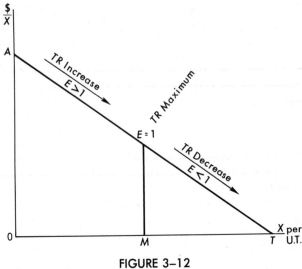

FIGURE 3–12

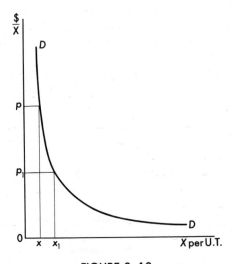

FIGURE 3–13

mand at all points on it is unitary. Such a curve is illustrated in Figure
3–13. Its basic characteristic is that price multiplied by quantity taken
results in the same total receipts regardless of what price is charged. For
price increases or for price decreases, total receipts remain unchanged;
i.e., $x \times p = x_1 \times p_1 = \ldots = x_n \times p_n$.

The businessman contemplating changes in the price of his product should be vitally concerned with its elasticity of demand for the price change. If demand were inelastic a price increase would be advisable but a price decrease would not. The former would increase his total receipts while at the same time it would cut his sales and his total costs. The latter would cut his total receipts but would increase his sales and his total costs.

Factors Influencing Elasticity of Demand

The major factors influencing elasticity remain to be considered. These are (1) the availability of good substitutes for the commodity under consideration; (2) the number of uses to which the commodity can be put; (3) the price of the commodity relative to consumers' incomes; and (4) whether the price established is toward the upper end of the demand curve or toward the lower end of the curve. These should be thought of as points to look for in trying to determine whether in the neighborhood of the ruling price demand will be more or less elastic.

The availability of substitutes is the most important of the factors listed. If good substitutes are available, demand for a given commodity will tend to be elastic. If the price of whole-wheat bread is decreased while the prices of other kinds remain constant, consumers will shift rapidly from the other kinds to whole wheat. Conversely, increases in the price of whole-wheat bread, the prices of other kinds remaining constant, will cause consumers to shift rapidly away from it to the now relatively lower-priced substitutes.

The wider the range of uses for a given commodity, the more elastic demand for it will tend to be. The greater the number of uses for a commodity the greater possibility there is for variation in quantity taken when its price changes. Suppose that aluminum could be used only in the making of airframes for aircraft. Not much possibility would exist for variation in quantity taken as its price varies, and demand for it would likely be inelastic. In reality aluminum can be put to hundreds of uses requiring a lightweight metal. The possible variation in quantity taken is quite large. Increases in its price subtract from and decreases in its price add to the list of its economically desirable uses. These possibilities tend to make demand for aluminum more elastic.

Demand for goods that take a large amount of the consumer's income is more likely to be elastic than demand for goods that are relatively unimportant to the consumer's income. Goods such as deep-freezers, which require large outlays, make consumers price-conscious and substitute-conscious. An increase in the price of deep-freezers will cause shifts toward use of commercial lockers. Quantity taken therefore is likely to vary considerably in response to price changes. For goods such as spices, which take a negligible part of consumers' incomes, changes in price are likely to have little effect on quantity taken.

If the ruling price is toward the upper end of the demand curve for a commodity, demand is more likely to be elastic than if it were toward the lower end. This is a purely mathematical determinant of elasticity, and its validity depends upon the shape of the curve. It stands on a completely different footing from that of the other three determinants.

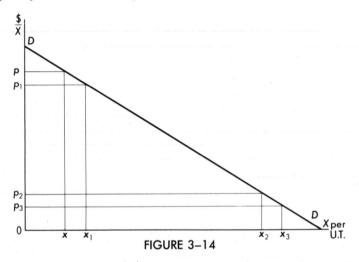

FIGURE 3–14

Figure 3–14 shows a linear demand curve.[4] If the original price is p and changes to p_1, and the original quantity is x and changes to x_1, the percentage change in quantity is large because the original quantity is small compared with the quantity change. The percentage change in price is small because the original price is large compared with the change in price. A large percentage change in quantity divided by a small percentage change in price means that demand is elastic. On the other hand, if the original price is p_2 and changes to p_3, and the original quantity is x_2 and changes to x_3, the reverse is the case. The percentage change in quantity is small because the original quantity is large. The percentage change in price is large because the original price is small. A small percentage change in quantity divided by a large percentage change in price means that demand is inelastic.

---

[4] The argument of this paragraph does not apply to a demand curve which is a rectangular hyperbola or to one which has greater convexity to the origin than has a rectangular hyperbola. It applies only to those with less convexity.

With the possible exception of the first point, these are not infallible criteria of elasticity of demand but are expressions of tendencies only. Additionally, they need not all work in the same direction at the same time. One or more may be working against the others and the magnitude of elasticity will depend upon the relative strengths of the opposing forces.

Cross Elasticity of Demand

Cross elasticity of demand measures the extent to which various commodities are related to each other. If we consider commodities X and Y, the cross elasticity of X with respect to Y equals the percentage change in quantity of X taken divided by the percentage change in the price of Y. This can be expressed mathematically by

$$\theta_{xy} = \frac{\Delta x/x}{\Delta p_y/p_y}$$

The relationships with which we are most concerned are those between substitute commodities and those between complementary commodities.

When commodities are substitutes for each other, the cross elasticity between them will be positive. Wieners and hamburger illustrate this situation. An increase in the price of wieners increases hamburger consumption. Or a decrease in the price of wieners decreases hamburger consumption. The percentage changes in the price of wieners and the consumption of hamburger are in the same direction, whether price moves up or down. In either case, cross elasticity will be positive.

Commodities that are complementary to each other have negative cross elasticities. Notebook paper and pencils serve as an illustration. An increase in the price of notebook paper cuts paper consumption and, consequently, the consumption of pencils. A decrease in the price of paper increases its consumption and, also, the consumption of pencils. The change in the price of notebook paper is accompanied by a change in the consumption of pencils in the opposite direction. Therefore, the cross elasticity of demand will be negative.

Cross elasticity of demand is frequently used to define the boundaries of an industry; however, its use in this respect has certain complications. High cross elasticities indicate close relationships or goods in the same industry. Low cross elasticities indicate remote relationships or goods in different industries. A commodity whose cross elasticity is low with respect to all other commodities is sometimes considered to be in an industry by itself. A commodity group with high cross elasticities within the group but with low cross elasticities with respect to other commodities is often said to constitute an industry. Various kinds of men's shoes will have high cross elasticities among each other, but low cross elasticities with other articles of men's clothing. Thus we have a basis for separating out a men's shoe industry.

One difficulty with cross elasticity as a means of determining industry boundaries is that of establishing how high must cross elasticities among commodities be if they are to be considered in the same industry. Cross elasticities among some foods are quite high — those among frozen peas, frozen green beans, frozen asparagus spears, and the like. Others, such as those between frozen vegetables and meat, are likely to be quite low. Is there a frozen food industry? Answers cannot be given unequivocally. Some general economic problems can best be solved by considering all frozen foods in the same industry. More narrow or more specific economic problems will require more narrow industry groupings — a frozen vegetable industry or perhaps even a frozen peas industry. Cross elasticities furnish a guide to, but not a hard and fast determination of, industry boundaries.

Another complication is that of chains of cross relationships. Cross elasticities may be high between passenger cars and station wagons, and between station wagons and pick-up trucks. But passenger cars and pick-up trucks may have low cross elasticities. Are they in separate industries or in the same industry? Again the nature of the problem we want to attack must be our guide to the proper definition of industry boundaries.

Elasticity of Supply

The concept of elasticity of supply is very similar to that of elasticity of demand. The formula for numerical measurement is the same; that is,

$$\eta = \frac{\Delta x/x}{\Delta p/p}$$

In the case of elasticity of supply, no confusion need result over the sign of the elasticity coefficient, except in the unusual situation of a downward sloping curve. A change in price will bring about a change in quantity in the same direction when the supply curve slopes upward to the right; hence Δx and Δp are either both positive or both negative. Therefore, the resulting coefficient of elasticity will be positive.

SUMMARY

The nature of pure competition and its role in economic analysis must be clearly understood. Pure competition is essentially the idea of smallness of the individual economic unit in relation to the markets in which it operates, the idea of freedom of prices to move in response to changes in demand and supply, and the idea that a considerable degree of mobility for both goods and resources exists in the economy.

The concept of pure competition does not provide an accurate description of the real world but this does not negate its usefulness. It supplies the logical starting point for economic analysis. Enough competition exists for it to give us valid answers to many economic problems. Additionally, it serves as a "norm" for evaluation of the actual performance of the economy.

Demand shows the quantities per unit of time which consumers will take of a commodity at alternative prices, other things equal. It can be represented as a demand schedule or a demand curve. We must distinguish carefully between changes in demand and movements along a given demand curve. Changes in demand result from changes in one or more of the "other things equal." Movements along a given demand curve assume that the "other things equal" do not change.

Supply shows the different quantities per unit time of a commodity that sellers will place on the market at all possible prices, other things equal, and, together with demand, determines the equilibrium price of the commodity. The equilibrium price of a commodity is that price which if attained will be maintained. Actions of sellers attempting to dispose of surpluses will push a higher than equilibrium price toward the equilibrium level. Actions of buyers attempting to buy short supplies will drive a lower than equilibrium price toward equilibrium.

Elasticity of demand measures the responsiveness of quantity taken of a commodity to changes in its price. It is defined as the percentage change in quantity divided by the percentage change in price when the price change is small. Arc elasticity is an approximate measure of elasticity between two separate points. Point elasticity measures elasticity at one single point on the demand curve. Elasticity of demand is the key element in determining what happens to total business receipts for a commodity when the price of the commodity changes, given demand. When demand is inelastic, increases in price increase total receipts, while decreases in price decrease total receipts. When demand is elastic, the opposite results occur when price is increased or decreased. The degree of demand elasticity for a certain good depends upon the availability of substitutes, the number of uses for the good, the importance of the good in consumers' budgets, and the region of the demand curve within which price moves.

Two other elasticity concepts are of importance in price theory.

These are cross elasticity of demand between products and elasticity of supply. High positive cross elasticities indicate a high degree of substitutability between products and are frequently used to mark off the boundaries of particular industries. High negative cross elasticities indicate a high degree of complementarity between products. Elasticity of supply shows the responsiveness of quantity placed on the market to price changes. It is defined as the percentage change in quantity supplied divided by the percentage change in price.

SUGGESTED READINGS

KNIGHT, FRANK H. *Risk, Uncertainty, and Profit.* Boston: Houghton Mifflin Company, 1921, chap. I.

MACHLUP, FRITZ. *The Political Economy of Monopoly.* Baltimore: The Johns Hopkins University Press, 1952, pp. 12–23.

MARSHALL, ALFRED. *Principles of Economics.* 8th ed.; London: Macmillan & Co., Ltd., 1920, bk. III, chap. IV, and bk. V, chaps. I-III.

STONIER, ALFRED W., and HAGUE, DOUGLAS C. *A Textbook of Economic Theory.* 3d ed.; New York: John Wiley & Sons, Inc., 1964, chap. I.

Individual Consumer Demand: The Utility Approach | 4

THE MARKET DEMAND CURVES of the preceding chapter originate with individual consumers. To round out our knowledge of demand and to understand market demand curves better we shall consider the theory of individual consumer behavior in this and the following chapter. Two approaches are presented. The older utility approach will be developed in this chapter and the more recent indifference curve approach will be deferred to the next. The two approaches are for the most part different ways of explaining the same thing. Some economists prefer one approach and some prefer the other. Regardless of personal preferences, both contribute toward a better understanding of demand.

The utility approach to the theory of individual consumer demand arose in the 1870s with the almost simultaneous publication of major works by three economists working independently. These were William Stanley Jevons of Great Britain, Karl Menger of Austria, and Léon Walras of France. Modern utility theory owes much to all three. The utility concept will be explained first, followed by the theory of individual consumer behavior. Then the theory of individual consumer behavior will be used to illustrate the gains from exchange and to establish individual consumer demand curves. Last, we shall convert individual consumer demand curves into market demand curves.

THE CONCEPT OF UTILITY

Utility theory starts with the observation that a consumer gets utility or satisfaction from the consumption of goods and services. We shall distinguish between the total utility and the marginal utility obtained from consuming various quantities of a good or service. The nature of each concept will be examined in turn.

Total Utility

Total utility refers to the entire amount of satisfaction obtained from consuming various quantities of a commodity. The more of the commodity a consumer consumes per unit of time, the greater will be his total utility or satisfaction up to a certain point. At some level of consumption total utility from the commodity will reach a maximum. The consumer will not be capable of enjoying any greater satisfaction from it even though more of the commodity were thrust upon him. This is called his saturation point for that commodity.[1]

A hypothetical total utility curve showing the properties explained above is drawn in Figure 4–1(a).[2] The saturation point is reached at a consumption level of six units of X per unit of time. Up to that level, total utility is increasing as consumption increases. Beyond it, total utility decreases.[3]

Marginal Utility

Marginal utility is defined as the change in total utility resulting from a one-unit change in consumption of the commodity per unit of time. In Figure 4–1(a), if the consumer were consuming two units per unit of time and increased his consumption to three, his total utility would increase from eighteen to twenty-four units of utility. Marginal utility of the third unit is thus six units of utility. Marginal utility of the third unit also is equal roughly to the average slope of the total utility curve between points A and B. The slope of the total utility curve between points A and B shows the increase in utility resulting from a one-unit increase in consumption and is equal to 6/1 if that segment of the curve is considered a straight line. The total utility curve is not necessarily a straight line between A and B, but the error involved in considering it as such is not significant and becomes progressively less the smaller the distance between the points. If the distance on the X axis that measures one unit of X is infinitesimal, marginal utility at any given level of consumption is equal to the slope of the total utility curve at that point.

---

[1] Conceivably, still more units of the good forced upon him can cause his total utility to decrease. If for no other reason, storage problems will cause it to decrease. However, the possibility of decreases in total utility beyond the saturation point is of no importance for our purposes.

[2] There has been considerable controversy in economic literature over whether or not utility can be measured. The theory presented here does not really require measurability, but requires only that the consumer be able to distinguish between greater amounts and lesser amounts of utility. However, for expositional purposes we shall treat it as though it can be measured.

[3] This assumes that the rate of consumption must be increased by discrete units. Total utility is maximum at five units of X as well as at six units per unit of time. However, there are pedagogical advantages to considering the maximum as occurring at six units.

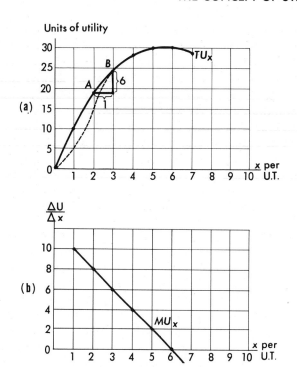

FIGURE 4-1

Marginal utility reflects the shape of the total utility curve as consumption is increased or decreased. From the total utility curve of Figure 4–1(a) we can see that marginal utility decreases as consumption per unit of time increases between zero and six. This can be restated by saying that each additional unit of consumption per unit of time adds less and less to total utility until, finally, the sixth unit adds nothing at all. Note also that as consumption per unit of time increases, the average slope of the total utility curve between any two consecutive consumption levels becomes smaller and smaller until, between five and six units of X, it becomes zero. The concept of diminishing marginal utility and the concavity of the total utility curve when viewed from below are the same thing.

Diminishing marginal utility need not be the case for all levels of consumption between zero and six units of X. The dotted curve in Figure 4–1(a) could conceivably be the total utility curve between zero and three. Suppose, for example, that a single television set in a home with several children causes so much friction over program selection that it adds little to the satisfaction of the family. Two sets — one for the parents and one for the children — may yield more than twice the satisfaction of one. But the successive increases in total utility yielded by three, four, and five sets will surely be successively smaller. Thus up to some certain consumption level marginal utility may increase as the consumption level increases, and the total utility curve will be convex downward. Beyond that consumption level marginal utility would be decreasing. If a saturation point for a commodity exists for a given consumer, as his consumption level approaches that point marginal utility must be decreasing even though it may have been increasing at lower levels of consumption.

Whether or not the marginal utilities of given commodities are decreasing at the quantities of them that consumers are likely to buy has been the source of considerable controversy among economists. We shall assume that the principle of diminishing marginal utility does hold.[4] This assumption does no violence to the end result of the theory of individual consumer demand while at the same time it greatly facilitates its exposition.

From the total utility curve of Figure 4–1(a) a marginal utility curve can be constructed. In Figure 4–1(b) the utility axis has been stretched out so that the vertical distance measuring one unit is greater than it is in Figure 4–1(a). The X axis is the same for the two diagrams. Marginal utility at each level of consumption is plotted as a vertical distance above that level of consumption on the X axis. At a consumption level of six in Figure 4–1(a) the average slope of the total utility curve between five and six is zero. Hence marginal utility is zero, also, and in Figure 4–1(b) the marginal utility curve hits the X axis at that consumption level. In Figure 4–1(b) a line MU_x joining the plotted marginal utilities at each level of consumption is the marginal utility curve for X.

A set of a consumer's marginal utility curves for different commodities gives us a graphic picture of the consumer's tastes and preferences at any given time. For those commodities with which the consumer is easily satiated, the marginal utility curves will slope off very rapidly, reaching zero at fairly low levels of consumption. For other commodities with which the consumer is not easily satiated, the marginal utility curves will slope off gradually and will reach zero at fairly high levels of

---

[4] Actually, all we need to assume is that the marginal utility of one good decreases *relative* to the marginal utilities of other goods as consumption of the one is increased in proportion to consumption of the others. Marginal utility of X could be increasing. However, if the additional consumption of X raises the marginal utilities of other goods more than it raises the marginal utility of X, the marginal utility of X has decreased *relative* to those of the other goods.

consumption.[5] Changes in consumer tastes and preferences will change the shapes and positions of the marginal utility curves for different commodities.

CONSUMER BEHAVIOR

The utility concept helps us explain the behavior of the individual consumer in the market place. The explanation presupposes rational action on the part of the consumer to achieve certain objectives subject to certain limitations imposed upon him. We shall consider the objectives of the typical consumer, the limitations confronting him, and the course of action he should follow to attain his objectives.

Objectives and Limitations

The objective usually postulated for the rational consumer is maximization of the amount of satisfaction or utility that he can get from his income. His tastes and preferences are shown by his utility curves for the various goods he desires and are given data for the consumer at any particular moment in time. The consumer's problem is to decide how much of each of the many different commodities to consume so as to secure the highest possible level of total utility with his available income. The limitations confronting the consumer in maximizing satisfaction are his available income and the prices of the goods he desires to consume. The consumer has a fixed amount of income per time period at his disposal. We shall include as income any sums which he may be able to borrow so that the term refers to whatever he has to spend per time period. Prices faced by the consumer will appear to him to be fixed, also, since he is typically a pure competitor in the purchase of goods. By himself he is unable to influence the market prices of most goods he buys. Limited then by his income and by the product prices he faces, the consumer sets out to maximize his utility or satisfaction.

Maximization of Utility

Suppose the consumer purchases two commodities — commodity X and commodity Y — the prices of which are p_x and p_y, respectively. As long as we consider p_x and p_y as fixed, a dollar's worth of X or a dollar's worth of Y represents a certain quantity of X or Y just as would quantity measurements such as bushels or pints. Suppose that the consumer's

---

[5] As a practical matter, no consumer will reach the saturation point for any good that commands a price, except by accident. The reason for this will become apparent in the next section of the chapter.

marginal utility schedules for X and Y — with quantities measured in terms of dollar's worth — are those of Table 4–1(a).[6]

TABLE 4–1
(a)

PRODUCT X		PRODUCT Y	
Quantity (*$'s worth*)	MU_x (*units of utility*)	Quantity (*$'s worth*)	MU_y (*units of utility*)
1	40	1	30
2	36	2	29
3	32	3	28
4	28	4	27
5	24	5	26
6	20	6	25
7	12	7	24
8	4	8	20

(b)

PRODUCT X		PRODUCT Y	
Quantity (*bu.*)	MU_x (*units of utility*)	Quantity (*pts.*)	MU_y (*units of utility*)
1	50	1	30
2	44	2	28
3	38	3	26
4	32	4	24
5	26	5	22
6	20	6	20
7	12	7	16
8	4	8	10

[6] In the analysis the marginal utility schedule of each commodity is assumed to be independent of the level of consumption of the other commodity. This assumption enables us to go directly and quickly to the conditions necessary for maximization of satisfaction. In reality X and Y are likely to be related to each other so that the marginal utility derived at various consumption levels of one will depend upon the consumption level of the other. Thus if X and Y were substitutes, the more of X consumed, the lower the marginal utility of Y would be at various consumption levels of Y. If they were complements, the more of X consumed, the higher the marginal utility of Y would be at various consumption levels of Y. These possibilities do not change the conditions necessary for maximization of satisfaction but they make numerical exposition of it virtually impossible.

How should the consumer allocate his income between X and Y? Suppose he has an income of $12 per unit of time. We can determine how he should allocate it by assuming first that he spends only $1 per unit of time. On which commodity should he spend it? A dollar spent on X will give him forty units of satisfaction while a dollar spent on Y will yield only thirty units; so, since he wants to maximize utility, he will take a dollar's worth of X. Now suppose he spends $2 per unit of time instead of $1. Where should the second dollar go? The second dollar spent on X will increase his total utility by thirty-six; whereas, if he spent it on Y, it would increase total utility by thirty units only. Therefore, he should spend the second dollar on X, also. If he spends $3 per unit of time the third dollar should go for X. When we assume he spends $4 per unit of time, we find that a fourth dollar spent on X increases total utility by twenty-eight units; but, if he should spend it on the first dollar's worth of Y, the increase would be thirty. The fourth dollar should be spent on Y. As his expenditure per unit of time is increased dollar by dollar, the fifth dollar should be spent on Y; the sixth and seventh, one each on X and Y; the eighth, ninth, and tenth on Y; and the eleventh and twelfth, one each on X and Y. So, when the consumer is spending all his income, he should be taking five dollars' worth of X and seven dollars' worth of Y. The general principle for maximization of consumer satisfaction is that with his given income he should buy those quantities of different goods and services at which the marginal utility per dollar's worth of any one is equal to the marginal utility per dollar's worth of each of the others. This principle can be extended to as many goods as confront the consumer and is not limited to the two commodities of the example.

We can show in an alternative way that this allocation of the consumer's income maximizes total satisfaction. Suppose he should transfer $1 per unit of time from X to Y. Giving up a dollar's worth of X will decrease total utility by twenty-four units. The additional dollar's worth of Y will increase total utility by twenty units, so the transfer results in a net loss of four units of satisfaction. If the transfer were made from Y to X, the net loss would be four units, also. No other allocation of the consumer's income will yield as much satisfaction as the one set out above.

Savings of an individual consumer appear to pose a problem, but they fit easily into the analysis just presented. To the consumer who saves, savings have utility. They can be thought of in terms of the purchase of security; or, if invested, they can be thought of as the purchase of future income. Whatever the motives of savers may be, the dollars saved serve to accomplish those motives and that accomplishment yields satisfaction to the saver. Further, the greater the savings from a given income, the smaller would be the marginal utility of each additional dollar of savings. Hence savings can be treated as a commodity. To maximize utility, the consumer should save that amount at which the marginal utility of a dollar's worth of savings to him is equal to the marginal utility of a dollar's worth of any commodity he consumes.

The foregoing type of problem can be set up using data in an alternative form. Suppose we have another consumer whose marginal utility schedules are listed in terms of bushels of X and pints of Y. The price of X is $2 per bushel and the price of Y is $1 per pint. The consumer's income is $15 per unit of time. His marginal utility schedules are those of Table 4–1(b).

Before solving the consumer's allocation problem it will be convenient to put into the form of equations the conditions necessary for maximizing satisfaction. Consider the fourth bushel of X. If the consumer were taking four bushels of X, the fourth bushel (like any other bushel) has a marginal utility of thirty-two units. The fourth bushel (like any other bushel) costs $2. Therefore, at this consumption level the marginal utility per bushel of X divided by the price of X, or MU_x/p_x, is the marginal utility per dollar's worth of X. The marginal utility per dollar's worth of X is sixteen units at this point. Likewise, the marginal utility per pint of Y at any consumption level divided by the price of Y, or MU_y/p_y, can be read as the marginal utility per dollar's worth of Y. The conditions necessary for maximizing satisfaction will be

$$\frac{MU_x}{p_x} = \frac{MU_y}{p_y} = \frac{MU_z}{p_z} = \cdots \qquad (4.1)$$

Equation 4.1 does not take into account the income restraint under which the consumer operates, but this can be easily remedied. The total expenditure of the consumer cannot exceed his income — which we shall designate as I. His total expenditure on commodity X is equal to the price of X multiplied by the quantity purchased. The same holds for each other commodity purchased and also for his "expenditure" on savings. The income restraint can be expressed in equation form as follows:

$$x \times p_x + y \times p_y + z \times p_z + \cdots = I \qquad (4.2)$$

Since the price of X is $2 per bushel and the price of Y is $1 per pint we must find some combination of X and Y at which the marginal utility per bushel of X is twice the marginal utility per pint of Y. This occurs at 6 bushels of X and 8 pints of Y. However, the total amount spent on X would be $12 and the total amount spent on Y would be $8. The consumer is exceeding his income, so the second condition for maximization of total utility is not met, although the first one is satisfied. Another possible combination is the one containing 4 bushels of X and 7 pints of Y. The first condition is met since $32/\$2 = 16/\$1$. The second condition is met, also, since 4 bu. $\times$ \$2 + 7 pts. $\times$ \$1 = \$15. Thus, the consumer should take 4 bushels of X and 7 pints of Y to maximize total utility.

Again, we can show that utility is maximized by transferring a dollar from X to Y. Giving up a dollar's worth of X, or half of the fourth bushel, reduces total utility by sixteen units. Spending the dollar for an eighth pint of Y increases total utility by ten. There is a net loss of six units. As before, a transfer of a dollar in the opposite direction also results in a net loss of utility — three units in this case.

The data confronting the consumer may not result in the even solution of the foregoing example. Suppose the consumer's income were $14 per unit of time instead of $15. How should he allocate the income? He could give up either a half bushel of X or a pint of Y. In either case his total utility would be decreased by sixteen units. If his income were $16 instead of $15, he would take half of the fifth bushel of X. The increase in total utility would be thirteen units; whereas, if he had taken the eighth pint of Y, his total utility would have increased by ten units only. Thus the consumer seeking maximum satisfaction should allocate his income among various goods so as to approach as nearly as he can the condition that the marginal utility of a dollar's worth of one good equals the marginal utility of a dollar's worth of any other good purchased.

Because the discussion so far has been rather abstract, suppose we consider how the theory would work for a typical family. Assume that the family budget is composed of the following items: food, clothing, housing, automobile, medical care, recreation, and education. Over a short period of time expenditures in some of the classifications are more or less fixed in amount. The mortgage payments, for example, are a fixed monthly amount. The grocery bill and medical expenditures are sometimes thought to be dictated by necessity rather than by choice. The other categories are likely to be more variable, but habit may be influential in determining them in the short run.

Over a longer period of time, however, expenditures on any or all of the budgeted items will be subject to change. The family seeking to get the greatest possible satisfaction from its limited income will reappraise its budget from time to time. The family car begins to rattle a little and at the same time it appears desirable to add a new room to the house for Junior. Both a new car and a new room are out of the question, so a choice must be made regarding the direction of expenditure. If either is to be obtained it will be necessary to cut down on educational expenses for the older daughter, who has been attending a private university. Should she be transferred to the state university where expenses are less? Food budgeting and clothing budgeting will be in order, too, to make the new car or the new room possible. Likewise, the family will need to economize on recreation — and even on medical expenses. When Junior has a minor illness he will have to get over it without the doctor's help. The whole chain of decisions will be made on the basis of marginal utility principles if maximum satisfaction for the family is to be attained. The family subjectively estimates the marginal utilities of dollars spent in each of the various directions. Transfer of expenditures from the items where marginal utility per dollar's worth is less toward items where marginal utility per dollar's worth is greater serves to increase total satisfaction.

EXCHANGE

A very large part of economic activity consists of exchange among individuals. Through the money medium goods are exchanged for goods;

TABLE 4–2

INDIVIDUAL A				INDIVIDUAL B			
Product X		Product Y		Product X		Product Y	
Quantity (bu.)	MU_x (units of utility)	Quantity (pts.)	MU_y (units of utility)	Quantity (bu.)	MU_x (units of utility)	Quantity (pts.)	MU_y (units of utility)
1	14	1	10	1	20	1	18
2	13	2	9	2	19	2	17
3	12	3	8	3	18	3	16
4	11	4	7	4	17	4	14
5	10	5	6	5	16	5	12
6	9	6	5	6	15	6	10
7	8	7	4	7	14	7	8
8	7	8	3	8	13	8	6
9	6	9	2	9	12	9	4
10	5	10	1	10	10	10	2

resources are exchanged for goods; and resources are exchanged for resources. A very common mistake on the part of many people is to think that one of the parties to a voluntary transaction gains while the other loses. In any voluntary exchange of goods among individuals, all parties to the exchange increase their satisfaction. It is the prospect of gain that causes voluntary exchange to occur. This point can be illustrated clearly by means of utility analysis. We shall limit ourselves to two consumers, A and B, who each hold stocks of two goods, X and Y. Marginal utility schedules for the two goods for each consumer are shown in Table 4–2.

Comparative marginal utilities of goods indicate the comparative worths or values of the goods to a consumer. Suppose consumer A has 5 bushels of X and 6 pints of Y. A bushel of X at this point contributes ten units of utility to his total satisfaction. A pint of Y contributes five units of utility. If he were to lose a bushel of X his loss in satisfaction would be ten units of utility; or if he were to lose a pint of Y his loss would be five units of utility. Thus a bushel of X to him is worth two pints of Y. Alternatively, we can say that a pint of Y is worth one-half bushel of X.

To illustrate the gains from exchange, assume that individual A initially has 9 bushels of X and 3 pints of Y, while individual B initially has 3 bushels of X and 9 pints of Y. Since for individual A the marginal utility of a bushel of X is six units of utility and that of a pint of Y is eight units of utility, a pint of Y is worth 1⅓ bushels of X to him. For individual B the marginal utility of a bushel of X is eighteen units of utility and that of a pint of Y is four units of utility. Thus for individual B a pint of Y is worth only 2/9 of a unit of X.

Under these circumstances both parties will gladly do some exchanging. Individual A will be willing to trade a bushel of X to individual B for a pint of Y and individual B will be willing to trade a pint of Y for a bushel of X. For individual A, the pint of Y gained would be worth 1⅓ times the bushel of X given up. For individual B the pint of Y given up would be worth only 2/9 of the bushel of X gained. To put it another way, in trading a bushel of X for a pint of Y, individual A would give up six units of utility in exchange for seven units, experiencing a net gain of one unit of utility. Individual B would give up four units of utility in exchange for seventeen units, experiencing a net gain of thirteen units of utility.[7]

---

[7] The one-for-one exchange ratio used here is not the only one at which the initial exchange could occur. Both parties can gain from any exchange ratio at which the amount of X that A is willing to give up to get a pint of Y exceeds the amount of X that B would require to give up a pint of Y.

Once this exchange has been consummated, an additional exchange could result in further gain for both parties. Individual A, with 8 bushels of X and 4 pints of Y, will no longer be willing to exchange on a bushel-for-a-pint basis since his loss would be greater than his gain from such a transaction. However, individual B can still gain from trading pints of Y for bushels of X. Since trade is no longer attractive to A on a bushel-for-a-pint basis, B will alter the terms of trade. If B, who now has 4 bushels of X and 8 pints of Y, were to give up 2 pints of Y for a bushel of X, he would give up fourteen units of utility, would gain sixteen units, and would still experience a two-unit net gain in utility. Individual A would find this offer attractive. It would get him eleven units of utility in exchange for seven such units.

Once the second exchange has occurred, no further gains are available from trade between the two parties and exchange will cease. Individual A has 7 bushels of X and 6 pints of Y with marginal utilities of eight and five units of utility, respectively. Individual B has 5 bushels of X and 6 pints of Y with marginal utilities of sixteen and ten units of utility, respectively. For A the unit of X is worth $1\frac{3}{5}$ units of Y. Individual B's relative valuations of X and Y are exactly the same; hence, neither can gain from further exchange.

The general principle underlying exchange is that for exchange to occur, two or more individuals must place different relative valuations on the goods involved. Relative valuations of goods by a single party depend upon relative marginal utilities of the goods. Thus for all holders of goods to be in equilibrium, that is, for no incentive to exchange to exist, each individual's holdings of goods must be such that the ratio of the marginal utilities of the goods for him is the same as it is for everyone else. In our simple example, for A and B to be in equilibrium, MU_x/MU_y for A must equal MU_x/MU_y for B. When these conditions do not hold, it becomes worthwhile for the parties to alter the terms of exchange and to engage in exchange until it does hold.

DEMAND CURVES

In addition to providing an explanation of consumer disposition of income and exchange, utility theory is useful in establishing individual consumer demand curves for commodities. A consumer's demand curve for a commodity should show the different quantities of it that he will take at various alternative prices, other things equal. Again we shall limit the consumer to a two-commodity world. We want to establish his demand curve for X. The "other things equal," or the factors that will be held constant, are the consumer's tastes and preferences (his utility curves), his income, and the price of Y. We shall vary the price of X and observe first what happens to the quantity of X taken and why. Next, we shall observe the effects of the price changes of X on the quantity of Y taken. Last, a distinction will be drawn between the income effects of a price change and the substitution effects resulting from it.

The Demand Curve[8] for X

To establish the consumer's demand curve for X suppose that initially the price of X is p_{x1} and the price of Y is p_{y1}. We shall assume that at all times the consumer is operating at the limit of his income restraint. The consumer will maximize satisfaction or be in equilibrium when he is taking that quantity of X and that quantity of Y at which

$$\frac{MU_{x1}}{p_{x1}} = \frac{MU_{y1}}{p_{y1}}$$

Thus at price p_{x1} the consumer is taking some definite quantity of X — that quantity which makes the marginal utility of a dollar's worth of X equal to marginal utility of a dollar's worth of Y. We shall call this quantity x_1.[9]

The consumer's initial position of equilibrium is shown graphically in Figure 4–2. Assuming that p_{x1} is twice p_{y1}, the consumer takes quantity x_1 of X and y_1 of Y. These quantities are such that MU_{x1} is twice MU_{y1}.[10] One point on the consumer's demand schedule or demand curve for X has been established now. At a price of p_{x1} the consumer will take a quantity of x_1.

The problem now is to establish the quantities of X the consumer will take at other prices of X when he is in equilibrium at each of those

---

[8] The analysis presented here is essentially that of Walras. See Léon Walras, *Abrégé des Eléments d'économie politique pure* (Paris: R. Pichon et R. Durand-Auzias, 1938), pp. 131–133.

The transition from the theory of consumer behavior to demand curves set out in the text differs from the usual Marshallian treatment. The usual Marshallian treatment considers the marginal utility of money constant and simply converts the marginal utility curve for a commodity into the demand curve for it. See Kenneth E. Boulding, *Economic Analysis* (3rd ed., New York: Harper & Row, Publisher, 1955), pp. 680–687. The Marshallian approach ignores income effects of price changes. The approach used in the text makes allowance for income effects as well as for substitution effects. This in turn makes the utility analysis of the present chapter more nearly parallel to the indifference curve analysis of the next chapter.

[9] He will also be taking some definite quantity y_1 of Y; however we are primarily concerned with the quantity of X that he takes.

[10] For any given ratio of p_x and p_y, quantities of X and Y taken must be such that $p_x/p_y = MU_x/MU_y$ or $MU_x/p_x = MU_y/p_y$.

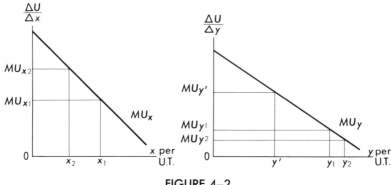

FIGURE 4–2

prices. The price of Y remains constant at p_{y1}. The consumer's marginal utility curves do not shift, that is, his tastes and preferences remain constant. His income remains constant also. Suppose now the price of X goes up to p_{x2}. Assume that he continues to take the same amount of X that he was taking before. The marginal utility per bushel of X will remain unchanged but the marginal utility per dollar's worth of X, MU_{x1}/p_{x2}, will have decreased. If at price p_{x2} the consumer continues taking quantity x_1, he will now be spending more of his income on X than before, leaving less to spend on Y. Since p_{y1} is the fixed price of Y, he will necessarily cut his purchases of Y to some quantity y'. The decrease in the number of pints of Y consumed causes the marginal utility per pint of Y to go up to $MU_{y'}$ (see Figure 4–2). This increases the marginal utility per dollar's worth of Y to $MU_{y'}/p_{y1}$. So now

$$\frac{MU_{x1}}{p_{x2}} < \frac{MU_{y'}}{p_{y1}}$$

that is, the marginal utility of a dollar's worth of X is less than the marginal utility of a dollar's worth of Y. The consumer is not maximizing satisfaction so, clearly, he will not continue to take quantity x_1 of X after the price has gone up to p_{x2}.

The consumer can increase satisfaction by transferring dollars from X to Y. His loss from taking a dollar away from X is the marginal utility of a dollar's worth of X. His gain from buying an additional dollar's worth of Y is the marginal utility of a dollar's worth of Y. Since $MU_{x1}/p_{x2} < MU_{y'}/p_{y1}$ the transfer will yield a net gain in total utility.

The transfer of dollars from X to Y will continue as long as the marginal utility of a dollar's worth of X is less than the marginal utility of a dollar's worth of Y. However, as the consumer gives up units of X the marginal utility per bushel of X increases, causing the marginal utility per dollar's worth of X to increase since price remains at p_{x2}. As the consumer buys additional units of Y the marginal utility per pint of Y declines, as does the marginal utility per dollar's worth of Y. The transfer will stop when the consumer has again equalized the marginal utility per dollar's worth of X with the marginal utility per dollar's worth of Y and is thus maximizing satisfaction. The quantity of Y taken will have increased from y' to some quantity y_2. The quantity of X taken will have decreased from x_1 to x_2. Quantities x_2 and y_2 must be such that

$$\frac{MU_{x2}}{p_{x2}} = \frac{MU_{y2}}{p_{y1}}$$

The quantities of X and Y that bring MU_x and MU_y into the proper relationship are shown in Figure 4–2 as x_2 and y_2. We now have another point on the consumer's demand curve for X. At a price of p_{x2} he will achieve equilibrium by taking quantity x_2 of X. The analysis has shown that an increase in the price of X causes a decrease in quantity taken.

Starting with $MU_{x2}/p_{x2} = MU_{y2}/p_{y1}$, the price of X can be changed again and we can trace through to the re-establishment of a new position of consumer equilibrium. At the new equilibrium position the quantity of X taken at the new price of X could be determined. By repeating the process, a whole series of price-quantity combinations for X can be listed in the form of a demand schedule and graphed as the individual consumer's demand curve. Such a curve is shown in Figure 4–3.

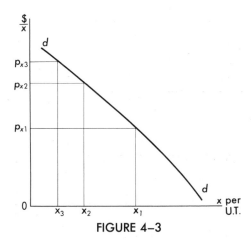

FIGURE 4–3

Quantities Taken of Other Goods

As a corollary to the foregoing analysis it may be instructive to take a closer view of what happens to the quantity of Y taken. When the price of X increases to p_{x2}, is the quantity of Y at the new equilibrium position greater than the original quantity as is shown in Figure 4-2? The answer is, "not necessarily." It depends upon the elasticity of demand for X. If demand for X is elastic, the increase in the price of X must decrease total spending on X, leaving more of the consumer's income to spend on Y. In this case quantity y_2 would be greater than quantity y_1, as shown in Figure 4-2. However, if elasticity of demand for X were unitary, total spending on X and total spending on Y would each remain constant and there would be no change in the quantity of Y taken. Should demand for X be inelastic, the price increase in X would increase total spending on X, decrease total spending on Y, and the quantity of Y taken would be smaller than y_1.

Income Effects and Substitution Effects

The decrease in quantity of a commodity taken when its price increases is the combined result of two forces: (1) the substitution effect, and (2) the income effect. The substitution effect causes the consumer to substitute relatively lower-priced goods for the relatively higher-priced good when its price goes up. Suppose, for example, that steak occupies a prominent place in a family's food budget. An increase in the price of steak relative to the price of other meats will cause the family to substitute the lower-priced meats for steak. The income effect stems from the decrease in the consumer's real income when the price of a commodity increases. The expenditure transfers from steak to other meats yield less satisfaction when spent on other meats than they did when spent on steak at its former price. Also, the dollars spent on steak at the now higher price yield less satisfaction than formerly because each dollar now purchases a smaller quantity of steak. The income of the consumer buys less satisfaction than before. The decrease in real income alone tends to cause quantities taken of different goods, including steak, to decrease a little. Usually the substitution effect is by far the stronger of the two, since a moderate increase in the price of any one commodity purchased does not decrease substantially the consumer's real income. The existence of good substitutes for the commodity will decrease further the magnitude of the income effect.

The income effect does not always operate in the same direction as the substitution effect. Only in the case of so-called normal goods will both work in the same direction. The quantity taken of a normal good will increase as the consumer's income increases, or vice versa. The quantity taken of an inferior good will decrease as the consumer's income increases, or vice versa. An example of the latter is chuck roasts. As the consumer's income increases, his purchases of chuck roasts will decrease while his purchases of top sirloin roasts and the better cuts of meat will expand. Given the consumer's money income, an increase in the price of chuck roasts will decrease his real income. The decrease in real income causes him to reduce consumption of better meat cuts and increase consumption of chuck roasts. At the same time the increase in the price of chuck roasts causes the consumer to substitute relatively lower-priced goods for them in his budget. Thus, the income effect and the substitution effect work in opposite directions. The income effect usually will be more than offset by the substitution effect.

MARKET DEMAND CURVES

The market demand curve for a commodity is composed of the individual consumers' demand curves for that commodity. We defined the demand curve of an individual consumer in much the same way as we defined a market demand curve. It shows the different quantities that the consumer will take at all possible prices, other things equal. Thus by summing the quantities that all consumers in the market will take at each possible price, we arrive at the market demand curve.

The process of summing individual consumer demand curves to obtain the market demand curve is illustrated in Figure 4–4. Suppose there are two consumers, only, who buy commodity X. Their individual demand curves are d_1d_1 and d_2d_2, respectively. At a price of p_1 Consumer I will be willing to take x_1 per unit of time while Consumer II will be willing to take x_1' per unit of time. Together they will be willing to take quantity $X_1(= x_1 + x_1')$ at that price and A is located as a point on the

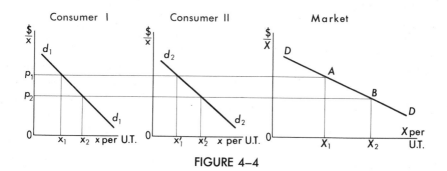

FIGURE 4–4

market demand curve. Likewise, at price p_2 Consumer I will be willing to take x_2 units per unit of time while Consumer II will be willing to take x_2'. Together they will be willing to take $X_2(= x_2 + x_2')$ at that price and B is located as a point on the market demand curve. Additional points can be located similarly and the market demand curve DD is drawn through them. The market demand curve for a commodity, then, is the horizontal summation of the individual consumer demand curves for the commodity.

SUMMARY

The concept of utility can be used to analyze individual consumer behavior and to explain individual consumer demand curves. The theory of individual consumer behavior and the downward slope to the right of individual consumer demand curves depend upon the principle of decreasing marginal utility.

We assume that a consumer seeks to maximize utility or satisfaction, given his income and the prices of the various goods available for him to buy. Maximum satisfaction will be obtained when he spends his income on different commodities in such a way that the marginal utility per dollar's worth of one will be equal to the marginal utility per dollar's worth of every other commodity available to him.

Marginal utility analysis can be used to show the basis of voluntary exchange among individuals. If for any individual the ratios of the marginal utilities of various goods differ from the corresponding ratios for other individuals, gains in satisfaction can occur from exchange. When the ratios of marginal utilities of various goods are the same for all individuals, equilibrium exists: there is no basis for voluntary exchange.

To establish the consumer's demand curve for a commodity we look first at his initial equilibrium position. At the initial price of the commodity he takes some definite quantity of it. The initial price and quantity form one point on his demand curve for it. Then we increase the price of the commodity. At the higher price the marginal utility per dollar's worth of it will have decreased, provided he takes the same quantity of it as before. The marginal utility per dollar's worth of other commodities will be higher than that of the commodity under consideration; consequently, expenditure will be shifted away from the latter and toward the former until marginal utilities per dollar's worth are once more equalized. Thus at the higher price, less of the commodity will be taken. A new point on the demand curve is formed by the new price and quantity. Additional points can be established and the resulting demand curve will be downward sloping to the right.

The decrease in quantity taken of a commodity when its price increases stems from two causal factors. One is called the substitution effect, which means that when the price of a commodity rises, the consumer tends to substitute now relatively lower-priced goods for it. The other is the income effect. The increase in price of the commodity decreases the consumer's real income, causing a tendency to cut purchases of all goods consumed.

The market demand curve for a commodity is built up from individual consumer demand curves for it. It is the horizontal summation of individual consumer demand curves.

SUGGESTED READINGS

MARSHALL, ALFRED. *Principles of Economics.* 8th ed.; London: Macmillan & Co., Ltd., 1920, bk. III, chaps. V and VI.

STIGLER, GEORGE J. "The Development of Utility Theory, I," *The Journal of Political Economy,* LVIII (August 1950), 307–324.

Individual Consumer Demand: The Indifference Curve Approach

5

INDIFFERENCE CURVE TECHNIQUE dates back to the 1880s; however, it was not developed and integrated into the main body of economic thought until the 1930s. A British economist, Francis Y. Edgeworth, first introduced the use of indifference curves in 1881.[1] Edgeworth's technique, with some modifications, was adopted by an Italian economist, Vilfredo Pareto, in 1906.[2] It remained for two British economists, John R. Hicks and R. G. D. Allen, to popularize and extend the use of indifference curve analysis in the 1930s.[3] It has since become a standard and necessary part of the economist's analytical equipment.

Indifference curve theory furnishes both an alternative and a supplement to the utility explanation of individual consumer behavior and individual consumer demand curves for commodities. Some economists find distasteful the quantifying of utility and the assumption of diminishing marginal utility which we used in the preceding chapter. Indifference curve analysis eliminates the necessity of making any such assumptions regarding the measurability of utility and the principle of diminishing marginal utility. Nevertheless, the utility theory of the preceding chapter and the indifference curve theory of the present chapter reach the same results. They complement each other and together should give us a better understanding of consumer behavior than will either one used exclusively. The order of exposition in the chapter is to treat first the nature of indifference curves; second, the maximization of consumer satisfaction; third, the gains from exchange; and fourth, the derivation of individual consumer demand curves and Engel curves. A section relating indifference curve analysis to utility analysis followed by a sec-

---

[1] Francis Y. Edgeworth, *Mathematical Psychics* (London: C. K. Paul & Co., 1881).

[2] Vilfredo Pareto, *Manuel d'économie politique* (Paris: V. Giard & E. Brière, 1909). The work was first published in Italian in 1906.

[3] John R. Hicks and R. G. D. Allen, "A Reconsideration of the Theory of Value," *Economica* (February, May 1934), 52–76, 196–219.

tion showing separation of income effects and substitution effects of price changes appear as appendixes to the chapter.

THE NATURE OF INDIFFERENCE CURVES

Indifference curves present a graphic picture of consumer tastes and preferences. Again we shall limit the consumer to choices between two commodities — commodity X and commodity Y. The indifference curves of a single consumer are obtained by confronting the consumer with a range of choices among various possible combinations of X and Y. The assumption on which indifference curve analysis rests is that the consumer can tell which of the various combinations yield equivalent satisfaction to him and which ones yield greater or less satisfaction. In this section we shall define indifference curves, or an "indifference map." Then we shall consider the basic characteristics of a system of indifference curves. Next, we shall observe the way in which indifference curves reflect the complementarity or substitutability of the goods under consideration.

Indifference Curves Defined

A single indifference curve shows the different combinations of X and Y that yield equal satisfaction to the consumer, or among which the consumer is indifferent. Suppose, for example, that it makes no difference to the consumer which of the combinations listed in Table 5-1 he

TABLE 5-1

X (Bu.)	Y (Pt.)
3	7
4	4
5	2
6	1
7	½

has. These combinations, shown graphically, are points on an indifference curve. In Figure 5-1, units of X per unit of time are measured on the horizontal axis and units of Y per unit of time are measured on the vertical axis. The combinations are plotted and joined to form indifference curve I.

Greater amounts of satisfaction than that obtained on indifference curve I are shown by higher indifference curves. Suppose we select a point

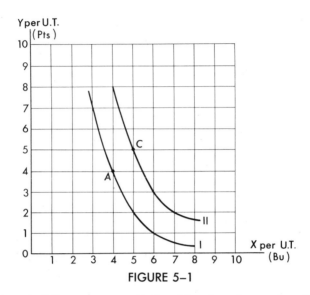

FIGURE 5–1

such as *A* on indifference curve I. Combination *A* contains 4 bushels of *X* and 4 pints of *Y*. If we add one bushel of *X* and one pint of *Y* to combination *A* we have combination *C*, containing 5 bushels of *X* and 5 pints of *Y*. Since it contains more *X* and more *Y*, combination *C* will yield greater satisfaction to the consumer than will combination *A*. Other combinations equivalent to *C* in satisfaction can be found and plotted to form indifference curve II. Innumerable indifference curves can be drawn on the diagram depicting all degrees of satisfaction. All combinations on one indifference curve are of equal satisfaction to the consumer. All combinations on higher indifference curves are preferable to those lying on lower indifference curves. We can make no inferences with regard to the amount of satisfaction gained in moving from a lower to a higher indifference curve — nor are such inferences necessary. The entire system of indifference curves for a consumer is called an indifference map.

Indifference Curve Characteristics

A system of indifference curves shows three basic characteristics. First, the curves slope downward to the right. Second, they are convex toward the origin of the indifference curve diagram. Third, indifference curves are nonintersecting. These will be considered in turn.

Those parts of indifference curves which are of importance to us slope downward to the right. If an indifference curve were horizontal, this would mean that the consumer is indifferent between two combinations, both of which contain the same amount of *Y*, but one of which contains a greater amount of X than the other. This could occur only if the consumer were receiving enough X to be saturated with it; that is, additional units of X alone would add nothing to his total satisfaction. Similarly, if an indifference curve were vertical, this would mean that the two combinations of X and Y, both with the same amount of X but with one containing more Y than the other, yield equivalent satisfaction to the consumer. This can occur only if the consumer has reached a saturation point for Y. The usual case will be that if the consumer's satisfaction is to remain constant when he gives up units of one commodity, the loss must be compensated for by additional units of another commodity. The result, shown graphically, is an indifference curve sloping downward to the right.

Indifference curves not only slope downward to the right, but are convex toward the origin of the indifference map. We can see this in better perspective by introducing first the concept of the marginal rate of substitution of one good for another. The marginal rate of substitution of X for Y (MRS_{xy}) is defined as the amount of Y the consumer is just willing to give up to get an additional unit of X. In Figure 5–1 suppose the consumer is taking 7 pints of Y and 3 bushels of X initially. To move to a consumption rate of 4 bushels of X he would just be willing to give consumption of 3 pints of Y per unit of time. Thus the marginal rate of substitution is three. The more Y and the less X the consumer has, the more important a unit of X is to him as compared with a unit of Y. Therefore, at point A in Figure 5–2, he would be willing to give

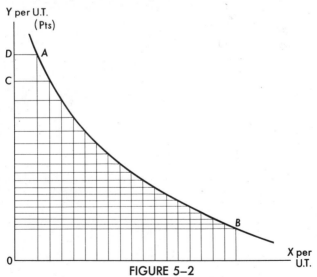

FIGURE 5–2

up a considerable amount of Y to get an additional unit of X. At point
B the consumer has a large amount of X and very little Y; hence a unit
of Y would be more important to him as compared with a unit of X than
it was at point A, and he would be willing to give up very little of Y to get
an additional unit of X. The X axis is marked off in equal quantity units
between A and B. At point A the indifference curve shows that the consumer is just willing to give up CD of Y to get an additional unit of X.
As we move from point A toward point B the consumer acquires more
of X per unit of time and less of Y. The importance of a unit of Y becomes progressively greater as compared with the importance of a unit
of X. The amount of Y he is just willing to give up to get additional units
of X becomes progressively smaller; that is, the marginal rate of substitution of X for Y is decreasing.[4] If the marginal rate of substitution of
X for Y is decreasing, the indifference curve must be convex toward the
origin. If it were constant, the amounts of Y the consumer would give
up to get additional units of X would be constant instead of decreasing,
and the indifference curve would be a straight line sloping downward to
the right. If the marginal rate of substitution were increasing, the indifference curve would be concave toward the origin.

Indifference curves are nonintersecting. This can be seen by considering again the indifference curves of Figure 5–1. All combinations
of X and Y shown on indifference curve II are preferable to all combinations on indifference curve I. Also, all combinations on indifference
curve I are equivalent to each other. Similarly, all combinations on
indifference curve II are equivalent to each other. Every combination on
indifference curve II can be shown to contain greater amounts of both
X and Y than corresponding combinations on indifference curve I. Thus,
the definition of indifference curves precludes their intersecting. Indifference curve II must lie above and to the right of indifference curve I.
This is not the same thing as saying that indifference curves are parallel
or that they are equidistant from each other. They may run farther apart
at some points and closer together at others. The only requirement is
that they do not intersect.

Complementary and Substitute Relationships

The complementarity and substitutability of commodities are reflected in the curvature of indifference curves.[5] Indifference curves show

---

[4] It may be helpful to work out MRS_{xy} arithmetically between different points on indifference curve I of Figure 5–1 before proceeding to the more abstract geometric representation of it in Figure 5–2.

[5] A more refined and considerably more complex discussion of complementary and
substitute relationships is presented in J. R. Hicks, *Value and Capital* (2d ed.; Oxford, England: The Clarendon Press, 1946), chap. III.

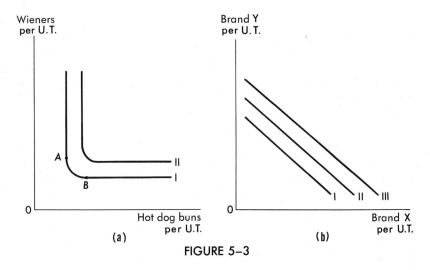

FIGURE 5–3

us also that we are not always correct in saying that commodities are either substitutes or complements. Consider indifference curve I in Figure 5–3(a). Within a certain range such as AB, wieners and hot dog buns can be substituted for each other. But the substitution process is possible within certain limits only. Above point A, the consumer is no longer willing to give up bun consumption per unit of time for additional quantities of wieners per unit of time. Similarly, to the right of point B, additional quantities of hot dog buns are of no value unless wieners come attached. Points A and B represent the limits within which they can be substituted for each other. Outside those limits the complementary relationships between the two commodities are the important ones.

The extent to which commodities are substitutes for each other is shown by the flatness or straightness of indifference curves. The indifference curves for perfect substitutes are downward sloping straight lines as shown by Figure 5–3(b). The consumer is indifferent as to which commodity he has. Suppose, for example, that X and Y are two different brands of milk chocolate and that the consumer is indifferent as to which he eats. Regardless of the amount of each he has, he is willing to substitute one for the other on a unit for unit basis.

There is no reason for differentiating between perfect substitutes. Goods that are perfect substitutes are the same commodity. But we have shown the extreme case. Indifference curves for goods which are substitutes, although not perfect substitutes, have some degree of convexity to the origin. The poorer substitutes they are for each other, the greater the degree of convexity. The better substitutes they are, the flatter or less convex the indifference curves will be.

MAXIMIZATION OF SATISFACTION

What the consumer is able to do has been left out of account so far. We have presented a picture of the consumer's tastes and preferences only. His set of indifference curves shows what he is willing to do with respect to different combinations of X and Y. What the consumer is able to do depends upon the respective prices of X and Y and the consumer's income. These opportunity factors — prices and income — are summed up in his "line of attainable combinations" which we have yet to discuss. The line of attainable combinations and his indifference map will show the combination of X and Y that will maximize his satisfaction.

The Line of Attainable Combinations

The consumer's opportunity factors are the price of X, the price of Y, and the consumer's income. The consumer regards these as fixed at the moment. Suppose the consumer's income is $100 per unit of time, the price of Y is $1 per unit, and the price of X is $2 per unit. With reference to Figure 5–4, if the consumer should spend all of his income on

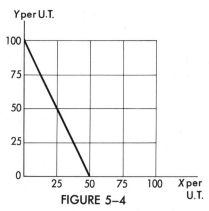

FIGURE 5–4

Y, he could buy 100 units of Y. Likewise, he could buy 50 units of X if he were to spend all of his income on X. A straight line joining these two points shows all combinations of X and Y that the consumer's income will allow him to take. This line is called the line of attainable combinations.[6]

---

[6] The line of attainable combinations is simply the budget restraint, $xp_x + yp_y = I$, plotted. If $p_x = \$2$, $p_y = \$1$, and $I = \$100$, and if the consumer is taking 100 units of Y and no X initially, then to get a unit of X, he would have to give up 2 units of Y. To get another unit of X he would have to give up 2 more units of Y. Substituting X for Y in this manner establishes the line of attainable combinations. The ratio of Y given up to get additional units of X is 2:1 and is constant as long as the price of X and the price of Y remain at $2 and $1, respectively. The consumer ends up with 50 units of X if the substitution process is continued to the point at which he is taking none of Y.

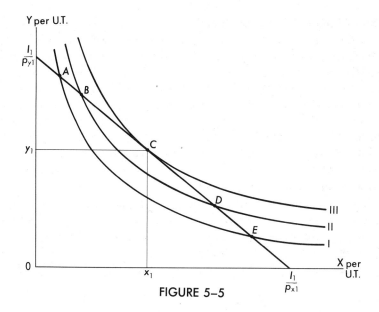

FIGURE 5-5

The slope of the line of attainable combinations depends upon the price of X and the price of Y. Suppose the consumer's income is I_1, the price of X is p_{x1}, and the price of Y is p_{y1}. If he should spend all of his income on Y, I_1/p_{y1} in Figure 5-5 shows the total number of units of Y that he could purchase. If he were to spend all of his income on X, I_1/p_{x1} shows the number of units of X that he could purchase. The line of attainable combinations joins the two extreme points. The slope of the line of attainable combinations is equal to

$$\frac{I_1/p_{y1}}{I_1/p_{x1}} = \frac{I_1}{p_{y1}} \times \frac{p_{x1}}{I_1} = \frac{p_{x1}}{p_{y1}}$$

Allocation of Income between X and Y

The consumer's taste factors (indifference curves) and his opportunity factors (line of attainable combinations) are brought together in Figure 5-5 to show how he should allocate his income between X and Y in order to maximize his satisfaction. The indifference curves show what he would like to do. The line of attainable combinations shows what he is able to do. The consumer can take any combination, such as A, B, C, D, or E, that lies on the line of attainable combinations. However, he would not take combination A. Combination B is also available to him and is on a higher indifference curve than is combination A. Combination C is on a still higher indifference curve. Combinations D and E are on lower indifference curves than is combination C. Combination C will give the consumer a higher level of satisfaction than will any other combination allowable with his given income and the given prices of X and Y. The consumer maximizes satisfaction by taking that combination of X and Y at which the line of attainable combinations is just tangent to an indifference curve. The indifference curve to which the line of attainable combinations is tangent is the highest one he can reach. He will take x_1 of X and y_1 of Y.

The income allocation that will maximize the consumer's satisfaction can be approached from a slightly different point of view. The slope of an indifference curve at any point represents the amount of Y the consumer *is willing* to give up to get an additional unit of X (that is, equals MRS_{xy}) at that point. The slope of the line of attainable combinations at any point represents the amount of Y he *would have* to give up in the market to get an additional unit of X at that point (p_x/p_y). At point A the slope of indifference curve I is greater than the slope of the line of attainable combinations. This means the amount of Y the consumer *is willing* to give up to get an additional unit of X is greater than the amount of Y he *would have* to give up to get an additional unit of X (that is, $MRS_{xy} > p_x/p_y$). The consumer would give up units of Y for additional units of X, because he can gain satisfaction by doing so. The same would be the case at point B. At point C the amount of Y the consumer is willing to give up to get an additional unit of X is equal to the amount of Y he would have to give up, or, the slope of indifference curve III is equal to the slope of the line of attainable combinations (that is, $MRS_{xy} = p_x/p_y$). At point D the slope of indifference curve II is less than the slope of the line of attainable combinations, which means that the amount of Y the consumer is willing to give up to get an additional unit of X is less than the amount he would have to give up (that is, $MRS_{xy} < p_x/p_y$). Therefore the consumer would not move beyond point C to such points as D and E, for such a movement would decrease his satisfaction. He is in equilibrium, or is maximizing satisfaction at point C where marginal rate of substitution of X for Y is equal to the ratio of their respective prices.

Suppose we put the matter in practical form. Say Figure 5–5 is a university student's indifference map for football games and movies, and he has a fixed yearly budget for the two. The Y axis measures movies per year and the X axis measures football games per year. At point A suppose he would be willing to give up four movies per year to see an additional football game. The marginal rate of substitution is four — one football game will substitute for four movies. Suppose the price of football games is $2 each while the price of movies is $1 each. He can attend an additional football game by sacrificing only two movies. Clearly it increases his satisfaction to make such a move. At point C, suppose our student is willing to give up two movies per year to see an additional football game. The marginal rate of substitution is two. At the same prices of football games and movies such a move will neither increase nor decrease his satisfaction. At some point such as D he is willing to sacrifice only one movie for an additional football game. But it would take a sacrifice of two movies to give him the price of admission to the additional football game. Such a move would decrease his total satisfaction. Thus our student maximizes satisfaction when his consumption of both is such that the rate at which he is willing to give up movies for football games is just equal to the ratio of the price of football games to the price of movies.

EXCHANGE

The forces giving rise to exchange of commodities among individuals can be readily explained in terms of indifference curve analysis. Suppose we consider two consumers, A and B, who each hold stocks of and consume two commodities, X and Y.

Individual A's tastes and preferences for X and Y are shown on the conventional part of Figure 5-6. The indifference map of B is rotated

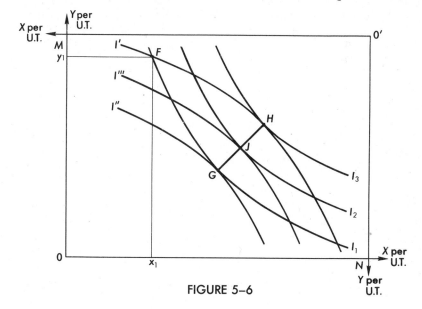

FIGURE 5-6

180° and is superimposed on that of A so that the axes of the two diagrams form a box. The diagram for B can be so placed that OM represents the combined stock of Y held by the two individuals and ON represents their combined stock of X. The indifference curves of A are convex to O, while those of B are convex to O'. Any point on or in the rectangle represents a possible distribution of the goods between the two individuals.

The initial distribution of X and Y between the two can be represented by some such point as F, lying within the rectangle formed by the two sets of axes. Individual A holds Oy_1 of Y and B holds y_1M. The amount of X held by A is Ox_1 and that held by B is x_1N. Individual A is on indifference curve I_1. Individual B is on indifference curve I'. For A the marginal rate of substitution of X for Y at point F is greater than it is for B. Individual A would be willing to give up more Y to get an additional unit of X than B would require to induce him to part with a unit of X. Thus the stage is set for exchange.

Either or both parties may gain from exchange when the initial holdings of the two commodities are represented by a point at which an indifference curve of A cuts through an indifference curve of B.[7] With F showing the initial distribution of X and Y, exchanges of Y by individual A to individual B for X could take place in such a way that indifference curve I_1 is followed downward to the right. Individual A would be made no worse off, but individual B would reach successively higher levels of satisfaction until the distribution of goods between the two is that represented by point G, at which indifference curve I_1 is tangent to indifference curve I''. No further exchange can occur without making one party or both parties worse off than they are at G. Similarly, individual A could exchange Y to individual B for X in such a way that indifference curve I' is followed downward to the right. Such exchanges would leave B no worse off than before but would place A on successively higher indifference curves, or at higher levels of satisfaction, until the distribution of goods is that represented by point H, at which indifference curve I' is tangent to indifference curve I_2. Any further exchanges would result in a decrease in satisfaction to one or both parties. Again, starting at F, both parties could gain from exchanges of Y by A to B for X if the exchanges were to follow a path from F to J, falling somewhere within the area bounded by FG and FH. Both parties would reach higher levels of satisfaction until some point J, at which an indifference curve of A is tangent to an indifference curve of B, is reached. Further exchanges would result in a decrease in satisfaction for one or both parties.

---

[7] It should be noted that every point in the box is either such an intersection point or is a point of tangency of an indifference curve of A with an indifference curve of B.

It becomes apparent that there are a number of distributions of the two goods between A and B at which there will be no further incentive for exchange to occur or at which equilibrium will exist. If the initial distribution of X and Y is that represented by point F, the possible equilibrium distributions trace out GH, a line formed by the points of tangency of A's indifference curves with those of B between G and H. This curve is called the contract curve. The distribution of X and Y on the contract curve at which the parties would ultimately arrive depends upon their comparative bargaining strengths. If A were in the stronger bargaining position, the end distribution of goods would be nearer point H; whereas if B were in the stronger bargaining position, it would be nearer G.

The necessary conditions for an equilibrium distribution of goods between the two parties are that MRS_{xy} for one party must be equal to MRS_{xy} for the other. If the maximum amount of Y that individual A is just willing to give up to get an additional unit of X is equal to the minimum amount of Y that B would accept in exchange for a unit of X, then no gain from such an exchange would occur for either party. These conditions are fulfilled at every point along the contract curve. At each such point an indifference curve of A is tangent to an indifference curve of B. Thus individual A's indifference curve has the same slope as does individual B's, or MRS_{xy} is the same for A as it is for B.

DEMAND CURVES AND ENGEL CURVES

Indifference curve analysis can be used to obtain the consumer's demand curve for a commodity and the consumer's Engel curve for a commodity. The demand curve shows the different quantities of one good that the consumer will take at various possible prices, other things equal. The Engel curve shows the different quantities of one good which the consumer will take *at various levels of income,* other things equal.[8] These will be considered in turn.

The Demand Curve

Suppose we concentrate on the demand curve for commodity X. The consumer's income, the price of Y, and the consumer's tastes and preferences (his indifference curves) are held constant. We shall vary the price of X and observe what happens to the quantity of X taken.

Changes in the price of X will change the consumer's line of attainable combinations. Suppose the initial line of attainable combina-

---

[8] Engel curves are named after Ernst Engel, a German pioneer of the last half of the 1800's in the field of budget studies. See George J. Stigler, "The Early History of Empirical Studies of Consumer Behavior," *The Journal of Political Economy,* LXII (April, 1954), 98–100.

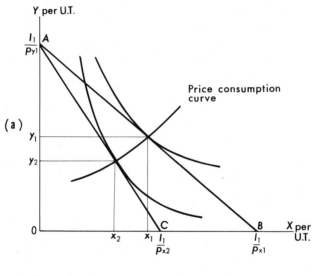

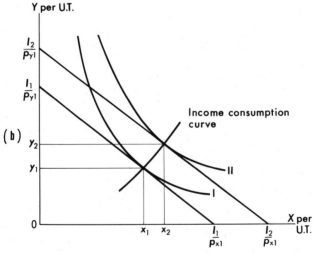

FIGURE 5–7

tions is AB in Figure 5–7(a). An increase in the price of X to p_{x2} would decrease the number of units of X he can buy to some quantity I_1/p_{x2}, if he were to spend his entire income on X. The new line of attainable combinations will be AC. It lies below line AB and has a steeper slope.[9]

_____
[9] Since the slope of line AB is equal to p_{x1}/p_{y1}, the increase in the price of X makes the slope of line AC steeper than that of AB and equal to p_{x2}/p_{y1}.

Line AC will necessarily be tangent to a lower indifference curve than was line AB, and the combination of X and Y that maximizes consumer satisfaction will differ from the original combination. Initially, the consumer maximized satisfaction by taking quantity x_1 of X and quantity y_1 of Y. The new combination will be x_2 of X and y_2 of Y. At various prices of X the line of attainable combinations will assume different positions with its focal point always remaining at A. Higher prices of X will rotate it clockwise, making it tangent to lower indifference curves. Lower prices of X will rotate it counterclockwise, making it tangent to higher indifference curves. The line joining points of consumer equilibrium at various prices of X is called the price consumption curve. Such a curve is shown in Figure 5-7(a). Note that in reality it shows no prices. It merely connects the combinations of X and Y that maximize satisfaction when the consumer's tastes and preferences, his income, and the price of one commodity are held constant and the price of the other commodity is varied.

The necessary quantity data for setting up the consumer's demand schedule and demand curve for X can be obtained from Figure 5-7(a). When the price of X is p_{x1}, the consumer will take quantity x_1 of X. This establishes one point on the demand schedule or demand curve. At the higher price of p_{x2}, the consumer will take the smaller quantity x_2 of X. This establishes a second point on the consumer's demand schedule or demand curve for X. The decrease in quantity taken is the combined income and substitution effect resulting from the increase in the price of X. Appendix II to the chapter shows how income effects and substitution effects can be separated. Additional price-quantity points can be established in a similar manner and the points can be plotted on the conventional demand diagram in the usual way. The resulting demand schedule or demand curve ordinarily will show that the higher the price of X, the lower will be the quantity taken, and vice versa.

Engel Curves

To obtain the Engel curves for X and Y, the prices of X and Y and the consumer's tastes and preferences are held constant, while income is changed. Given the price of X at p_{x1} and the price of Y at p_{y1}, an increase in income from I_1 to I_2 will shift the line of attainable combinations to the right parallel to itself as pictured in Figure 5-7(b). The consumer could take more units of Y than before at price p_{y1} if he were to spend his entire income on Y. Likewise, if he were to spend his entire income on X at price p_{x1}, he could take more units of X than before. The new line of attainable combinations thus lies to the right and above the old

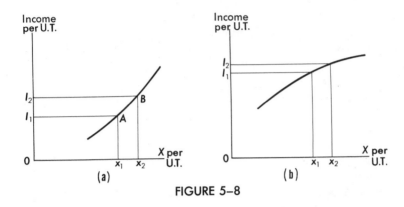

FIGURE 5-8

one. Since both lines of attainable combinations have slopes equal to p_{x1}/p_{y1}, the two must be parallel. If X and Y are normal goods, the increase in income increases the amount of X taken from x_1 to x_2, and the amount of Y taken from y_1 to y_2. The line joining all points of consumer equilibrium as income changes is called the income consumption curve.

Engel curves for X and Y can be plotted from the data provided from an indifference curve diagram such as Figure 5-7(b). Two typical Engel curves are shown in Figure 5-8. Income is measured on the vertical axes of the diagrams, while quantities of X per unit of time are measured on the horizontal axes. Now, from Figure 5-7(b), we can read that at an income level of I_1, the consumer will take quantity x_1 of X. This is plotted as point A on Figure 5-8(a). From Figure 5-7(b) we note that when income is I_2, the consumer will take quantity x_2 of X. We plot this as point B on Figure 5-8(a). If other lines of attainable combinations resulting from other levels of income were shown in Figure 5-7(b), the corresponding quantities of X he would take could be determined and plotted on Figure 5-8(a). Assuming X is a normal good, the higher the income, the greater will be the quantity of X taken.

Engel curves provide valuable information regarding consumption patterns for different commodities and for different individuals. For certain basic commodities such as food, as the consumer's income increases from very low levels his consumption may increase considerably at first. However, as his income continues to increase, the increases in consumption become less than proportional to the income increases. A pattern of this type is illustrated in Figure 5-8(a). For certain other items such as housing, as the consumer's income increases, expenditures on the items increase in greater proportion than does income. Figure 5-8(b) reflects a situation of this type.

Elasticity of Demand and the Price Consumption Curve

If we let the Y axis of an indifference curve diagram represent dollars and the X axis represent units of a certain commodity,[10] the slope of the price consumption curve indicates whether elasticity of demand for the commodity is unitary, greater than one, or less than one. In Figure 5–9(a), the indifference curves are such that the price consumption curve is parallel to the X axis, or has a slope of zero. As the price of X rises from p_{x1} to p_{x2}, the portion of his income *not spent* on X remains constant at Oy_1. Thus the amount of income spent on X remains constant also. If a rise in the price of X causes no change in total income spent on X, then demand for X has unitary elasticity for the price increase.

Figure 5–9(b) shows an upward sloping price consumption curve which tells us that demand for X is inelastic. A rise in the price of X from p_{x1} to p_{x2} brings about a decrease in the portion of income not spent on X (that is, from Oy_1 to Oy_2). This means that more of his income will be spent on X. An increase in expenditures on X as the price of X rises can result only when demand for X is inelastic for the price increase.

Figure 5–9(c) shows a downward sloping price consumption curve, indicating that demand for X is elastic. The rise in the price of X

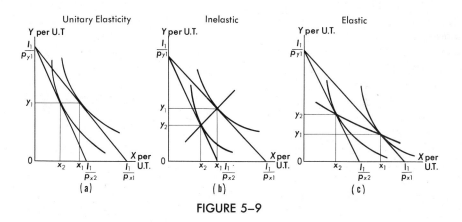

FIGURE 5–9

---

[10] A given indifference curve will show the combinations of money and commodity X among which the consumer is indifferent.

The line of attainable combinations is drawn in the usual way. The price of money, or p_{y1}, in dollars is, of course, \$1 a unit. Hence I_1/p_{y1} equals the consumer's income. Since the slope of the line of attainable combinations equals p_{x1}/p_{y1} and p_{y1} equals \$1, that slope is equal to p_{x1}.

increases the portion of income not spent on X from Oy_1 to Oy_2. Therefore, less is spent on X. An increase in the price of X that decreases total expenditure on X results from an elastic demand curve for X between the two prices.

SUMMARY

Indifference curve analysis offers an alternative way to describe individual consumer behavior and to establish individual demand curves for particular commodities. This analysis is preferred by some economists to utility theory because it does not require the assumptions that utility is measurable and that marginal utility is diminishing. Consumer tastes and preferences are represented by the indifference map. The consumer's opportunity factors — his income and the prices of goods he buys — are represented by the line of attainable combinations. The point at which the line of attainable combinations allows the consumer to reach the highest possible indifference curve shows the combination of goods that maximizes the consumer's satisfaction.

The consumer's demand curve for one good is obtained by varying the price of the good while holding constant his tastes and preferences, his income, and the prices of other goods. The resulting points of consumer equilibrium trace out the price consumption curve for the commodity. Data for the demand curve can be taken from the indifference curve diagram.

Engel curves for commodities can be obtained by varying the consumer's income, holding his tastes and preferences and the prices of all goods constant. The points of consumer equilibrium form the income consumption curve. The indifference curve diagram furnishes the necessary data for setting up Engel curves.

The slope of the price consumption curve for a commodity indicates the elasticity of demand when the commodity under consideration is measured on the X axis and money is measured on the Y axis. A horizontal price consumption curve means that demand has unitary elasticity. When the price consumption curve slopes upward to the right, demand is inelastic. When it slopes downward to the right, demand is elastic.

SUGGESTED READINGS

HICKS, JOHN R. *Value and Capital.* 2d ed.; Oxford, England: The Clarendon Press, 1946, chaps. 1 and 2.

RYAN, W. J. L. *Price Theory.* London: Macmillan & Co., Ltd., 1958, chap. 1.

Indifference Curve Analysis and Utility Analysis

This brief postscript to indifference curve analysis translates the indifference curve conditions necessary for maximization of individual consumer satisfaction into utility terms. It requires, however, that we think in terms of measurable utility. According to indifference curve analysis, satisfaction is maximized with the combination of X and Y at which the line of attainable combinations is just tangent to an indifference curve of the consumer. At this point

$$MRS_{xy} = \frac{p_x}{p_y}$$

Utility analysis tells us that the consumer maximizes satisfaction when he spends his income so that

$$\frac{MU_x}{p_x} = \frac{MU_y}{p_y}$$

MRS_{xy} at any point on an indifference curve is equal to the slope of the indifference curve at that point. It shows the amount of Y the consumer is just willing to give up to get an additional unit of X. If X is to be substituted for Y without loss of satisfaction, then, in terms of utility theory, the amount of utility lost by giving up some of Y must be equal to the amount gained by obtaining an additional unit of X. Letting Δy equal the amount of Y given up, the loss in utility will be equal to $MU_y \times \Delta y$. Letting Δx equal the additional unit of X, the gain in utility will be equal to $MU_x \times \Delta x$. Since the gain must equal the loss, then

$$MU_y \times \Delta y = MU_x \times \Delta x \qquad (5.1)$$

or

$$\frac{\Delta y}{\Delta x} = \frac{MU_x}{MU_y} \qquad (5.2)$$

Or at any point on an indifference curve

$$MRS_{xy} = \frac{MU_x}{MU_y} \qquad (5.3)$$

For the consumer to be in equilibrium,

$$MRS_{xy} = \frac{p_x}{p_y} \qquad (5.4)$$

From (5.3) and (5.4),

$$\frac{MU_x}{MU_y} = \frac{p_x}{p_y} \qquad (5.5)$$

Or

$$\frac{MU_x}{p_x} = \frac{MU_y}{p_y} \qquad (5.6)$$

Thus, indifference curve analysis as well as utility analysis tells us that the combination of goods that maximizes consumer satisfaction is the one at which the marginal utilities of the goods are proportional to their respective prices, or is the one at which the marginal utility of a dollar's worth of one good is equal to the marginal utility of a dollar's worth of every other good purchased.

Income Effects and Substitution Effects

With respect to a given demand curve, the price of the product and the quantity of it taken per unit of time vary inversely with each other because of substitution effects and income effects. An increase in the price of one commodity causes consumers to turn to relatively lower priced substitutes. Additionally, the increase in price decreases the consumer's real income or purchasing power, thereby tending to cut his consumption of all goods to some extent. Indifference curve analysis enables us to separate readily the income effect of a change in price of a commodity from the substitution effect of the price change.

The separation of income effects and substitution effects is illustrated in Figure 5–10. The consumer's income is I_1 and the prices of X and Y are p_{x1} and p_{y1}, respectively. Combination A, containing x_1 of X and y_1 of Y, maximizes the consumer's satisfaction. Suppose the price

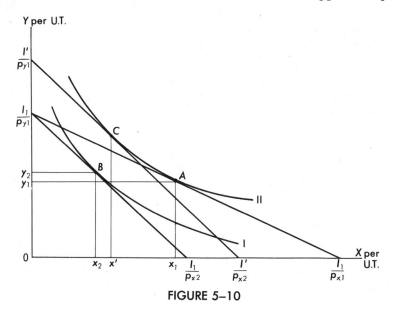

FIGURE 5–10

85

of X rises to p_{x2}. This rotates the line of attainable combinations clockwise with I_1/p_{y1} as its focal point. It now cuts the X axis at I_1/p_{x2}. Note that the slope of the new line of attainable combinations is greater than that of the old one. This, of course, results from the increase in the price of X. The slope of the original line of attainable combinations is p_{x1}/p_{y1}, while that of the new one is p_{x2}/p_{y1}. Combination B, containing x_2 of X and y_2 of Y, maximizes consumer satisfaction after the rise in the price of X.

The consumer's real income has been decreased by the increase in the price of X. This is illustrated graphically by the fact that combination B lies on a lower indifference curve than does combination A. However, the movement from combination A to combination B, and the reduction in quantity of X taken from x_1 and x_2 is the combined income and substitution effect.

In order to isolate the substitution effect and determine its magnitude, suppose we increase the consumer's income enough to compensate him for his loss in purchasing power. The additional purchasing power of the "compensating increase in income" will move the line of attainable combinations to the right parallel to itself; and when just enough compensation has been given the consumer to offset his loss, it will lie tangent to indifference curve II at point C. Combination C yields the same satisfaction to the consumer as did combination A; however, in maximizing satisfaction the consumer has cut his consumption of commodity X (and increased his consumption of commodity Y) because the price of X with which he is confronted is now higher relative to the price of Y than it was originally. The income effect of the increase in the price of X has been eliminated by the compensating variation in the consumer's income; hence the movement from A to C, or the decrease in X taken from x_1 to x', is the substitution effect. It results solely from the change in the price of X relative to the price of Y.

The income effect, apart from the substitution effect, can be determined by taking the compensating variation in income away from the consumer. The line of attainable combinations shifts to the left, and the highest indifference curve to which it is tangent is indifference curve I. Combination B, y_2 of Y and x_2 of X, is the position of maximum satisfaction. The movement from C to B is the income effect and reduces quantity of X taken from x' to x_2.

The movement of the consumer from combination A to combination B when the price of X increases thus is broken down into two steps, one showing the substitution effect and the other showing the income effect. Usually they operate in the same direction. If X is an inferior good, however, the income effect will work in the opposite direction from the substitution effect. In such a case the increase in the price of X causes a tendency on the part of the consumer to substitute relatively lower priced goods for X, but at the same time the lower real income of the consumer may tend toward an increase in the consumption of X.

With regard to the magnitude of the income effect compared with the substitution effect, the substitution effect is usually much the stronger of the two. A consumer who purchases a great many goods will not ordinarily experience a large drop in real income when the price of one of the goods rises. He may experience a large substitution effect, however, when good substitutes are available for the commodity in question.

Market Classifications and the Demand Curve Faced by the Firm | 6

IN THIS CHAPTER we look at demand from a different viewpoint — that of the individual business firm desiring to produce and sell a product. The discussion of demand in the preceding chapters was oriented toward consumers with whom demand does in fact originate. But we turn now to demand as it appears to the individual business firm.

No special definition of the firm is necessary at this point, but a little description may be in order. The concept of the firm used here is the ordinary concept of an individual business concern. It may be a single proprietorship, a partnership, or a corporation. To simplify exposition we shall assume that a single firm produces one product only.

The demand curve faced by a firm for its product shows the various amounts which it can sell at different possible prices, other things equal, and could appropriately be called a sales curve. The nature of such a curve depends upon the type of market in which the firm sells. Selling markets usually are classified into four different types. The bases of the classification are the importance of individual firms in relation to the entire market in which they sell and whether or not the products sold in a particular market are homogeneous. The market types are (1) pure competition, (2) pure monopoly, (3) oligopoly, and (4) monopolistic competition. Markets of the real world do not necessarily fall neatly within one classification or another, but may be a mixture of two or more. However, it will clarify our thinking to analyze the demand curve faced by the firm in each of the four theoretical or pure classifications. Detailed analysis of pricing and output under each will follow in Chapters 9–12.

PURE COMPETITION

The conditions necessary for pure competition to exist in a market were outlined in Chapter 3. There will be many firms selling identical products with no one firm large enough relative to the entire market to be able to influence market price. If one firm drops out of the market, supply will not be decreased enough to cause price to increase perceptibly. Neither will it be feasible for one firm to expand output enough to cause any perceptible decrease in market price. No single seller feels that he affects or is affected by other sellers in the market. No rivalries arise. There will be no reactions of other firms to actions taken by any one firm. Relationships among firms will be entirely impersonal.

The Demand Curve

Under these circumstances the demand curve facing the firm is horizontal at the prevailing market or equilibrium price. At any price above the prevailing market price, it can sell nothing. Since all firms of the industry sell identical products, consumers will turn to firms charging the market price if one firm raises its selling price above that level. The proportion of the total market filled by one seller is so small that the firm can dispose of its entire output at the prevailing market price; hence there is no necessity of lowering price below that of other sellers. Any firm attempting to do so will find itself swamped with buyers who promptly bid the price back up to the equilibrium level.

A producer of potatoes would face this sort of demand curve. When he hauls his potatoes to market he receives the going market price. If he asks for more than the market price and sticks to his request he will undoubtedly haul the potatoes home again. On the other hand no amount of potatoes that he alone could bring to market would drive the price down. He can sell all he desires to sell at the going market price.

Diagrammatically, the nature of the demand curve faced by the firm is illustrated by dd on the left-hand side of Figure 6–1. The market

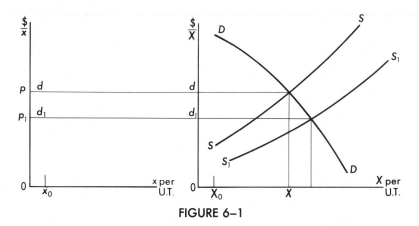

FIGURE 6–1

or industry demand curve and the industry supply curve are DD and SS, respectively. Market price is p and establishes the horizontal infinitely elastic demand curve faced by the firm. The price axes of the two diagrams are identical; however, quantity measurements of the industry diagram are compressed considerably as compared with those of the firm diagram. For example, if x_0 measures 10 units of X for the firm, suppose that X_0 measures 10,000 units of X for the industry.

In reality the demand curve faced by the firm is an infinitesimal segment of the industry demand curve in the neighborhood of quantity X stretched out over the firm diagram. Any one firm can be thought of as supplying the last small portion of quantity X. Stretching this small segment out over the firm diagram makes the demand curve faced by the firm appear horizontal.

Influence of the Firm on Demand, Price, and Output

Any forces that change market demand or market supply will change market price of the product and, consequently, the demand curve faced by the firm. The firm by itself can do nothing about either the demand curve faced by it or market price. It must accept both as given data. If industry supply increases to $S_1 S_1$, market price decreases to p_1 and the demand curve faced by the firm shifts downward to $d_1 d_1$. Any such change is completely beyond control of the individual firm. The firm can adjust only its output and will gear its output to the prevailing market price.

PURE MONOPOLY

Pure monopoly is a market situation in which a single firm sells a product for which there are no good substitutes. The firm has the mar-

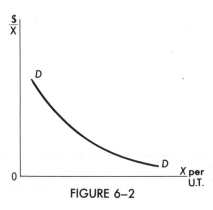

FIGURE 6–2

ket for the product all to itself. There are no similar products whose price or sales will influence the monopolist's price or sales perceptibly, and vice versa. Cross elasticity of demand between the monopolist's product and other products will be either zero or small enough to be neglected by all firms in the economy. The monopolist does not believe that actions of his will evoke retaliation of any kind from firms in other industries. Similarly, he does not consider that actions taken by firms in other industries are of sufficient importance to warrant his taking them into account. The monopolist is the industry from the producing point of view. The supplier of telephone service to a particular community is a case in point.

The Demand Curve

The market demand curve for the product is also the demand curve faced by the monopolist. Figure 6–2 shows the market demand curve for product X which is produced and sold by a monopolist. It shows the different quantities of X that buyers will take off the market at all possible prices of X. Since the monopolist is the only seller of product X, he can sell at different possible prices exactly the amounts that buyers will buy at those prices.

Influence of the Firm on Demand, Price, and Output

The monopolist is able to exert some influence on price, output, and demand for his product. The market demand curve marks off the limits of the monopolist's market. Faced by a given demand curve, he can increase sales if he is willing to lower his price, or he can increase his price if he is willing to restrict his sales volume. Additionally, he may be able to affect the demand curve itself through sales promotion activities of various kinds. He may be able to induce more people to buy his product, thus increasing demand, and he may be able to make demand less elastic if he can convince enough people that they cannot afford to be without the product. It follows that if the monopolist is able to increase demand he can increase sales to some extent without lowering price, or, alternatively, he can increase price to some extent without restricting his sales volume.

OLIGOPOLY

An oligopolistic industry is one in which the number of sellers is small enough for the activities of a single seller to affect other firms and for the activities of other firms to affect him. Changes in the output and price of one firm will affect the amounts which other sellers can sell and the prices which they can charge. Hence other firms will react in one way or another to price-output changes on the part of one. Individual sellers are not independent as they are under pure competition or under pure monopoly. Oligopolistic sellers are *interdependent*.

Typically the firms in an oligopolistic industry produce and sell "differentiated products." The products of all firms in the industry are very good substitutes for each other — they have high cross elasticities of demand — but that of each firm has its own distinguishing characteristics. The differences may be real or fancied. They may consist of differences in quality and design as is the case in the automobile industry, or they may consist merely of differences in brand names as is the case in the sale of aspirin tablets. The term *differentiated oligopoly* is applied to such industries.

Some industries approach a situation called *pure oligopoly*. Here the firms of the industry produce virtually identical products. Purchasers have little cause for preferring the product of one firm to that of another on any basis except price. Examples of industries approaching the pure oligopoly category are the cement industry, the aluminum industry, and the steel industry.

The Demand Curve

There is no typical demand situation facing an oligopolistic firm. The interdependence of sellers in an oligopolistic market makes the determination of the single seller's demand curve difficult. In some situations the demand curve faced by the firm is indeterminate. In others it can be located with some degree of accuracy.

The oligopolistic seller's demand curve will be indeterminate when he cannot predict what the reactions of his rivals will be to price and output changes on his part. The output that the one firm can sell if it changes its price depends upon the manner in which other firms react to its price change. The range of possible reactions is fairly broad. Rivals may just meet the price change, they may change price in the same direction but by less than the change of the original seller, they may undercut the price change, they may improve the quality of their products, they may engage in extensive advertising campaigns, or they may react in many other ways. Inability of the individual seller to predict which reactions will occur and in what degree amounts to inability to determine the demand curve faced by him.

When the single seller knows with some accuracy how his rivals will react to price changes on his part, the demand curve faced by him becomes correspondingly determinate. If he can form reliable judgments

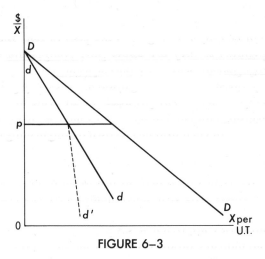

FIGURE 6–3

with regard to the probable effect of rivals' reactions on his own sales, he can take these into account. However, each different reaction by each different rival will result in different quantities which the single seller can market. Consequently, ascertaining the effects of rivals' reactions on the quantities that can be sold at different prices is at best a complex process for the individual firm. A few examples should improve our grasp of the problems involved.

Suppose that there are two producers in a particular oligopolistic industry and that price changes by either will be just matched by the other. Suppose also that the producers are of approximately equal size and prestige and produce virtually identical products. The market demand curve is *DD* in Figure 6–3. If each knows the other will just match his price changes, at any given price each will expect to get approximately half the market. Each will face a fairly determinate demand curve *dd* for his output and such a demand curve will lie about halfway between *DD* and the price axis.

Suppose now that one producer doesn't behave in the way described above. With an initial price of *p*, suppose that when Firm A cuts price, Firm B cuts price still more. Firm B will take part of Firm A's customers away from it. Hence the demand curve faced by Firm A will not follow *dd*, but will follow some path such as the broken line *d'*. Firm A, since its rival reacts by cutting price still more, will lose a part of its share of the market when it cuts price. Firm A, of course, will not take this lying down. It may undercut B's price again and the situation may degenerate into a price war — an indeterminate situation.

Suppose that the producers in a given oligopolistic industry form a cartel. Under the cartel arrangement the firms of the industry act as a single unit, each having some voice in the setting of price, output, and other industry policies. When all firms act as a unit, the amount that one firm can sell at different possible prices becomes irrelevant. The cartel is concerned with how much the industry as a whole can sell at different possible prices. Thus the cartel is in much the same position as is a pure monopolist, and is faced by the industry demand curve. The demand curve faced by a single firm fails to put in an appearance.

These examples provide a small sample of the possible demand situations faced by an oligopolistic seller. Additional illustrations will be presented in Chapter 11. Our goal at this point is to show that when the demand curve faced by one seller is determinate, its position and its shape will depend upon what the reactions of rivals will be to price changes on the part of the one.

Influence of the Firm on Demand, Price, and Output

Generally the oligopolist is able to influence in some degree the demand curve faced by him, his price, and his output. Through sales promotion efforts he may be able to shift the demand curve for his product to the right — partly by increasing consumer demand for this type of product, but mostly by inducing consumers to desert his rivals and to buy his own brand. He may be able to accomplish this result through advertising or through design and quality changes, provided such changes give his brand more customer appeal. Rivals will not be sitting idly by in such cases and may retaliate by vigorous campaigns of their own. The

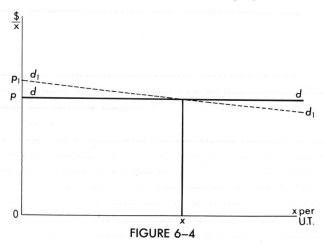

FIGURE 6–4

firms with the most successful campaigns will be the ones which succeed in increasing demand for their brands.

Whether the firm does or does not face a determinate demand curve, it knows that in general its demand curve slopes downward to the right. To increase sales it must usually lower price — unless the sales increase is made possible by a shift to the right of the demand curve. Higher prices can be obtained at the expense of sales, unless they are obtained through or in conjunction with increases in demand. Generally, the demand curve faced by an individual oligopolist will be fairly elastic because of the existence of the good substitutes produced by other firms in the industry. Elasticity of demand, however, as well as the position of the demand curve will depend upon rivals' reactions to the price and output changes of the single seller.

MONOPOLISTIC COMPETITION

Monopolistic competition is a market situation in which there are many sellers of a particular product, but the product of each seller is in some way differentiated in the minds of consumers from the product of every other seller. As in pure competition there are enough sellers, and each is small enough relative to the entire market so that the activities of one will have no effects on the others. Relationships among firms are impersonal. Product differentiation may take the form of brand names, trade-marks, quality differences, or differences in conveniences or services offered to consumers. The products are good substitutes for each other — their cross elasticities are high. Examples of industries approaching monopolistic competition include the women's full-fashioned hosiery industry, various textile products, and the service trades in large cities.

The Demand Curve

The shape of the demand curve faced by the firm under monopolistic competition comes from product differentiation. The influence of product differentiation can be seen readily if first we assume its absence. This assumption leaves us with the case of pure competition and a horizontal demand curve such as *dd* in Figure 6–4. Now we shall introduce the concept of product differentiation and observe how *dd* is affected. When products are differentiated, consumers become more or less attached to particular brand names. At any given price for commodity X some consumers will be on the margin of switching to other brands while others are attached to X at that price with varying degrees of tightness. Suppose that for the monopolistic competitor quantity x will be taken at price p. If the firm raises price, those consumers on the verge of switching to other brands will make the switch since the other brands are now relatively lower in price. The higher the firm raises its price, the more customers it will lose to relatively lower-priced brands. Since other brands will usually be very good substitutes for that of the firm under consideration, the rise in price necessary for the firm to lose all its customers (pp_1) will not be large. For price increases above p the demand curve faced by the firm will be the dotted line. Similarly, if the firm lowers price below p, it will pick up marginal customers of other sellers since its price is now relatively lower as compared with other firms' prices. It will not have to lower price much to pick up all the additional customers it can handle. Thus for decreases in price below p the dotted line shows the demand curve faced by the one firm. The entire demand curve faced by the monopolistic competitor is one such as d_1d_1.

It may appear offhand that decreases in price by one firm that attract customers away from the other firms in the industry will evoke some kind of retaliatory action on the part of the other firms, as in the case of oligopoly. We must keep in mind, however, that there are many firms in the monopolistically competitive industry. The firm decreasing its price will attract so few customers from each of the others that the other firms will not notice or feel the loss. Nevertheless, for the one firm the total increase in customers will be substantial.

Likewise, it may seem that price increases by the one firm which drive customers away would increase demand for the products of the other firms. Again, we must remember that customers shifting to other firms will be widely scattered among those firms. Not enough will go to any other single firm to cause any perceptible increase in demand for its product, even though the loss of customers to the price-raising firm is substantial.

Influence of the Firm on Demand, Price, and Output

The individual firm under conditions of monopolistic competition may be able to influence demand for its own product to some perceptible degree through advertising. However, the existence of many good substitutes will preclude much success in this direction.

The firm is subjected to highly competitive forces, but is to a small extent a sort of monopolist. It is a sort of monopolist since it has some discretion in setting price and output. However, if the firm raises price very much it loses all its customers, and it does not have to lower price very far to secure all the customers it can handle. Within that limited price range the firm has price-setting discretion. Outside that price range it is subject to competitive forces. The demand curve faced by the firm under monopolistic competition will be highly elastic throughout its relevant range. The cause is not hard to find. The products of all firms in the industry, even though differentiated, are very good substitutes for each other.

SUMMARY

Analysis of the demand situation facing the individual business firm is organized around four market classifications. The conditions of demand facing the individual firm differ from classification to classification. The differences stem from two sources: (1) the importance of the individual firm in the market in which it sells, and (2) product differentiation or product homogeneity.

Pure competition stands at one extreme of the classification and pure monopoly stands at the other. Purely competitive firms sell homogeneous products and each is so small relative to the entire market that by itself it cannot influence market price. Hence the demand curve faced by the firm is horizontal at the equilibrium market price. A monopolist is a single seller of a product not closely related to any other product. He faces the market demand curve for his product.

Oligopoly and monopolistic competition fill the gap between the two extremes. Monopolistic competition differs from pure competition in one respect only — products of different sellers are differentiated. This fact gives the monopolistic competitor a small amount of control over his price; however, each firm is so small relative to the entire market that by itself it cannot affect other firms in the industry. It faces a downward sloping highly elastic demand curve.

With regard to the number of firms in the industry, oligopoly lies between the extremes of pure competition and monopolistic competition on the one hand and pure monopoly on the other. Its primary characteristic is that there are few enough firms in the industry for the activities of one firm to have repercussions on the price and sales of the other firms. Hence rivalries develop under oligopoly. The demand curve faced by a single seller depends upon what the reactions of rivals will be to market activities on the part of the one. If the reactions of rivals cannot be predicted, the demand curve faced by the firm cannot be determined.

SUGGESTED READINGS

FELLNER, WILLIAM. *Modern Economic Analysis.* New York: McGraw-Hill Book Company, Inc., 1960, chap. 17.

MACHLUP, FRITZ. "Monopoly and Competition: A Classification of Market Positions," *American Economic Review,* XXVII (September 1937), 445–451.

The Principles of Production | 7

THE PRINCIPLES OF PRODUCTION provide the foundation for analysis of costs of production and supplies of particular goods. The theory of costs in the next chapter builds upon the foundation laid here. The ensuing four chapters bring demand theory and production theory together to give us our first detailed view of product pricing and output. Additionally, the principles of production are a fundamental element in the analysis of resource pricing and employment, resource allocation among alternative employments in the economy, and distribution of the economy's product.

The theory of production parallels in many respects the theory of consumer demand. The economic unit under analysis is the individual firm rather than the individual consumer. Whereas the individual consumer attempts to maximize satisfaction by the way in which he spends his income on consumer goods, the individual firm attempts to maximize the product output it can obtain with any given cost outlay by the way in which it secures and combines resource inputs. A fundamental difference between the two theories is that while the disposable income of the consumer is fixed, the possible outlays of the firm are variable. The difference will not concern us much here but will be of importance in subsequent chapters. As in the theory of demand, two alternative approaches to the theory of production are in common use. The first one, which we shall call the traditional approach, parallels the utility approach to demand theory. The second one is the *isoquant-isocost* approach, and it parallels the indifference curve approach to demand theory. The traditional approach will be developed in the chapter proper. Appendix II to the chapter presents the fundamentals of the isoquant-isocost approach.

The traditional approach to the principles of production begins with the nature of the production function. Next, the law of diminishing returns is considered. Third, resource product curves and the efficiency of various resource combinations are analyzed. Fourth, the firm's selection of the least-cost combination of resources is discussed.

98

THE PRODUCTION FUNCTION

The term *production function* is applied to the physical relation between a firm's inputs of resources and its output of goods or services per unit of time, leaving prices aside. It can be expressed in general mathematical terminology as

$$x = f(a, b, c)$$

The output of goods is represented by x and the inputs of resources are represented by $a, b,$ and c. The equation can be expanded readily to include as many different resources as are used in the production of any given commodity. It furnishes a convenient way of relating product output to resource inputs.

The product output that a firm can produce depends upon the quantities of resources used. The firm can increase or decrease output by increasing or decreasing the quantities of all resources used. Or, since resources usually can be combined in varying proportions to produce a commodity, output also can be increased up to some maximum level by increasing the quantity of one resource while holding the quantities of other resources constant. For example, since various combinations of land, labor, seed, and fertilizer can be used to produce wheat, we would expect increases in the quantity of fertilizer, holding the quantities of the other resources constant, to increase wheat yields up to some maximum level. We shall return to this point shortly while discussing the law of diminishing returns.

The product output achieved by a firm also depends upon the techniques of production used. Given the firm's cost outlay for resources, the more efficient the techniques used, the greater will be the firm's output. The less efficient the techniques used, the smaller will be its output. We shall continue to assume that whatever the cost outlay made by the firm, the techniques used will be the most efficient ones available.

THE LAW OF DIMINISHING RETURNS

Definition

The law of diminishing returns describes the direction and the rate of change which the firm's output takes when the input of one resource only is varied. It states that *if the input of one resource is increased by equal increments per unit of time while the inputs of other resources are held constant, total product output will increase, but beyond some point the resulting*

TABLE 7–1

(1)	(2)	(3)	(4)	(5)	
			MARGINAL		
		TOTAL	PHYSICAL	AVERAGE	
		PRODUCT	PRODUCT	PRODUCT	
LAND	LABOR	(LABOR)	(LABOR)	(LABOR)	
1	1	3	3	3	
1	2	7	4	3½	Stage I
1	3	12	5	4	
1	4	16	4	4	
1	5	19	3	3⅘	
1	6	21	2	3½	Stage II
1	7	22	1	3⅐	
1	8	22	0	2¾	
1	9	21	(–)1	2⅓	Stage III
1	10	15	(–)6	1½	

output increases will become smaller and smaller.[1] If input increases of the variable resource are carried far enough, total product will reach a maximum and may then decrease. The law is consistent with observations that there are limits to the output that can be obtained by increasing the quantity of a single resource applied to constant quantities of other resources.

The law of diminishing returns may or may not be operative for the first few units of the variable resource used with the fixed quantities of other resources. Diminishing returns or diminishing total product increases may be evident with the first few increases in the variable resource. This occurs frequently with the application of larger quantities of fertilizer to a given complex of seed, land, labor, and machinery. On the other hand, a stage of increasing returns may characterize the initial increases in the variable resource before diminishing returns begin. An example here is that of labor used to operate a factory of given size. Smaller quantities of labor than that for which the factory is designed tend to operate inefficiently because of the multiplicity of jobs to be performed by each individual and because of time lost in changing from one job to another. Equal increments in labor used bring about successively greater

---

[1] The different inputs of the variable resource refer to *alternative* quantities used with constant amounts of other resources, not to a chronological application of additional units.

increments in total product up to some point. Beyond that point, increases in the quantity of labor used lead to diminishing returns.

We shall illustrate the product curves of a variable resource and the law of diminishing returns both numerically and graphically. The illustration will be reduced to its simplest form. Suppose that a single resource — call it land — is fixed in quantity. Suppose alternative quantities of a variable resource — labor — are applied to a unit of land and that the ensuing product outputs are observed and recorded.

A Numerical Illustration

The results of the hypothetical experiments are listed in Table 7–1. The total product column shows increasing returns (larger and larger successive increases in total product) for the first three units of labor.[2] Beginning with the fourth unit of labor the law of diminishing returns becomes operative. Eight units of labor produce the maximum amount of product obtainable from the unit of land.

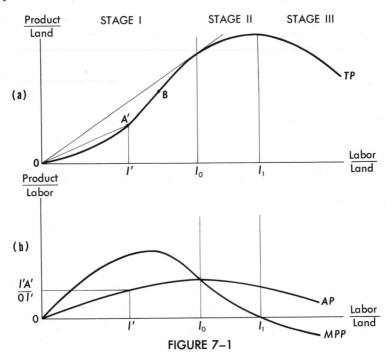

FIGURE 7–1

***

[2] Whether we assume that diminishing returns occur at the outset or whether we assume first increasing and then diminishing returns is not of paramount importance. The latter assumption probably is more general and will be used here.

Use of the phrase "successive increases (or decreases) in total product" is awkward. Instead, we should refer to *marginal physical product* of labor. The marginal physical product of a resource is defined as the change in total product resulting from a one-unit change in the quantity of the resource used per unit of time. Thus, the law of diminishing returns could as well be called the law of diminishing marginal physical product. Column 4 of Table 7–1 lists the marginal physical product of labor.

The average product of labor is shown in column 5. Average product for any given quantity of labor is found by dividing total product of that quantity of labor by the quantity of labor itself. Since total product of labor is positive in sign, average product must be positive, too.

A Graphic Illustration

A graphic illustration of the product curves and the law of diminishing returns is presented in Figure 7–1. The vertical axis of Figure 7–1(a) measures total product produced on a unit of land; that is, Product/Land. The vertical axis of Figure 7–1(b) measures product per unit of labor; that is, Product/Labor. The horizontal axes of both diagrams measure different quantities of labor used per unit of land and are properly designated as Labor/Land.

The total product curve of Figure 7–1(a) shows the same type of information as the total product schedule of Table 7–1.[3] Note that it is drawn concave upward for the first several units of labor. This illustrates the situation in which a very small quantity of a variable resource used with a given quantity of a fixed resource will tend to be inefficient, or, in other words, the variable resource is being used too sparsely with the given amount of fixed resource. Increasing the quantity of the variable resource will bring about successively greater increments in total product or increasing returns up to some point such as B. At point B the law of diminishing returns takes effect and equal increments in labor result in successively smaller increments in total product. When l_1 units of labor are used on the unit of land, total product reaches a maximum. In the illustration still more units of labor per unit of land cause total product to decrease.

---

[3] The total product curve of Figure 7–1 begins at the origin of the diagram, but this is not necessary. For some resources not absolutely essential in the production of the product, it may begin above the origin — cottonseed meal fed to cows to increase milk production is a case in point. In other cases no product may be obtained until several units of the variable resource are applied to the fixed complex of other resources. For example, one man in a steel mill will produce nothing. Two men can do no better. A certain minimum complement of labor is necessary before any production can be obtained. In this case the total product curve of labor begins to the right of the origin.

The average product curve for labor can be derived easily from the total product curve and is drawn in Figure 7–1(b). Since average product equals total product divided by the number of units of labor used, then average product at l' units of labor equals $l'A'/Ol'$ or the slope of the line OA'.[4] As the number of units of labor is increased from zero to l_0 the slopes of the corresponding OA lines increase and hence the average product of labor increases. At l_0 units of labor the slope of line OA_0 is greater than that of any other OA line drawn from the origin to the total product curve. Thus, the average product of labor will be maximum at this point. Beyond l_0 units of labor, average product will decrease, but it will remain positive as long as total product is positive. The average product curve obtained from the total product curve of Figure 7–1(a) is shown as AP in Figure 7–1(b).

Since the marginal physical product of labor is defined as the change in total product per unit change in the quantity of labor used, the slope of the total product curve at any given quantity of labor will be equal to marginal physical product at that quantity of labor.[5] Marginal physical product reaches a maximum at point B where the total product curve turns from concave upward to concave downward. At quantity l_1 of labor, total product is maximum; hence marginal physical product is zero. Beyond l_1, additional units of labor cause total product to decrease, so marginal physical product is negative.

An additional guide to the proper location of the marginal physical product curve is its relationship to the average product curve. When average product is increasing, marginal physical product is greater than average product. When average product is maximum, marginal physical product equals average product. When average product is decreasing, marginal physical product is less than average product.[6] These relationships can be verified by reference to columns 4 and 5 of Table 7–1.

---

[4] See pages 152–155 for the similar derivation of an average cost curve from a total cost curve.

[5] See pages 48–51 for the similar derivation of a marginal utility curve from a total utility curve.

[6] To illustrate these relationships, consider a succession of men entering a room, each taller than the one who preceded him. As each man enters, the average height of the men in the room increases; however, except for the first man, average height will be less than that of the man currently entering. The height of each man as he enters is marginal height and is analogous to marginal physical product. Average height is analogous to average product. Thus for average product (height) to be increasing, marginal physical product (height) must exceed the average. Now suppose that additional men enter, each successively shorter than the one preceding him and all shorter than was average height before they entered. Average height will decrease but will not be as low as marginal height. Where average height is maximum the height of the last man who entered must have been equal to average height since he caused neither an increase nor a decrease in average height.

PRODUCT CURVES AND THE EFFICIENCY OF RESOURCE COMBINATIONS

The three product curves just described provide a means for determining how efficient various resource combinations will be in the process of production. We shall assume that both land and labor are completely divisible with respect to quantities used, and that techniques of production are such that the same techniques will be used for any given ratio of labor to land regardless of the absolute amount of the resources used. To put this another way, we shall assume that the same techniques would be used if two units of labor work one unit of land as would be used if one unit of labor works one-half unit of land or if four units of labor work two units of land. A situation of this kind is called constant returns to scale — proportional changes in the quantities of all resources used change product output in the same proportion.

Our major concern is with the *ratio* of the "variable" resource to the "fixed" resource. In arriving at the product curves we are not really limited to one unit of land or whatever quantity the "fixed" resource happens to be. We can think of the firm as using any amount of land it wishes to use, but in establishing the product curves we convert our observations into terms of product obtainable from one unit of the "fixed" resource. For example if ten units of labor working two units of land produce thirty-eight units of product per unit of time, for purposes of establishing the product curves, we would convert the data to a one unit of land equivalent — that is, five units of labor working one unit of land produce an output of nineteen units of product per unit of time. An increase in the quantity of land used while labor is held constant in quantity is equivalent to a decrease in the quantity of labor with the quantity of land being held constant.

The Three Stages

The product schedules of Table 7–1 and the product curves of Figure 7–1 can be divided into three stages. In each of the three stages the average product curve of labor and the total product curve provide information with regard to how efficiently the resources are used for various labor-land ratios. As the ratio of labor to land is increased, that is, as more and more labor per unit of land is used, the average product curve provides information regarding the amount of product obtained per unit of labor for the various ratios. The total product curve provides information regarding the amount of product obtained per unit of land.

Stage I is characterized by increases in the average product of labor as more labor per unit of land is used. The increases in average product are the same thing as increases in the efficiency of labor — the product per worker increases. The total product obtained per unit of land as larger quantities of labor are applied to it also increases in Stage I. The increases in total product show us that the efficiency of land increases, too, in Stage I. Thus increases in the quantity of labor applied to a unit of land in Stage I increase the efficiency with which both labor and land are utilized.

Stage II is characterized by decreasing average product and decreasing marginal physical product of labor. But marginal physical product is positive since total product continues to increase. In Stage II, as larger quantities of labor per unit of land are used, the efficiency of labor — product per worker — decreases. However, the efficiency of land — product per unit of land — continues to increase.

In Stage III the application of larger quantities of labor to a unit of land decreases average product of labor still more. Additionally, marginal physical product is negative and total product is decreasing. The efficiency of labor and the efficiency of land both decrease when the firm pushes into Stage III combinations.

In looking over the three stages we note two things. The combination of labor and land that leads to maximum efficiency of labor lies at the boundary line between Stage I and Stage II. The combination of labor and land leading to maximum efficiency of land is the one at the boundary line between Stage II and Stage III.

Stage II Combinations

The foregoing discussion suggests that Stage II ratios will be more efficient than Stage I or Stage III ratios. By introducing resource costs into the picture we can clinch the case. Suppose that land is so plentiful that it costs nothing at all while labor is scarce enough to command some price. Since whatever cost outlay the firm makes will go for labor, the firm will achieve greatest economic efficiency (lowest cost per unit of product) at the ratio of labor to land that maximizes product per unit of labor. This ratio occurs at the boundary between Stage I and Stage II. The output per unit expenditure will increase through Stage I and decrease through Stage II and Stage III.

Suppose that labor can be had for the asking and that land is a scarce resource which commands a price. In this case the entire cost outlay goes for land and economic efficiency is greatest when the ratio of labor to land is such that product per unit of land is maximum. Stage I is again ruled out of consideration since product per unit of land (and per unit expenditure) increases through Stage I ratios. Stage II is ruled out for the same reason. Note, however, that economic efficiency of the firm increases through both Stage I and Stage II. In Stage III product per unit expenditure decreases along with the decrease in product per unit of land. Thus economic efficiency will be greatest at the boundary line between Stage II and Stage III.

Suppose now that both labor and land are economic resources — that is, both are scarce enough to command a price. Increases in the ratio of labor to land in Stage I increase both the product per unit of labor and the product per unit of land. This increases the product obtained per unit of expenditure on both; hence the firm will move at least to the boundary between Stage I and Stage II. If the firm moves into Stage II the product per unit expenditure on labor decreases while that per unit expenditure on land increases. Which is more important — the increasing efficiency of land or the decreasing efficiency of labor? We shall return to the question in a moment. Should the firm move into Stage III the product per unit expenditure on land and on labor both decrease; hence when both resources have costs, the firm should not go beyond the boundary line between Stage II and Stage III.

Labor to land ratios of Stage I and Stage III are ruled out of the firm's consideration under all circumstances. The firm will not operate in Stage I when land is free and when labor has costs, or when labor is free and land has costs, or when both resources command prices. The same thing applies to Stage III. Stage II is left as the possible range of relevant ratios of labor to land.

What ratio of labor to land falling within Stage II will the firm use? The answer depends upon the comparative costs or prices per unit of land and labor. We have observed already that if land is free and labor must be paid, the firm will use the ratio at which Stage II begins. If land must be paid and labor is free, the firm will use the ratio at which Stage II ends. From this we can deduce that the less the price of land relative to the price of labor, the closer the ratio should be to the beginning of Stage II. The less the price of labor relative to the price of land the closer the ratio should be to the end of Stage II. Generalizing, for any resource that a firm uses, we can say that the firm should use some ratio of that resource to other resources which falls within Stage II for that resource.

THE LEAST-COST COMBINATION

We can go beyond the simple case and adopt one a little more realistic. The simple case has the virtue of placing the principles of production in proper focus and those principles will be carried over into the more complex example. Suppose that we have a manufacturing firm

TABLE 7–2

RESOURCE A (Physical units)	MPP_a (Units of X)	RESOURCE B (Physical units)	MPP_b (Units of X)
5	10	7	6
6	9	8	5
7	8	9	4
8	6	10	3
9	3	11	1
10	0	12	0

operating a factory of a given size. Assume that the quantities of resources comprising the factory's physical plant do not change during the time period under consideration. Two resources, A and B, are used in the factory, and more or less of both together or of each individually can be used in the production of product X.

The problem facing the firm is that of using resources A and B in such proportions or in such a ratio that whatever the output produced the cost outlay made for A and B will be as small as possible for that particular output. We shall put this the other way around in order to get at the way in which the firm should solve the problem. We can say that the firm should use that combination of A and B which will produce the greatest amount of product for a given cost outlay. Suppose that the price of A is $2 per unit and the price of B is $1 per unit. The cost outlay to be made by the firm on the two resources is $26 per day. The daily marginal physical product schedules in Stage II for each resource are listed in Table 7–2.[7]

The problem faced by the firm in this case is the same type of problem as that faced by the consumer in maximizing utility with his given income. The consumer maximizes satisfaction by spending his income on different goods in such a way that the marginal utility per dollar's worth of one good is equal to the marginal utility per dollar's worth of every other good purchased. Similarly, the firm will maximize total

---

[7] The numerical example assumes that MPP_a is independent of MPP_b. This will not be the case usually. If A and B are complementary resources, the greater the quantity of A used, the higher will be the MPP_b schedule; and the greater the quantity of B used, the higher will be the MPP_a schedule. If they are competitive or substitute resources, the marginal physical product schedules of each will shift inversely to the quantity of the other resource used. We are interested in the end result — the ratio in which the two resources are finally combined. The assumption of independence allows us to move directly and simply to that result and in no way vitiates it.

product by distributing its cost outlay among different resources in such a way that the marginal physical product of a dollar's worth of one resource is equal to the marginal physical product of a dollar's worth of every other resource used. Letting p_a and p_b represent the price per unit of resources A and B, respectively, the conditions necessary for maximization of product with a given cost outlay can be expressed as follows:

$$\frac{MPP_a}{p_a} = \frac{MPP_b}{p_b}$$

These conditions can be extended to include as many variable resources as the firm uses.

Since the price per unit of A is \$2 and the price per unit of B is \$1, the combination of A and B used should be such that the marginal physical product of A is twice that of B when the firm is spending the \$26. This occurs at eight units of A and ten units of B. The marginal physical product per dollar's worth of each resource is three units of product.

To prove that output is maximized for the given cost outlay assume that a dollar is shifted from resource A to resource B. At eight units of A the marginal physical product per dollar's worth of A is three units of product. Therefore, withdrawal of the dollar from resource A decreases total product by three units. Spending the additional dollar on B enables the firm to take the eleventh unit of B, which adds only one unit to the firm's total product. The transfer causes the firm's total product to decrease by two units. Similarly, starting from the equilibrium position, the transfer of a dollar from B to A will occasion a net loss in total product.

The statement that the firm obtains maximum product from a given cost outlay means the same thing as the statement that the firm obtains a given amount of product at the least possible cost. If we consider the maximum amount of product obtained by the firm for its \$26 cost outlay as the given amount of product, then obviously the \$26 cost outlay is the least cost for which that amount of product can be produced.

The principles just discussed constitute formalized common sense. They are not limited to manufacturing establishments but are quite general in their application. Consider an accounting firm. To accomplish its work it can use labor of varying skills, or machines of various kinds, or different combinations of labor and machines. Its work is to be turned out at the least possible cost. How should the correct combination of labor and machines be determined? If a dollar's worth of labor adds less to output than a dollar's worth of machines, a combination of less labor and more machines will lower the costs of the firm. As the ratio of machines to labor is increased, the marginal physical product per dollar's worth of machines decreases while that of labor increases. When the ratio is such that a dollar's worth of labor adds the same amount to output as a dollar's worth of machines, cost of the firm's output is minimized.

SUMMARY

The principles of production lay the foundation for analysis of costs, resource pricing and employment, resource allocation, and product distribution. These will be met in later chapters.

The term *production function* is applied to the physical relation between resource inputs and product output of a firm. Product output is determined partly by the quantities of resource inputs and partly by the techniques of production used by the firm.

The law of diminishing returns describes the general nature of the production function when product output is varied by using variable quantities of one resource together with fixed quantities of all other resources. We distinguished among total product, marginal physical product, and average product of the variable resource. The product schedules or product curves of the variable resource were divided into three stages. Stage I is characterized by increasing average product. In Stage II average and marginal physical product of the variable resource are decreasing, but its marginal physical product is still positive. In Stage III the marginal physical product of the variable resource is negative. We deduced that only those ratios of the variable resource to other resources lying within Stage II may be economically efficient for the firm to use.

The precise combination of variable resources that the firm should use depends upon the marginal physical products of those resources and upon their respective prices. To maximize product with a given cost outlay or to minimize cost for a given amount of product, resources should be combined in ratios such that the marginal physical product per dollar's worth of one equals the marginal physical product per dollar's worth of each other resource used.

SUGGESTED READINGS

CASSELS, JOHN M. "On the Law of Variable Proportions," *Explorations in Economics.* New York: McGraw-Hill Book Company, Inc., 1936, pp. 223–236. Reprinted in *Readings in the Theory of Income Distribution.* Philadelphia: The Blakiston Company, 1946, pp. 103–118.

HEADY, EARL O. *Economics of Agricultural Production and Resource Use.* New York: Prentice-Hall, Inc., 1952, chap. 2.

KNIGHT, FRANK H. *Risk, Uncertainty, and Profit.* Boston: Houghton Mifflin Company, 1921, pp. 94–104.

The Symmetry of Stage I and Stage III

The product schedules of Table 7–1 and the product curves of Figure 7–1 can be reworked, using labor as the fixed resource and land as the variable resource. The process will show that the original Stage I for labor is Stage III for land, that the original Stage III for labor is Stage I for land, and that the original Stage II for labor is also Stage II for land. We shall assume as before that techniques of production are such that proportional increases in both resources will increase total product proportionally; that is, sixty men working ten acres of land use the same techniques as six men working one acre of land and will produce ten times as much product.

Again, it is the ratios of labor to land used that are important. Reading the horizontal axes of Figure 7–1 in the usual way, the farther to the right we move the greater is the ratio of labor to land. If we move from right to left on the horizontal axes the ratio of labor to land decreases. This means precisely the same thing as increases in the ratio of land to labor. Therefore, if we want to show the effects of increasing the ratio of land to labor we must rework the diagram from right to left. Similarly we must rework Table 7–1 from bottom to top.

THE PRODUCT SCHEDULES

We shall rework Table 7–1 first, listing the results in Table 7–3. Starting at the bottom of Table 7–1, ten units of labor are used per unit of land. In a ratio sense this means the same thing as using one tenth of a unit of land per unit of labor. These numbers are shown in columns 1 and 2 in the last row of Table 7–3. Similarly, in terms of ratios, nine units of labor per unit of land are the same as one ninth of a unit of land per unit of labor, and so on up through the table until we reach the top, where one unit of land is used with one unit of labor. The ratios of land and labor are the same throughout Table 7–3 as they are in Table 7–1.

TABLE 7–3

(1) LAND	(2) LABOR	(3) TOTAL PRODUCT (LAND)	(4) MARGINAL PRODUCT (LAND)	(5) AVERAGE PRODUCT (LAND)	
1	1	3	(−)1	3	
½	1	3½	(−)3	7	Stage III
⅓	1	4	0	12	
¼	1	4	4	16	
⅕	1	3⅘	9	19	Stage II
⅙	1	3½	15	21	
⅐	1	3⅐	22	22	
⅛	1	2¾	30	22	
⅑	1	2⅓	75	21	Stage I
⅒	1	1½	15	15	

Next, the total product schedule for variable amounts of land applied to one unit of labor can be determined. From Table 7–1 we see that ten units of labor applied to one unit of land produce fifteen units of product. Obviously, then, one tenth of a unit of land applied to one unit of labor should produce a total product of 15/10 or 1½ units of product. The total product of one tenth of a unit of land is listed in the last row of column 3 in Table 7–3. Since nine units of labor applied to one unit of land produce twenty-one units of product, one ninth of a unit of land applied to one unit of labor will produce a total product of 2⅓. Total product of the larger quantities of land used with one unit of labor is computed in a similar way to complete column 3.

The marginal physical product schedule for land should show the increments in total product per full unit increment in land at the various ratios of land to labor used. The first one tenth of a unit of land used increases total product from zero to 1½ units. Therefore, at this ratio of land to labor the marginal physical product of a unit of land is $1½ ÷ 1/10 = 3/2 \times 10 = 15$ units of product, which is listed in column 4 in the last row of Table 7–3. An increase in land from one tenth of a unit to one ninth of a unit increases total product from 1½ to 2⅓. The product increment is $7/3 − 3/2 = 14/6 − 9/6 = 5/6$ of a unit of product. The land increment is $1/9 − 1/10 = 10/90 − 9/90 = 1/90$ of a unit of land. Marginal physical product of a unit of land at this point is

THE PRODUCT SCHEDULES   113

$5/6 \div 1/90 = 5/6 \times 90 = 75$ units of product. By similar computations on up through columns 1 and 3 of Table 7–3, column 4 is determined.

Column 5 of Table 7–3, read from bottom to top, presents average product per unit of land for the various land to labor ratios. Average product of land for each ratio is obtained by dividing total product of land by the quantity of land used. Since one tenth of a unit of land produces 1½ units of product, average product of land equals $1½ \div 1/10$ equals fifteen at this point. Similarly, 2⅓ units of product divided by one ninth of a unit of land shows that average product of land at this point is twenty-one units. The other figures of column 5 are determined by similar computations.

When Table 7–1 is compared with Table 7–3, two columns of Table 7–1 are seen to be identical with two columns in Table 7–3. First, the total product schedule of labor applied to one unit of land (see Table 7–1, column 3) has become the average product schedule of land applied to one unit of labor (see Table 7–3, column 5). Second, the average product schedule of labor applied to one unit of land (see Table 7–1, column 5) has become the total product schedule of land applied to one unit of labor (see Table 7–3, column 3). A little reflection will reveal that this is as it should be. The total product of more and more labor applied to one unit of land is the average product of land (or the product per unit of land) as the ratio of labor to land is increased. Likewise, the average product of labor (product per unit of labor) is necessarily the total product of various quantities of land applied to one unit of labor.

A further observation can be made. Stages I, II, and III are marked off approximately for labor in Table 7–1.[1] Stages I, II, and III for land are marked off approximately in Table 7–3. That which is Stage I for labor in Table 7–1 has become Stage III for land in Table 7–3. That which is Stage III for labor in Table 7–1 has become Stage I for land in Table 7–3. Stage II for labor is also Stage II for land in both tables.

THE PRODUCT CURVES

The product curves for land per unit of labor are shown graphically in Figure 7–2. The product curves for both labor applied to a unit of land and for land applied to a unit of labor are drawn in the diagram. Reading the horizontal axes from left to right the ratio of labor to land is increasing, giving rise to the three familiar product curves for labor [TP (Labor) in Figure 7–2(a); AP (Labor) and MPP (Labor) in Figure 7–2(b)]. Reading the horizontal axes from right to left, the ratio of

---

[1] The boundary lines between stages must be approximations when product schedules are set up in table form. Only on continuous graphs can the exact boundaries between the stages be established.

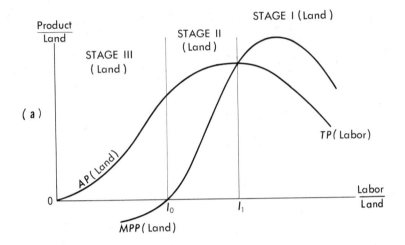

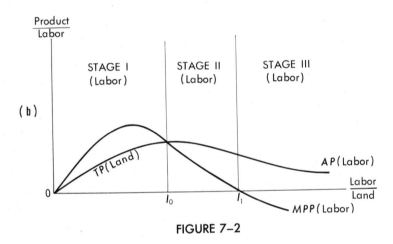

FIGURE 7–2

land to labor is increasing. The total product curve of labor when the ratio of labor to land is increased becomes the average product curve for land when the ratio of land to labor is increased. The average product curve for labor when the ratio of labor to land is increased becomes the total product curve for land when the ratio of land to labor is increased. Note that the marginal physical product curve for land, reading from right to left in Figure 7–2(a), lies above the average product curve for land when average product is increasing, cuts the average product curve at its maximum point, and lies below the average product curve when that curve is decreasing. Note also that the marginal physical

TABLE 7–4

LABOR PRODUCTIVITY WHEN THE RATIO OF LABOR TO LAND IS INCREASED		LAND PRODUCTIVITY WHEN THE RATIO OF LAND TO LABOR IS INCREASED	
Stage I	Increasing *AP*	Negative *MPP*	Stage III
Stage II	Decreasing *AP* and *MPP*, but *MPP* is positive	Decreasing *AP* and *MPP*, but *MPP* is positive	Stage II
Stage III	Negative *MPP*	Increasing *AP*	Stage I

product curve for land reaches zero at the ratio of land to labor at which total product of land is maximum. Marginal physical product of land is negative where increases in the quantity of land per unit of labor lead to decreases in total product of land. The three stages for both land and labor are shown in Figure 7–2.

We can observe now why the firm will not operate in either Stage I or Stage III for labor or in Stage I or Stage III for land. We can determine why Stage II, which is common for both land and labor, contains all the relevant ratios of labor to land for the firm. The three stages — their relationships and their characteristics — are summed up in Table 7–4. We noted earlier that in Stage I for labor, labor is used too sparsely on the land and that increases in the ratio of labor to land will increase its average product. We can observe further that in Stage I for labor (Stage III for land), the marginal physical product of land is negative. Too little labor per unit of land means precisely the same thing as too much land per unit of labor. The firm should increase the ratio of labor to land used (or decrease the ratio of land to labor used) at least to the point at which the average product of labor will no longer increase and the marginal physical product of land will no longer be negative. Such an increase will place the firm in Stage II. In Stage III for labor, the marginal physical product of labor is negative, which means that too much labor is used per unit of land or that too little land is used per unit of labor. The ratio of labor to land should be decreased at least to the point at which the marginal physical product of labor is no longer negative. Decreases in the ratio of labor to land (increases in the ratio of land to labor) will increase the average product of land. A decrease in the ratio of labor to land sufficient to make the marginal physical product of labor no longer negative and to make the average product of land no longer increase will place the firm in Stage II. Thus, the firm will use resource combinations lying within Stage II for each resource that it uses.

If it does otherwise, marginal physical product of some resource will be negative, which means that total product can be increased by using less of that resource.

We can draw a fundamental generalization from the analysis presented above. Whenever a resource is used so sparingly that its average product rises as more of it is used, some other resource (or resources) is being used so heavily that its marginal physical product is negative. This can be put the other way around. Whenever any resource is used so heavily that its marginal physical product is negative, some other resource (or resources) is being used so sparingly that an increase in its quantity will increase its average product.

Isoquants and Isocosts

The isoquant-isocost approach to production theory, like the traditional approach, explains the principles that underlie costs, resource pricing and employment, resource allocation, and product distribution. In some respects it is an alternative to the traditional approach. In other respects it shades into and supplements the traditional approach. We shall use the traditional theory of the text to help explain isoquant-isocost analysis wherever possible.

Again, the principles of production are developed with respect to the individual firm. Isoquants, which represent the firm's production possibilities, are developed first. Then resource costs and the firm's outlay are introduced in the form of isocosts. Following logically from these is the determination of the firm's least-cost resource combinations.

ISOQUANTS

The exposition of isoquants is divided into three parts. First, the concept of isoquants is explained. Second, product curves are derived from a firm's set of isoquants. Third, isoquants are used to enlarge upon and generalize Stages I, II, and III of the product curves of the firm's resources.

The Concept of Isoquants

DEFINITION • An isoquant is the same general type of curve as an indifference curve. An indifference curve shows the different combinations of two products that will yield equal satisfaction to the consumer. An isoquant shows the different combinations of two resources with which a firm can produce equal amounts of product. In Figure 7–3 the curve designated x_6 is an isoquant. Points along the isoquant show the combinations of resource A and resource B that will produce x_6 units of product X. The firm can obtain x_6 units of product by using b_5 units of resource B together with a_4 units of resource A, or by using b_1 units of re-

117

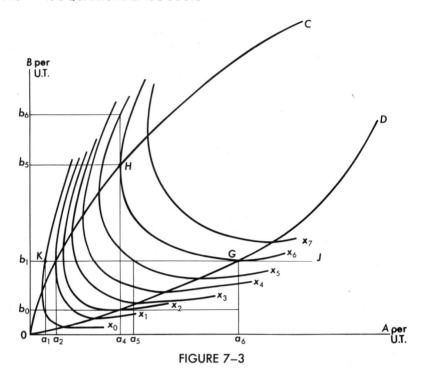

FIGURE 7–3

source B together with a_6 units of resource A, or by using any other combination of A and B shown on that isoquant.

Greater amounts of product are represented by higher isoquants. Isoquant x_7 shows the different combinations of A and B necessary to produce quantity x_7 of product X, where quantity x_7 is greater than quantity x_6. Similarly, quantities x_5, x_4, x_3, x_2, and x_1 are lower isoquants for smaller quantities of product X.

CHARACTERISTICS • The general characteristics of isoquants are the same as those of indifference curves. Two isoquants will not intersect. For all combinations of resources A and B that the firm could use rationally to produce a given output, the isoquant will slope downward to the right. Additionally, isoquants are convex to the origin of the diagram.

Nonintersection of two isoquants hardly necessitates discussion. Were two isoquants to intersect, the intersection point would mean that two different quantities of the product could be produced with the same resource combination. This is impossible if the firm uses the most efficient productive techniques available at all times — and we assume throughout our analysis that the most efficient techniques are used.

The downward slope of an isoquant from left to right depends upon the technical substitutability of one resource for the other, that is, upon the ability of one resource to substitute for the other in the productive process. Although exceptions may occur, generally the combination of resources necessary to produce a given amount of product can be varied by substituting quantities of one resource for another.[1] Labor can be substituted for capital and vice versa. When resources are technical substitutes, if less of one is used more of the other must be used to compensate for its loss if total product is to remain constant. This means that the isoquant will slope downward from left to right. With reference to Figure 7–3, those segments of the isoquants lying outside lines OC and OD do not slope downward to the right. After we have considered convexity to the origin we shall show that the use of resource combinations forming those segments would be economic nonsense for the firm.

Convexity of an isoquant to the origin stems from the fact that while different resources may be technical substitutes for each other, they are not perfect substitutes. Consider labor and capital, for example, used in digging a ditch of a certain length, width, and depth. Within limits they can be substituted for each other. But the more labor and the less capital used to dig the ditch, the more difficult it becomes to substitute additional labor for capital. Additional units of labor will just compensate for smaller and smaller amounts of capital. The same reasoning applies to other resources. The more of resource A and the less of resource B the firm uses to produce a constant amount of product X, the more difficult it becomes to substitute additional units of A for B; that is, additional units of A will just compensate for smaller and smaller amounts of B. This is called the principle of diminishing marginal rate of technical substitution of A for B. The marginal rate of technical substitution of A for B is measured at any point on an isoquant by the slope of the isoquant at that point. It is the amount of B the loss of which will just be compensated for by an additional unit of A at that point.

The marginal rate of technical substitution of A for B also can be thought of as the ratio of the marginal physical product of A to the marginal physical product of B, or MPP_a/MPP_b. Suppose the marginal

---

[1] One such exception is the case in which certain quantities of one resource are essential to obtain certain product outputs. For example, the production of pasteurized milk requires certain inputs of raw milk per unit output of the final product. Machinery or labor could hardly be substituted for raw milk in producing a certain quantity of the pasteurized product. For analysis of such exceptions see Sidney Weintraub, *Intermediate Price Theory* (Philadelphia: Chilton Books, 1964), pp. 34, 40–42.

physical product of B is one-half unit of X at a certain point on an iso-quant and that the marginal physical product of A is one unit of X. An additional unit of A at this point will just compensate for the loss of two units of B. Hence the marginal rate of technical substitution equals $MPP_a/MPP_b = 1/\frac{1}{2} = 2$.

RELEVANT SECTORS • Suppose we return to the isoquant segments in Figure 7–3 which slope upward to the right. For any given amount of product per unit of time — say quantity x_6 — there will be some minimum amount of B required for its production. This is shown by point G at which the slope of the isoquant becomes zero. Resource A has been substituted for resource B as far as such substitution is possible in the production of quantity x_6 of the product. The marginal physical product of resource A is zero at this point, meaning simply that the last unit of A used per unit of time adds nothing to total product. The marginal rate of technical substitution of A for B is zero. Quantities of A larger than a_6 used with quantity b_1 of B will be worse than useless. Marginal physical product of A will be negative and total product will decrease. Or, if total product is to be maintained at x_6, larger quantities of B must be used also with the larger quantities of A, and the isoquant turns upward to the right. The use of resource combinations on the up-ward sloping part of the isoquant would be economic nonsense, since it would cause production costs to be higher than necessary for quantity x_6 of the product.

The line OD joining the points at which the isoquants in Figure 7–3 are horizontal is called a ridge line. Among other things it shows the minimum amounts of resource B necessary to produce the different quantities of product. It is also the boundary line between combinations of A and B that the firm may conceivably use and those combinations that the firm would never rationally select.

Line OC is the ridge line joining the points at which the isoquants are vertical. An isoquant becomes vertical at the point where it is no longer possible to substitute resource B for resource A. The marginal physical product of B is zero at this point, and the marginal rate of sub-stitution of A for B is infinite. If larger quantities of B were used, the marginal physical product of B would be negative; consequently, to maintain product at a constant level, larger quantities of A would have to be used, also, causing the isoquant to turn upward to the right. Again, the use of such combinations would be foolish. The same amount of product could be produced with smaller amounts of both resources at a smaller total cost. Line OC shows the minimum quantities of resource A necessary for the production of various quantities of X and separates the resource combinations which the firm should never use from those which may be economically desirable. All rational combinations of A and B for the firm lie between ridge lines OC and OD.

Isoquants and Product Curves

Product schedules and product curves for either resource A or resource B can be derived from the firm's system of isoquants. With reference to Figure 7–3, assume the firm uses b_1 of resource B and, starting from a zero quantity of A, uses more and more of resource A per unit of time with the fixed amount of B. Increasing the quantity of A used moves the firm along the line b_1J. Total product obtained from each amount of A used with b_1 of B is read off the isoquant interesected by line b_1J at each particular quantity of A. Thus, when a_5 of A is used with b_1 of B, total product will be x_5. The greater the amount of A used, the greater will be total product until the firm is using a_6 of A. With the use of more than a_6 units of A, line b_1J intersects lower and lower isoquants, indicating that total product decreases and that the marginal physical product of A is negative. Thus the firm would never use more than a_6 of A with b_1 of B, even if A were free. The total product curve for increasing quantities of A used with the fixed amount of B will increase at first, will reach a maximum at a_6 of A, and will then decrease.

For quantities of A between zero and a_2 used with b_1 of B, average product of A will be increasing. Consider for a moment combination K composed of b_1 units of B and a_1 units of A. The combination lies outside ridge line OC and the isoquants in this section of the diagram slope

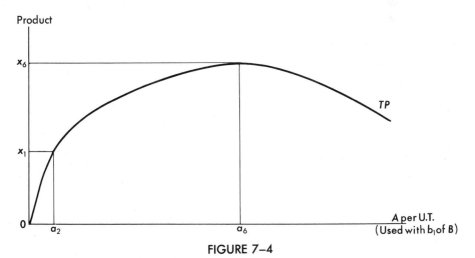

FIGURE 7–4

upward to the right. If units of resource B were taken away from combination K, total product would increase; or if units of B were added to combination K, total product would decrease. The marginal physical product of resource B at combination K is negative for increases in B. Consequently, average product of A must be increasing for increases in A.[2] For all quantities of A between zero and a_2, used with b_1 of B, marginal physical product of B will be negative and average product of A will be increasing.

The total product curve shown by Figure 7–4 is drawn on the basis of the above analysis. Up to quantity a_2 of A it is drawn so that average product of A will be increasing. Total product reaches a maximum at a_6 and will decrease as larger quantities of A are used with the fixed amount of B.

The isoquants of Figure 7–3 enable us to do more, however, than to derive the total product curve of one resource used in conjunction with a constant amount of another resource. Any number of total product curves for A can be established from them — one for each possible quantity of B. For each such product curve the end of Stage I and the beginning of Stage II occur at the ridge line OC. The end of Stage II and the beginning of Stage III occur at the ridge line OD. The larger the quantity of resource B used, the farther to the right Stage II will lie on the product diagram for resource A.

If we consider a fixed amount of resource A, say quantity a_4, and assume that the firm uses more and more of resource B in conjunction with it, we can derive a total product curve for B in exactly the same manner as we derived the total product curve for A. If a smaller quantity of B than b_0 is used with a_4 of A, an increase in the quantity of B used will increase average product of B. Thus, Stage I for B extends from a zero quantity to b_0 of B. From quantity b_0 to b_5, Stage II of B's total product curve will occur. Greater amounts of B than b_5 will cause its total product to decrease. As many total product curves for B can be derived as there are quantities of A with which varying amounts of B can be used.

The Three Stages

Isoquants are of material value in production analysis in visualizing the symmetry between Stage I and Stage III for two resources. We need not resort to working backward through the product curves of one resource used in conjunction with one unit of another resource. We can see readily that for any quantity of A to the right of ridge line OD used

---

[2] See pages 114–116 above.

with a fixed amount of B, marginal physical product of A is negative. Correspondingly, for any amount of B below ridge line OD used with a fixed amount of A, average product of B will increase when the quantity of B is increased. For any amount of B above ridge line OC used with a fixed amount of A, marginal physical product of B is negative. Also, for any amount of A to the left of ridge line OC used with a fixed amount of B, average product of A will increase when the quantity of A is increased. The region to the left and above OC is a generalized Stage I for resource A and Stage III for resource B. The region bounded by the ridge lines is a generalized Stage II for both resources. The region to the right and below ridge line OD is a generalized Stage III for A and Stage I for B.

ISOCOSTS AND LEAST-COST COMBINATIONS

In this subsection the nature of isocosts is explained first. Next, the firm's isocosts and isoquants are brought together to show the least-cost resource combinations for given product outputs. Last, necessary conditions for a least-cost combination as determined by the isoquant-isocost approach are shown to be the same as those determined by the traditional approach.

The Nature of Isocosts

An isocost curve shows the different combinations of resources that the firm can purchase, given the cost outlay to be made by the firm and the price per unit of each resource. We shall continue to limit the firm to two resources, A and B. Their respective prices are p_a and p_b. The total cost outlay of the firm is T. In Figure 7–5, units of resource A are measured along the horizontal axis and units of resource B are measured

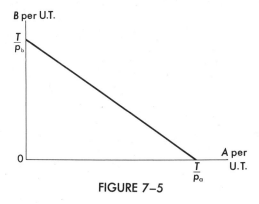

FIGURE 7–5

along the vertical axis. If the firm uses resource A only, it can purchase T/p_a units of A. If it uses resource B only, it can purchase T/p_b units of B. A straight line joining the two points marked on the A and B axes shows all combinations of A and B which the firm can purchase with its given cost outlay and is called an isocost curve.[3] The slope of the isocost curve is

$$\frac{T/p_b}{T/p_a} = \frac{T}{p_b} \times \frac{p_a}{T} = \frac{p_a}{p_b}$$

The Least-Cost Combination of Resources

The problem faced by a firm making a given cost outlay is that of getting on the highest possible isoquant that its isocost curve will allow; that is, it is that of getting the greatest amount of product from the given cost outlay on resources. In Figure 7–6 the greatest amount of product which the firm can get from a cost outlay of T will be quantity x_3 of X. The firm will use a_1 of A and b_1 of B. Any other combination of A and B obtainable for a cost outlay of T will move the firm up or down the isocost curve to a lower isoquant.

Alternatively, combination a_1 of A and b_1 of B can be thought of as the resource combination that produces quantity x_3 at the least possible cost. Cost outlay T is the least possible cost of producing output x_3. In Figure 7–6 we can see that a greater cost outlay would be necessary if some other resource combination were used to produce x_3; that is, resource combinations to the right of the isocost would have to be used, and these would involve greater cost outlays.

Changes in the firm's cost outlay, given the prices of resources A and B, will shift the isocost curve parallel to itself. If the cost outlay were a smaller amount T_0, the isocost curve would shift to the left as shown in Figure 7–6. Thus T_0 would be the least possible cost of producing output x_2. If the cost outlay were a greater amount T_2, the isocost curve would shift to the right and T_2 would be the least possible cost of producing output x_4. The line GH joining all points of equilibrium (least-cost resource combinations) for each possible cost outlay is called the expansion path of the firm.

Isoquant-Isocost Results Translated into Traditional Terms

A slight extension of the analysis thus far will show that the isoquant-isocost approach to the principles of production reaches the same end

---

[3] An isocost curve is the same type of curve for the firm purchasing resources as is the line of attainable combinations for the consumer purchasing consumer goods.

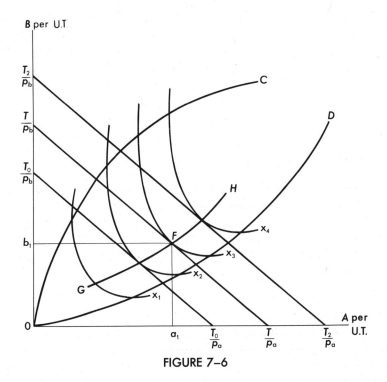

FIGURE 7–6

result as does the traditional approach. With reference to Figure 7–6, at any given point on a given isoquant the marginal rate of technical substitution of A for B is equal to MPP_a/MPP_b and is also equal to the slope of the isoquant at that point. At point F the slope of the isoquant x_3 equals the slope of the isocost tangent to it at that point. We have seen already that the slope of the isocost equals p_a/p_b. Therefore at F, the least-cost resource combination for producing x_3, $MPP_a/MPP_b = p_a/p_b$. Rearranging the equation, we can write $MPP_a/p_a = MPP_b/p_b$. Thus to secure a given output at the least possible cost, the marginal physical product of a dollar's worth of one resource must be equal to the marginal physical product of a dollar's worth of every other resource used.

SUGGESTED READINGS

SCITOVSKY, TIBOR. *Welfare and Competition.* Chicago: Richard D. Irwin, Inc., 1951, pp. 109–126.

WEINTRAUB, SIDNEY. *Intermediate Price Theory.* Philadelphia: Chilton Books, 1964, chap. 3.

Costs of Production | 8

SUPPLIES OF PARTICULAR COMMODITIES are determined by costs of production; therefore, to understand supply we must understand costs. Cost analysis is rooted in the principles of production. We shall start with the meaning of costs and shall follow through with the short-run and long-run cost curves of the individual firm.

THE CONCEPT OF COSTS

The costs of production incurred by a firm frequently are thought to consist of the money outlays that the firm must make for resources used to produce its product. However, the firm's actual expenditure on resources, or its "expenses," constitutes only a part of the cost picture. It will help at the outset to consider briefly two important aspects of costs: (1) the alternative cost doctrine, and (2) explicit and implicit costs.

The Alternative Cost Doctrine

Since supplies of economic resources in the economy are limited in relation to human wants, when resources are used by a firm in the production of a product, certain quantities of other products which those resources aid in producing must be forgone by society. Suppose that units of a certain kind of labor can be used in the production of either washing machines or refrigerators. If some are used in the production of washing machines, then society necessarily forgoes or gives up the refrigerators that these units could have produced. Or steel may be used in the making of automobiles, locomotives, buildings, and many other products. Thus, when steel is used in the making of automobiles some value of alternative products is sacrificed.

Economists define costs of production of a particular product as the value of the forgone alternative products that resources used in its

126

production could have produced. The costs of resources to a firm are their values in their best alternative uses. This is called the alternative cost doctrine or the opportunity cost doctrine. The firm, in order to secure the services of resources, must pay them amounts equal to what they can earn in those alternative uses. In the foregoing example of labor, the cost of the labor in the manufacture of washing machines is the value of refrigerators that the labor could have produced. Unless the manufacturer of washing machines pays that amount for the labor, it will go into or remain in refrigerator production. The steel example is similar. Automobile manufacturers must pay enough for steel to attract or hold the desired amounts away from alternative employments of steel — and this is its cost to the automobile firm from the economist's point of view.

Explicit and Implicit Costs

Explicit costs of production are those outlays made by a firm that we usually think of as its expenses. They consist of explicit payments for resources bought outright or hired by the firm. The firm's payroll, payments for raw and semifinished materials, payments of overhead costs of various kinds, and payments into sinking funds and depreciation accounts are examples of explicit costs. They are the costs that accountants list as the firm's expenses.

Implicit costs of production are those costs of self-owned, self-employed resources which are frequently overlooked in computing the expenses of the firm. The salary of a single proprietor who sets aside no salary for himself but who takes the firm's "profits" as payment for his services is an excellent example. A still more common implicit cost is the return to owners of a firm on their investment in plant, equipment, and inventories.

The firm owner's salary as a cost can be easily explained. In accordance with the alternative cost doctrine the cost of the single proprietor's services in producing his product is the forgone alternative product which would have been produced had he worked for someone else in a similar capacity. We consider as a part of the firm's costs, then, a salary for the proprietor equal to the value of his services in his best alternative employment. This is an implicit cost which does not take the form of an "expense" outlay.

The return on investment as a cost of production is more tricky. Return on investment usually is thought of as coming from the firm's profit rather than as being a cost of production. In the simplest case consider a single proprietor who has invested in (purchased) the land, building, and equipment for his business establishment. A return on his investment equal to what he could have earned had he invested the same amount elsewhere in the economy is an implicit cost of production. Had he invested elsewhere his investment would have purchased resources to produce other goods. What those resources could earn in those alternative uses would determine the return on investment which he could have earned had he invested there.

The same principle on a larger scale applies to a corporation. Stockholders are the real owners of the corporation's land, plant, equipment, and inventories[1] — they have invested money in resources used by the corporation. Dividends equal to what stockholders could earn had they invested elsewhere in the economy are implicit costs of production from the point of view of the economist. The costs of resources obtained by the firm with stockholders' investments are, according to the alternative cost doctrine, the value of the alternative products forgone by holding the investment where it is. To hold the investment where it is the corporation must pay a return to stockholders equal to what they could earn if they should invest elsewhere in the economy.

Costs, Resource Prices, and Efficiency

Costs of production incurred by the firm consist of both explicit and implicit obligations to resource owners. These obligations are just large enough to obtain and hold resources in the employment of the firm. Usually the firm's "expenses" include the explicit obligations only. Thus costs of production as viewed by the economist differ somewhat from (will usually be larger than) the firm's accounting "expenses."

The discussion of costs in this chapter will be oversimplified to some extent. We shall be concerned with a firm's costs of production at various alternative product outputs. Costs at each output depend upon (1) how much the firm must pay for resources; that is, resource prices, and (2) the efficiency with which the firm uses resources; that is, the quantities necessary to produce the output. We shall eliminate the problem of resource pricing by assuming that the firm is a pure competitor in the purchase of resources. The single firm takes such a small proportion of the total amount of any given resource in existence that by itself it cannot influence resource price. The firm can get all it wants of any one resource at a constant price per unit. Thus differences in costs at different output levels result from differences in the efficiency with which

---

[1] Additionally, they may have borrowed money by selling bonds to increase plant and equipment. Thus bondholders, too, have invested money in the corporation. However, interest payments on the bonds — the return on the bondholders' investments — are explicit payments and hence are recorded as costs by the corporation as well as by the economist.

the firm can use resources at each of those outputs. The effects on costs of possible changes in resource prices as a result of output changes on the part of a firm can be taken into consideration later on after resource pricing has been discussed.

COSTS AND THE TIME VIEWPOINT

The way in which costs of production of the firm change as the firm varies its output per unit of time will differ with differences in the period of time under consideration. In cost analysis a distinction is made between the time period called the short run and the time period called the long run. These concepts will be examined in turn.

The Short Run

The short run is a time period so short that the firm is unable to vary the quantities of some resources used. We could, if we so desired, think of a time period so short that no resource could be varied in quantity. Then, as we lengthen the time period under consideration, it becomes possible for the firm to vary the quantity of one. As the time period is progressively lengthened, more and more resources become variable in quantity until ultimately they all fall into the variable category. Any time period between that in which no resources can be varied in quantity and that in which all resources but one are variable could legitimately be called the short run. However, to facilitate exposition we shall use a more restricting definition.

The possibilities of varying the quantities of different resources depend upon their nature and their terms of hire or purchase. Some, such as land and buildings, may be leased by the firm for given time periods; or, if they are owned outright, it may take some time to acquire additional quantities or to dispose of a part of the quantities already owned. The quantity of top management required is not ordinarily readily variable. Heavy machinery, especially designed for the firm's use, cannot be quickly increased or decreased in quantity. Typically, the time period required for variation in the quantities of such resources as power, labor, transportation, raw materials, and semifinished materials will be shorter than that required for variation in the quantities of land, buildings, heavy machinery, and top management.

The short-run concept which we shall use will be a time period so short that the firm does not have time to vary in quantity such resources as land, buildings, heavy machinery and top management. These are the firm's short-run "fixed resources." Our short run will be long enough to allow variation in the quantities of such resources as labor, raw materials, and the like. These are the firm's "variable resources."[2]

The length of the time period which we call the short run will vary from industry to industry. For some industries the short run may be very short indeed. This will be the case where the quantities of "fixed" resources used by a firm in the industry are typically small or can be added to or subtracted from in a short space of time. The various textile industries are cases in point. For other industries the short run may be a year or more. It takes time to add to the productive capacity of an automobile firm or a basic steel firm.

The quantities of fixed resources used determine the size of the firm's plant, or its *scale of plant*.[3] The scale of plant sets the upper limit to the amount of output per unit of time which the firm is capable of producing. It can, however, vary its output up to that limit by increasing or decreasing the quantities of variable resources used in the fixed scale of plant. The fixed resources or the scale of plant may be compared with a meat grinder. The variable resources will be analogous to the meat put through it. The output of ground meat per unit of time can be varied by varying the input of unground meat. However, there will be some upper limit beyond which the output cannot be increased regardless of how much unground meat is on hand to push through it. Or the land and labor example of the preceding chapter can be viewed in a short-run context. We can think of the fixed amount of land as the fixed scale of plant and the variable quantities of labor as the variable resources used with it.

The Long Run

The long run presents no definitional difficulties. It is a period of time long enough for the firm to be able to vary the quantities per unit of time of all resources used. Thus, all resources are variable. No problem of classifying resources as fixed or variable exists. The firm has sufficient time to vary its scale of plant as it desires from very small to large or vice versa. Infinitesimal variations in size are usually possible.

---

[2] The dividing line between fixed and variable resources is not always clear-cut. In particular cases some of the resources listed above as "variable" may require more time for alterations in quantity taken than some listed as "fixed." For example, contractual arrangements for the purchase of power or labor may be such that their quantities cannot be readily varied. Or, on the other hand, it may be possible for the firm to lease out, sublease, or sell some part of its "fixed" resources on short notice.

[3] The term *plant* is used here in a broad context to cover the whole scope of the firm's operations. A firm may operate several establishments at different locations; however, we shall view them all together as the firm's "plant."

SHORT-RUN COST CURVES

Classification of resources in the short run as fixed and variable enables us to classify their costs as fixed costs and variable costs. Fixed costs are the costs of fixed resources. Variable costs are the costs of variable resources. The distinction between fixed and variable costs will be basic for the discussions of total costs, average costs, and marginal costs which follow.

Total Cost Curves

Three concepts of total cost are important for short-run price and output analysis. These are total fixed cost, total variable cost, and total cost. Total fixed cost and total variable cost are the component parts of the firm's total cost. The three concepts will be examined in turn.

TOTAL FIXED COSTS • Total fixed costs refer to the entire obligation per unit of time incurred by the firm for fixed resources. Since the firm does not have time to vary quantities per unit of time of fixed resources used, total fixed cost will remain at a constant level regardless of the

TABLE 8–1

QUANTITY OF X	TOTAL FIXED COST	TOTAL VARIABLE COST	TOTAL COST
1	$100	$ 40	$140
2	100	70	170
3	100	85	185
4	100	96	196
5	100	104	204
6	100	110	210
7	100	115	215
8	100	120	220
9	100	126	226
10	100	134	234
11	100	145	245
12	100	160	260
13	100	180	280
14	100	206	306
15	100	239	339
16	100	280	380
17	100	330	430
18	100	390	490
19	100	461	561
20	100	544	644

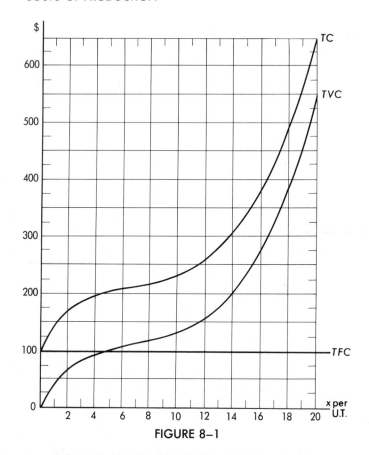

FIGURE 8–1

output produced per unit of time. Suppose, for example, that the firm occupies a certain amount of land. If it owns the land outright the cost must be amortized over the expected life of the firm. The amortization costs are a fixed amount per unit of time and are independent of the firm's output. The same principle applies to buildings and heavy machinery. Top management salaries are also fixed — usually by contract — for the short run and are independent of the firm's output. A hypothetical total fixed cost schedule is presented in Table 8–1; the corresponding total fixed cost curve is plotted in Figure 8–1. Note that the total fixed cost curve is parallel to the quantity axis and lies above it by the amount of total fixed costs.

TOTAL VARIABLE COSTS • Total variable costs are a different matter. They must necessarily rise as the firm's output increases, since larger outputs require larger quantities of variable resources and, hence, larger cost obligations. For example, the larger the output of an oil refinery, the larger the quantity of crude oil it must purchase; hence the larger will be crude oil costs. Table 8–1 lists a hypothetical total variable cost schedule; *TVC* in Figure 8–1 is the corresponding total variable cost curve. These show a characteristic usually typical of a firm's total variable cost. Up to a certain output level their rates of increase decrease as the firm's output of product and input of variable resources increase. Beyond that output level the rate of increase in total variable cost increases. Thus, up to seven units of output in Table 8–1 and in Figure 8–1, the successive increases in total variable cost are smaller and smaller. Beyond eight units of output the successive increases become larger and larger.

The changes in total variable cost shown in Table 8–1 and the shape of the total variable cost curve shown in Figure 8–1 result directly from increasing and diminishing returns of variable resources. With a given scale of plant there will be some quantities of variable resources — say labor and raw materials — small enough for the efficiency of those resources to suffer; that is, the firm using very small quantities of them will be in Stage I for those resources. Increasing the quantities of variable resources increases the efficiency with which they are used. Successive increases in the quantities of variable resources increase their respective marginal physical products or lead to successively larger increases in product output for equal increments in total variable cost. Thus, for output increases in the range of increasing returns, the total variable cost curve will be concave downward.

As larger quantities of variable resources are used with the fixed scale of plant and as product output per unit of time increases, the law of diminishing returns comes into play. The marginal physical products of the variable resources decline. Product increases resulting from equal increments in total variable cost decline; or, in the region of diminishing returns for variable resources, the total variable cost curve is concave upward. At some output level the fixed scale of plant will have reached its absolute maximum capacity. Here the total variable cost curve will turn straight up. Increased obligations incurred for still larger quantities of variable resources will lead to no increases in output at all.

TOTAL COSTS • Total costs of the firm for various outputs are the summation of total fixed costs and total variable costs for those outputs. The total cost column of Table 8–1 is obtained by adding total fixed cost and total variable cost at each output. Likewise, in Figure 8–1, the total cost curve is obtained by summing the *TFC* curve and the *TVC* curve vertically. The *TC* curve and the *TVC* curve must necessarily have the same shape since each increase in output per unit of time increases total cost and total variable cost by the same amount. The output increase does not affect total fixed cost. The *TC* curve lies above the *TVC* curve by an amount equal to *TFC* at all outputs.

Per Unit Cost Curves

Per unit cost curves are used extensively for price and output analysis — more so than are the total cost curves. Essentially they show the same kind of information that total cost curves show, but they show it in a different, and frequently more usable, form. The per unit cost curves are the average fixed cost curve, the average variable cost curve, the average cost curve, and the marginal cost curve.

AVERAGE FIXED COSTS • <u>Average fixed costs or fixed costs per unit of product at various levels of output are obtained by dividing total fixed cost by those outputs.</u> Thus, the average fixed cost column of Table 8–2 is computed by dividing the total fixed cost column of Table 8–1 by the different quantities of *X*. The average fixed cost schedule is plotted in Figure 8–2 as the *AFC* curve.

TABLE 8–2

QUANTITY OF X	AVERAGE FIXED COST	AVERAGE VARIABLE COST	AVERAGE COST	MARGINAL COST
1	$100.00	$40.00	$140.00	—
2	50.00	35.00	85.00	30
3	33.33	28.33	61.66	15
4	25.00	24.00	49.00	11
5	20.00	20.80	40.80	8
6	16.67	18.33	35.00	6
7	14.29	16.43	30.72	5
8	12.50	15.00	27.50	5
9	11.11	14.00	25.11	6
10	10.00	13.40	23.40	8
11	9.09	13.18	22.27	11
12	8.33	13.33	21.66	15
13	7.69	13.85	21.54	20
14	7.14	14.72	21.86	26
15	6.67	15.93	22.60	33
16	6.25	17.50	23.75	41
17	5.88	19.41	25.29	50
18	5.55	21.67	27.22	60
19	5.26	24.27	29.53	71
20	5.00	27.20	32.20	83

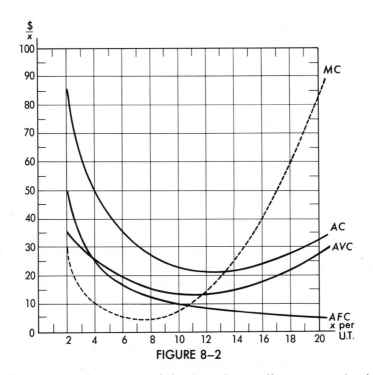

FIGURE 8–2

The greater the output of the firm the smaller average fixed cost will be. Since total fixed cost remains the same regardless of output, fixed costs are spread over more units of output and, consequently, each unit of output bears a smaller share. Therefore the average fixed cost curve is downward sloping to the right throughout its entire length. As output per unit of time increases it approaches but never reaches the quantity axis. Thus it becomes apparent that firms with large fixed costs — the railroads, for example, with their tremendous fixed charges on roadbeds and rolling stock — can reduce substantially their fixed costs per unit by producing larger outputs.

AVERAGE VARIABLE COSTS • Variable costs per unit of output are computed in the same way as fixed costs per unit of output. The average variable cost column of Table 8–2 is obtained by dividing total variable cost in Table 8–1 at various outputs by those outputs. Plotted graphically, the average variable cost column of Table 8–2 becomes the *A VC* curve of Figure 8–2.

The average variable cost curve usually will have a ∪ shape. Its ∪ shape can be explained in terms of the principles of production. Suppose, for example, that a factory is designed to employ in the neighborhood of one hundred workers. The scale of plant is fixed and labor is the only variable resource. The amount of product produced if only one man is employed will be extremely small, but if an additional man is employed the two can split up the jobs to be performed and can more than double the single man's output. This means, of course, that the average product of labor increases with the employment of the additional man. If a doubling of labor (variable) costs will more than double output, labor costs per unit of output (average variable costs) will decrease. Thus, throughout Stage I for labor, the average product per worker increases and average variable costs decrease. When enough men are employed to go into Stage II, average product of labor decreases, or, what amounts to the same thing, average variable costs increase. Thus the average variable cost curve in this case is a sort of monetized mirror reflection of the average product curve for labor.

The same general principles apply when a complex of several variable resources is used by the firm. For small inputs of the complex, product per unit cost or "average product" of the complex will be increasing, which means that average variable costs will be decreasing. As inputs are increased, "average product" reaches a maximum and then decreases. Average variable costs correspondingly reach a minimum and then increase.

When a complex of variable resources is used by the firm, combinations or ratios of the variable resources to each other must be considered also. Suppose the firm for which the cost curves of Figure 8–2 are drawn uses three variable resources — A, B, and C — with its given scale of plant. Resource prices are p_a, p_b, and p_c, respectively. If the firm's output is to be six units of product and if its average variable cost is to be as low as possible ($18.33) for that output, the variable resources must be combined in such proportions that

$$\frac{MPP_a}{p_a} = \frac{MPP_b}{p_b} = \frac{MPP_c}{p_c}$$

If they are not so combined, average variable cost for that output will exceed $18.33. Similarly, each point on the average variable cost curve can be attained only if the firm combines variable resources in the proper proportions for each and every output at which those points are located. Failure to do so will result in higher costs.

AVERAGE COSTS • Average cost or the over-all cost per unit of output can be obtained in either of two ways. Total cost at various outputs in Table 8–1 divided by the respective outputs gives us the average cost column of Table 8–2. Alternatively, in Table 8–2, average fixed cost and average variable cost added together for each of the various outputs produce the average cost column. Graphically, the AC curve in Figure 8–2 represents the average cost column of Table 8–2 plotted against outputs. The AC curve is also the vertical summation of the AFC curve and the AVC curve.

The average cost curve, too, is usually thought to be a ∪-shaped curve. Its ∪ shape depends upon the efficiency with which both fixed and variable resources are used. Given the scale of plant, the greater the output of the firm the greater the efficiency of the fixed resources as a group; that is, the smaller average fixed cost becomes. In Figure 8–2 variable resources are used more and more efficiently until output reaches eleven units. Up to this output average cost must be decreasing, since the efficiency of both fixed and variable resources is increasing. Between eleven and thirteen units of output, average fixed cost decreases but average variable cost increases as variable resources become less efficient. However, the decreases in average fixed cost more than offset the increases in average variable cost so that average cost continues to decrease. Beyond thirteen units of output per unit of time, decreases in the efficiency of variable resources more than offset increases in the efficiency of fixed resources and average cost rises. We should note an obvious fact in passing: the minimum point on the average variable cost curve lies at a lower output level than does the minimum point on the average cost curve.

MARGINAL COST • Marginal cost is defined as the change in total cost resulting from a one-unit change in output. It could be defined just

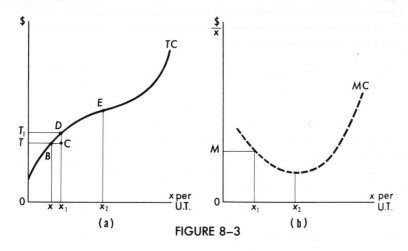

FIGURE 8–3

as accurately as the change in total variable cost resulting from a one-unit change in output. This will be the case since a change in output changes total variable cost and total cost by exactly the same amounts. Marginal cost depends in no way upon fixed cost. The marginal cost column of Table 8–2 can be computed from either the total variable cost column or the total cost column of Table 8–1. It is plotted graphically as MC in Figure 8–2.

Frequently it is helpful to be able to visualize the marginal cost curve corresponding to or derived from a given total cost curve. Consider output x on the total cost diagram of Figure 8–3(a). Total cost at that output is T. Now increase output by one unit to x_1. Total cost increases to T_1. Marginal cost of the x_1th unit is $T_1 - T$. The marginal cost of a unit of output at any level of output can be found in the same way. The marginal cost values plotted against outputs in Figure 8–3(b) form the marginal cost curve. At any given output on the marginal cost diagram, marginal cost at that output is measured by the distance from the base line up to the marginal cost curve. Thus, at output x_1 marginal cost of the x_1th unit is M dollars. This represents the same number of dollars as does $T_1 - T$ on the total cost diagram.

The marginal cost curve usually is ∪-shaped and its shape comes from that of the TC curve. Out to output x_2 the TC curve is concave downward, or, what amounts to the same thing, each additional unit of output per unit of time up to that point will increase total cost by a smaller amount than did the preceding unit. Hence marginal cost is decreasing as output is increased to that level. Point E on the TC curve is called the point of inflection. At output x_2, at which the point of inflection occurs, marginal cost takes on its minimum value. At outputs greater than x_2 the total cost curve is concave upward, meaning that each additional unit of output per unit of time increases total cost by more than did the preceding unit. Therefore, marginal cost will be increasing at outputs beyond that level.

Marginal cost at any given output can be thought of geometrically as the slope of the total cost curve at that output. The approximate slope of the total cost curve of Figure 8–3(a) between B and D is CD/BC. BC is equal to one unit of output and CD is equal to $T' - T$ or marginal cost of the x_1th unit. The slope of the total cost curve between B and D is thus equal to marginal cost of the x_1th unit. For the typical firm, one unit of output is measured by an infinitesimal distance along the quantity axis. The large size of the unit of output (x to x_1) in Figure 8–3(a) is for purposes of illustration only. If one unit of output is measured by an infinitesimal distance along the quantity axis, marginal cost at any given

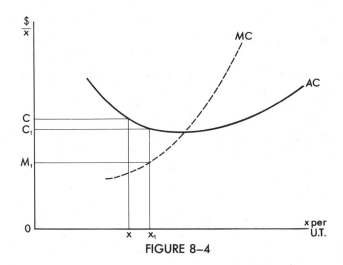

FIGURE 8–4

output is numerically equal to the slope of the total cost curve at that output. The slope of the TC curve of Figure 8–3(a) is decreasing between zero and output x_2 (although TC is rising) and is increasing beyond x_2. Thus marginal cost first decreases and then increases as output increases.[4]

Relationship of MC to AC and to AVC

The marginal cost curve bears a unique relationship to the average cost curve which is derived from the same total cost curve. When AC is decreasing as output increases, MC is less than AC. When AC is increasing as output increases, MC is greater than AC. It follows that at the output at which AC is minimum, MC is equal to AC. These relationships are shown in Figure 8–4. For example, suppose the firm's output is x. Its average cost is OC. We know that average cost at any output equals total cost of that output divided by the output; so $OC = TC/x$ at output x. Suppose now that output is increased by one unit to x_1 and that the addition to total cost is OM_1, which is marginal cost of the x_1th unit. Suppose, as we have shown in Figure 8–4, that marginal cost of the x_1th unit is less than the average cost OC of x units. Since the additional unit of output per unit of time adds a lesser amount to total cost than was the average cost of x units, the average cost of x_1 units must be less than the average cost of x units. However, average cost of x_1 units will not be pulled down as low as the marginal cost of the x_1th unit. Thus $OC_1 < OC$, but

---

[4] Compare the relationship of MC to TC with the relationship of marginal utility to total utility on pages 48–51, and with the relationship of the marginal physical product of labor to the total product of labor on page 103.

$OC_1 > OM_1$ or, when average cost is decreasing, marginal cost is necessarily less than average cost. Similarly, when an additional unit of output adds an amount to total cost equal to the old average cost, the new average cost will equal the old and will also be equal to marginal cost of the additional unit of output. Also, when an additional unit of output adds a greater amount to total cost than was the original average cost, the new average cost will be greater than the original, but will be less than the marginal cost of the additional unit.[5] These relations can be verified by reference to Table 8–2 and Figure 8–2.

The relations between marginal cost and average variable cost will be identical with the relations between marginal cost and average cost, and for the same reasons. When average variable cost is decreasing, marginal cost will be less than average variable cost. When average variable cost is minimum, marginal cost and average variable cost will be equal. When average variable cost is increasing, marginal cost will be greater than average variable cost. These relations can also be verified by Table 8–2 and Figure 8–2.

The complete set of short-run per unit cost curves is pictured in Figure 8–2. The marginal cost curve cuts the average variable cost curve and the average cost curve at their respective minimum points. An increase in fixed costs would shift the average cost curve upward and to the right in such a way that the marginal cost curve would still intersect it at its minimum point. No change in the marginal cost curve would be involved since marginal cost is independent of fixed cost.

The Optimum Rate of Output

The output at which short-run average cost is lowest is the output at which a given scale of plant is most efficient. Here the value of the inputs of resources per unit output of product is least. This output is called the optimum rate of output. The term *optimum* as we use it means "most efficient." Whatever the scale of plant built by the firm, the output of minimum average cost is the optimum rate of output for that scale of plant. As we shall see later, the optimum rate of output for a given scale of plant is not necessarily the output at which the firm makes the greatest profits. Profit depends upon revenue as well as upon costs.

As we have presented them, the variations in the component parts of short-run costs as the firm varies output depend in no way upon changes in the price paid per unit for each of the various resources used by the firm. We assumed at the outset that the firm can get all it wants

---

[5] The relations between MC and AC are exactly the same as the relations between the marginal physical product of labor and the average product of labor explained on page 103.

of any resource at a constant price per unit; that is, it buys them under conditions of pure competition. The shapes of the short-run curves as they are presented here are solely reflections of the efficiency with which resources are used. Efficiency in the use of resources varies among the alternative outputs obtainable with a given scale of plant.

Still, in the real world we observe such things as quantity discounts on resources purchased in large quantities by the firm. This represents a departure from pure competition in the buying of resources or a departure from the assumptions on which our cost curves are based. Should quantity discounts occur, the total variable cost curve and the total cost curve will increase less as output is increased than they would otherwise. Correspondingly, quantity discounts would cause the average variable cost curve and the average cost curve to show greater decreases, then smaller increases, than they would otherwise show as output is increased. Further modifications of short-run cost analysis will be developed in Chapters 13 and 14.

LONG-RUN COST CURVES

In the long run the firm can build any desired scale of plant. All resources are variable. The firm can change the quantities used per unit of time of land, buildings, machinery, management, and all other resources. There will be no average fixed cost curve. We need to concern ourselves with the long-run average cost curve, the long-run total cost curve, and the long-run marginal cost curve.

It will be helpful to think of the long run as a series of alternative short-run situations into any one of which the firm can move. If we look at the firm's situation at any given moment, we are viewing a short-run situation. Yet, looked at from the point of view of a long period of time, the firm has opportunity to change the short-run picture. The long run may be compared with the action sequence of a motion picture. If we stop the film and look at a single picture we have a short-run concept.

Long-Run Average Cost

Suppose that it is possible for the firm to build only three alternative scales of plant. These are represented by SAC_1, SAC_2, and SAC_3 in Figure 8–5. Each SAC curve is the short-run average cost curve for a given scale of plant. In the long run the firm can build any one of the possible scales of plant, or it can shift from one to another.

Which scale of plant should the firm build? The answer depends upon, and will vary with, the long-run output per unit of time to be produced. Whatever the output is to be, the firm will want to produce at an

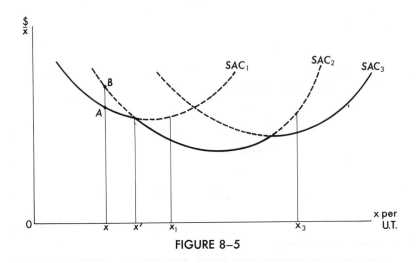

FIGURE 8–5

average cost as low as possible for that output. Suppose output is to be x. The firm should construct the scale of plant represented by SAC_1 since it will produce output x at a smaller cost per unit, xA, than will the other possible scales of plant. Costs would be xB per unit if SAC_2 were used. For output x', the firm would be indifferent between SAC_1 and SAC_2, but for output x_1, it would prefer to use SAC_2. For output x_3, the firm would want to construct and use the scale of plant represented by SAC_3.

We are now in a position to define the long-run average cost curve. It shows the least possible cost per unit of producing various outputs when the firm has time to build any desired scale of plant. In Figure 8–5 the solid portions of the SAC curves form the long-run average cost curve. The broken line portions of the SAC curves are irrelevant. The firm would never operate on the broken line portions in the long run since it could reduce costs by changing scale of plant instead.

The possible scales of plant which a firm can build as a long-run undertaking usually are unlimited in number. For every conceivable scale of plant there will be another scale of plant infinitesimally larger or infinitesimally smaller. A series of SAC curves such as those of Figure 8–6 results, and even here any number of additional SAC curves can be drawn between any two of those in the diagram. The outer portions of the SAC curves form a solid line which is the long-run average cost curve. Since the long-run average cost curve is made up of very small segments of the various SAC curves, it can be considered just tangent to all possible SAC curves representing the different scales of plant which

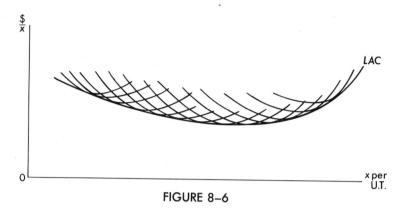

FIGURE 8–6

the firm conceivably could build. Mathematically it is called an envelope curve to the *SAC* curves.

The long-run average cost curve also can be viewed in terms of least-cost resource combinations. For any given output, long-run total cost and long-run average cost are least when *all* resources used are combined in proportions such that the marginal physical product per dollar's worth of one equals the marginal physical product per dollar's worth of every other resource used. This means that a dollar spent on management must add the same amount to total product as a dollar spent on raw materials. A dollar spent on labor and a dollar spent on machinery must both yield the same addition to total product, and so on for all resources. Should these conditions not be fulfilled — if a dollar spent on management adds less to total product than a dollar spent on machines — then some shifts in expenditures from management to machines will increase total product without increasing total cost. This, of course, amounts to the same thing as a decrease in total cost or a decrease in average cost, holding total product constant. Thus the cost levels shown by the long-run average cost curve for various outputs can be attained by the firm only if the least-cost resource combination is used for each output.

Economies of Scale

The long-run average cost curve is thought to be a ∪-shaped curve, usually. This would be the case if scales of plant were to become successively more efficient up to some particular scale or range of scales, and if scales of plants were then to become successively less efficient as the range of plant scales from very small to very large is considered. Increasing efficiency, associated with larger and larger scales of plant, is

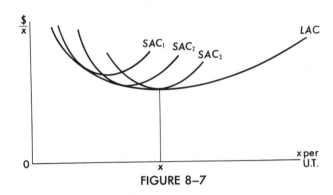

FIGURE 8–7

reflected by *SAC* curves lying successively at lower levels and farther to the right. Examples are provided by SAC_1, SAC_2, and SAC_3 in Figure 8–7. Decreasing efficiency, associated with still larger scales of plant, would be shown by *SAC* curves lying successively at higher levels and farther to the right. The resulting *LAC* curve would thus have a general U-shape.

The forces causing the *LAC* curve to decrease for larger outputs and scales of plant are called economies of scale. Two important economies of scale are (1) increasing possibilities of division and specialization of labor, and (2) increasing possibilities of using advanced technological developments and/or larger machines. These will be discussed in turn.

DIVISION AND SPECIALIZATION OF LABOR • The advantages of division and specialization of labor have long been known to both economists and the general public.[6] A small scale of plant employing few men cannot specialize the men on particular operations as readily as can a larger scale of plant employing a larger work force. In the small scale of plant the typical worker performs several different operations in the process of producing the commodity. He may not be particularly proficient at some of them. In addition he may lose time in changing from one set of tools to another in performing the different operations. However, with a larger scale of plant, greater specialization may be possible with the worker performing that process at which he is most adept. Specialization on a particular process eliminates the time lost in changing from one set of tools to another. Also, the worker performing a single type of operation develops short cuts and speed in performing it. Thus, the efficiency of the worker is likely to be higher and cost per unit of output correspondingly lower where division and specialization of labor

---

[6] See Adam Smith, *The Wealth of Nations* (Edwin Cannan, ed.; New York: The Modern Library, 1937), bk. I, chaps. I-III.

are possible. A word of warning may be necessary here, though. In some cases it may be possible to carry specialization to the point at which monotony of the task begins to counteract increases in the efficiency of the individual's performance.

TECHNOLOGICAL FACTORS • The possibility of lowering costs per unit of output by technological methods increases as the scale of plant is increased. In the first place, the cheapest way of producing a small output will usually not be one employing the most advanced technological methods. Consider, for example, the production of automobile hoods. If the output were to be two or three hoods per week, then certainly large automatic presses would not be used. The cheapest way to produce the hoods probably would be to hammer them out by hand. However, the cost per unit would still be comparatively high. There would be no cheap way of producing the small output or of operating the small scale of plant for the production of a small output. For larger outputs and scales of plant mass production technological methods can be used to effect reductions in per unit costs. In the foregoing example, if output were to be several thousand units per week, then a larger scale of plant with automatic presses could be installed, and costs per unit would become substantially lower than was possible with the small scale of plant.

In the second place, technological considerations are usually such that in order to double the capacity of a machine to produce, a doubling of material, construction, and operating costs of the machine are not necessary. For example, it is cheaper to build and operate a 600-horsepower diesel motor than it is to build and operate two 300-horsepower diesel motors. The 600-horsepower motor has no more working parts than a single 300-horsepower motor. Additionally, the 600-horsepower motor does not require twice the amount of materials used in building a single 300-horsepower motor. The same type of example can be made of almost any machine. Technological possibilities represent a very important explanation of the increasing efficiency of larger and larger scales of plant up to some limit.

Diseconomies of Scale

The question now arises as to why, once the scale of plant is large enough to take advantage of all economies of scale, still larger scales of plant are likely to result in less efficiency. It would appear, offhand, that the firm would be able at least to maintain the economies of scale. The answer usually given to the question is that there are limitations to the efficiency of management in controlling and coordinating a single firm. These limitations are called diseconomies of scale.

As the scale of plant is increased, management, like the lower echelons of labor, may become more efficient through division of tasks and specialization in particular functions; but the argument commonly made is that beyond some certain size the difficulties of coordinating and controlling the firm multiply rapidly. The contacts of top management with the day to day operations of the business become more and more remote, causing operating efficiency in production departments to decrease. Decision-making responsibility must be delegated and coordination must be established among the decision-making subordinates. The paper work, travel expenses, telephone bills, and additional employees necessary for coordination pile up. Occasionally plans of separate decision-making subordinates fail to mesh and costly slowdowns occur. To the extent that increasing difficulties of coordination and control reduce the efficiency per dollar outlay on management as the scale of plant is increased, per unit costs of production will increase.

The discussion so far may be interpreted to mean that as the scale of plant is increased, economies of scale cause the long-run average cost curve to decrease, and then, when all economies of scale are realized, diseconomies of scale straightway begin. However, this is not necessarily the case. Once the scale of plant is large enough to take advantage of all economies of scale, there may be a range of larger scales of plant for which diseconomies are not yet evident. The long-run average cost curve will have a long horizontal series of minimum points rather than the single minimum point of the conventional long-run average cost curve. When the scale of plant has become sufficiently large for diseconomies of scale to become apparent, the long-run average cost curve turns upward to the right. Another possibility is that some diseconomies begin to occur in a scale of plant too small to realize all economies of scale. If the economies of scale for larger scales of plant more than offset the diseconomies, the long-run average cost curve slopes downward to the right. Where diseconomies of scale more than offset economies of scale, the long-run average cost curve slopes upward to the right.

The Optimum Scale of Plant

The term *optimum scale of plant* is applied to the most efficient of all scales of plant that the firm can build. The optimum scale of plant is the one whose short-run average cost curve forms the minimum point of the long-run average cost curve. It can also be thought of as that scale of plant with a short-run average cost curve tangent to the long-run average cost curve at the minimum points of both. The short-run average cost curve of the optimum scale of plant in Figure 8–8 is *SAC*.

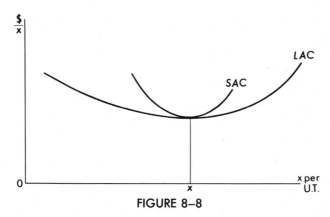

FIGURE 8–8

   Firms will not invariably construct optimum scales of plant and operate them at optimum rates of output. As we shall see, they will do so under conditions of pure competition in the long run; however, under pure monopoly, oligopoly, and monopolistic competition, they are not likely to do so. The scale of plant that will operate at the lowest cost per unit for given outputs will vary with the output to be produced. For example, in Figure 8-8, scale of plant *SAC* will produce output *x* cheaper than will any other scale of plant, and output *x* can be produced at a lower cost per unit than can any other output. But for outputs greater or less than *x*, per unit costs will necessarily be higher. Scales of plant other than the optimum scale of plant will produce such outputs at lower costs per unit than will the optimum scale of plant.

   To illustrate determination of the scale of plant to be constructed for a particular output, consider Figure 8-9. Suppose the firm is produc-

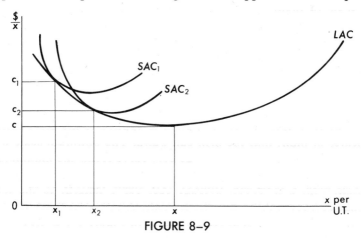

FIGURE 8–9

ing output x_1 with scale of plant SAC_1. Scale of plant SAC_1 is being operated at less than its optimum rate of output. Now output is to be increased to x_2. The increase can be accomplished in either of two ways: (1) by increasing the output rate with scale of plant SAC_1, or (2) by changing the scale of plant to a larger size. Which method should the firm use? Either method will allow the firm to reduce costs per unit. Method 1 will cause SAC_1 to be used at its optimum rate of output. Costs are lower than c_1. However, if the firm should use method 2, economies of scale from the larger scale of plant will allow even greater per unit cost reductions for output x_2 than will method 1. Costs per unit will be c_2 with scale of plant SAC_2, and this is the lowest cost at which that output can be produced. For outputs between zero and x, the firm will achieve lowest per unit costs for any given output by using a less than optimum scale of plant at less than the optimum rate of output. Similarly, for any given output greater than x, lowest cost per unit will be achieved if the firm uses a greater than optimum scale of plant at a greater than optimum rate of output. The applicable general principle is this: To minimize cost for any given output, the firm should use the scale of plant whose short-run average cost curve is tangent to the long-run average cost curve at that output.

LONG-RUN TOTAL COST AND LONG-RUN MARGINAL COST

Most analyses of individual firm behavior pay little attention to the long-run total cost curve (LTC) of the firm; nevertheless, it is a useful concept for at least two reasons. In the first place the long-run marginal cost curve (LMC) of the firm can be derived from it. In the second place it provides a means for establishing the correct relations between the firm's long-run marginal costs and its short-run marginal costs for any given scale of plant.

The LTC curve of a firm can be constructed from its LAC curve. Suppose that the LAC curve of the firm is that of Figure 8–9. At output levels x_1, x_2, and x, long-run total costs will be $x_1 \times c_1$, $x_2 \times c_2$, and $x \times c$, respectively. Long-run total costs can be computed from other output levels in the same way. We would expect that the resulting LTC curve would look like that of Figure 8–10, starting at the origin of the diagram and moving upward to the right in much the same fashion as a total variable cost curve. The LTC curve as we have drawn it reflects decreasing long-run average costs between zero and x and increasing long-run average costs for outputs greater than x.[7]

The long-run marginal cost curve shows the change in long-run total cost per unit change in the firm's output when the firm has ample time

---

[7] See pp 153–155.

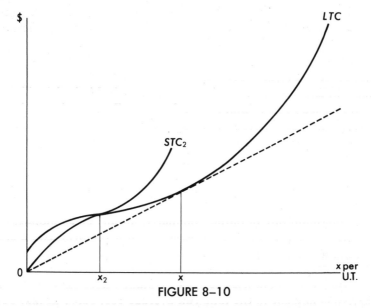

FIGURE 8–10

to make the output change by making the appropriate adjustments in the quantities of all resources used, including those which constitute its plant. Or, we can think of it as measuring the slopes of the *LTC* curve at various output levels.

From the *LTC* curve of Figure 8–10 we can deduce that *LMC* would be less than *LAC* where *LAC* is decreasing — that is, from zero to output x — and would be greater than *LAC* for output levels beyond x where *LAC* is increasing. At output x, *LMC* and *LAC* are equal. These relationships are shown in Figure 8–11 by the *LAC* and *LMC* curves. The

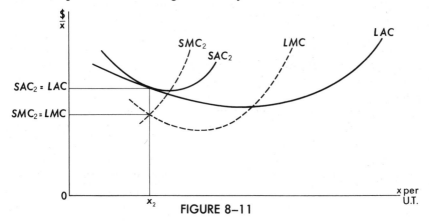

FIGURE 8–11

LMC curve bears the same relationship to its LAC curve that any given SMC curve bears to its SAC curve.

Relationships between LMC and SMC

When the firm has constructed the proper scale of plant for producing a given output, short-run marginal cost will equal long-run marginal cost at that output. Suppose for example that the given output is x_2 in Figure 8–11. The firm would use the scale of plant represented by SAC_2, which is tangent to the LAC curve at that output. The corresponding total cost curves would be STC_2 and LTC in Figure 8–10. We can verify that STC_2 would lie above LTC at output levels below x_2 since SAC_2 is greater than LAC at those output levels. At output x_2, STC_2 would be equal to LTC since SAC_2 and LAC are equal. At outputs greater than x_2, STC_2 would again exceed LTC since SAC_2 for those outputs again lies above LAC. At output x_2 where SAC_2 is tangent to LAC, STC_2 must also be tangent to LTC. At outputs in the neighborhood of, but below, x_2, the STC_2 curve must have a smaller slope than the LTC curve. At outputs in the neighborhood of, but above, x_2 the STC_2 curve must have a greater slope than the LTC curve. At x_2, where STC_2 is tangent to LTC, both curves have the same slope. Since slope of the STC_2 curve is short-run marginal cost for that scale of plant and since the slope of LTC is long-run marginal cost, it follows that $SMC_2 < LMC$ at outputs just smaller than x_2, $SMC_2 > LMC$ at outputs just larger than x_2, and SMC_2 equals LMC at output x_2. These relationships are shown in Figure 8–11.

SUMMARY

Costs of production are the obligations incurred by the firm for resources used in the production of its product. The cost of any given resource is determined by its value in its best alternative use. This is called the alternative cost doctrine. Costs of production differ from the usual concept of the firm's "expenses." "Expenses" of the firm usually coincide with explicit resource costs. In addition implicit resource costs must be included. The analysis of costs presented in the chapter assumes that the firm by itself cannot influence the price of any resource which it buys.

In the short run, resources used by the firm are classified as fixed and variable. The obligations incurred for them are "fixed costs" and "variable costs." Total fixed costs and total variable costs for different outputs are the component parts of total costs. From the three total cost curves we derived the corresponding per unit cost curves — average fixed cost, average variable cost, and average cost. The short-run average cost curve shows the least per unit cost of producing different outputs with a given scale of plant and is a ∪-shaped curve. In addition, we derived the marginal cost curve. The output at which average cost is least is called the optimum rate of output for the given scale of plant.

All resources can be varied in quantity by the firm in the long run; consequently, all costs are variable. The long-run average cost curve shows the least per unit cost of producing various outputs when the firm is free to change its scale of plant to any desired size. It is the envelope curve to the short-run average cost curves of all possible scales of plant and is usually ∪-shaped. The factors causing its ∪ shape are called economies of scale and diseconomies of scale. The long-run marginal cost curve shows the change in total costs resulting from a one-unit change in output when the firm is free to vary the quantities used of all resources. The scale of plant which is the most efficient of all scales of plant is called the optimum scale of plant.

For whatever output the firm produces in the long run, if the least per unit cost is to be obtained for that output, the scale of plant must be such that its short-run average cost curve is tangent to the long-run average cost curve at that output. For such a scale of plant short-run marginal cost will equal long-run marginal cost at the output of tangency.

SUGGESTED READINGS

STIGLER, GEORGE J. *The Theory of Price.* Rev. ed.; New York: The Macmillan Company, 1952, chap. 6.

VINER, JACOB. "Cost Curves and Supply Curves," *Zeitschrift für Nationalökonomie,* III (1931), 23–46. Reprinted in American Economic Association, *Readings in Price Theory.* Edited by George J. Stigler and Kenneth E. Boulding. Chicago: Richard D. Irwin, Inc., 1952, pp. 198–232.

The Geometry of Short-run per Unit Cost Curves

The relationships between total cost curves and per unit cost curves can be shown geometrically. Using the three total cost curves as a starting point, we shall derive the corresponding per unit cost curves from them. Then we shall show geometrically the relationship between the average cost curve and the marginal cost curve.

THE AVERAGE FIXED COST CURVE

The average fixed cost curve of Figure 8–12(b) is derived from the total fixed cost curve of Figure 8–12(a). The quantity scales of the two diagrams are the same. The vertical axis of Figure 8–12(a) measures total fixed costs, whereas that of Figure 8–12(b) measures fixed cost per unit. Consider output x in Figure 8–12(a). At that output total fixed cost is measured by xA. Now consider the straight line OA. The slope of OA equals xA/Ox, which is numerically equal to average fixed cost at output x. Likewise, at output x_1, average fixed cost equals the slope of OA_1 or x_1A_1/Ox_1. At successively larger outputs the slopes of the corresponding OA lines become smaller and smaller, showing that average fixed cost decreases as output increases; however, it can never reach zero. The numerical slopes of the OA lines plotted against the respective outputs for which they are drawn comprise the average fixed cost curve of Figure 8–12(b).

Geometrically, the AFC curve is a rectangular hyperbola. It approaches but never reaches both the dollar axis and the quantity axis. It is convex to the origin of the diagram. The distinguishing feature of a rectangular hyperbola is that at any point on the curve, such as L, the values represented on each axis when multiplied together produce the same mathematical product as the multiplication of the corresponding values at any other point on the curve, such as M. In other words, $Ox \times OR = Ox_1 \times OR_1$. This must necessarily be the case for the average fixed cost curve. Since total fixed costs are constant and since average

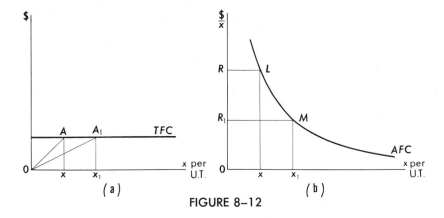

FIGURE 8–12

fixed cost at any output times that output equals total fixed cost, the mathematical product of any output times its corresponding average fixed cost must equal the mathematical product of any other output times its corresponding average fixed cost.

THE AVERAGE VARIABLE COST CURVE

The average variable cost curve in Figure 8–13(b) is derived from the total variable cost curve in Figure 8–13(a). The process of derivation is similar to that used in obtaining the AFC curve. At output x, TVC equals xB; hence AVC at output x equals xB/Ox equals the slope of line

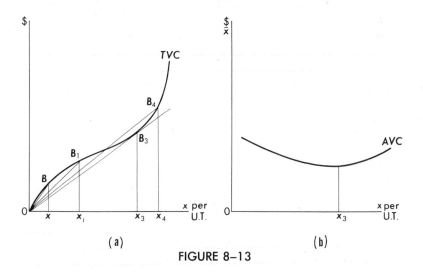

FIGURE 8–13

OB. At x_1, AVC equals x_1B_1/Ox_1 equals the slope of OB_1. At x_3, AVC equals x_3B_3/Ox_3 equals the slope of OB_3. At x_4, AVC equals x_4B_4/Ox_4 equals the slope of OB_4. The numerical slopes of the OB lines plotted against their respective outputs trace out the AVC curve of Figure 8–13(b).

The geometric derivation of the AVC curve makes clear that it takes its shape from the TVC curve. Between zero output and output x_3, the OB line for each successively larger output must have a smaller slope than the one for the preceding output. Hence, between zero and x_3, the AVC curve must be decreasing. At output x_3, line OB_3 is just tangent to the TVC curve and thus has a smaller slope than any other OB line possibly can have. At x_3, AVC is as low as it can get. At outputs greater than x_3, the OB lines will increase in slope, meaning that AVC is increasing. The AVC curve must have a $\cup$ shape if we have correctly established the shape of the TVC curve.

THE AVERAGE COST CURVE

The average cost curve in Figure 8–14(b) is derived from the total cost curve in the same way that the AVC curve is derived from the TVC curve. At output x, TC equals xC, so AC equals xC/Ox equals the slope of line OC. At output x_1, AC equals x_1C_1/Ox_1 equals the slope of OC_1 At output x_4, AC equals x_4C_4/Ox_4 equals the slope of OC_4. At output x_5, AC equals x_5C_5/Ox_5 equals the slope of OC_5. The slopes of the OC lines plotted against the corresponding outputs locate the AC curve in Figure 8–14(b).

If the shape of the TC curve is correct, the AC curve must be a $\cup$-shaped curve. The OC lines decrease in slope as output increases up to

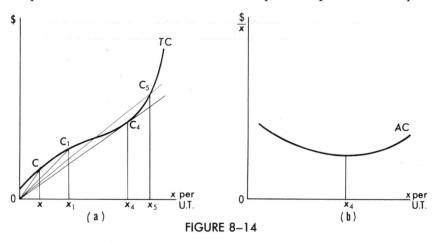

FIGURE 8–14

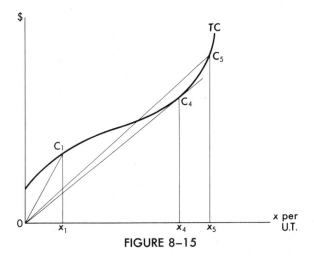

FIGURE 8–15

x_4. This tells us that AC is decreasing up to output x_4. At output x_4, OC_4 is tangent to the TC curve and, consequently, is the one of least slope. Here AC is minimum. At greater outputs, the slopes of the OC lines are increasing; that is, AC is increasing.

THE RELATIONSHIP OF AC AND MC

The relationship between AC and MC can be shown geometrically with the aid of the TC curve of Figure 8–15. Consider output x_1. Average cost at x_1 is equal to the slope of line OC_1. Marginal cost at output x_1 is equal to the slope of the TC curve at that output. The line OC_1 has a greater slope than does the TC curve at output x_1; hence average cost at x_1 is greater than marginal cost at the same output. This will be the case for any output up to x_4. At output x_4 the slope of line OC_4 is equal to the slope of the total cost curve at that output, meaning that average cost and marginal cost are equal at that output. As we have seen already, average cost is minimum at output x_4. At output x_5, the slope of line OC_5 is less than the slope of the TC curve, which means that marginal cost is greater than average cost at that output. This relationship will hold at any output above x_4; that is, at outputs for which average cost is increasing. Thus when average cost is decreasing, marginal cost is less than average cost. When average cost is minimum, marginal cost equals average cost. When average cost is increasing, marginal cost is greater than average cost.

Pricing and Output under Pure Competition 9

THE ANALYSES OF DEMAND, production, and costs are brought together in this chapter to explain pricing and output under market conditions of pure competition. The models to be developed present a rather
detailed tentative view of how production is organized in a free enterprise economy. As well as being useful in their own right, the principles
underlying the models provide a convenient point of departure for the
study of various degrees of monopoly in the following three chapters.

NB —> Pure competition was defined in Chapter 3. Its prime characteristics are (1) product homogeneity among the sellers of an industry; (2)
many sellers of the product — that is, enough sellers so that no one is
large enough relative to the entire market to influence product price; (3)
an absence of artificial restraints on demand, supply, and product price;
and (4) mobility of goods and of resources.

THE VERY SHORT-RUN

Very short-run analysis explains pricing and sales in situations
where certain amounts of product are already in existence. For example,
demand for a product may be seasonal, with production scheduled ahead
of the season in which the product is to be sold. The clothing industries
are cases in point. Spring, summer, fall, and winter production are based
on estimated seasonal demands and occur well in advance of the season
of sales. Another very short-run example occurs in fresh fruit and
vegetable retail markets. Retailers purchase stocks of perishable goods.
Once the stocks are on hand they must be disposed of before they spoil.
Still a third example is that of a product produced seasonally for a demand that continues the year around. Production of wheat and other
farm crops is typical of this type of situation. Two basic problems must
be solved by the economy in the very short run. First, how are the existing supplies of goods to be allocated or rationed among the many con-

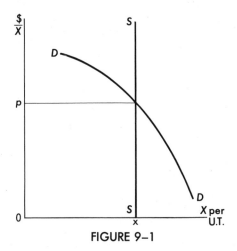

FIGURE 9–1

şumers who want them? Second, how are the given supplies to be rationed over their entire very short-run periods?

Rationing among Consumers

Price is the mechanism for rationing or allocating a fixed supply
among the consumers who want it. Suppose the period during which the
supply is fixed is one day and that we draw the demand curve of Figure
9–1 to show the different quantities per day that consumers will take off
the market at different possible prices. The supply curve is vertical since

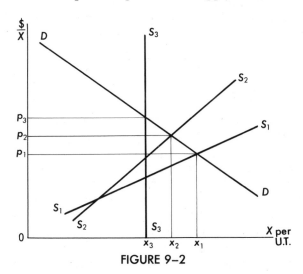

FIGURE 9–2

the supply for the day is fixed. A price of p will clear the market. Everyone who wants the commodity at that price will receive it in the desired amounts. At a price below p, a shortage will develop and consumers will drive the price up. At a price above p, a surplus will exist and sellers will lower price to get the commodity off their hands. At price p consumers voluntarily limit themselves to the fixed supply.

Rationing over Time

Prices also serve to ration a fixed supply over time, but the rationing process is more complex. Suppose that the period of the very short run is one year. Suppose, however, that the demand curve of Figure 9–2 is applicable to a four-month period, only. To simplify matters we shall suppose further that the demand curves for each of the three four-month periods of the year are alike. Suppose that sellers correctly anticipate the market for each four-month period and sell or hold their supplies accordingly.

Since the diagram applies to a four-month period only, the supply curve for the first four-month period will not be vertical. Sellers have a choice of selling during either the first or second four-month period, or of holding their supplies over to the last four-month period of the year. The higher the price offered during the first four-month period the greater the quantity sellers would be expected to place on the market during that period. Thus, the supply curve for the first four-month period will be an upward sloping curve such as $S_1 S_1$. Market price will be p_1 and quantity sold will be x_1.

The supply curve for the second four-month period would be expected to lie above $S_1 S_1$, except at low prices, and to be less elastic. It would lie above $S_1 S_1$ because sellers, to be induced to hold quantities over, would require sufficiently higher prices for different quantities to cover storage costs and a normal rate of return on investment in the goods carried over. At extremely low prices, however, the second four-month period supply curve may lie to the right of $S_1 S_1$. The possibility of low prices in the second period would be more serious to sellers than would a similar possibility in the first period since the opportunities for disposing of supplies held over have been narrowed. Consequently, sellers may be induced to place more on the market during the second period at low prices than they are willing to place on the market at those same prices in the first period. The smaller elasticity at various prices also is a result of the narrowing of opportunities for disposing of the supplies held over. The periods during which supply can be disposed of now have been narrowed to two. The supply curve for the second period would look something like $S_2 S_2$. Price would be p_2 and quantity sold would be x_2.

The third four-month period will be identical with the case shown in Figure 9–1. The remaining supply must be disposed of in the third period; consequently, the supply curve will be S_3S_3 in Figure 9–2. Note that S_3S_3 lies above S_2S_2, except at low prices, and that it is less elastic than S_2S_2. In fact, S_3S_3 is completely inelastic. Price will be p_3 and quantity sold will be x_3.

The successively higher prices for the three-month periods will occur as shown only if sellers correctly anticipate demand and the amounts that should be held over. If sellers misjudge the future market and hold large quantities over to the second and third periods, the prices during those periods may fall below that of the first period. If sellers' anticipations are correct, the price for each successive period should be sufficiently higher than that of preceding periods to pay storage costs, a normal rate of return on investment in held-over supplies, and sums for the risks involved in holding supplies over to the succeeding periods.

Thus, price is the rationer of fixed supplies over time. Sellers, or speculators, as the case may be, in holding supplies off the market during the early part of the period of the very short run, cause price to be held up during that time above what it would otherwise have been. By selling held-over supplies in the latter part of the very short-run period, sellers drive price below what it would otherwise have been. Thus, by their speculative activity, they smooth out both prices and quantities sold over the entire period. In the absence of any speculative activity, large quantities would be placed on the market early in the period, driving price low. Small quantities available in the latter part of the period would cause price to be high. The speculative activity described above, while not eliminating the price trend from lower to higher, does much to narrow the differential between the early and the late parts of the period. Activity of this type occurs regularly in the markets for those storable farm products lying outside the price support program.

A Corollary

A corollary to the foregoing discussion is that once a good is on the market in fixed quantity, costs of production play no part in the determination of its price. Price will be determined solely by the fixed supply, together with demand for the product.[1] It will be futile for holders of such a product to try to recoup production costs. Any seller who cannot consume the product himself will prefer to dispose of his holdings at almost any price above zero rather than to keep them indefinitely. Old bread and overripe bananas are cases in point. Costs of

---

[1] Note that in the example of Figure 9–2, market supply is fixed at an absolute quantity for the third period only.

production enter the picture only when there is some possibility of varying the supply produced over the time period under consideration. Such a possibility exists in both the short run and the long run, both of which we have yet to consider.

THE SHORT RUN

Short-run price and output analysis treats situations in which the firm is free to vary its output but does not have time to change its scale of plant. The number of firms in the industry will be fixed because new firms will not have time to enter nor will existing firms have time to leave. Any changes in industry output must come from the plant capacity of existing firms. Since each firm is too small relative to the market in which it sells to be able to affect the market price of the product, the problem facing the firm is that of determining the output to produce and sell. With regard to the entire market, the market price and market output are to be determined.

The Firm

We shall assume that the firm's primary objective is to maximize its profits or to minimize its losses if it cannot make profits. These need not be the firm's sole objectives; however, they furnish a simple and con-

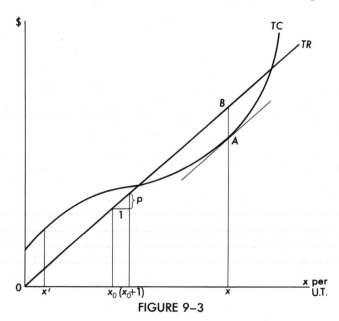

FIGURE 9–3

venient starting point for the theory of the firm. Profit will be the difference between the firm's total receipts and its total costs.

PROFIT MAXIMIZATION: TOTAL CURVES • Profit maximization involves a comparison of total costs with total receipts at various possible outputs and choice of the output at which total receipts exceed total costs by the greatest amount. Total receipts, or total revenue at different outputs, are plotted against short-run total costs at various outputs in Figure 9–3. The total cost curve is the short-run total cost curve we met in the preceding chapter. The total receipts curve needs further elaboration.

Since the firm can sell either large or small outputs at the same price per unit, its total receipts curve will be a linear upward sloping curve starting at zero. If sales of the firm are zero, total receipts will be zero, too. If sales are one unit of output per unit of time the firm's total receipts will equal the price of the product. At two units of output and sales, total receipts will be twice the price of the product. Each one-unit addition to the firm's sales per unit of time will increase total receipts by a constant amount — the price per unit of product — hence the total receipts curve is upward sloping and linear.

Profits of the firm are maximum at output x, where the vertical spread between TR and TC is greatest. The amount of profit is measured by the vertical distance AB. At output x the slopes of the two curves are equal. At outputs just smaller than x, the slope of TR exceeds that of TC; hence the two curves spread farther and farther apart as output increases. At outputs just greater than x, the slope of TC exceeds that of TR; hence the two curves come closer and closer together as output increases.

The amount by which the firm's total receipts change when sales are changed by one unit is called *marginal revenue*. Under conditions of pure competition, since product price is fixed, the change in total receipts brought about by a one-unit change in sales is necessarily equal to product price. Marginal revenue and product price for the purely competitive seller are the same thing. In Figure 9–3, an increase in sales from x_0 to $(x_0 + 1)$ increases TR by an amount equal to p. Thus, marginal revenue and product price are equal to the slope of the TR curve.[2]

The necessary conditions for profit maximization can be restated in terms of marginal revenue and marginal cost. Since marginal cost is equal to the slope of the TC curve and marginal revenue is equal to the slope of the TR curve, profits are maximized at the output at which marginal cost

---

[2] The relationship between marginal revenue and total revenue is the same as that between marginal utility and total utility, between marginal physical product and total product of a resource, and between marginal cost and total cost.

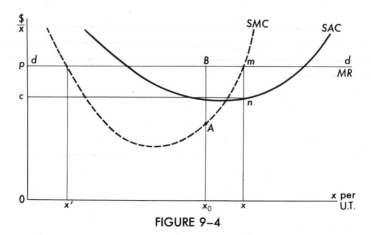

FIGURE 9–4

equals marginal revenue.[3] At outputs smaller than x, we can see that marginal revenue is greater than marginal cost. This means that larger outputs up to x will add more to the firm's total receipts than to the firm's total costs and, therefore, will make net additions to profit. Beyond output x, marginal cost is greater than marginal revenue. Thus, larger outputs beyond x add more to total costs than to total receipts and cause profits to decrease.

PROFIT MAXIMIZATION: PER UNIT CURVES • Analysis of the firm's profit-maximizing output is usually put in terms of per unit cost and revenue curves. The basic analysis is the same as above but the diagrammatic treatment is in a different form. The firm's short-run average cost curve and short-run marginal cost curve are shown in Figure 9–4, as is the demand curve faced by the firm. Since marginal revenue is equal to price per unit, the marginal revenue curve coincides with the demand curve faced by the firm. Both are equal at all possible outputs of the firm to the market price of the product.

Profits are maximum at the output at which marginal cost equals marginal revenue; that is, at output x where SMC equals MR.[4] At any output less than x, say x_0, marginal revenue $x_0 B$ exceeds marginal cost $x_0 A$. Larger outputs up to x will increase total receipts more than they increase total costs; hence profits will increase up to that point. Beyond

---

[3] This statement must be used with caution. Consider output x' in Figure 9–3. At output x' *losses* are maximized rather than profits, but marginal cost equals marginal revenue. This matter will be clarified in the discussion of per unit curves which follows.

[4] MC equals MR at output x' but this is an output of maximum loss. For profit maximization, MC must equal MR and *additionally* the MC curve must intersect the MR curve from *below*.

output x, SMC is greater than MR, which means that movement to those larger outputs will increase total costs more than they increase total receipts. This will cause profits to decrease. Therefore, x is the output of maximum profits.

Total profit of the firm appears in Figure 9–4 as the area of the rectangle $cpmn$. Profit per unit is price p minus average cost c at output x. Total profit is equal to profit per unit multiplied by sales; that is, total profit equals $cp \times x$. Note that at output x, profit per unit is not maximized, nor is there any reason why it should be. The concern of the firm is with total profit, not with profit per unit.

LOSS MINIMIZATION • If it should happen that market price of the product is less than short-run average costs at all possible outputs, the firm will incur losses instead of making profits. Since the short run is defined as a time period so short that the firm cannot change its scale of plant, liquidation of the plant in the short run is not possible. The choices open to the firm are (1) whether to produce at a loss, or (2) whether to discontinue production. Fixed costs will be incurred even if the second alternative is chosen.

The firm's decision will rest on whether or not price of the product will cover average variable costs (or whether total receipts will cover total variable costs). Suppose market price of the product is p_0 in Figure 9–5. If the firm produces output x_0, at which SMC equals MR_0, total receipts equal $p_0 \times x_0$. Total variable costs also equal $p_0 \times x_0$; hence total receipts just cover total variable costs. Total costs are equal to total variable costs plus total fixed costs; therefore, if variable costs are just covered, the firm's loss will be equal to total fixed costs. It will make no difference whether the firm produces or not. In either case losses will equal total fixed costs.

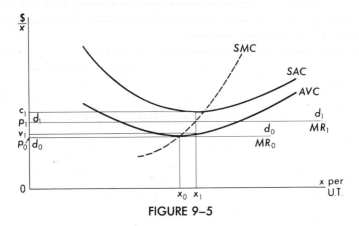

FIGURE 9–5

If market price is less than minimum average variable costs the firm will minimize losses by discontinuing production. The loss will equal total fixed costs when the firm produces nothing. If the firm should produce at a price less than p_0, average variable costs would be greater than price and total variable costs would be greater than total receipts. Losses would equal total fixed costs plus that part of total variable costs not covered by total receipts.

At a price greater than minimum average variable costs but less than minimum SAC, it will pay the firm to produce. At such a price as p_1, an output of x_1 will result in losses less in amount than total fixed costs. Total receipts will be $p_1 \times x_1$. Total variable costs will be $v_1 \times x_1$. Total receipts exceed total variable costs by an amount equal to $v_1 p_1 \times x_1$. The excess of total receipts over total variable costs can be applied against total fixed costs, thus reducing losses to an amount less than total fixed costs. Loss in this case equals $p_1 c_1 \times x_1$.

To give the analysis a practical application, suppose the firm under consideration is a wheat farmer who owns his farm and his machinery. The farm is mortgaged and the machinery is not yet paid for. Mortgage and machinery payments constitute his fixed costs and must be met wether or not he produces wheat. Outlays for seed, gasoline, fertilizer, and his own labor represent his variable costs. If he produces nothing there is no necessity for making outlays on variable resources. Under what circumstances should he produce nothing at all and hire his labor out to someone else? If expected receipts from the wheat crop are not sufficient to cover the costs of seed, gasoline, fertilizer, and his own labor, he should not produce. If he should produce under these circumstances, his losses will equal mortgage and machinery payments plus that part of his variable costs not covered by his receipts. If he does not produce, his losses will equal mortgage and machinery payments only. Thus he should not produce. Under what circumstances will it be to his advantage to produce even though incurring losses? If expected receipts will more than cover the variable costs, the excess can be applied to the mortgage and machinery payments and production should be undertaken. Under these circumstances, a decision not to produce means the loss will be the full amount of the fixed costs. If he produces, his loss will be less than his total fixed costs.

At output x_1 when market price is p_1, equality between SMC and MR shows that losses are minimum. At a lower output, MR is greater than SMC and increases in output will add more to total receipts than to total costs. This will reduce losses. Beyond output x_1, SMC is greater than MR, which means that increases in output add more to total costs than to total receipts. These increases in output will increase the losses. Hence losses are minimum at the output where *SMC* equals *MR*.

To summarize the analysis, the firm maximizes profits or minimizes losses by producing the output at which *SMC* equals *MR* or price. There is one exception. If market price is less than the firm's average variable costs, losses will be minimized by stopping production altogether, leaving losses equal to total fixed costs.

SHORT-RUN SUPPLY CURVE OF THE FIRM • That part of the firm's *SMC* curve that lies above the *AVC* curve is the firm's short-run supply curve for the product. The *SMC* curve shows the different quantities that the firm will place on the market at different possible prices. At each possible price the firm will produce the amount at which *SMC* equals *p* (and *MR*) to maximize profits or minimize losses. Supply drops to zero at any price below *AVC*.

The Industry

Market or industry price has been taken as given so far, but we now have the necessary tools to see how it is determined. Industry price emerges from the interactions between demanders of a good on the one hand and suppliers of the good on the other. We discussed the forces underlying an industry demand curve in previous chapters, but we have yet to establish the industry supply curve. The short-run industry supply curve for a commodity is a short step beyond the individual firm supply curve. After we establish it we shall consider short-run equilibrium for an entire industry.

SHORT-RUN SUPPLY CURVE OF THE INDUSTRY • As a first approximation we can think of the industry short-run supply curve as the hori-

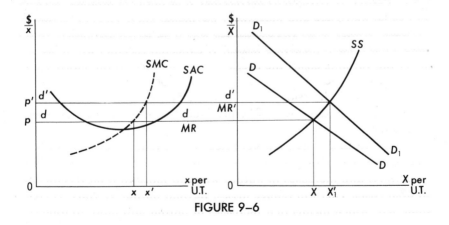

FIGURE 9–6

zontal summation of the short-run supply curves of all firms in the industry. It shows the quantities of the commodity that all firms together will place on the market at various possible prices. Such an industry short-run supply curve is valid if resource supplies to the industry as a whole are perfectly elastic; that is, expansion of resource inputs and product output by all firms simultaneously has no effect upon resource prices. We shall return to this point shortly.

SHORT-RUN EQUILIBRIUM • Diagrammatically, Figure 9–6 shows determination of market price, industry output, and the output of one representative firm of the industry. The output axis of the industry diagram is considerably compressed as compared with that of the firm diagram. The price axes of the two diagrams are identical. The industry demand curve for the product is shown as DD in the industry diagram. The SAC and SMC curves of the representative firm are drawn in the firm diagram. The horizontal summation of all individual firm supply curves establishes the industry short-run supply curve SS. The short-run equilibrium market price will be p. The demand curve and the marginal revenue curve faced by the firm will be horizontal at that level. To maximize profits, the representative firm, and each firm in the industry, will produce the output at which $SMC = MR = p$. The firm output is x. The combined output of all firms is the industry output X. The industry as a whole and each individual firm in the industry are in short-run equilibrium.

An increase in industry demand for the product to D_1D_1 will increase the short-run equilibrium price and output. The increase in demand will cause a shortage of the good at the old price p. Price will be driven up by consumers to p'. The demand curve and marginal revenue curve faced by the firm shift up to the level of the new market price. To maximize profits, each firm in the industry will increase output up to the point at which its SMC equals its new marginal revenue and the new market price. The new output for the representative firm will be x' and the new industry output will be X'.

SUPPLY CURVE MODIFICATIONS • When expansion or contraction of resource inputs by all firms acting simultaneously cause resource prices to change, the industry short-run supply curve is no longer the horizontal summation of individual firm supply curves. Even though one firm cannot affect resource prices through expansion or contraction of the quantities it buys, all firms acting at the same time may be able to do so. If expansion of industry output and resource inputs increases resource prices, individual firm cost curves will shift upward. If expansion decreases resource prices, firm cost curves will shift downward. The possibility exists, too, that some resource prices will increase and some will decrease. The effect may be to change the shape of the cost curves slightly and to cause some shift up or down depending upon whether resource price increases or resource price decreases are predominant.

The net effect of resource price increases when expansion occurs will be to make the industry short-run supply curve less elastic. In Figure 9-6 the increase in demand increases price and marginal revenue, inducing firms to expand output. But suppose the output expansion causes resource prices to increase, shifting *SAC* and *SMC* upward. The upward shift in *SMC* is also a shift to the left, which means that the new *SMC* curve will equal marginal revenue or price at a smaller output than would be the case had the *SMC* curve not shifted. Similarly, resource price decreases resulting from expansion of industry output will cause the industry supply curve to be more elastic than the industry supply curve shown in Figure 9-6. The industry short-run supply curve in this case is obtained by summing individual firm profit maximizing outputs at each possible level of industry price.

THE LONG RUN

The possibilities of output variation in a purely competitive indus- try are much greater in the long run than in the short run. In the long run, output can be varied through increases or decreases in the utiliza- tion of existing plant capacity — as is the case in the short run. But more important, in the long run firms have time to increase or decrease their scales of plant and there is ample time and opportunity for new firms to enter or for existing firms to leave the industry. The two latter possibilities greatly increase the elasticity of the long-run industry supply curve as

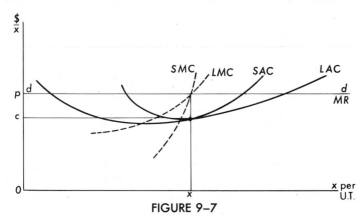

FIGURE 9–7

compared with the short-run industry supply curve. Long-run adjustments in scale of plant by individual firms will occur simultaneously with the entrance or exit of firms to and from the industry, but they can be more easily understood if they are considered first by themselves.

The Firm

SCALE OF PLANT ADJUSTMENTS • The firm's determination of the scale of plant to use can be put into proper focus by assuming that entry into the industry is blocked in some way. Suppose the firm is faced with a certain market price, say p in Figure 9–7. Its long-run average cost curve and long-run marginal cost curve are LAC and LMC, respectively. To maximize long-run profits the firm should produce output x at which long-run marginal cost equals marginal revenue. The scale of plant that enables the firm to produce output x at the least possible cost per unit is SAC, and for that scale of plant short-run marginal cost also is equal to marginal revenue. Profits of the firm are $cp \times x$.

DIGRESSION ON PROFITS • A note on profits is in order before proceeding further. The concept of profit is ambiguous enough to require explicit definition. Economic profit is a pure surplus or excess of total receipts over all costs of production incurred by the firm. Included as costs are obligations incurred for all resources used equal to what those resources could earn employed in their next best alternative use; that is, the "opportunity costs" of all resources used. These costs include returns to the owners of capital used equivalent to what they could get had they invested in capital elsewhere in the economy. They include implicit returns to labor owned by the operator of the business. Thus, profit is so much "gravy" for the firm.

The contrast between the concept of economic profit as defined above and the accountant's concept of a corporation's "profit" should help make the definition clear. Corporation income taxes will be ignored. A corporation's "profit" is determined by the accountant as follows:

$$\left\{ \begin{array}{l} \text{Gross income} \\ - \text{ Expenses (including interest payments on bonds, amortization} \\ \quad \text{expenses, depreciation expenses, and so on)} \\ \hline \text{Net income or "profit"} \end{array} \right.$$

However, from the point of view of economics, certain costs are left out of consideration. Obligations incurred to the owners of the corporation's capital (that is, its stockholders) are as much costs of production as are those incurred for labor or for raw materials. The corporation is usually thought to make payments to capital owners in the form of dividends from the corporation's "profit," but from the point of view of economic theory this is incorrect. To arrive at economic profit, dividend payments equal to what investors could earn had they invested elsewhere in the economy should be subtracted from the corporation's net income as follows:

$$
\begin{array}{l}
\text{Net income or ``profit''} \\
- \text{ Average dividends} \\
\hline
\text{Economic profit}
\end{array}
$$

What happens to profits made by an individual firm? They accrue primarily to the owners of the firm in the form of higher returns to investors in the business or in the form of increases in the value of owners' holdings. The former means higher than average dividends to stockholders in the case of the corporation, or a higher income in the case of a single proprietor or partner than he could have earned had he invested and/or worked elsewhere. The latter means that some of the economic profits are plowed back into the firm to expand or improve it. This, of course, increases the value of the owners' holdings. Secondarily, profits may be used to some extent to pay other resources returns above their opportunity costs.

The Firm and the Industry

LONG-RUN EQUILIBRIUM • By dropping the assumption of blocked entry into the industry the nature of long-run equilibrium for the industry under conditions of pure competition can be determined. The firm with plant SAC in Figure 9–7 is making pure profits. It pays a greater rate of return to its investors than they can earn elsewhere; hence new investors and new firms will be attracted into the industry with the expectation that they, too, can do the same thing. The entry of new firms increases the supply of product X and causes price to move downward from its original level, $p_;$ Each individual firm in the industry, faced with

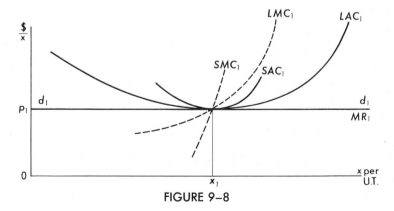

FIGURE 9–8

a downward shifting demand curve and marginal revenue curve, will cut output below x and will reduce scale of plant below SAC. In the interests of maximizing profits outputs will be cut to levels at which the long-run marginal cost curve cuts the successively lower marginal revenue curves.

Pure profits can be made by firms in the industry until enough firms have entered to drive price down to p_1 as shown in Figure 9–8. At that point individual firms will have cut their scale of plant back to SAC_1, the optimum scale of plant, and will be operating SAC_1 at the optimum rate of output. Pure profit has been eliminated by the entry of new firms and there is no incentive for more firms to enter. No losses are being incurred, so there is no incentive for firms to leave the industry. The firms in the industry are doing satisfactorily. They are earning returns for all resources equal to what those resources could earn in alternative employments.[5]

The industry is in long-run equilibrium when all firms of the industry are in the position shown in Figure 9–8. Industry equilibrium implies that there are neither incentives for firms to enter nor incentives for firms to leave; that there are no profit possibilities for firms in the industry; and that no losses are being incurred. For every firm, $LAC = SAC = p$ at the output being produced, and at no other output can lower average

---

[5] In the discussion of the long run we shall assume that for all firms, both in the industry and potentially in it, the minimum points of the LAC curves lie at the same level. This condition is a necessary one for defining the long-run equilibrium position of an industry.

As a practical matter, long-run equilibrium is never likely to be achieved in any industry. It is a will-o'-the-wisp which industries forever chase but never catch. Before an industry can reach equilibrium, conditions defining the equilibrium position change. Demand for the product changes or costs of production change as a result of resource price changes or changes in techniques of production. Thus the chase goes on toward a new equilibrium position. The long-run (and other) equilibrium concepts are important, however, because they show us the motivation for and the direction of the chase. Additionally, they show us how the chase works toward (in most cases) solution of the economic problem.

The argument usually made regarding equality of minimum long-run average costs of firms in the industry rests on the alternative cost doctrine. Initial inequalities in such costs may result from superior management of particular firms, from favorable locations of certain firms with respect to power, markets, and sources of raw and semifinished materials, or from other similar causes. According to the alternative cost doctrine, these differentials will not persist. The superior manager who can make profits for his firm could do the same for other firms in the industry and, perhaps, in others outside the industry. His prospective value to other firms becomes his cost to the firm in which he works; thus, the cost of his services to the one firm increases to the point at which he can make pure profits for none. The same argument applies to a favorable location. The cost of the favorable location becomes its value to other firms which could use it to advantage. Its value to other firms is the capitalized value of the returns it could earn for them. Hence the profits it can earn for any one firm disappear as its cost is correctly determined.

costs be obtained. Also for each firm there is no incentive to increase or decrease scale of plant or output since $LMC = SMC = MR$.

For long-run industry equilibrium to exist, individual firms must also be in long-run equilibrium. However, the converse of this will not hold. An individual firm could be in long-run equilibrium while making profits — as in Figure 9–7, for example. But in this case the industry would not be in equilibrium. The existence of long-run industry equilibrium requires long-run individual firm equilibrium at a no-profit no-loss level of operation.

Similarly, long-run industry and individual firm equilibrium requires that short-run equilibrium exist at the same time. But short-run individual firm and industry equilibrium can exist even though there is long-run individual firm and/or industry disequilibrium. Long-run equilibrium of an industry is a more general concept than is either long-run equilibrium for a firm or short-run equilibrium for both a firm and an industry.

The foregoing analysis serves to introduce the concept of long-run equilibrium in a purely competitive industry, but it is by no means a complete analysis of the long-run adjustments within the industry that occur as a result of some disturbing force. Usually cost changes as well as price changes will occur as new firms, attracted by profits, enter an industry. The nature of the cost adjustments, if any, will depend upon whether the industry is one of increasing costs, constant costs, or decreasing costs. Each of these will be analyzed in turn.

INCREASING COSTS • Consider first an industry of increasing costs. The nature of increasing costs will become evident as we move through

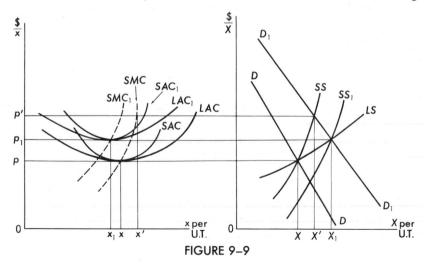

FIGURE 9–9

the analysis. Suppose that the industry is initially in long-run equilibrium. Then suppose that the disturbing force is an increase in demand for product X. We shall trace through the short-run effects and the long-run effects of the increase in demand. Then the long-run industry supply curve for the product will be established.

Long-run equilibrium diagrams for the industry and for a representative firm of the industry are shown in Figure 9–9. The industry demand curve is DD and the industry short-run supply curve is SS. The firm's long-run average cost curve and short-run average cost curve are LAC and SAC, respectively. The firm's short-run marginal cost curve for scale of plant SAC is SMC. The long-run marginal cost curve is omitted. It is not essential for the analysis and unduly complicates the diagram. Since the industry and the firm are in long-run equilibrium, they are necessarily in short-run equilibrium, too. Therefore, we can think of the market demand curve and the market short-run supply curve as establishing the industry price p. The demand curve and the marginal revenue curve faced by the firm are horizontal and are equal to price p at all levels of output for the firm. The firm produces the output at which SMC (and LMC) equals marginal revenue or price. Individual firm output is x. Industry output X is the summation of individual firm outputs at price p. There are just enough firms in the industry to make price equal to minimum short-run and long-run average costs for the firm at output x. The firm is using the optimum scale of plant at the optimum rate of output. There are no pure profits or losses being incurred.

Now suppose we consider the short-run effects of an increase in demand to D_1D_1. Industry price will rise to p'. The firm, in order to maximize profits, will increase output to x', the output at which SMC equals the new marginal revenue. Industry output will increase to X'. The firm will be making profits equal to output x', multiplied by the difference between price p' and short-run average costs at output x'. The short-run effects of the increase in demand are (1) an increase in price, and (2) some increase in output as existing plant capacity is worked with greater intensity.

Turning now to the long-run effects, the existence of profit will bring new firms into the industry. As new firms enter, increasing the industry's productive capacity, the industry short-run supply curve will shift to the right. The more firms that enter, the farther to the right it will move. The increase in supply will cause price to move downward from the short-run high of p'. As price goes down, individual firms will cut output back from the short-run high of x'.

In an increasing cost industry the entry of new firms causes the whole set of cost curves for existing firms to shift upward. This will occur in an industry that uses significant proportions of the total supplies available of the resources necessary for making its product. Suppose, for example, that one such resource is a special steel alloy. The entry of new firms increases the demand for such resources thus increasing their prices. As resource prices rise the set of cost curves shifts upward accordingly.

Any given set of cost curves presupposes that the firm can get all it wants of any one resource at a constant price per unit. No single firm causes the prices of resources to change. One firm alone does not take a large enough amount of any resource to be able to do this. It is the greater demand for resources brought about by the entry of new firms into the industry and also, perhaps, by the simultaneous expansion of output by existing firms that causes resource prices to rise. The forces causing resource prices to rise lie completely outside the control of the individual firm, or are said to be *external* to the firm. The increases in resource prices and the consequent upward shifts of the cost curves thus are the result of *external diseconomies* of increasing production in the industry.

A two-way squeeze is put on profits by the entry of new firms as price falls and costs rise. Eventually enough firms enter so that price decreases enough and costs rise enough for price to be equal again to minimum long-run average costs for individual firms. All profit is squeezed out. In Figure 9–9 the new price is p_1 and the new cost curves are LAC_1, SAC_1, and SMC_1. The entry of new firms stops and the industry is once more in long-run equilibrium. The new long-run industry price of p_1 lies between the original long-run price of p and the short-run high of p'. The new firm output is x_1 at which SMC_1 is equal to the new long-run marginal revenue and price. Industry output will have increased to X_1 since the increased capacity of the industry has moved the short-run supply curve to SS_1.[6]

---

[6] To keep an already complex exposition as simple as possible, a long-run development of a transitory nature has been ignored in the argument of the text. The short-run high price, resulting from the increase in demand for the product, not only attracts profit-seeking new firms into the industry, but also creates an incentive for existing firms to increase their scales of plant beyond the optimum. This will be the case since, for the individual firm, maximum long-run profits are obtained at the output at which long-run marginal cost equals marginal revenue and price (see Figure 9–7). Then, as the entrance of new firms lowers price, the output at which long-run marginal cost equals price becomes smaller. The firm is induced to reduce scale of plant. When enough firms have entered to eliminate profit, the firm once more will be building the optimum scale of plant.

Some question may arise with regard to the new long-run output of the firm. Will it be equal to, greater than, or less than the old long run output of x? The answer depends upon the way in which the cost curves shift upward. Whether the cost curves shift straight up, a little to the left, or a little to the right depends upon the comparative price increases of different classes of resources. If all resource prices increase proportionally, the same combinations of resources will be the least-cost combinations. The cost curves will shift straight up and the new long-run firm output will be equal to the old. Suppose, however, that short-run fixed resources go up relatively more in price than do those which are considered variable in the short run. The firm will want to economize on the now relatively more expensive fixed resources. The proportions of the relatively more expensive fixed resources to the relatively cheaper variable ones will be decreased to secure least-cost combinations. The optimum scale of plant will tend to be slightly smaller in the new long-run equilibrium position than it was in the old. Hence the new long-run equilibrium firm output will tend to be smaller than the old, as is shown in Figure 9–9. If short-run fixed resources increase proportionally less in price than do short-run variable resources, least-cost combinations favor larger scales of plant. The firm will want to economize on the now relatively more expensive resources and use larger proportions of those which constitute scale of plant. The new optimum scale of plant and the new output will tend to be larger than the old.

The long-run industry supply curve is LS in Figure 9–9. It joins all points of long-run equilibrium for the industry. Alternatively, the industry long-run supply curve can be thought of as the horizontal summation of the minimum points of all individual firm LAC curves as the entry of new firms shifts their cost curves upward. It shows the industry outputs that will be forthcoming at different possible prices when there is ample time for scale of plant adjustments as well as for entry and exit of firms.

CONSTANT COSTS • The pattern of analysis for an industry of constant costs is basically the same as that for an industry of increasing costs. Starting from the position of long-run equilibrium shown in Figure 9–10, suppose that an increase in demand occurs. The short-run effects are the same as before. Price will increase to p'; firm output will increase to x'; and industry output will increase to X'. Pure profits will be made by the individual firms of the industry.

New firms will be attracted into the industry in the long run. As before, the industry short-run supply curve will shift to the right as new firms enter, causing price to decrease.

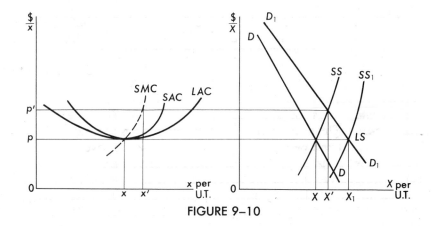

FIGURE 9–10

In a constant cost industry the entry of new firms does not increase market demands for resources sufficiently to cause their prices to increase. Of the total supplies of resources necessary for the production of X this industry takes a small enough part so that no influence is exerted on their prices by the new firms coming in. If the entry of new firms has no effect on resource prices, the cost curves of existing firms will remain as they were before. Profits will be made until enough firms have entered to bring the price back down to p. Price and minimum long-run average costs will be equal and long-run equilibrium will be reestablished. The new short-run supply curve will be SS_1. Individual firm output will be that at which SMC equals marginal revenue and price p. The entry of new firms will have increased industry output substantially to X_1. The long-run supply curve will be LS and will be horizontal at the level of minimum long-run average costs.

DECREASING COSTS • Decreasing cost cases are probably rather rare. Analytically they parallel increasing and constant cost cases. As before, we start with an industry and its firms in long-run equilibrium and then assume demand increases. The short-run effects are the same as before. In Figure 9–11, industry price will increase to p', firm output goes up to x', and industry output increases to X'. Pure profits equal to x' times the difference between p' and SAC at output x' will be made by the representative firm.

New firms will be attracted into the industry in the long run because of the pure profits available. The industry short-run supply curve moves to the right as new firms add to the industry's productive capacity. Price goes down as new firms enter.

In a decreasing cost industry, the entry of new firms must cause

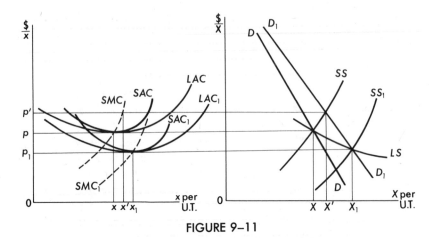

FIGURE 9–11

resource prices to fall. The decrease in resource prices as new firms enter causes the cost curves to shift downward. Both price of X and costs of production are decreasing. Eventually the declining product price overtakes the declining cost curves and profit is squeezed out. The new long-run equilibrium price is p_1 and is less than the original price of p. Individual firm output is x_1, at which both short-run and long-run marginal costs equal marginal revenue or price. The new industry output is X_1. The long-run supply curve LS will be downward sloping to the right.

What are the circumstances that could conceivably give rise to decreasing costs? Suppose the industry in question is a young one growing up in a new territory.[7] Transportation facilities and the organization of markets, both for resources and the final product, may not be well developed. An increase in the number of firms in the industry and, consequently, in the size of the industry may make feasible the development of improved transportation and marketing facilities that will substantially reduce the costs of individual firms. For example, industrial growth of an area may stimulate development and improvement of railway, highway, and air transportation service into and from the area. Explanations of decreasing costs are rather hard to find. Whatever the specific explanations given for particular cases, they must stem basically from improvements in qualities of resources furnished or from greater efficiencies developed in the resource-furnishing industries.

Decreasing costs, or *external economies* of increasing production, as discussed above should not be confused with the *internal economies*

---

[7] However, in this case, the chances of its being one of pure competition are small.

of scale possible for a single firm with a smaller than optimum scale of plant. The individual firm has no influence over external economies. They result solely from expansion of the industry or from forces outside the control of the firm. Internal economies of scale are under the control of the firm. The firm can secure them by enlarging its scale of plant.

Probably increasing cost industries are the most prevalent of the three cases analyzed. Decreasing costs are most unlikely to occur. Industries of constant cost and of decreasing cost are likely to become industries of increasing cost as they become older and well established. Granting the possibility of decreasing costs, once the decreasing costs or external economies of increasing production have been taken advantage of, the industry must surely become one of constant or increasing costs.

The disturbing force triggering the foregoing chains of adjustments was assumed to be an increase in demand for the product. It could just as well have been a decrease in demand, in which case losses would occur for individual firms and exit from the industry would have occurred until long-run equilibrium was again established. Or, in lieu of changes in demand, we could have assumed that major technological developments caused disequilibrium to occur and these would induce new firms to enter the industry until long-run equilibrium was re-established.

THE ORGANIZATION OF PRODUCTION

The theory of pure competition can be used to put into more detailed and complete form our thinking with regard to the organization of production in a free enterprise economy. In the rather idealistic purely competitive world there are no obstructions to the adjustment of productive capacity to consumer desires. We shall assume that all industries in the economy are purely competitive, that long-run equilibrium exists initially, and that all industries operate under increasing cost conditions.

Suppose now that consumer tastes and preferences shift away from commodity Y and toward commodity X. Demand for X increases and demand for Y decreases. How does the realignment of the economy's productive capacity to meet the change occur? The process can be discussed from both a short-run and a long-run point of view.

The Short Run

The short-run adjustments will fall more heavily on prices and less heavily on output for the industries involved. The increase in demand for X increases the price of X considerably and increases the output of X to a limited extent. Price bears the major burden of adjustment since output increases must come from the existing plant capacity of the industry. Similarly, the decrease in demand for Y decreases the price of Y considerably and decreases output to a limited extent. Since firms do not have time to leave the industry they continue to produce if they can cover variable costs. Thus the changes in consumers' comparative valuations of X and Y show up for the most part in the relative prices of the two commodities.

The changes in the relative prices of X and Y are signals to producers that reallocation of productive capacity or reallocation of resources is in order. Industry X, because of the relatively higher price for X, shows short-run profits. Industry Y, because of the relatively lower price of Y, shows short-run losses. Some reallocation of resources occurs, even in the short run. To expand output, producers in industry X offer slightly higher prices for the necessary variable resources. In industry Y, output contraction decreases demand for variable resources used in that industry, which in turn depresses the prices offered for those variable resources. To the extent that industry X and industry Y use the same kinds of variable resources, voluntary reallocation by resource owners from the lower-paying to the higher-paying uses sufficient to equalize their remuneration in the two uses will occur. If the two industries use different kinds of variable resources, a general reallocation of variable resources may occur throughout the economy. Reallocation may occur from industry Y to other industries which can use the kinds of variable resources used in producing Y. In turn, reallocation of the kinds of resources used in industry X from other industries to industry X may occur. The over-all short-run resource reallocation which occurs will be limited, however, by existing plant capacity in the industries concerned.

Even when short-run equilibrium is reestablished in the two industries, neither will be producing as efficiently as it is capable of producing. At the higher price of X, firms in industry X operate at the output at which their respective short-run marginal costs equal marginal revenue and product price — at greater than optimum rates of output. In industry Y, the outputs at which individual firm short-run marginal costs equal marginal revenue and product price are less than optimum rates of output.

The Long Run

In the long run the shift in demand from Y to X will be met by greater output adjustments and smaller price adjustments than those which occurred in the short run. There is ample time for existing firms to leave industry Y and for new firms to enter industry X. The motivating forces will be the short-run profits of industry X and the short-run losses of industry Y.

The short-run losses of industry Y bring about rates of return on investment in that industry below what investment elsewhere in the economy will earn. Consequently, disinvestment in industry Y will occur — primarily through failure to take care of depreciation on plant and equipment and through the eventual liquidation of some existing firms. As firms leave industry Y, the supply of Y decreases, causing price to rise above its short-run low level. The decreased demands for resources in industry Y lower their prices, decreasing costs of production of individual firms. Exit of firms will cease when the decreasing supply has increased price and lowered costs enough so that losses are no longer being incurred. A smaller number of firms in Y will be producing with optimum scales of plant and optimum rates of output, but in total they produce a smaller combined output at a lower price than before.

At the same time, short-run profits in industry X will be attracting resources (productive capacity) into that industry. The profits indicate a higher return on investment than investors can earn elsewhere in the economy. This is a lucrative field in which to invest. New firms are established in the industry. Increasing demands for resources raise resource prices and the cost curves, both of entering firms and firms already in the industry. The entry of new firms increases industry supply, driving price below its short-run high level. New firms enter until the increasing supply lowers price to the level of increasing average costs. Entry stops when pure profits appear to be no longer obtainable to entering firms. Firms will be forced to use optimum scales of plant and operate them at optimum rates of output to avoid losses. More firms are in the industry, their combined outputs are greater, and the product price is somewhat higher than it was before the shift in demand occurred.

The reallocation of resources may be direct or indirect. If the plant capacity of firms in industry Y can be easily converted to the production of product X, firms in industry Y may simply switch over to producing the more profitable X. Or, if the production processes of the two industries are unrelated, reallocation will be of the indirect nature described above, with firms folding in industry Y and new firms emerging in industry X. In either case profits and losses, and differential prices for resources in the two industries, bring about the desirable reallocation of resources or productive capacity.

With the reestablishment of long-run equilibrium, the two industries again achieve the greatest possible economic efficiency. Individual firms in each industry operate optimum scales of plant at optimum rates of output. Consumers receive units of each product at prices equal to the minimum obtainable average cost per unit. Some of the economy's resources or productive capacity has been switched from the production of one commodity to another in response to changes in consumer tastes and preferences.

EFFECTS OF PURE COMPETITION

Since the various types of market situations frequently are compared with respect to their relative impacts on the economy, certain long-run economic effects of pure competition will bear repetition and emphasis. First, where pure competition exists, consumers get products at prices equal to their average costs of production. Second, economic efficiency *in industries where pure competition can exist* will be at a maximum. Third, sales promotion effort and expenditures likely will be negligible.

Prices and Average Costs

Ease of entry into purely competitive industries ensures that product prices will equal their average costs of production. When product prices exceed average costs of production, pure profits exist. The appearance of profits motivates the entrance of new firms. The entrance of new firms brings prices and average costs together, causing the profits to disappear.

Equality of product prices with average costs of production usually is thought to be desirable. The goal of economic activity is maximum consumer satisfaction, and since outputs of products are expanded under pure competition to the point at which these prices equal their costs, the consumer gains both from a high volume of production and from low prices. The significance of this point will become clear when we have studied the other three types of market situations.

Economic Efficiency

Pure competition provides the largest possible degree of economic efficiency in those industries in which it can exist. For pure competition to exist in an industry the product market must be large relative to the optimum rate of output of the optimum scale of plant for individual firms in the industry. There must be room for enough such firms so that no one firm alone can influence product price. In such a situation, with each firm forced to operate an optimum scale of plant at the optimum rate of output, maximum economic efficiency is obtained. To put the matter in a different way, the product will be produced at the least possible cost per unit of product.

Sales Promotion

No necessity exists for individual firms to engage in aggressive activities to promote sales when they sell in purely competitive markets. One firm alone cannot influence product price, and the products produced by all firms in the industry are homogeneous. Since the individual firm can sell all it wishes to sell at the going market price, sales promotion to increase volume is unnecessary. The homogeneity of product produced by all sellers largely precludes sales promotional activities on the part of one to raise his price. Buyers have so many alternative sources of supply that price increases on the part of one seller cause his sales to drop to zero.

SUMMARY

The present chapter draws together the analysis of demand and the analysis of costs to show how the price system organizes production under the special conditions of pure competition. Pricing and output are discussed from the time viewpoints of the very short run, the short run, and the long run.

Supplies of goods are fixed in amount in the very short run. Price serves to ration existing supplies among consumers. Additionally, it rations the fixed supply over the duration of the period of the very short run.

Individual firm outputs can be varied within the limits of their fixed scales of plant in the short run. In order to maximize profits, individual firms produce the outputs at which their short-run marginal costs equal marginal revenue or product price. Industry price of a product is determined by the interactions of all consumers and all producers of the product. Individual firms may make profits or incur losses in the short run.

In the long run, additional firms will enter industries that make profits, and some existing firms will leave industries in which losses occur. Thus, productive capacity expands in the former industries and contracts in the latter. Expansion of productive capacity lowers market price of the product and decreases individual firm profits. Contraction of productive capacity increases market price and reduces losses. Long-run equilibrium exists in each industry when the number of firms in the industry is just sufficient for profits not to be made nor losses incurred. When an industry is in long-run equilibrium, product price equals average cost of production. Each firm must be operating an optimum scale of plant at the optimum rate of output if losses are to be avoided.

Industries may be characterized as increasing cost, constant cost, or decreasing cost industries. Increasing costs occur when the entrance of new firms into an industry increases the prices of resources used to produce the product. The resulting higher costs are called external diseconomies. In constant cost industries the entrance of new firms does not increase demand for resources enough to raise their prices. Consequently, no changes in the costs of existing firms occur. Decreasing costs, which must be rare in the real world, occur when the entrance of new firms causes resource prices and costs of production to fall. These are termed external economies.

Pure competition has certain economic effects or implications on the basis of which it frequently is compared with the other three types of markets. In the first place, consumers get products at prices equal to their average costs of production. Second, pure competition, where pure competition can exist, results in greatest economic efficiency. Third, there is little motivation for sales promotion efforts on the part of individual firms.

SUGGESTED READINGS

BOULDING, KENNETH E. *Economic Analysis.* 3d ed.; New York: Harper & Row, 1955, chaps. 26 and 27.

MARSHALL, ALFRED. *Principles of Economics.* 8th ed.; London: Macmillan & Co., Ltd., 1920, bk. V, chaps. IV and V.

VINER, JACOB. "Cost Curves and Supply Curves," *Zeitschrift für Nationalökonomie,* III (1931), 23–46.

Pricing and Output under Pure Monopoly | 10

THE NATURE OF PURE MONOPOLY was explained in Chapter 6; however, it may be well to recount its essential characteristics. Pure monopoly is a market situation in which there is a single seller of a particular product for which there are no good substitutes. The product sold by the monopolist must be clearly different from other products sold in the economy. Changes in prices and outputs of other goods sold in the economy must leave the monopolist unaffected. Conversely, changes in the monopolist's price and output must leave the other producers of the economy unaffected.

Pure monopoly in the real world is rare. Local public-utility industries approximate it. Other industries that approach pure monopoly include aluminum prior to World War II, shoe machinery, nickel, molybdenum, magnesium, telephone communications, Pullman cars, and a few others.[1] But despite complete control or 90 percent control of a particular product by a single firm, monopoly is not complete unless substitutes are nonexistent. In the public utility field, gas and electricity are to some extent substitutes. Aluminum also has substitutes, as do the metal alloys produced with the aid of molybdenum and magnesium.

Whether or not monopoly exists in pure form, the principles of pure monopoly provide an indispensable tool for analyzing problems of pricing, output, and resource allocation. In the first place, monopoly tools of analysis are the most fruitful ones to apply to industries approaching pure monopoly or which act in many instances in a monopolistic fashion. Second, monopoly tools of analysis and modifications of them are invaluable in the study of oligopoly and monopolistic competition. We shall discuss first some of the basic concepts of monopoly analysis. This will be followed by a discussion of short-run and long-run

---

[1] Clair Wilcox, *Competition and Monopoly in American Industry,* Temporary National Economic Committee Monograph No. 21 (Washington, D. C.: Government Printing Office, 1940).

183

TABLE 10–1

(1) Price	(2) Quantity per unit time	(3) Total Revenue	(4) Marginal Revenue
10	1	$10	10
9	2	18	8
8	3	24	6
7	4	28	4
6	5	30	2
5	6	30	0
4	7	28	(−)2
3	8	24	(−)4
2	9	18	(−)6
1	10	10	(−)8

pricing and output. Control of monopoly pricing will then be considered. Finally, we shall turn our attention to price discrimination.

COSTS AND REVENUES UNDER MONOPOLY

Costs of Production

For analysis of pure monopoly we use the same cost concepts that we built up in Chapter 8 and that we used in the case of pure competition. Pure monopoly differs from pure competition with respect to product sales, not with respect to costs of production. We shall assume that the monopolistic seller of product is a purely competitive buyer of resources and has no effect on resource prices.[2] He can get as much of any resource as he desires without affecting its price per unit.

Revenues

The difference between the purely competitive firm and the monopolist lies on the selling side. The pure competitor can sell all he wants to sell at the going market price; hence his marginal revenue and price are equal. The monopolist faces the market demand curve for his product; hence the more he sells per unit of time the lower must be his price. This has important implications for the monopolist's marginal revenue in relation to his price.

---

[2] Modifications of cost curves to take account of a single firm's influence on resource prices are deferred to Chapter 14. The modifications, if used here, would make no essential difference in the development of the chapter.

Marginal revenue at different levels of sales per unit of time for the monopolist will be less than price per unit at those sales levels. Consider Table 10–1. A typical demand schedule faced by a monopolist is shown by columns 1 and 2. Total revenue at different levels of sales is listed in column 3, and at any given level of sales equals price multiplied by quantity sold. The marginal revenue column shows the changes in total receipts resulting from one-unit changes in sales per unit of time. With the exception of the first unit, marginal revenue is less than price at each level of sales. Suppose the firm's current level of sales is three units of X per unit of time. Price per unit is $8 and total receipts are $24. Now suppose the firm desires to increase sales per unit of time to four units of X. It must reduce price per unit to $7 in order to expand sales. The fourth unit sells for $7. However, the firm takes a $1 loss per unit on its previous sales volume of three units. The total loss of $3 must be deducted from the selling price of the fourth unit in order to compute the net increase in total receipts resulting from the one-unit increase in sales. Thus, marginal revenue at a sales volume of four units is seen to be $7 − $3 = $4.

When the demand schedule and marginal revenue schedule of Table 10–1 are plotted on the same diagram the marginal revenue curve lies below the demand curve. In fact, the marginal revenue curve bears the same relationship to the demand curve as does any marginal curve to its corresponding average curve. The demand curve is the firm's average revenue curve. When any average curve — average product, average

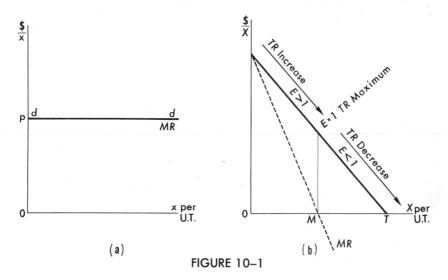

(a)

(b)

FIGURE 10–1

cost, or average revenue — decreases as the firm's output increases, the corresponding marginal curve lies below it.[3]

A useful proposition[4] in economic analysis states that at any given level of sales by the firm, marginal revenue equals price minus the ratio of price to elasticity of demand at that sales level; that is, $MR = p - p/\varepsilon$. The proposition ties together the relationships among the firm's marginal revenue, total revenue, price, and elasticity of demand. Consider the demand curve faced by a purely competitive firm as shown in Figure 10-1(a). Elasticity of demand at all outputs approaches infinity (∞). Since $MR = p - p/\varepsilon$ and since $\varepsilon \to \infty$, p/ε approaches zero and MR approaches p; that is, for all practical purposes $MR = p$ at all outputs. Now consider a monopolist faced by the straight line demand curve of Figure 10-1(b). At output M, halfway between zero and T, $\varepsilon = 1$. At smaller outputs $\varepsilon > 1$ and at larger outputs $\varepsilon < 1$.[5]

We noted in Chapter 3 that an increase in sales when $\varepsilon > 1$ causes TR to increase. This means that when $\varepsilon > 1$, MR must be positive. The equation $MR = p - p/\varepsilon$ states the same thing. If $\varepsilon > 1$, then p/ε must be less than p and MR must be positive. The greater ε is, the smaller p/ε will be, and the smaller will be the difference between p and MR. At the output where $\varepsilon = 1$, TR is maximum and MR should be zero. The formula supports this point. If $MR = p - p/\varepsilon$ and $\varepsilon = 1$, then $MR = p - p = 0$. We learned in Chapter 3 that increases in sales when $\varepsilon < 1$ cause TR to decrease. MR must be negative in this case. If $MR = p - p/\varepsilon$ and $\varepsilon < 1$, then $p/\varepsilon > p$ and MR is negative. The formula is consistent with our earlier observations regarding the relationships between elasticity and total revenue when sales are increased.

THE SHORT RUN

Profit Maximization: Total Curves

Pricing and output under conditions of pure monopoly follow basically the same rules as those applying to the firm under pure competition when the objective of the firm is profit maximization. When plotted, the total receipts schedule of Table 10-1 becomes a total receipts curve similar to that of Figure 10-2. Note the difference between the monopolist's TR curve and that of a purely competitive firm. The difference results from the fact that to sell greater outputs the monopolist

---

[3] See Appendix I to this chapter for a geometric method of establishing the marginal revenue curve for a given demand curve.

[4] This proposition is proved geometrically in Appendix II to this chapter.

[5] See pages 37–39.

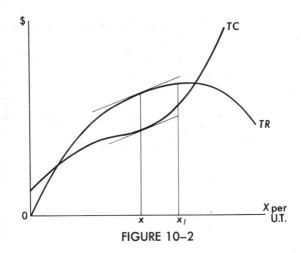

FIGURE 10–2

must lower price. This means that at some output such as x_1 he will have reached maximum total receipts. Still larger sales will cause total receipts to decrease rather than to increase. The monopolist will maximize profits at output x, where the difference between *TR* and *TC* is greatest. The output at which the difference between the *TR* and *TC* curves is greatest is that at which their slopes are equal (tangents to the curves at this output are parallel). Since the slope of the *TC* curve is marginal cost and the slope of the *TR* curve is marginal revenue,

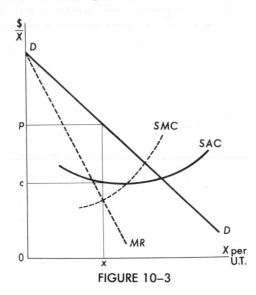

FIGURE 10–3

profits are maximized at the output at which marginal revenue equals marginal cost.

Profit Maximization: Per Unit Curves

Diagrammatic representation of short-run profit maximization by a monopolist in terms of per unit costs and receipts is presented in Figure 10–3. Profits are maximized at the output at which *SMC* equals *MR*. Price per unit which the monopolist can get for an output of *x* is *p*. Average cost at that output is *c* and profits are equal to *cp* multiplied by *x*. At outputs smaller than *x*, *MR* is greater than *SMC*; thus, larger outputs up to *x* add more to total receipts than to total costs and increase profits. At outputs beyond *x*, *MR* is less than *SMC*; hence larger outputs beyond *x* add more to total costs than to total receipts and cause profits to decrease.[6]

Two Common Misconceptions

There is a common misconception that a monopolist necessarily makes profits. Whether or not profits are made depends upon the relationship between the market demand curve faced by the monopolist and his conditions of cost. The monopolist may incur losses in the short run and, like the purely competitive firm, continue to produce if price more than covers average variable costs. In Figure 10–4 the monopolist's costs

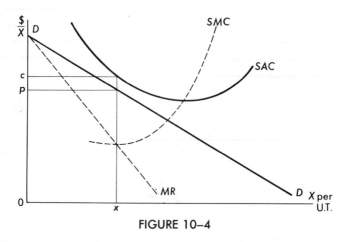

FIGURE 10–4

---

[6] The intersection of *MR* and *SMC* tells us nothing other than that profits are maximum or losses are minimum at that output. Price is shown by the demand curve at that output and not by the *MR* curve. Profits are determined by price and *average cost*, not by price and *marginal cost*.

are so high and his market is so small that at no output will price cover average costs. His losses are minimum, provided price is greater than average variable costs, at output x, at which SMC equals MR. Losses are equal to $pc \times x$.

Another common misconception is that the demand curve faced by a monopolist is inelastic. Most demand curves, with the exception of those faced by firms under conditions of pure competition, range from highly elastic toward their upper ends to highly inelastic toward their lower ends.[7] Hence most demand curves cannot be said to be either elastic or inelastic. They are usually both, depending upon the sector of the demand curve under consideration. The output that maximizes a monopolist's profits will always be within the elastic sector of his demand curve if he has any costs of production. Marginal cost is always positive; therefore, at the output at which marginal cost equals marginal revenue, marginal revenue must also be positive. If marginal revenue is positive, then the elasticity of demand must be greater than one.

THE LONG RUN

Entry into the Industry

Whereas entry of new firms into an industry of pure competition is easy in the long run, entry into a monopolistic industry is blocked. The monopolist must be able to forestall entry of new firms when profits are being made or he does not remain a monopolist. Entry into the industry will change the market situation in which the firm operates.

The monopolist may block entry into his field in several ways. He may control the sources of raw materials necessary for the production of his product. The Aluminum Company of America, for example, prior to World War II was reputed to own or control over 90 percent of the available supplies of bauxite, the basic raw material used in the making of aluminum.[8] Or he may hold certain patents which prevent other firms from duplicating his products. In the manufacture of shoe machinery a single company has held patents simultaneously on virtually all equipment used in the manufacture of shoes. Instead of selling machinery outright to shoe manufacturers, the company leased it to them and collected royalties. The shoe manufacturer who obtained any equipment from another source would then find himself unable to obtain key equip-

---

[7] The situation could conceivably be reversed, but this would be unusual. A demand curve that is inelastic toward the upper end and elastic toward the lower end would necessarily be one with a greater degree of curvature than that of a rectangular hyperbola.

[8] Wilcox, *Competition and Monopoly in American Industry*, pp. 69–72.

ment from the company.[9] <u>Or the market of a monopolist may be so
limited relative to the size of his optimum scale of plant that even
though the one firm makes profits, the entry of another would drive
prices so low that both would incur losses.</u> Thus entry is blocked. Still
other methods of blocking entry occur. In the public-utility field exclusive franchises granted by the governmental unit concerned will do the
job. These are some of the more important monopolizing devices. [10]

The necessity that entry be completely blocked in order to maintain a position of pure monopoly helps explain why pure monopoly is
rare. Except in cases where the government blocks entry it is extremely
difficult for a monopolist to suppress the rise of substitutes when profits
can be made in his field. Patents similar to those of the monopolist can
be secured, although putting them to use in producing substitute products may be a difficult procedure in some cases. Or patents may become
obsolete as new ideas and processes supersede those of the past. Where
sole ownership of raw materials is the monopolizing device used, substitute raw materials frequently can be developed to make a product
which is a reasonably good substitute for the original.

Scale of Plant Adjustments

<u>Since entry into the industry is blocked the monopolist adjusts his
long-run output through scale of plant adjustments. Three possibilities
exist. First, the relation between the monopolist's market and his long-
run average costs may be such that he will build a less than optimum
scale of plant. Second, the relation may be such that he will build an
optimum scale of plant. Third, the monopolist may, under certain circumstances, be induced to build a greater than optimum scale of plant.</u>

LESS THAN OPTIMUM SCALE OF PLANT • Suppose the monopolist's
market is so limited that his marginal revenue curve cuts his long-run
average cost curve to the left of its minimum point. Figure 10–5 illustrates this situation. <u>Long-run profits will be maximum at the output at
which LMC equals MR. The output will be x and price will be p. The
monopolist should build the scale of plant that will produce output x at
the least possible average cost.</u> Its short-run average cost curve SAC
should be tangent to the LAC curve at output x. If SAC is tangent to
LAC at output x, SMC is necessarily equal to LMC at that output.[11] Also,
since output x is the output at which LMC equals MR, SMC is equal to

---

[9] *Ibid.,* pp. 72–73.

[10] A more complete list of devices for restricting entry into particular industries is given
on pages 232–235.

[11] See Chapter 8, pp. 148–150.

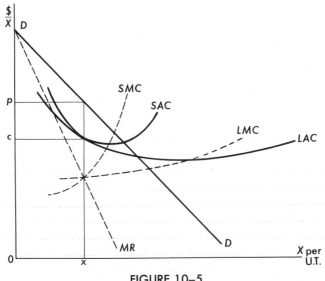

FIGURE 10–5

MR at the same output. Thus a monopolistic firm in long-run equilibrium is necessarily in short-run equilibrium, too. Profits are equal to $cp \times x$. Any change in scale of plant or in the rate of output of SAC will decrease profits.

The monopolist will build a less than optimum scale of plant and operate it at less than the optimum rate of output in this case. His market is not large enough for him to expand scale of plant sufficiently to take advantage of all economies of scale. The scale of plant that he uses will have some excess capacity. If he were to decrease his scale of plant below SAC so that no excess capacity occurs he would at the same time lose some of the economies of scale which SAC offers. The loss would more than offset any "gains" from fuller utilization of a smaller scale of plant.

Local power companies in small- and medium-sized towns often operate smaller than optimum scales of plant at less than the optimum rate of output. The limited local market for electricity limits the generating plant to a size too small to use the most efficient generating equipment and techniques. Yet the well-planned plant will have some excess capacity — both to take advantage of economies of scale and to meet peak output requirements.

OPTIMUM SCALE OF PLANT • Suppose the monopolist's market and his cost curves are such that his marginal revenue curve hits the mini-

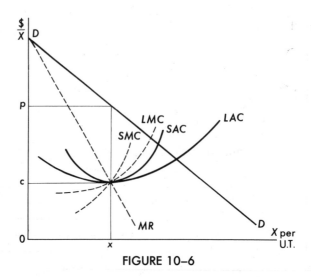

FIGURE 10–6

mum point of his *LAC* curve as in Figure 10–6. The long-run profit maximizing output is *x*, at which $LMC = MR$; this will necessarily be the output at which *LAC* is minimum. The monopolist, to produce *x* at the least possible cost per unit for that output, should build scale of plant *SAC*, the optimum scale of plant. In this case $SMC = LMC = MR = SAC = LAC$ at output *x*. The firm is in both short-run and long-run equilibrium. Price is *p*, average cost is *c*, and profit is equal to $cp \times x$. Under

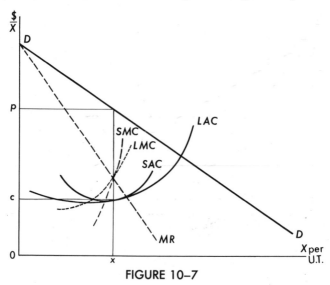

FIGURE 10–7

the assumed conditions the firm operates the optimum scale of plant at the optimum rate of output.

GREATER THAN OPTIMUM SCALE OF PLANT • Suppose the monopolist's market is large enough for his marginal revenue curve to cut his LAC curve to the right of its minimum point. This situation is diagramed in Figure 10–7. The long-run profit maximizing output will be x. The proper scale of plant to build is SAC, which is tangent to LAC at output x. At output x, $LMC = SMC = MR$; hence the monopolist is in short-run equilibrium as well as in long-run equilibrium.

Under the assumed conditions the monopolist builds a larger than optimum scale of plant and operates it at more than the optimum rate of output if he is to maximize profits. His scale of plant is so large that diseconomies of scale occur. It pays him to use a plant a little smaller than the one that would produce output x at its most efficient rate of output. By operating SAC beyond its most efficient rate of output he can obtain a lower per unit cost than would be possible with a larger plant. The diseconomies of scale of a still larger plant are of a greater cost magnitude than is the operation of SAC beyond its optimum rate of output.

REGULATION OF MONOPOLY

The tools of monopoly analysis so far discussed can provide some indications as to how monopoly might be regulated. We shall consider

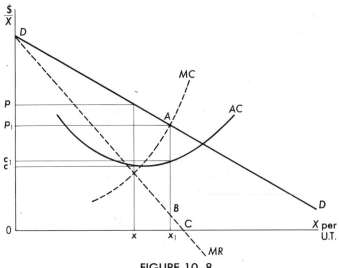

FIGURE 10–8

two possible governmental regulatory devices: (1) direct regulation of monopoly price, and (2) regulation through taxation.

Price Regulation

Authority is frequently invested in state regulatory commissions to govern the rates or prices charged by public utilities such as gas and electric power companies. The economic problem involved is determination of the rate that will induce the monopolist to furnish the greatest amount of product consistent with his costs and with consumer demand.[12]

The profit maximizing output of the monopolist in the absence of price regulation is shown in Figure 10–8.[13] The monopolist maximizes profits at the output where marginal cost equals marginal revenue. The price he wants to charge is p and the output he wants to produce is x. Since entry into the industry is blocked, the profits may exist over time.

By establishing a maximum price below p, the regulatory commission can induce the monopolist to increase output. Suppose a maximum price of p_1 is established — at the level at which the marginal cost curve cuts the demand curve. The demand curve faced by the monopolist becomes p_1AD. Between outputs of zero and x_1, sales will be made at p_1 per unit. The monopolist cannot charge more, but the public will take his entire output within those limits at the price of p_1. For outputs greater than x_1 the monopolist must lower price to clear the market; hence the industry demand curve applies for such outputs.

The change in the demand curve faced by the firm alters the marginal revenue curve too. Between zero and x_1 the new demand curve is infinitely elastic — it is the same as the demand curve faced by a firm under pure competition — and marginal revenue equals p_1. Beyond output x_1, the market demand curve and the original marginal revenue curve are relevant. After the maximum price is established, the marginal revenue curve of the monopolist becomes p_1ABC.

The monopolist's profit-maximizing position must be reexamined in view of the altered demand and marginal revenue situation. With the establishment of the maximum price, output x is no longer the profit maximizing output. Profits will be maximized at the output at which marginal cost equals the new marginal revenue. At output x, marginal revenue exceeds marginal cost; consequently, increases in output up to

---

[12] Economic aspects of the problem frequently are subordinated to political aspects, but we shall omit the latter.

[13] The analysis can be presented in either long-run terms or short-run terms. A short-run explanation has the virtue of being less complex.

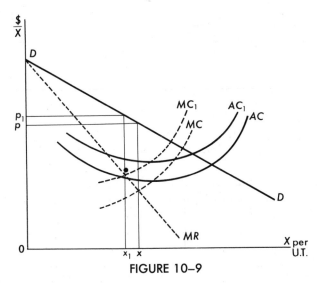

FIGURE 10–9

x_1 increase profits. At outputs beyond x_1, marginal cost would exceed marginal revenue — which drops off sharply, or is said to be "discontinuous" at x_1 — causing profits to decrease. The new profit maximizing output is x_1 — a larger output than before. Profits will be $c_1 p_1 \times x_1$.

Establishment of the maximum price benefits consumers through a lower price per unit and a greater volume of goods available for consumption. It prevents the monopolist from receiving all the advantages of his monopoly position. It forces him to expand output to the point at which marginal cost equals product price, provided the maximum price is set as low as p_1. Some profit may continue to exist, but the spread between price and average cost is narrower than before.

Taxation

Taxes levied on monopolists are often thought to be an appropriate regulatory device to prevent their reaping the full benefits of their monopolistic positions. We shall consider two types of taxes: (1) a specific tax or a fixed tax per unit on the monopolist's output,[14] and (2) a lump sum tax levied without regard to the monopolist's output.[15]

A SPECIFIC TAX • Suppose a specific tax is levied on the monopolist of Figure 10–9. His original average cost and marginal cost curves are

---

[14] The general effects would be the same if an ad valorem tax — a fixed percentage of the product price — were levied.

[15] The general effects would be the same if the tax were a fixed percentage of the monopolist's profits.

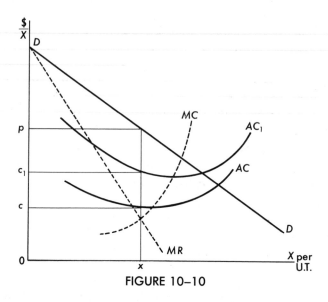

FIGURE 10–10

AC and MC, respectively. His original price and output are p and x. The tax is a variable cost and shifts the average and marginal costs upward by the amount of the tax. Faced with the new cost curves AC_1 and MC_1, the monopolist cuts his output to x_1 and raises price to p_1 in order to maximize profits.

The monopolist is able to pass a part of the specific tax to the consumer through a higher price and a smaller output. At the same time the monopolist's profits will be smaller after the tax than before. Before-tax profits were $cp \times x$. After-tax profits are $c_1 p_1 \times x_1$. To make certain that after-tax profits are smaller than before-tax profits think for a moment of the firm's total revenue and total cost curves. Total receipts of the monopolist at various outputs are unchanged by the tax, but total costs at all outputs will be greater. Profits at all possible outputs will be smaller than before and maximum profits after the tax necessarily will be smaller than they were before. If all the monopolist's profits were taxed away through specific taxes, still higher prices and smaller outputs than are shown in Figure 10–9 would result.

A LUMP SUM TAX • Suppose a lump sum tax is imposed upon the monopolist of Figure 10–10 — for example, a license fee imposed by a city on its only swimming pool. The original average and marginal cost curves are AC and MC. The original price and output are p and x. Since the lump sum tax is independent of output it is a fixed cost to the monopolist. It shifts the average cost curve to AC_1 but it has no effect on the marginal cost curve. Consequently, the profit maximizing price and output remain at p and x. But profits fall from $cp \times x$ to $c_1p \times x$.

The lump sum tax must be borne by the monopolist alone. He is unable to pass any part of it to the consumer through higher prices and smaller outputs. Attempts to do so will decrease his profits even more. All of the monopolist's profits may be taxed away in this manner with no effect whatsoever on output and price.

PRICE DISCRIMINATION

In some cases a monopolist may find it possible and profitable to separate and keep separate two or more markets for his product. Under such conditions he will charge a different price for his product in each of the markets. Two conditions are necessary for such *price discrimination* to occur. First, he must be able to keep the markets apart; otherwise, his product will be purchased in the market with the lower price and resold in the market with the higher price. This will iron out the price differential the monopolist attempts to establish. Second, for price discrimination to be profitable, the elasticities of demand at each price level must differ among the markets. The reason for this will emerge as the analysis progresses.

Distribution of Sales

Suppose we look first at the way in which a discriminating monopolist should distribute his sales between two (or more) markets. For any

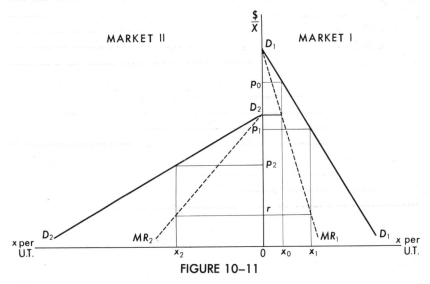

FIGURE 10–11

given volume of sales, ignoring costs for the moment, he should always sell in the market in which an additional unit of sales per unit of time adds most to his total receipts. This amounts to saying that he should distribute his sales among the markets in such a way that marginal revenue in each market is equal to marginal revenue in the other market(s). This will bring him the greatest total receipts from a given volume of sales.

Diagrammatically, suppose the monopolist can sell in the two separate markets of Figure 10–11. The demand curves are D_1D_1 and D_2D_2, respectively. For convenience, the quantity axis of Market II is reversed. Units of X are measured from right to left instead of from the usual left to right. If the volume of sales is below x_0 he should sell the entire amount in Market I, since the additions to his total receipts on sales in that market will exceed any addition to his total receipts made from selling in Market II. If his total volume of sales equals x_1 plus x_2, he should sell x_1 in Market I and x_2 in Market II so that marginal revenue in Market I equals marginal revenue in Market II. The level of marginal revenue will be r in each market. We can show that this distribution brings in greatest total receipts by assuming that he cuts his sales volume in one market by one unit and increases his sales volume in the other market by one unit. Cutting sales by one unit in either market will reduce his total receipts from that market by an amount equal to r. Increasing sales by one unit in the other market will add less to total receipts than r since marginal revenue from an additional unit of sales per unit of time in that market will be less than r. With the proper distribution of sales, price in Market I will be p_1 and price in Market II will be p_2.

We can observe now why elasticity of demand at each possible price must differ between the two markets. Since $MR = p - p/\varepsilon$, if elasticities were the same in the two markets at equal prices the corresponding marginal revenues would also be the same. The distribution of sales that makes marginal revenue in Market I equal to marginal revenue in Market II would make the price in Market I equal to the price in Market II. If this were the case there would be neither point nor profit in separating the markets.

Profit Maximization

The monopolist's cost curves, together with the marginal revenue curve for his total sales volume, are needed to solve his profit-maximizing problem. Suppose that his average cost curve and his marginal cost curve are those of Figure 10–12. They are operative for his entire output regardless of how it is distributed. The marginal revenue curve for the entire sales volume when sales are properly distributed is ΣMR in

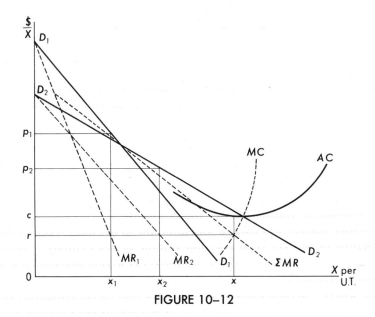

FIGURE 10–12

Figure 10–12. The demand curve and marginal revenue curve for Market II have been drawn in the regular way. Then MR_1 and MR_2 are summed horizontally to obtain ΣMR.

The profit-maximizing problem is reduced now to a simple monopoly problem. The total output of the monopolist should be x, at which $MC = \Sigma MR$. The distribution of sales and the prices charged should be x_1 in Market I, sold at price p_1, and x_2 in Market II, sold at price p_2. Marginal revenue in Market I equals marginal revenue in Market II equals r with this distribution of sales. If total output and sales were less than x, marginal revenue in one market or the other (or both) would be greater than r and marginal cost would be less than r. Increases in production up to x would therefore add more to total receipts than to total costs and would increase profits. If total output and sales were expanded beyond x, marginal cost would exceed r and marginal revenue in one market or the other (or both) would be less than r. Such increases in production would add more to total costs than to total receipts and would decrease profits. With output x properly distributed between the two markets, profit in Market I will equal $cp_1 \times x_1$, and profit in Market II will equal $cp_2 \times x_2$. Total profit will be $cp_1 \times x_1$ plus $cp_2 \times x_2$.

Examples of Price Discrimination

Price discrimination is frequently encountered in public-utility industries. Electric power companies usually separate commercial from domestic users of electricity. Use of a separate meter for each user enables the company to keep the markets apart. Elasticity of commercial users' demand for electricity is higher than that of domestic users; consequently, a lower rate is charged commercial users. This discrimination stems from the greater possibilities of their using substitutes for the power company's product. Large commercial users may find it possible not only to use substitute sources of power but to generate their own electric power. Although domestic users may, and sometimes do, generate their own electric power, generating plants for their power needs are so small that costs per unit tend to be prohibitive.

Another example of price discrimination occurs in the field of foreign trade in the classic case of "dumping." Here goods are sold abroad for a lower price than the domestic or home price. The markets are separated by transportation costs and tariff barriers. Elasticity of the demand curve facing the seller in the foreign market is usually higher than that in the domestic market. Although the seller may be a monopolist in the domestic market, he may find himself confronted abroad with competitors from other countries. Substitutes for his product on the world market increase the elasticity of the foreign demand curve he faces.

EFFECTS OF PURE MONOPOLY

A comparison of the effects of pure monopoly with the effects of pure competition will help us assess the impact of pure monopoly on the operation of a free enterprise economy. We shall make comparisons with regard to prices and outputs, prices and average costs, economic efficiency, and sales promotion.

Prices and Outputs

If an industry *which could be one of pure competition* were to be monopolized, monopolization would result in higher prices and a smaller output than would occur under conditions of pure competition. In examining this proposition, we shall assume that minimum average costs of production will be the same regardless of whether pure competition or monopoly prevails. Actually, we would expect such a monopolist's cost curves to be at a higher level than those of purely competitive firms. If the industry could be and were one of pure competition, individual firms would operate scales of plant large enough to take advantage of all economies of scale; that is, they would operate optimum scales of plant. Monopolization could bring about no further economies of scale, but on the contrary would be expected to bring about diseconomies of scale. However, we shall give the monopolist the benefit of any doubt by

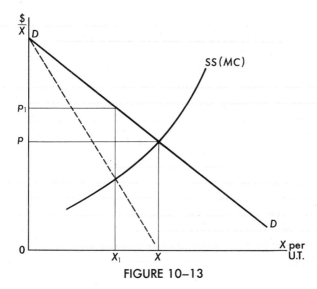

FIGURE 10–13

assuming away disadvantages which may accrue from diseconomies of scale.

Figure 10–13 illustrates the point. The industry demand curve is *DD* and, if the industry were one of pure competition, the short-run industry supply curve would be *SS*. Industry price would be *p* and output would be *X*. At price *p*, each firm in the industry would face a horizontal marginal revenue curve equal to that price at all outputs and would produce an out put at which its $SMC = MR = p$. All firms together would produce an output of *X*.

If the industry were to become monopolized, marginal revenue for the monopolist would differ from that which each of the pure competitors had faced. Since the monopolist would be faced with the downward sloping industry demand curve, his marginal revenue curve would lie below the demand curve; hence marginal revenue would be less than price at all industry outputs. If the monopolist takes over intact the physical facilities of the purely competitive industry, the former *SS* curve of the competitive situation (the horizontal summation of individual firm marginal cost curves) becomes the marginal cost curve of the monopolist.[16] The profit maximizing price and output for the monopolist

---

[16] In all probability, diseconomies of scale would result and would shift the monopolist's marginal cost curve above *SS*. However, the purpose of the analysis is to show the effects on price and output brought about by the change in what constitutes marginal revenue for the firm when the viewpoint changes from one of pure competition to one of monopoly. Therefore, any diseconomies which may result are ignored.

are located at the point at which his marginal cost is equal to his marginal revenue. Output would be X_1 and price would be p_1.

Prices and Average Costs

Since price may exceed average cost in the long run, long-run profits may occur under pure monopoly, whereas under pure competition they will disappear. The difference between the two market situations on this point turns on the conditions of entry under each. Entry of new firms when profits are made in a purely competitive industry causes the profits to disappear. In the industry of pure monopoly, blocked entry makes long-run profits possible. Where profits occur, consumers pay more for the product than the costs of its production; that is, they pay more for the product than is necessary to induce the required quantities of resources to remain in the industry.

Blocked entry and monopoly profits have important implications for the organization of production. The existence of profits in a free enterprise economy provides the signal and the incentive for expansion of output in the industries where they occur. Monopoly prevents the expansion of output from occurring to the desired degree. The individual monopolist may, of course, expand his scale of plant in response to an increase in demand for his product, but his profit-maximizing output is short of the output at which his profits will be zero. Where monopoly profits and blocked entry are found, resources cannot move into those industries in the desired quantities but must necessarily remain in other employments where their contributions to consumer wants are smaller.

Economic Efficiency

The monopolistic firm ordinarily will not use resources at their peak potential efficiency. The purely competitive firm in long-run equilibrium uses the optimum scale of plant at the optimum rate of output. The scale of plant and the output that maximize the monopolist's long-run profits are not necessarily the optimum scale of plant or the optimum rate of output of the scale of plant that he does build.[17] However, if monopoly is to be compared with pure competition on this point, the comparison is legitimate only for industries in which pure competition can exist. In an industry with a limited market relative to the optimum rate of output of the optimum scale of plant, monopoly may result in lower costs or greater efficiency than would occur if there were many firms, each with a considerably less than optimum scale of plant. In such a case, even though monopoly may give greater efficiency than any other type of

---

[17] See pages 190–193.

market organization, resources still are not used at peak potential efficiency.

Sales Promotion

It may be to the advantage of the monopolist to engage in some sales promotion activities, whereas under pure competition there is little point in activities of this kind. The monopolist may use sales promotion activities to enlarge his market; that is, to shift his demand curve to the right. Also, if he can convince the public that consumption of his product is highly desirable or indispensable, elasticity of demand at various prices may be decreased. Additionally, such activities may be used to shield him from potential competition and to protect his monopoly position. His objective in this case will be to get his firm name so closely tied to his product that potential competitors will find it futile to attempt to enter.

SUMMARY

Pure monopoly is rare in the real world; however, the theory of pure monopoly is applicable to those industries in which it is approximated and to firms that act as though they were monopolists. Additionally, it furnishes necessary tools of analysis for the study of oligopoly and monopolistic competition.

The differences between the theory of pure monopoly and the theory of pure competition rest on the demand and revenue situations faced by the firm and on the conditions of entry into industries in which profits are made. Marginal revenue is less than price for the monopolist. His marginal revenue curve lies below the demand curve which he faces. Entry into monopolistic industries is blocked.

The monopolist maximizes short-run profits or minimizes short-run losses by producing the output and charging the price at which marginal revenue equals short-run marginal cost. Monopolists may incur losses and, if so, continue to produce if price exceeds average variable cost. The monopolist operates within the elastic sector of his demand curve.

In the long run the monopolist maximizes profits at the output at which long-run marginal cost equals marginal revenue. The scale of plant to be used will be the one with its short-run average cost curve tangent to the long-run average cost curve at the profit-maximizing output. Short-run marginal cost will equal long-run marginal cost and marginal revenue at that output.

The theory of monopoly throws some light on effective means of monopoly regulation. A maximum price set below the monopoly price will benefit consumers through both the lower price and an increased product output. A specific tax levied on the monopolist's product will be shifted partly to consumers through output restriction and higher prices. A lump sum tax must be borne entirely from the monopolist's profits.

A monopolist finds it profitable to practice price discrimination when he can keep markets for his product separate and when elasticity of demand for each market is different at each possible price. The price-discriminating monopolist produces an output and distributes it among his markets in such a way that marginal revenue in each market equals marginal revenue in every other market and is also equal to his marginal cost.

As compared with the effects of pure competition on the economy's operation, pure monopoly has some important implications. In particular industries where pure competition could function, it leads to output restriction and higher prices. The possibility of long-run profits under monopoly exists because of blocked entry into monopolized industries. Where profits occur consumers pay more for products than is necessary to hold the resources making those products in the industries concerned. Blocked entry limits transfer of resources into and expansion of output by the monopolized profit-making industries. Monopolistic firms are not likely to operate optimum scales of plant at optimum rates of output. Some sales promotion efforts may be made to enlarge the monopolist's market, to decrease elasticity of demand for his product, and to discourage potential competition.

SUGGESTED READINGS

HARROD, R. F. "Doctrines of Imperfect Competition," *Quarterly Journal of Economics,* XLVIII (May 1934), 442–470.

MARSHALL, ALFRED. *Principles of Economics.* 8th ed.; London: Macmillan & Co., Ltd., 1920, bk. V, chap. XIV.

ROBINSON, JOAN. *The Economics of Imperfect Competition.* London: Macmillan & Co., Ltd., 1933, chaps. 2, 3, 15, 16.

Derivation of the Marginal Revenue Curve

The geometric method presented here of deriving the marginal revenue curve from a given demand curve helps materially in keeping the relations between the two curves straight. We shall use a straight-line demand curve to develop the method; then we shall modify it to apply to a nonlinear demand curve.

STRAIGHT-LINE CURVES

Consider first the real nature of a marginal revenue curve. In Figure 10–14 the quantity units are purposely large. Suppose a single unit of sales adds an amount OK to the firm's total receipts. Both total receipts and marginal revenue are equal to Area I, or $OK \times 1$. When sales are increased to two units of X per unit of time, suppose total receipts increase by an amount OL. Marginal revenue of a unit now equals Area II, or $OL \times 1$. Area II does not overlap Area I but lies entirely to

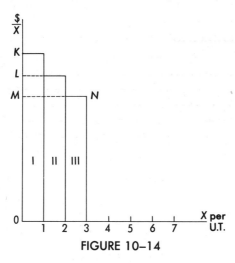

FIGURE 10–14

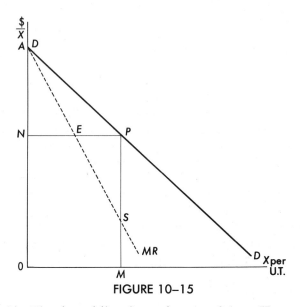

FIGURE 10–15

the right of it. The dotted line from the top of Area II to point L is a reference line only, to assist us in reading marginal revenue from the dollar axis. Total revenue from the two units equals marginal revenue when sales are one unit plus marginal revenue when sales are increased to two units, or equals Area I plus Area II. Marginal revenue when sales are increased to three units per unit of time equals OM, or, what amounts to the same thing, equals Area III. Total revenue is now equal to Area I plus Area II plus Area III. The stairstep curve from K to N is the marginal revenue curve for the firm through three units of sales.

For a typical firm a single unit of output is measured by an infinitesimal distance along the X axis. If the distance measuring a single unit of output is infinitesimal, the marginal revenue curve no longer looks like the discontinuous or stairstep curve of Figure 10–14, but looks as smooth as does the MR curve in Figure 10–15. The point to be made from Figure 10–14 is that at any given level of sales, total receipts are equal to the area under the marginal revenue curve up to that quantity. In Figure 10–14 total receipts from three units of sales equal the sum of Areas I, II, and III. Likewise in Figure 10–15, total receipts when sales are OM are equal to Area $OASM$.

Assume that the demand curve faced by a monopolist is the straight-line DD of Figure 10–15 and that we want to determine marginal revenue at sales level OM. Ignore the MR curve of the diagram temporarily. Price at quantity OM will be MP or ON. Suppose now that MR

is drawn in Figure 10–15 as a tentative marginal revenue curve. It should start from the vertical axis at a common point with the demand curve.[1] Reference to Table 10–1 shows that the marginal revenue curve for a straight-line demand curve also will be a straight line spreading away from the demand curve as the sales level increases.

What conditions must be fulfilled if marginal revenue is to be correctly measured at sales level OM? If MR were the marginal revenue curve, Area $OASM$ would equal total receipts. Likewise Area $ONPM$ (that is, price times quantity) equals total receipts. Hence Area $ONPM$ must equal Area $OASM$. Area $ONESM$ is common to both the larger areas, and if subtracted from each, the area of triangle ANE must be equal to the area of triangle EPS. Angle NEA equals angle SEP because the opposite angles formed by two intersecting straight lines are equal. Since triangle ANE and triangle EPS are right triangles, with an additional angle of one equal to the corresponding angle of the other, they are also similar triangles. If MR is correctly drawn, triangle ANE and triangle EPS are equal in area as well as similar and thus will be congruent. If they are congruent, SP must equal NA since corresponding sides of congruent triangles are equal. Therefore, to locate correctly marginal revenue at sales level OM, we must measure the distance NA and set point S below point P such that SP equals NA. Marginal revenue at OM will be MS.

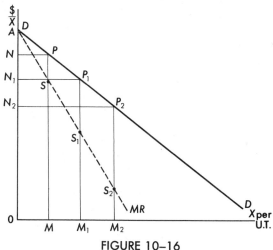

FIGURE 10–16

[1] Actually, it coincides with the demand curve at a sales level of one unit. However, if the distance measuring a unit of sales on the quantity axis is infinitesimal we can assume that both curves start from a common point on the vertical axis.

Use of the geometric method for deriving marginal revenue from a given demand curve is much simpler than the proof. Suppose we locate the marginal revenue curve for demand curve DD in Figure 10–16. Select several points such as P, P_1, and P_2 at random on the demand curve. The corresponding levels of sales are OM, OM_1, and OM_2. Corresponding prices will be ON, ON_1, and ON_2. Now drop below P by an amount equal to NA and call the newly located point S. Marginal revenue at sales level OM is MS. Drop below P_1 by an amount equal to N_1A. Call this point S_1 and marginal revenue at OM_1 equals M_1S_1. Repeat the process at P_2 so that S_2P_2 equals N_2A. A line joining the S points is the marginal revenue curve.

NONLINEAR CURVES

The procedure with a slight modification can be used to locate the marginal revenue curve for a nonlinear demand curve. Suppose the demand curve is DD in Figure 10–17. The demand curve and the marginal revenue curve start from a common point on the vertical axis and we should locate marginal revenue at several different sales quantities, say OM, OM_1, and OM_2. The corresponding points on the demand curve are P, P_1, and P_2. The corresponding prices are ON, ON_1, and ON_2. Now draw a tangent to the demand curve at point P so that the tangent cuts the vertical axis. Call this point A. If the tangent were the demand

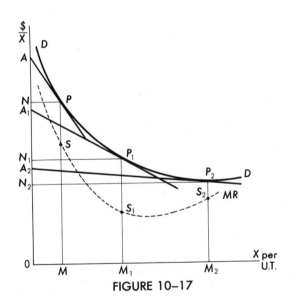

FIGURE 10–17

curve we could easily find marginal revenue for it at sales level OM. We would drop below P by an amount equal to NA and set point S so that SP equals NA. Actually the tangent and demand curve DD are the same curve and have the same slope at the point of tangency. Therefore, MS will be marginal revenue for DD at sales level OM as well as being marginal revenue for the tangent when the tangent is thought of as being the demand curve. Marginal revenue at sales OM_1 can be found by drawing a tangent to DD at P_1. The tangent intersects the vertical axis at A_1. Drop below P_1 by an amount equal to N_1A_1 and marginal revenue at OM_1 is M_1S_1. Repeat the procedure at P_2, so that S_2P_2 equals N_2A_2. Marginal revenue at OM_2 is M_2S_2. A line joining the S points is the marginal revenue curve for DD. Note that when the demand curve is not a straight line the A points on the vertical axis shift as different levels of sales are considered.[2]

---

[2] A common mistake in locating the marginal revenue curve for a given demand curve is that of merely drawing the marginal revenue curve so that it bisects the distance between the demand curve and the vertical axis. This procedure will locate the marginal revenue curve accurately for a linear demand curve only. If the demand curve has any curvature to it — i.e., is convex or concave when viewed from below — such a procedure is not valid. If the demand curve is convex from below, the marginal revenue curve will lie to the left of a line bisecting the distance between the vertical axis and the demand curve. If the demand curve is concave from below, the marginal revenue curve will lie to the right of such a line.

Even in the case of a linear demand curve the procedure described here is correct in a mathematical sense only. It is not sound logically from the point of view of economics. For example, in Figure 10–15 point E lies on the marginal revenue curve for demand curve DD. Sales level OM (or NP) and price ON (or MP) are used in locating point E. However, there is no economic reason why sales level OM or price ON (or MP) should have any connection at all with marginal revenue at one half of sales level OM. The connection is purely a mathematical one stemming from the fact that DD is a straight line. With regard to sales level OM and price ON, the only marginal revenue value which could be derived from them logically is marginal revenue at that sales level and that price.

Price, Marginal Revenue, and Elasticity of Demand

The proposition that marginal revenue equals price minus the ratio of price to elasticity of demand at that price is proved geometrically with the aid of Figure 10–18. Suppose the sales level is OM. The demand curve

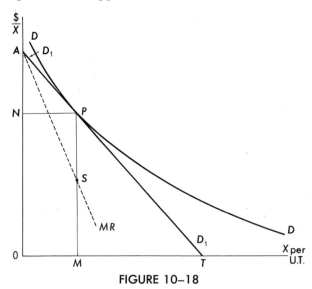

FIGURE 10–18

is either DD or D_1D_1 — which are tangent at that level of sales. At sales level OM, the elasticity of both curves is the same and the corresponding marginal revenues will also be the same. For convenience, draw the marginal revenue curve corresponding to D_1D_1. Elasticity of demand at OM equals MT/OM. However, MT/OM is equal to PT/AP, since a line parallel to one side of a triangle cuts the other two sides proportionally. Likewise, $PT/AP = ON/NA$. Since $ON = MP$ and $NA = SP$, $ON/NA = MP/SP$. Elasticity of demand at OM is equal to $MT/OM = PT/AP =$

$ON/NA = MP/SP$, or $\varepsilon = MP/SP$. Dividing through by ε and multiplying through by SP, $SP = MP/\varepsilon$. From the diagram it can be seen that $MS = MP - SP$. Since $SP = MP/\varepsilon$, then $MS = MP - MP/\varepsilon$, or

$$\text{marginal revenue} = \text{price} - \frac{\text{price}}{\text{elasticity}}$$

Pricing and Output under Oligopoly | 11

Market situations in which there are few enough sellers of a particular product for the activities of one to be of importance to the others are called oligopoly situations. A single seller occupies a position of sufficient importance in the product market for changes in his market activities to have repercussions on the others. Other sellers react to the market activities of the one and their reactions in turn have repercussions on him. The individual seller is aware of this and in changing his price, output, sales promotional activity, or quality of his product he must take the reactions of others into account.

The analysis of pricing and output under oligopoly lacks the neatness and precision of the theory of pure competition and the theory of monopoly. This is partly because of what we shall call oligopolistic uncertainty — in many cases an oligopolist cannot be sure what his rivals' reactions will be to various kinds of activities on his part — and partly because oligopoly covers such a wide range of cases, each with its own unique characteristics. There is not now nor is there likely to be in the foreseeable future a general theory of oligopoly. Consequently, in this chapter, we shall try to get some "feel" of the problems and principles involved in analysis of oligopolistic industries. Several selected models will be developed with this objective in mind.

First, we shall discuss briefly costs, demand, and product differentiation as they are to be used in the analysis. Next, we consider collusion versus independent action by oligopolists. Then we turn to short-run pricing and output, long-run pricing and output, and non-price competition. Finally, we examine the effects of oligopolistic market structures on the operation of the economy.

COSTS, DEMAND, AND PRODUCT DIFFERENTIATION

Costs of Production

The oligopolistic firm may buy its resources competitively and we shall assume for the present that it does. Thus, its cost curves will be similar to those of the purely competitive firm and the pure monopolist. When we have considered the effects of monopsony in resource buying, appropriate modifications in cost curves can be made wherever necessary with little difficulty.

Demand

Differences in the conditions of demand as seen by the individual firm probably constitute the main feature setting oligopoly apart from the other market situations. What one firm is able to do in attempting to make its profits as large as possible is conditioned by the ways in which other firms react to the market activities of the one. The extent of oligopolistic uncertainty is highly variable from case to case. In some situations the firm is quite knowledgeable as to the reactions to expect from other firms and can determine the demand curve it faces with some confidence. In other situations this is not so and the position and shape of the demand curve facing the firm is highly conjectural. Interdependence of demand among the firms of an industry and oligopolistic uncertainty give rise to a whole host of problems and strategies on the part of the firms that is not encountered in the other market classifications.

Pure and Differentiated Oligopoly

The distinction between differentiated oligopoly and pure oligopoly will not play a prominent role in the analysis. As a practical matter, sellers in most oligopolistic industries sell differentiated products.[1] Nevertheless, some of the fundamental principles of differentiated oligopoly as well as of pure oligopoly are seen most clearly when we assume that pure oligopoly exists. For example, instead of a single market price for a product produced under differentiated oligopoly, a cluster of prices may occur. Automatic toasters may range in price from $19.95 to $29.95. The various price levels reflect consumers' views regarding the respective qualities of the different sellers' wares and the availability of different makes. Analysis may be simplified and basic pricing principles not distorted seriously if we assume that pure oligopoly exists, thus reducing the cluster of prices to a single market price for the product.[2] Wherever

---

[1] Industries approaching pure oligopoly include cement, basic steel, and most of the metal-producing industries. Even here there are elements of differentiation among the products sold in a particular industry. Locational factors, service, and even personal friendships may differentiate the products of the various sellers in an industry.

[2] One such distortion is that product differentiation may affect control of the individual seller over price. Attachment of consumers to the products of single sellers will reduce the changes in quantities sold for price adjustments upward or downward within a certain price range; i.e., it will make the demand curve faced by the individual seller less elastic within that price range.

necessary, we shall specify whether differentiated or pure oligopoly is assumed.

COLLUSION VERSUS INDEPENDENT ACTION

Oligopolistic market structures invite collusion among the firms in an industry, but at the same time collusive arrangements are difficult to maintain. There are at least three major incentives leading oligopolistic firms toward collusion. In the first place, by decreasing the amount of competition among the firms it can enable them to act monopolistically and increase their profits by so doing. In the second place, it can decrease oligopolistic uncertainty. If the firms act in concert they can reduce the likelihood of any one firm taking actions detrimental to the interests of the others. In the third place, collusion among the firms already in an industry will facilitate blocking newcomers from entering the industry. At the same time, once a collusive arrangement is in existence, any single firm is provided with a strong profit incentive to break away from the group and to act independently. These forces will be examined in some detail throughout the chapter.

Classification of oligopolistic situations according to the degree of collusion occurring will facilitate discussion of representative oligopolistic models. We shall distinguish among cases of perfect collusion, cases of imperfect collusion, and cases characterized by independent action on the part of individual firms.[3]

Perfect Collusion

Cases of perfect collusion consist primarily of cartel arrangements. A cartel is a formal organization of the producers within a given industry. Its purpose is to transfer certain management decisions and functions of individual firms to a central association with the expectation that profit positions of individual firms will be improved by the transfer. Overt formal cartel organizations are generally illegal in the United States, but have existed extensively in countries outside the United States and on an international basis.[4] However, even in the United States voluntary tacit organization and collusion may give certain industries most of the characteristics of a cartel.

The extent of the functions transferred to the central association varies in different cartel situations. We shall consider two representative

---

[3] Cf./Fritz Machlup, *The Economics of Sellers' Competition* (Baltimore: The Johns Hopkins Press, 1952), pp. 363–365.

[4] See George W. Stocking and Myron W. Watkins, *Cartels in Action* (New York: The Twentieth Century Fund, 1946).

cartel types.[5] The first, selected to illustrate almost complete cartel control over member firms, will be called the centralized cartel. The second illustrates cases in which fewer functions are transferred to the central association. It will be designated as the market-sharing cartel.

In the centralized cartel, we shall assume that decision making with regard to pricing, output, sales, and distribution of profits is accomplished by the central association. The central association markets the product, determines prices, determines the amount that each firm is to produce, and divides profits among the member firms. Member firms are represented in the central association, and cartel policies presumably result from exchange of ideas, negotiation, and compromise. However, a firm's power to influence cartel policies is not necessarily proportional to its representation in the central association. Its economic power in the industry may significantly influence cartel policies.

The market-sharing cartel is a somewhat looser form of organization. We shall assume that firms forming the cartel agree on market shares with or without an understanding regarding prices. Member firms do their own marketing but are careful to observe the cartel agreement.

Imperfect Collusion

Imperfect collusive cases are made up for the most part of tacit informal arrangements under which the firms of an industry seek to establish prices and outputs and yet escape prosecution under the antitrust laws. The price leadership arrangements of a number of industries — steel, tobacco, oil, and others — are typical of the class. But tacit unorganized collusion can occur in many other ways. Gentlemen's agreements of various sorts with regard to pricing, output, market sharing, and other activities of the firms within the industry can be worked out on the golf course and on "social" occasions of different kinds.

Independent Action

Cases of independent action are just what the name implies. Individual firms of an industry each go it alone. In some industries independent action often touches off price wars when the reactions of rivals to actions of one are retaliatory in nature. In other industries independent action may be consistent with industry stability over time. Firms may have learned by experience what the reactions of rivals will be to actions on their part and may voluntarily avoid any activity that will rock the boat. Or it may be that the management of each firm is reasonably well

---

[5] For an excellent discussion of cartel types see Karl Pribram, *Cartel Problems* (Washington, D.C.: The Brookings Institution, 1935), pp. 41–58.

satisfied with present prices, outputs, and profits and is content to let things continue as they are rather than chance starting a chain reaction.

Classification Limitations

Collusion is a matter of degree with cases of perfect collusion and cases of independent action at the polar limits. We cannot with certainty say that all price leadership cases or all gentlemen's agreements fall under the heading of imperfect collusion. Ordinarily we would expect this to be so but in some such cases terms of agreement and adherence to those terms may be strict enough to present us with a case of perfect collusion. Similarly, cartel arrangements may not always be enforced strictly enough to warrant calling them perfect collusion, but rather may fall in the category of imperfect collusion.

Reference to the number of firms in an industry is conspicuously absent from the foregoing classification. However, the degree of collusion achieved corresponds to some extent to the number of firms involved. The greater the number of firms in a given industry, the harder it will be ordinarily to achieve a high degree of collusion.[6] The smaller the number of firms involved, the easier it is for the activities of individual firms to come under the scrutiny of the others. Small numbers are more easily policed by the group as a whole; hence collusive arrangements are less likely to be violated by individual firms.

THE SHORT RUN

We turn now to specific oligopoly cases in the short run. We shall examine typical examples under each of the three classifications of the preceding section to obtain a general grasp of the fundamental problems and principles involved in oligopolistic situations. In the short-run analysis of the present section we should keep in mind that individual firms do not have time to change their scales of plant, nor is it possible for new firms to enter the industry. The number of firms in the industry under consideration will be fixed.

Perfect Collusion

THE CENTRALIZED CARTEL • The centralized cartel case with all of its restraints on individual member firms illustrates collusion in its most compete form. With it the principles involved in joint or monopolistic

---

[6] State intervention has made collusion possible in some industries even though there are large numbers of producers involved. Certain agricultural crops — wheat, citrus fruits, and tobacco — are cases in point. See Arman A. Alchian and William R. Allen, *University Economics* (Belmont: Wadsworth Publishing Company, Inc., 1964), pp. 395–400.

maximization of industry profits by the several firms of an industry can be developed. "Ideal" or complete monopolistic price and output determination by a cartel will rarely be achieved in the real world although it may be approached in some instances.

Suppose that individual firms of a certain industry have surrendered to a central association the power to make price and output decisions. Quotas to be produced are determined by the association, as is the distribution of industry profits. Policies adopted are to be those which will contribute most to total industry profits. To simplify the analysis we shall assume that the firms of the industry produce homogeneous products.

Maximization of the cartel's profits is essentially a monopoly problem since in reality a single agency is making decisions for the industry as a whole. Profits will be maximized at the industry output and price at which industry marginal revenue equals industry marginal cost. We need to develop the nature of these two concepts.

The association is faced with the industry demand curve for the product; the industry marginal revenue curve is derived from it in the usual manner. The industry marginal revenue curve shows how much each additional unit of sales per unit of time by the cartel will increase industry total receipts. The industry demand curve and the industry marginal revenue curve are shown by DD and MR, respectively, in Figure 11-1.

The industry marginal cost curve is constructed from the short-run marginal cost curves of individual firms of the industry. A two-firm case is presented in Figure 11-1 for illustrative purposes. For any given output the central agency should minimize industry costs. This can be done by allocating quotas to the member firms in such a way that the marginal cost of each firm when producing its quota is equal to the marginal

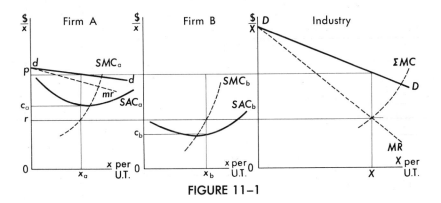

FIGURE 11-1

cost of every other firm when producing their respective quotas. If quotas are allocated to individual firms in any other way, industry costs for the given output will not be minimized. Suppose, for example, that the quota of Firm A with respect to the quota of Firm B is such that Firm A's marginal cost is greater than that of Firm B. Industry costs could be decreased by reducing Firm A's quota and by increasing Firm B's. Reducing Firm A's production rate by one unit will reduce industry total cost by an amount equal to Firm A's (higher) marginal cost. Increasing the production rate of Firm B by one unit will increase industry total cost by an amount equal to Firm B's (lower) marginal cost. Thus, the reduction of Firm A's quota will reduce total cost by more than the increase in Firm B's quota will increase it. When quotas are correctly allocated for each possible industry output, the industry marginal cost curve will be the horizontal summation of the individual firm short-run marginal cost curves. The industry marginal cost curve is ΣMC in Figure 11–1.

The profit maximizing price for the cartel will be p and the industry output will be X. Each individual firm should produce the quota at which its short-run marginal cost is equal to industry marginal revenue r. The quota of Firm A will be x_a and that of Firm B will be x_b. Ignore dd and mr in the Firm A diagram for the present. If industry output exceeds X, marginal costs of one or more firms will be greater than r and industry marginal revenue will be smaller. More will be added to industry total costs by these outputs than to industry total receipts; hence profits will decrease. If industry output is less than X, some or all firms' short-run marginal costs will be less than r while industry marginal revenue will exceed r. Larger outputs up to X will add more to industry total receipts than to industry total costs, and profits will increase.

Profits can be computed on a firm-by-firm basis and then totaled for the industry. Profit per unit of output for a single firm will equal industry price minus the firm's average cost at the output that the firm produces. Profit per unit multiplied by the firm's output equals the profit that the firm contributes to total industry profits. Profit of Firm A is $c_a p \times x_a$ while that of Firm B is $c_b p \times x_b$. Total industry profits are the sum of the profits contributed by all individual firms. Industry profits may be distributed among firms on the "as earned" basis, or according to any other scheme deemed appropriate.

The foregoing "ideal" monopolistic determination of industry output and price from the point of view of the cartel is not likely to be achieved in practice. Decisions made by the association are the results of negotiation, give-and-take, and compromise among the particular points of view and interests of the cartel members. Hence, it is not probable that the association would act precisely as would a monopolist who had the industry to himself. Profits, for example, may be distributed according to production quotas assigned individual firms. Those firms able to exert the greatest pressure on the central association may receive the larger quotas, even though additional output per unit of time may run their marginal costs above those of other firms. This would serve to increase industry costs and decrease industry profits. Also, pressure on the central association to increase particular firm quotas may result in decisions to increase industry output beyond the profit maximizing level. Prices and profits below the monopolistic level would result. Additionally, inefficient high-cost firms may be assigned quotas which run their marginal costs substantially above industry marginal revenue, even though principles of economy may indicate that such firms should be shut down completely. These possibilities by no means exhaust the field, but they do serve to illustrate that political decisions on the part of the association, made to placate certain member firms, may take precedence over economic considerations to some extent.[7]

The larger the number of firms forming the cartel, the harder it will be to hold the cartel together, particularly if the individual firms' shares of the industry profits are small. There exists a strong incentive for individual firms to leave the cartel and operate independently. With the larger part of the industry adhering to the cartel price, an individual firm operating independently would be faced with a demand curve for its output much more elastic than the industry demand curve in price ranges around the cartel price. Consider Firm A in Figure 11-1 for example. If Firm A could break away from the cartel it would be faced with a demand curve such as *dd,* provided other firms in the cartel adhere to price *p.* The demand curve facing any one individual firm under these circumstances would be much more elastic than the industry demand curve at the cartel price since a cut in price by the individual firm would attract buyers away from the rest of the cartel. Consequently, marginal revenue for Firm A, operating independently at output level x_a, would be higher than marginal revenue for the cartel at output level X. Firm A's marginal revenue would exceed its marginal costs at output x_a and the firm could increase its own profits by expanding its output beyond x_a. Thus the firm that can break away successfully from a cartel can increase its profit possibilities if other firms do not try the same thing. If all try it, the cartel falls apart and all end up with smaller profits.

---

[7] Cf. Machlup, *The Economics of Sellers' Competition,* pp. 476–480.

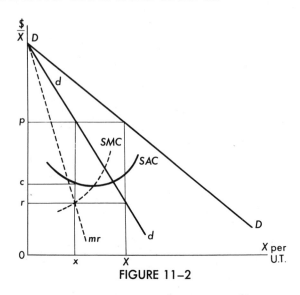

FIGURE 11–2

THE MARKET-SHARING CARTEL • Market sharing of one type or another is characteristic of many cartel arrangements. Under certain conditions, it can result in "ideal" monopoly price and output for the industry; that is, the industry profit maximizing level of price and output. In practice it is likely to deviate from the monopoly position.

Suppose that the firms of the industry produce a homogeneous product and agree upon the share of the market that each is to receive at each possible price. Homogeneity of the product will establish the rule of a single price in the product market. To simplify the analysis, assume further that there are only two firms in the industry. The two firms have equal costs and agree to share the market half and half.

Under the assumed conditions, the two firms will have identical views regarding the price to charge and the output to produce. The industry demand curve for the product is DD in Figure 11–2. Each firm faces demand curve dd for its own output. Each has a short-run average cost curve and a short-run marginal cost curve of SAC and SMC, respectively. The marginal revenue curve faced by each firm is mr. The profit-maximizing output for each firm will be x at which SMC is equal to mr. Each firm will want to charge price p. Profits for each firm will equal $cp \times x$. Together the firms will produce an industry output of X that will fill the market at price p. This will be the case since dd lies halfway between the market demand curve and the price axis.

The market-sharing cartel under the assumed conditions, like the centralized cartel, will determine price and output at the levels which a monopolist would set were he in complete control of the producing facilities of the industry. Such a monopolist's marginal cost curve would be the horizontal summation of the two SMC curves of the two plants — it would lie twice as far to the right at each price level as does the *SMC* curve of Figure 11-2. The monopolist would face the industry demand curve *DD* and at output *X* industry marginal revenue will be at level *r* — the same level as was individual firm marginal revenue at output *x*. This will be so because *DD* has the same elasticity at price *p* as does *dd*.[8] At output X, industry marginal cost will be at level *r*. Output *X* would be the profit maximizing output for the monopolist since in-industry marginal revenue and industry marginal cost are equal at that output. The monopolist would sell output *X* at price *p* per unit.

But several factors may stand in the way of achievement of an "ideal" monopolistic price and output. Costs of production for the individual firms are likely to differ rather than being identical as we assumed they are. Market sharing largely precludes the transferring of output quotas from firms with higher marginal costs to those with lower marginal costs at the outputs produced by each. Differing points of view and differing interests of the firms comprising the cartel may result in compromises which stand in the way of maximization of industry profits. Individual firms, assigned market shares and given a product price, may deliberately or may in good faith overestimate the quantities of product which constitute their respective proportions of the total market and thus may encroach upon the markets of others.[9] Additionally, the degree of independent action left to individual firms may whet their desires to break away from the cartel and may increase the possibilities of their doing so.

Under a market-sharing cartel arrangement, markets need not be shared equally. High-capacity firms may receive larger market shares than low-capacity firms. Market sharing may be accomplished on a regional basis, with each firm allocated a particular geographic area instead of sharing a common market. A whole host of difficulties may arise as a result of different demand elasticities at particular prices: different costs, inferior territories, encroachment upon each other's terri-

---

[8] Two demand curves with equal elasticities at each of various price levels are said to be *isoelastic*. Demand curves are isoelastic when the quantities taken at each of various prices form a constant ratio to each other. See Joan Robinson, *The Economics of Imperfect Competition* (London: Macmillan & Co., Ltd., 1933), p. 61. Since *dd* lies halfway between *DD* and the price axis at different prices, the quantities taken as shown by *dd* are in constant ratio to the quantities taken as shown by *DD*. The ratio is one half.

[9] To minimize sales in excess of market shares or quotas, most cartels exact penalties from the member who exceeds his quota.

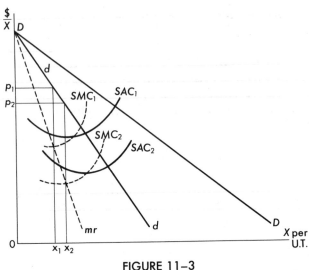

FIGURE 11–3

tories, and so on — all of which make pricing and output problems much more uncertain than they appear to be in the model.

Imperfect Collusion

PRICE LEADERSHIP BY A LOW-COST FIRM • In the absence of a formal cartel arrangement, price leadership by one firm in the industry frequently becomes the means of colluding. We shall suppose that there are two firms in the industry, that a tacit market-sharing arrangement has been established with each firm assigned half the market, that the product is undifferentiated, and that one firm has lower costs than the other.

A conflict of interest occurs with regard to the price which should be charged. The market demand curve is DD in Figure 11–3. Each firm faces demand curve dd. The cost curves of the high-cost firm are SAC_1 and SMC_1. Those of the low cost firm are SAC_2 and SMC_2. The marginal revenue curve of each firm is mr. The high-cost firm will want to produce an output of x_1 and charge a price of p_1, whereas the low-cost firm will want to produce an output of x_2 and charge a price of p_2.

Since the low-cost firm can afford to sell at a lower price than can the high-cost firm, the latter will have no recourse other than to sell at the price set by the low-cost firm. Thus, the low-cost firm becomes the price leader. This type of situation has several ramifications depending upon the comparative costs of the firms, the number of firms in the industry, the shape and position of the market demand curve, and the share of the market which each firm is to receive.[10]

PRICE LEADERSHIP BY A DOMINANT FIRM • In many oligopolistic industries, one or more large firms will be found, together with a number of small firms. To avoid large-scale price cutting, tacit collusion may occur in the form of price leadership by one or more of the large firms.[11] We shall simplify our analysis by assuming that there is a single large dominant firm in the industry and a number of small firms. Suppose the dominant firm sets price for the industry and allows the small firms to sell all they desire to sell at that price. The dominant firm then fills out the market.

Each small firm will behave as though it were in a competitive atmosphere. It can sell all it wants to sell at the price set by the domi-

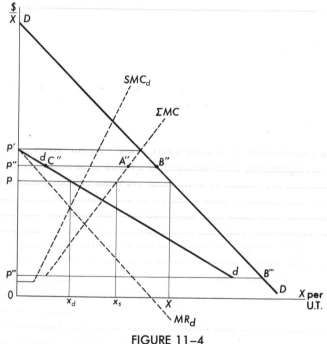

FIGURE 11–4

[10] See Kenneth E. Boulding, *Economic Analysis* (3d ed.: New York: Harper & Row, 1955), pp. 641–645.

[11] Price leadership has been common in the fabrication of nonferrous alloys, steel, agricultural implements, newsprint paper, and other industries. For brief accounts see Wilcox, *Competition and Monopoly in American Industry*, pp. 121–132.

nant firm; therefore it faces a perfectly elastic demand curve at the level of the established price. The marginal revenue curve of the small firm coincides with the demand curve faced by it; hence, to maximize profits, the small firm should produce the output at which its marginal cost equals marginal revenue and the price set by the dominant firm.

A supply curve for all small firms combined can be established by summing horizontally the marginal cost curves of all the small firms. It shows how much all small firms together will place on the market at each possible price. This curve is labeled ΣMC in Figure 11–4.

We can derive now the demand curve faced by the dominant firm. The market demand curve DD shows how much of the product consumers will take off the market at each possible price, whereas the ΣMC curve shows how much the small firms combined will sell at each possible price. The horizontal differences between the two curves at all possible prices show how much the dominant firm can sell at those prices. The demand curve faced by the dominant firm is dd and is obtained by subtracting horizontally the ΣMC curve from the DD curve. To show in detail how dd is obtained, suppose the dominant firm should set a price of p'. At this price, or any higher price, the small firms would fill the market, leaving no sales for the dominant firm. At a price of p'', the small firms would sell quantity $p''A''$ leaving $A''B''$ for the dominant firm to sell. In order to place the demand curve for the dominant firm's product in proper relationship to the quantity and dollar axes of the diagram, we can set point C'' so that $p''C''$ equals $A''B''$. This process can be repeated at various assumed prices. A line joining all points thus established will be dd, the demand curve faced by the dominant firm. At any price below their respective average variable costs, the smaller firms will drop out of the market leaving the entire market to the dominant firm.

Determination of the profit-maximizing price and outputs follows established principles. The marginal revenue curve of the dominant firm is MR_d and its marginal cost curve is SMC_d. Profits will be maximized for the dominant firm at an output of x_d at which SMC_d equals MR_d. Price charged by the dominant firm will be p. Each small firm will maximize profits by producing the output at which its marginal cost is equal to its marginal revenue, and marginal revenue for each small firm is equal to price p. Total output for the small firms combined will be x_s, the output at which ΣMC equals p. Total industry output will be x_d plus x_s, which equals X. Profit for the dominant firm will be x_d times the difference between price p and the dominant firm's average cost at output x_d. Profit for each small firm will equal its output times the difference between price p and its average cost at that output. Average cost curves are left off Figure 11–4 to avoid undue cluttering of the diagram.

 Many variations of the dominant-firm model are possible. For example, if there are two or more large firms surrounded by a cluster of small firms, the small firms may look to one or all of the large firms for price leadership. The large firms collectively may estimate the amounts which the small firms will sell at various prices and may then proceed to share the remaining market or to divide the remaining market in any one of the various possible ways. Our analysis assumes no product differentiation. However, product differentiation may occur in similar price leadership cases, causing price differentials for the products of the various firms. The gasoline industry furnishes a case in point. Retail prices of the major companies — one or more of which often serve as the price leader — will be very close together in a given locality, while those of the small independents will tend to be two or three cents per gallon below that of the majors.

Independent Action

PRICE WARS AND PRICE RIGIDITY • A persistent danger of price wars occurs in oligopolistic industries characterized by independent action on the part of individual firms. Little of a precise analytical nature can be said about these. One seller may lower his price to increase sales. But this takes customers away from rivals and the rivals may retaliate with a vengeance. The price war may spread throughout the industry with each firm trying to undercut the others. The end result may well be disastrous for some individual firms.

The specific causes of price wars are varied, but they stem basically from the interdependence of sellers. A new filling station breaking into a given locality or an existing one attempting to revive lagging sales may be the initiating factor. Surplus stocks at existing prices and limited storage facilities have touched off price wars in the sale of crude oil in the petroleum industry. In a young industry sellers may not have learned what to expect of rivals, or they may be scrambling to secure an established place in the industry and may inadvertently start a price war.

Maturity on the part of an industry may substantially lessen the dangers of price wars. Individual firms may have learned at least what not to do and may carefully avoid any activities that conceivably could touch off price wars. They may have established a price or a cluster of prices that is tolerable to all from the point of view of profits. Such prices are frequently thought to be rather rigid over time, although there is no clear cut evidence that this is the case. Individual firms are thought to

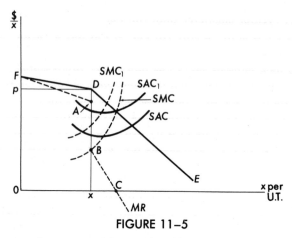

FIGURE 11–5

engage in nonprice competition rather than in price rivalry in order to increase their respective shares of the market and their profits. Soft drinks and cigarettes are frequently cited as examples of mature rigid-price industries.

THE "KINKED" DEMAND CURVE • An analytical device frequently used to explain oligopolistic price rigidity is that of the kinked demand curve. The kinked demand curve case is thought to occur when certain assumptions concerning the industry and the firms in the industry are fulfilled. First, the industry is a mature one, either with or without product differentiation. A price or a cluster of prices fairly satisfactory to all has been established. Second, if one firm lowers price, other firms will follow or undercut it in order to retain their shares of the market. Thus, for price decreases, the individual firm cannot hope to do more than hold its former share of the market — and may not succeed in doing that. Third, if one firm increases price, other firms will not follow the price increase. The customers of the price-raising firm will shift to the other now relatively lower-priced firms and the price-raising firm will lose a part, if not all, of its share of the market.

The demand curve faced by a single firm in such a situation is pictured diagrammatically in Figure 11–5 as FDE. The firm has established a price of p. If it decreases price below p, other firms follow and it retains its share only of the market. For price decreases, then, the demand curve faced by the firm is DE and will have about the same elasticity at different prices as the market demand curve. Should the firm increase price above p, other firms will not follow and it loses a part or all of its share of the market to the other firms. The demand curve faced by the firm for price increases is FD, and at each possible price it will have a considerably greater elasticity than the market demand curve. The demand curve FDE is not a smooth curve, but has a "kink" in it at the established price p.

The kinked demand curve has important implications for the marginal revenue curve of the firm. The marginal revenue curve is discontinuous at output x; that is, it has a gap in it at that point. We can establish that this will be the case by imagining first that the FD portion of the demand curve stands alone and by drawing the appropriate marginal revenue curve for it. Second, imagine that the DE portion of the demand curve extends smoothly on up to the price axis; then draw the appropriate marginal revenue curve for it. Since the imagined part of the DE curve does not exist, neither does a marginal revenue curve exist for it at outputs less than x. Since the FD part of the demand curve does not go beyond x, neither does the marginal revenue curve for it. The two nonvertical sections of the marginal revenue curve shown can be thought of as the appropriate marginal revenue curves for two distinct continuous demand curves and there would be no reason to expect them to be equal to each other at output x.

The discontinuous marginal revenue curve can be thought of also in terms of elasticity of demand. If the demand curve were a continuous curve, elasticity would be changing continuously as we move from higher to lower prices. Since $MR = p - p/\varepsilon$, the marginal revenue curve would also be continuous as we move down the demand curve. However, at D the demand curve breaks. Elasticity at an output infinitesimally below x is substantially greater than elasticity at an output infinitesimally above x. Thus, marginal revenue must drop sharply at output x.

Cost curves SAC and SMC show a situation such that at price p some profit can be made. The marginal cost curve cuts the marginal revenue curve within its discontinuous part. Output x and price p are, in fact, the firm's profit maximizing output and price. If output were less than x, marginal revenue would exceed marginal cost and the firm's profits would be increased by expanding output to x. For outputs exceeding x, marginal cost exceeds marginal revenue and profits will decrease.

A factor which may result in fairly rigid pricing policies on the part of individual firms of the industry now becomes apparent. Suppose the oligopolist's costs increase because of increases in the prices he must pay for resources. The cost curves will shift upward to some position such as SAC_1 and SMC_1. However, as long as the marginal cost curve continues to cut the discontinuous part of the marginal revenue curve, there is no incentive for the oligopolist to change either price or output. The reverse situation also holds. Resource price decreases will move the cost curves downward, but as long as the marginal cost curve cuts the marginal revenue curve in its discontinuous part, no price-output changes will occur. If costs should go up enough for the marginal cost curve to cut the *FA* segment of the marginal revenue curve, the oligopolist will restrict output to the point at which marginal cost equals marginal revenue and will raise price. Likewise, if costs decrease enough for the marginal cost curve to cut the *BC* segment of the marginal revenue curve the oligopolist will lower price and increase output up to the point at

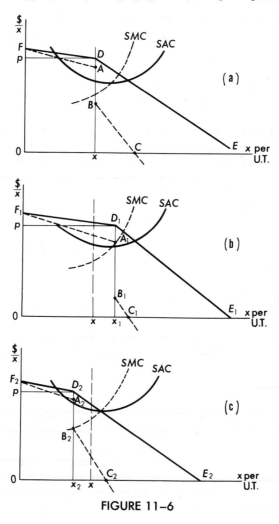

FIGURE 11-6

which marginal cost equals marginal revenue. Thus, there is room for the cost curves to shift up or down without changing the oligopolist's profit maximizing price and output. This will be the case as long as the marginal cost curve cuts the marginal revenue curve in its discontinuous part.

A second factor which may result in a fairly rigid pricing policy likewise becomes apparent. The initial position of the oligopolist is pictured by Figure 11–6(a). Assume his costs do not change and market demand for the product increases. The demand curve faced by the oligopolist shifts to the right to $F_1 D_1 E_1$ as shown in Figure 11–6(b) but it remains kinked at price p. The marginal revenue curve moves to the right, also, with its discontinuous segment always occurring at the output at which the demand curve is kinked. If the increase in demand is limited enough so that the marginal cost curve still cuts the marginal revenue curve in the discontinuous segment $B_1 A_1$, the firm will continue to maximize profits at price p, but at a larger output x_1. If the increase in market demand should shift the firm's demand curve farther to the right than $F_1 D_1 E_1$, the marginal cost curve would cut the marginal revenue curve's $F_1 A_1$ segment, and to maximize profits the firm should increase price as well as output. A decrease in market demand shifts the firm's demand curve to the left to $F_2 D_2 E_2$ as shown in Figure 11–6(c). Here there is no incentive to change price, although output decreases, until the demand curve shifts far enough to the left for the marginal cost curve to intersect the $B_2 C_2$ segment of the marginal revenue curve. This would induce the firm to lower price as well as to decrease output.

We should remember that the case of the kinked demand curve is only one of many possible oligopolistic situations and rests on a special set of assumptions regarding the behavior of rivals when confronted with certain actions on the part of the firm under analysis. This warning is necessary because students (and some professors) are frequently intrigued with the case and tend to think of it and the term "oligopoly" as being synonymous. We want to avoid that error in our thinking.

THE LONG RUN

Two types of adjustment are possible in oligopolistic industries in the long run. In the first place, individual firms are free to build any desired scale of plant; thus, the relevant cost curves for the firm are the long-run average cost curve and the long-run marginal cost curve. Second, some industry adjustments may be possible in the form of entry of new firms into the industry or exit of old firms from the industry. These will be considered in turn.

Scale of Plant Adjustments

The scale of plant which the individual firm should build depends upon its anticipated rate of output. For any given anticipated rate of output, we can say as a first approximation that the firm would attempt to produce that output at the least possible average cost; i.e., it would build the scale of plant which has its short-run average cost curve tangent to the long-run average cost curve at that output.

Under perfect collusion, and often under imperfect collusion, quotas, market shares, and outputs of individual firms may be predictable with some degree of accuracy. In such cases the firm would be expected to adjust its scale of plant accordingly. Not much can be said with regard to whether the scale of plant would be of optimum size, less than optimum size, or greater than optimum size. It may be any one of the three, depending upon the nature of the particular oligopolistic situation involved. Certainly, there is no reason for expecting that the firm would ordinarily construct an optimum scale of plant.

For a firm in an industry characterized by independent action, there will be no more certainty regarding the scale of plant to build than there is regarding the output to produce and the price to charge. Growth possibilities of the industry may influence decisions of the firm to a large extent. The existence of a large growth potential would make the individual firm optimistic with respect to anticipated sales and would result in plant enlargements. "Live and let live" policies or fear of "rocking the boat" on the part of individual firms may lead to fairly determinate outputs and consequently to some degree of certainty as to the scales of plant to build. Again there is no reason for believing that optimum scales of plant would be built.

Entry into the Industry

When individual firms of an industry make profits or when they incur losses, incentives exist for new firms to enter the industry or for old firms to leave the industry. Exit from an oligopolistic industry will usually be much easier than entry into the industry and need not detain us here. Ease or difficulties of entry are much more important. The very existence of oligopolistic markets depends to some extent upon whether or not entry into the industry can be partially or completely blocked. Also, the degree of collusion which can be attained or maintained within an industry tends to be an inverse function of the ease of entry.

ENTRY AND THE EXISTENCE OF OLIGOPOLY • If entry into a currently oligopolistic industry is comparatively easy, it may not remain oligopolistic in the long run. Whether it does or does not will depend upon the extent of the market for the product as compared with the optimum scale of plant of the individual firm. Profits will attract new firms in, lowering the market price or the cluster of prices as industry output increases. When price no longer exceeds long-run average costs for individual firms, entry will cease. If the market is limited, the number of firms may still be small enough to make it necessary for each firm to take account of the actions of the others. If so, the market situation remains one of oligopoly. If the market is so extensive that the number of firms can increase to the point at which each firm no longer considers that its activities affect the other firms, or that the activities of other firms affect it, the market situation will have become one of either pure or monopolistic competition.

ENTRY AND COLLUSION • Easy entry tends to break down collusive arrangements. We have seen already that in a collusive arrangement a strong incentive exists for any one individual firm to break away from the group. The same sort of incentive operates to attract new firms into a cartelized industry and to induce entering firms to remain outside the cartel. The entering firm, if it remains outside the group, will face a demand curve more elastic at various prices than that of the group and, consequently, will be confronted with higher marginal revenue possibilities. At prices slightly below the cartel price it can pick up many of the cartel's customers. At prices slightly above the cartel price it can sell little or nothing. Entering firms which remain outside the collusive group will encroach more and more upon the profits of that group or will cause it to incur losses and will force its eventual dissolution.

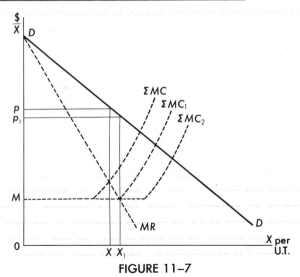

FIGURE 11-7

Even when the entering firms are taken into the cartel a strong presumption exists that dissolution of the cartel will follow eventually. Referring to Figure 11-7, suppose that ΣMC is the horizontal summation of individual firm short-run marginal cost curves. Price will be p and industry output will be X. The entry of new firms will move the ΣMC curve to the right,[12] increasing the industry profit maximizing output and lowering the profit maximizing price. When enough firms have entered to shift industry marginal cost to ΣMC_1, forcing prices down to p_1 and increasing output to X_1, profits for the industry may still exist. More firms will enter, shifting industry marginal cost to some position ΣMC_2; however, industry profits will decrease if output is expanded beyond X_1. Industry marginal revenue for additional output will be less than industry marginal cost. The more profitable course of action for the cartel is to keep the additional firms idle and simply cut them in on the industry's profits. Plant costs of additional firms augment industry total costs and eventually enough firms will have entered the industry to cause all industry profit to be eliminated. A strong incentive now exists for individual firms to break away from the cartel. Any single firm, if it markets its own output, faces a more elastic demand curve in the neighborhood of cartel price than does the cartel. Marginal revenue for the firm exceeds marginal revenue for the cartel. Also, average cost for the firm is lower than average cost for the cartel.[13] The firm which can break away can make profits, provided others remain in the cartel and cartel price is maintained. The temptations facing each individual firm are likely to result in a breakup of the cartel.[14]

BARRIERS TO ENTRY • Since ease of entry into an industry tends to be the nemesis of collusive oligopoly, collusion usually can be maintained only when entry is restricted and it has as one of its purposes the erection of barriers to potential entrants. Barriers to entry of new firms may be inherent in the nature of the industry or they may be established by the existing firms of the industry. These will be called "natural" barriers and "artificial" barriers, respectively. Natural barriers to entry may be inevitable in particular industries. Artificial barriers conceivably can be removed.

Probably the most important natural barrier to entry is smallness of the product market in relation to the optimum scale of plant for a

---

[12] Assume that M is the minimum price at which any firm will enter the industry.

[13] This will be so since the cartel is holding plant capacity of a number of firms idle — which adds to cartel average costs.

[14] See Don Patinkin, "Multiple-Plant Firms, Cartels, and Imperfect Competition," *Quarterly Journal of Economics,* LXI (February, 1947), 173–205.

firm in the industry. Suppose, for example, that there are two firms in the industry and each is operating with a scale of plant somewhere near the optimum. Price exceeds average costs for each and some profit exists. Heretofore we have considered the existence of profit as the signal for new firms to enter. Prospective entrants eye the profit and consider the possibility of entering. They discover that if a new firm enters with a considerably smaller than optimum scale of plant, average costs of the entrant will be so high that no profit could be made. Further, if a new firm enters with an optimum scale of plant, industry output will be increased to the extent that price will be below average costs both for existing firms in the industry and for the entrant. Therefore, no new firms will enter.

Another natural barrier to entry is the necessity of constructing and maintaining a large and complex scale of plant, together with the difficulty of obtaining funds in some situations to build it. The automobile industry is a case in point. The initial investment outlay for a potential entrant is extremely high. Large amounts of space, buildings, and specialized heavy equipment must be obtained. Highly skilled and expensive personnel are necessary. A nation-wide organization of dealership, maintenance, and repair facilities must be established. The difficulties of entry are so great that only a few have had the financial backing to tackle it since World War II despite record profits in the industry. This is not the only barrier to entry into the automobile industry, but it has been a major one.

Among the artificial barriers to entry, those enforced or supported by the state loom large. Patent rights to particular key machines or technological processes may be obtained by certain firms of an industry. Those firms may then maintain control of the machines or processes by leasing them to a limited number of other firms.[15] Or through cross-licensing arrangements the firms of an industry may give each other access to the patents of each but refuse to allow any new firms to use them.[16]

Government-supported barriers to entry exist extensively in the field of transportation. On a local basis taxicab companies and bus companies operate under franchises guaranteeing limited "competition" in the industry. Entry into the interstate public transportation field, with

---

[15] Entry into the glass-container industry has been controlled in this manner. See Wilcox, *op. cit.,* pp. 73–78.

[16] Cross-licensing arrangements have been used extensively in the domestic branch of the electric lamp industry. See Stocking and Watkins, *op. cit.,* pp. 325–327, especially footnote 75.

the exception of air carriers, is regulated by the Interstate Commerce Commission. The Civil Aeronautics Board regulates entry into the air transportation field.

Local governments regulate entry into a host of local oligopolistic industries. Building codes of many cities prevent the entrance of firms producing prefabricated houses or parts of houses. Local licensing laws are used frequently to limit the number of barbers, plumbers, morticians, and others in service trades. Rationalization of such restrictive devices runs in terms of maintaining standards of competency, keeping undesirables out of the trades, and otherwise protecting the public.

A second artificial barrier to prospective entrants is control by the firms already in the field of strategic sources of raw materials necessary for producing the product. This barrier will be of greatest importance where raw material sources are highly concentrated geographically, or, at least, where the better sources are highly concentrated. Concentration of raw material sources facilitates concentration of ownership. Magnesium, nickel, molybdenum, and aluminum provide examples.

Third, price policies of the established firms in an industry may barricade the door. The prospects of entry by new firms may set the established firms in motion. The established firms may frighten away prospective entrants by threatening to lower price enough to eliminate profit possibilities. Or if new firms should be bold enough to enter, underselling by the established firms may promptly drive them out again. The classic example here has been the Standard Oil case of the late 1800's. Additionally, recurrent price wars may create such an atmosphere of uncertainty about the profit possibilities of an industry that new firms will steer clear of it.

Fourth, product differentiation may form an artificial barrier to entry. The industry's product may have become so closely identified with particular sellers' names that consumers will refuse to buy "off brands." Even though standard brands are differentiated from each other, the standard brands are well known to all consumers. What consumers fear and refuse to consume are the new, unknown, and consequently "inferior" brands. This, too, is an important barrier to entry into the automobile industry.

Restricted entry into an oligopolistic industry makes it possible for profits to exist in the long run for the firms of the industry. This is not the same thing as saying that pure profits will always exist in oligopolistic industries. Losses can and do occur. Or the firms of an industry may be just covering average costs, showing neither profit nor loss. When no profits are being made, entry will not be desired, regardless of whether it is restricted or open. The possibility of profits provides the motivation for entry, and when entry is restricted, profits may persist over time. Restricted entry prevents profits from playing their essential role in the organization of productive capacity in a free enterprise economy.

NONPRICE COMPETITION

While oligopolists may be reluctant to encroach upon each other's market shares by lowering product price, they appear to have little hesitancy in using other means to accomplish the same results. Undercutting openly the price(s) of rivals leaves open the prospects of price wars which may be disastrous to individual firms. Product differentiation offers a more subtle and a much safer way of accomplishing approximately the same results. Product differentiation occurs in two major forms: (1) advertising, and (2) variation in design and quality of product. Both forms may and do occur simultaneously, but for purposes of analysis we shall treat them separately.

Advertising

The primary purpose of advertising is to shift to the right the demand curve faced by the single seller and to make it less elastic. This will enable the seller to sell a larger volume at the same or perhaps a higher price without the danger of touching off a price war. Each seller tries to encroach upon the markets of others through advertising instead of through price cutting. When one firm launches an ingenious and successful advertising program, ordinarily there will be a time lag before rivals can embark on similar programs and profits can result during the time lag interval.

Frequently the products of sellers in an industry can be differentiated effectively by advertising alone. Each seller attempts to attract customers to his particular brand name, although basically the product of each seller may be the same as that of other sellers in the industry. The success of sellers in this respect is especially evident in the aspirin industry. Basically all five-grain aspirin tablets conform to certain U.S.P. specifications and one is as effective on the patient as another; nevertheless, some nationally known sellers are able to attract and hold customers at prices far greater than those of other sellers in the same industry.

In some instances rival advertising campaigns succeed only in increasing the costs of individual sellers. Attempts on the part of a single seller to encroach upon the markets of others may be anticipated by the other sellers. They launch counteradvertising campaigns of their own and all sellers succeed only in holding their original places in the market. The over-all market for the product may not be expanded at all by the advertising activity — the present-day cigarette industry is a case in point. But once rival advertising is started, no single seller can withdraw without losing his place in the market. The advertising outlays become "built-in" in the cost structures of the individual firms and lead to higher product prices than would otherwise prevail.

How far should nonprice competition through advertising be carried by the individual seller seeking to maximize profits? The same principles which have guided us thus far in profit maximization apply in this case too. Advertising outlays are expected to add to the seller's total receipts, but successively larger outlays per unit of time beyond some point will add successively less. Marginal revenue from advertising will decrease as outlays increase. Similarly, larger advertising outlays add to the seller's total costs; i.e., marginal costs of advertising are positive. The profit maximizing outlay on advertising will be that outlay at which the marginal cost of advertising is equal to the marginal revenue received from it.[17]

Differences in Quality and Design

Variations in quality and design of particular products are usually used along with advertising to differentiate the product of one seller from another. Usually the objective of variations on the part of one seller is that of causing consumers to prefer his product over that of the other sellers; i.e., to shift his demand curve to the right (or to enlarge his share of the total market) and to make his demand curve less elastic. Additionally, quality variation may be used to extend the market vertically — different qualities to appeal to different classes or groups of buyers.

When quality and design variations are used to increase individual firm market shares we would not expect rival firms to sit by idly while their markets shrink. Retaliation by the rivals will occur. Successful innovations will be imitated and improved upon. Individual firms may succeed in increasing their market shares temporarily, but if a permanent increase is to be obtained such firms must be able to keep ahead of their rivals.

---

[17] In practice probably less is known about the effects of advertising outlays than about the effects of any other cost outlays made by the firm. Nevertheless, any intelligent approach by management to the "correct" magnitude of the advertising budget must be made on the basis of estimated marginal revenue and estimated marginal cost resulting from its contraction or expansion.

The automobile industry furnishes an excellent example of product variation to increase market shares of particular firms. One producer initiates power steering. Consumers "take" to the innovation and other producers follow to regain their market positions. Another mounts the motor on rubber and the process is repeated. Low-pressure tires, automatic transmissions, high horsepower, and many other "improvements," both real and fancied, are introduced initially to enlarge the market share of the particular producer and are in turn copied by other producers to regain or hold their shares of the market.

When quality differences are introduced to extend the market vertically for a particular product we may find the same firm producing different product qualities to sell to different groups of buyers at different prices, or we may find different firms specializing in particular qualities of the product. Initially a product, say de luxe air conditioners, may be produced for middle-income group markets. Sellers find that by producing "super de luxe" models the market can be expanded into the upper income levels. Likewise, by stripping the de luxe model of fancy gadgets and expensive cabinets, a standard model can be sold to lower income groups at a lower price. When different firms each specialize in a particular quality of the product, quality differences may become the basis of market sharing.

Product variation often operates in the best interests of consumers. When it passes along to the consuming public the fruits of industrial research in the form of an improved product, consumer desires may be more adequately met than before. The electric mixer in lieu of the old hand-driven egg beater, the more portable and more versatile tank type of vacuum cleaner in lieu of the upright model, the no-frost refrigerator, the high-fidelity sound system, the self-starter on the automobile, and many other variations in product probably represent more accurate fulfillment of consumer wants.

However, some product variation falls in the same class with retaliatory advertising. It adds to costs but adds little to demand or to fulfillment of consumer desires. Design changes adding nothing to the quality of the product may occur. Say the purpose of the design change is to differentiate a 1966 from a 1965 model. Each seller believes that other sellers will make some changes and feels that he should do the same to hold his share of the market. The costs of the change must be borne by the consumer.

The principles of profit maximization with respect to design and quality changes are the familiar ones. Any changes which will add more to total receipts than to total costs will increase profits (or reduce losses).

Or any changes which will reduce total costs more than total receipts are reduced will increase profits (or reduce losses). To maximize profits with respect to changes in the product, the firm should carry them to the point at which the marginal revenue from the changes is equal to the marginal cost of making the changes.

EFFECTS OF OLIGOPOLISTIC MARKETS

Despite the uncertainties clouding oligopolistic analysis, we can draw certain conclusions regarding the effects of the oligopolistic type of market structure on the economy. We shall consider its effects with respect to (1) prices and outputs, (2) prices and average costs, (3) individual firm efficiency, (4) sales promotion, and (5) the range of products available to consumers.

Output and Prices

It appears likely that some output restriction and increase in prices will occur in oligopolistic markets as compared with purely competitive markets. But again this comparison is legitimate only for industries in which pure competition could exist. In oligopolistic industries demand curves faced by individual firms slope downward to the right, or are less than perfectly elastic. This much seems certain, whether or not individual firm demand curves can be located with accuracy. Consequently, marginal revenue for individual firms will be less than price. An individual firm, attempting to maximize profits or minimize losses, seeks the output at which marginal cost equals marginal revenue. Since the purely competitive firm maximizes profits at the output at which marginal cost equals price (and marginal revenue), the oligopolistic firm by comparison restricts output and charges a higher price.

Prices and Average Costs

Since entry into an oligopolistic industry may be partially or completely blocked, prices may exceed average costs and profits may exist in the long run. To the extent that profits occur, consumers pay more for products than is necessary to hold the resources making them in the industries concerned. Blocked and partially blocked entry in the case of oligopoly, as in the case of monopoly, has important implications with regard to the organization of production in the economy. The existence of profits in an industry means that consumers desire an expansion in the output of the product concerned as compared with the output of other products in the economy. But resources are not free to move out of production of products desired less into the production of the products more urgently desired. Thus, organization of the economy's productive capacity will not follow consumer desires as closely as would be the case if pure competition could and did exist throughout the economy. However, since entry is only partially blocked in many oligopolistic industries, oligopolistic market structures generally are preferable to markets of pure monopoly in this respect.

Efficiency of the Firm

The maximum potential economic efficiency for individual firms in the production of particular products is realized when those firms are induced to build optimum scales of plant and operate them at optimum rates of output. As we have observed, there is no automatic tendency for this to occur in the long run under oligopoly. The firm's output depends upon its quota, its market share, or its anticipations with regard to its marginal revenue and its long-run marginal costs. Once a long-run output is decided upon, the firm will want to produce that output as cheaply as possible; i.e., it will build the scale of plant whose short-run average cost curve is tangent to the long-run average cost curve at that output. Coincidence of the desired output with the output of an optimum scale of plant operated at the optimum rate of output would be sheer accident.

It should be emphasized, however, as it was in the case of pure monopoly, that firms of an oligopolistic type of market, even though they do not use optimum scales of plant operated at optimum rates of output, may provide more efficiency in producing a certain product than would firms of any other type of market organization. The optimum scale of plant may be large enough in comparison with the market for the product so that there is not room in the industry for enough firms to make the market one of pure competition. If the firms of the industry were broken up or atomized so that no one firm could appreciably influence market price, each may have a much smaller than optimum scale of plant. Consequently, average costs and the market price(s) of the product may be higher with such an arrangement than they would be with an oligopolistic market structure.

Sales Promotion

Firms in oligopolistic markets engage in extensive sales promotional activities designed primarily to extend their own markets at the expense of the markets of rivals. The major forms of such activities consist of advertising and changes in product quality and design. To the extent that they add nothing to consumer satisfaction, resources used in those activities are wasted. Often, however, they yield certain satisfactions to consumers in the forms of entertainment and improved product quality. In such cases the important question with regard to economic efficiency is whether or not the additional satisfactions obtained from resources used in sales promotional activities are equal to their costs — i.e., equal to the satisfactions that the resources could have produced in alternative employments. A strong case can be made that, since decisions regarding entertainment and higher product quality are made by business firms rather than by consumers in the market places of the economy, expenditures on resources so used will be overdone and that the value of consumer satisfaction obtained will be less than the resource costs of providing it. To the extent that this occurs, economic waste will be the result.

Range of Products

Differentiated oligopoly provides consumers with a broader range of products among which they can choose than does either pure competition or pure monopoly. Rather than being limited to a single kind and quality of automobile, each consumer can choose the kind and quality which best suits his needs (and his income). The same observations apply to television receivers, washing machines, refrigerators, or even entertainment. Gradations in product qualities, with each lower quality selling at a correspondingly lower price, increase the divisibility of the consumer's purchases of particular items. Consequently, his opportunities for allocating his income among different products may be so enhanced that he can achieve a higher level of want satisfaction than would otherwise be possible. Additionally, product differentiation enables consumers to give vent to their own individual tastes and preferences with regard to alternative designs of a particular product. The range of products available under differentiated oligopoly appears to work in the consumer's favor.

SUMMARY

Under conditions of oligopoly there are few enough firms in the industry for the activities of a single firm to influence and evoke reactions from other firms. The demand curve faced by a single firm will be determinate when the firm can predict with accuracy what the reactions of rivals will be to market activities on his part. Otherwise it will be indeterminate.

We classified oligopolistic industries according to the degree of collusion which exists among firms of each of the industries. Under perfect collusion we included groups of firms such as cartels. Under imperfect collusion we included situations typified by price leadership and gentlemen's agreements. Under independent action we included noncollusive cases.

In the short run, perfectly collusive oligolopistic cases approximate the establishment of monopoly price and monopoly output for the industry as a whole. The less the degree of collusion, usually the lower will be price and the greater will be output. In industries characterized by independent action on the part of individual firms, price wars are likely to be prevalent. As the industry matures, the situation may become collusive or it may develop into a "live and let live" attitude on the part of the firms of the industry. In the latter case price rigidity may occur. Firms may be afraid to change price for fear of touching off a price war.

In the long run the firm can adjust its scale of plant to any desired size and new firms can enter the industry unless entry is blocked. The scale of plant chosen by the firm will be the one which will produce its anticipated output at the least possible average cost for that output. Easy entry into the industry is largely incompatible with a high degree of collusion. Collusion exists partly to block entry. Barriers to entry may be classified as "natural" and "artificial." Restricted entry may enable firms of the industry to make long-run pure profits.

The firms of particular oligopolistic industries frequently engage in nonprice competition through product differentiation to avoid touching off price wars. Nonprice competition takes two major forms: (1) advertising, and (2) quality and design variation. To the extent that firms using them succeed only in holding their respective market shares, costs of production and product prices will tend to be higher than they would otherwise be. The firm desiring to maximize profits will use each to the point at which the marginal revenue from it equals the marginal cost of extending its use.

Some effects of oligopolistic markets on the economy are these: (1) output may be restricted and prices may be increased as compared with pricing and output under pure competition; (2) with entry partially or completely blocked, pure profits and interferences with the organization of production occur; (3) individual firms are not induced to produce at maximum potential efficiency, although in many cases they produce more efficiently than they would if the industry were atomized; (4) some sales promotion wastes occur; and (5) the range of products available to consumers is broader under differentiated oligopoly than it would be under pure competition or pure monopoly.

SUGGESTED READINGS

BAIN, JOE S. *Pricing, Distribution, and Employment.* Rev. ed.; New York: Henry Holt and Company, 1953, chap. 6.

MACHLUP, FRITZ. *The Economics of Sellers' Competition.* Baltimore: The Johns Hopkins Press, 1952, chaps. 4, 11–16.

PATINKIN, DON. "Multiple-plant Firms, Cartels, and Imperfect Competition," *Quarterly Journal of Economics,* LXI (February, 1945), 173–205.

WILCOX, CLAIR. *Competition and Monopoly in American Industry.* Temporary National Economic Committee Monograph No. 21. Washington, D.C.: U. S. Government Printing Office, 1940.

Pricing and Output under Monopolistic Competition | 12

THERE ARE MANY SELLERS of a particular kind of product in a market situation characterized by monopolistic competition, and the product of each seller is in some way differentiated from the product of every other seller. A question may well arise with regard to what "many sellers" means. How can we distinguish between differentiated oligopoly and monopolistic competition? How many sellers must there be in an industry to warrant calling the case one of monopolistic competition? These questions cannot be answered objectively in terms of numbers alone. When the number of sellers is large enough so that the actions of any one have no perceptible effect upon the other sellers and their actions have no perceptible effect upon him, the industry becomes one of monopolistic competition.

The theory of monopolistic competition provides us with few new analytical tools. The analysis of it is very similar to that of pure competition. It furnishes a better description of those competitive industries in which product differentiation occurs — food processing, men's clothing, cotton textiles, the service trades in large cities, and many others — in that it recognizes small monopoly elements and the consequent different prices charged by different sellers of a particular type of product.

FUNDAMENTAL POINTS

Two fundamental points in the analysis of monopolistic competition are worth mentioning at the outset. These are the conditions of demand facing the individual firm and the limitations of graphic analysis in this market situation. With regard to costs of production and ease or difficulty of entering an industry, monopolistic competition usually will be similar to pure competition.

Demand

Conditions of demand faced by the firm set monopolistic competition apart from the three market situations discussed previously. Product

243

differentiation leads some consumers to prefer the products of particular sellers over those of other sellers. Consequently, the demand curve faced by an individual seller has some downward slope to it and enables the seller to exercise a small degree of control over his product price. Ordinarily, the demand curve faced by the firm will be very elastic within its relevant range of prices because of the numerous good substitutes available for his product.

Limitations of Graphic Analysis

Differentiation of the products of the sellers in an industry increases the difficulty of presenting the analysis in graphic terms. For example, in the analysis of pure competition we drew industry demand curves and industry supply curves. Under monopolistic competition, construction of industry curves is a rather unsatisfactory practice. Product differentiation makes the product units sold by one seller somewhat different from the product units sold by another. Tubes of toothpaste differ from cans of tooth powder. Bottles of liquid dentifrice are still different. Unless all of these can be converted into terms of a common denominator, difficulty in constructing the quantity axis for the industry curves will be encountered. Then an additional difficulty arises. No single price prevails for the differentiated products of the industry. Different sellers will receive somewhat different prices, depending upon consumers' judgments with regard to comparative qualities of the differentiated products. These problems make it appear preferable to confine diagrammatic analysis to the individual firm. The market as a whole is there, but we shall discuss it in linguistic rather than in graphic terms.

THE SHORT RUN

Short-run analysis of monopolistic competition is very similar to that of the other market situations. It is primarily an analysis of individual firm adjustment to the conditions it faces. The firm does not have time to change its scale of plant; therefore there is insufficient time for new firms to enter the industry. Individual firms can make price and output adjustments. Additionally, they may be able to bring about small changes in demand for their particular products through advertising and through slight variation of product quality and design.

Profit maximization with respect to output and price by the individual firm follows established principles and is shown graphically in Figure 12–1. Assume the firm's short-run average cost curve and short-run marginal cost curve are SAC and SMC, respectively. The demand curve faced by the firm is dd. Since dd is less than perfectly elastic, mar-

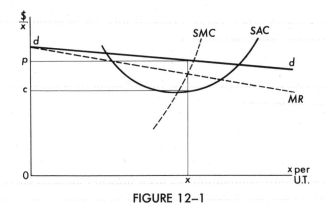

FIGURE 12–1

ginal revenue for each possible level of sales is less than price and the marginal revenue curve lies below the demand curve. The firm maximizes profits (or minimizes losses if the *SAC* curve lies above *dd* for all possible outputs) by producing output *x* at which marginal cost equals marginal revenue. Profits per unit are *cp*. Total profits are *cp* × *x*.

The firm may also attempt to maximize profits with respect to advertising outlays and outlays on product variation; however, the existence of many good substitutes for the product of the individual firm will preclude carrying either very far. To the extent that the firm does engage in them, the principles involved are the familiar ones. Each should be carried to the point at which its marginal revenue is equated to its marginal cost if profit maximization is the firm's objective.

Short-run equilibrium does not imply that all firms charge identical prices. Identity of prices would not be expected since the firms of the industry do not produce homogeneous products. Each firm seeks its own profit-maximizing position. Each equates its own marginal cost to its own marginal revenue. However, the prices charged by different producers will not be far apart. In short-run equilibrium we would expect prices to be clustered but not necessarily equal. Although each producer has some discretion in setting his own price, he is subjected to the restrictive effects of the many close substitutes for the product he produces.

THE LONG RUN

All resources used by the firm are variable in the long run; consequently, two types of adjustment are possible. First, the firm can build any desired scale of plant. Second, unless entry into the industry is blocked, it will be possible for new firms to enter when profits are being made by existing firms. In the event losses are being incurred, existing firms can exit from the industry.

Adjustments with Entry Blocked

Blocked entry into an industry characterized by monopolistic competition clearly will not be the usual case; however, it may and sometimes does occur. Where it does occur it usually is the result of legislative activity of one kind or another. Owners or operators of the firms in a particular industry may belong to a trade association which has some political influence on a local, state-wide, or perhaps even a nation-wide basis. The industry may be fairly profitable, and the trade association may foresee the possibility of wholesale entry into the industry. Therefore, it may use its influence to secure the enactment of legislation which it rationalizes as ensuring an adequate supply of the commodity at prices allowing those in the trade to make fair and reasonable profits. Among the service trades in a particular city or state one can easily find licensing laws that tend to block entry.[1]

In such situations individual firms would seek to adjust their respective scales of plant to the size required for long-run profit maximization. The long-run average cost curve and the long-run marginal cost curve are the relevant ones for the firm. These are shown as LAC and LMC in Figure 12–2. The demand curve faced by the firm is dd and the marginal revenue curve is MR. Profits will be maximized at output x, at which long-run marginal cost equals marginal revenue. Output x can be sold for price p per unit. To produce output x at the least possible cost

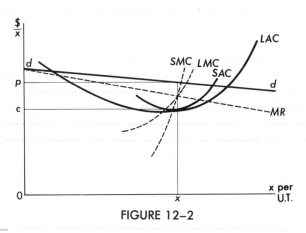

FIGURE 12–2

[1] Cf. Machlup, *The Economics of Sellers' Competition*, pp. 336–344.

per unit, the firm should build the scale of plant which has its short-run average cost curve tangent to the long-run average cost curve at that output. Since SAC is tangent to LAC at output x, short-run marginal cost is equal to long-run marginal cost and to marginal revenue at that output. Profits are equal to $cp \times x$. If the firm should deviate from output x by increasing or decreasing its rate of output with the given scale of plant, SMC would be greater than or less than MR and profits would decline. If it should increase or decrease its rate of output by increasing or decreasing the scale of plant, LMC would be greater than or less than MR and profits would decline. Long-run equilibrium for the firm when entry into the industry is blocked means that the firm produces the output at which SMC equals LMC equals MR and at which SAC equals LAC.

Adjustments with Entry Open

Ordinarily, we would expect entry into or exit from a monopolistically competitive industry to be fairly easy. Existing firms without the benefit of a trade association are likely to feel unconcerned about a few firms more or less in the industry; or, in the event they are concerned about the entry of a number of new firms, they feel powerless to do anything about it. The mere fact that a large number of firms exist in the industry suggests that the size of each firm is something less than gigantic and that effective collusion without government support will be extremely difficult. Thus, most of the bars to entry that exist under oligopoly are not effective in a situation of monopolistic competition.

When pure profits exist for firms in the industry and potential entrants believe that they, too, can make pure profits, entry will be attempted. As new firms enter they encroach upon the markets of existing firms, causing the demand curve and the marginal revenue curve faced by each to shift downward. The downward shift of each firm's demand curve results from the increase in industry supply of the product as new firms enter. The increase in supply (and in the number of suppliers) pushes the whole cluster of price ranges for individual firms downward.[2]

The entry of new firms into the industry will affect costs of production of the existing firms. As in pure competition (and in oligopoly to the extent that entry is possible) we can classify industries as increasing cost, constant cost, and decreasing cost industries. If the industry were one of increasing costs, the entry of new firms would cause resource prices to rise, which would shift the cost curves of existing firms upward

---

[2] This analysis parallels that of pure competition. Larger market supply under pure competition shifts demand curves faced by individual firms downward.

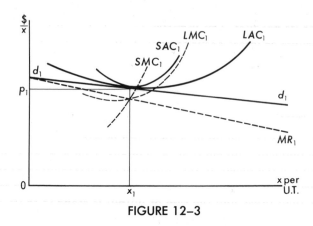

FIGURE 12-3

and would raise the level of costs of entering firms. Under constant costs, the entry of new firms would have no effects upon resource prices and upon the cost curves of individual firms. In the unlikely case of decreasing costs, entry of new firms would cause resource prices to decrease and the cost curves to shift downward. We shall analyze the case of increasing costs only.

The entry of new firms will shift the demand curves faced by individual firms downward and cost curves of the firms upward. This will cause profits to decrease, but new firms will continue to enter as long as profit possibilities remain. Eventually enough firms will have entered to squeeze out pure profits.

This situation for the individual firm is pictured graphically in Figure 12-3 as compared with Figure 12-2. The demand curve faced by the firm has shifted downward as new firms enter from dd in Figure 12-2 to $d_1 d_1$ in Figure 12-3. The long-run cost curves have shifted upward to LAC_1 and LMC_1. The short-run cost curves have also shifted upward and adjustments in the scale of plant have occurred as well. When enough firms have entered to cause the demand curve faced by each firm to be just tangent to its long-run average cost curve, firms of the industry will no longer be making profits and entry will stop.

Long-run equilibrium will be achieved by individual firms and by the industry as a whole when each firm in the industry is in the position shown by Figure 12-3. For each individual firm, long-run marginal cost and short-run marginal cost equals marginal revenue at some output such as x_1. Any deviation from that output with scale of plant SAC_1 will cause losses to be incurred. Any change in the scale of plant will cause losses to be incurred. Short-run average cost equals long-run average cost at that output and both are equal to the price per unit received by the firm for its product. The industry as a whole will be in equilibrium since no profits or losses occur to provide the incentive for entry into or exit from the industry.

EFFECTS OF MONOPOLISTIC COMPETITION

Output and Prices

Some slight restriction of output and increase in prices may occur under monopolistic competition as compared with pure competition. The demand curve faced by the monopolistic competitor, though very elastic, is less than perfectly elastic. Marginal revenue for the individual firm is less than price, and the rate of output is stopped short of that at which marginal cost equals price. The more elastic the demand curve faced by the firm the less will be the deviation from purely competitive price and output.

Prices and Average Costs

In the long run, price will equal average costs of production unless entry into the industry is blocked. When entry is free and easy — and this appears to be the usual case — new firms enter the profit-making industries and reduce profits to zero. Consumers pay just enough to enable firms to hold the desired quantities of resources in the production of the product. Organization of the economy's productive capacity can follow consumer tastes and preferences with a high degree of accuracy.

When entry into profit-making industries is blocked, the consequences with respect to prices and average costs are much the same as they are under pure monopoly and oligopoly. Productive capacity of the economy cannot be organized to conform accurately to consumer tastes and preferences. Additional quantities of resources are prohibited from moving into the profit-making industries where they would be more productive than they are in alternative employments.

Efficiency of Individual Firms

There will be some inefficiency of individual firms in the long run when entry into the industry is easy; that is, the firm will not be induced to build the optimum scale of plant or to operate the one it does build at the optimum rate of output. This can be seen best by reference to Figure 12–3. An optimum scale of plant would involve the firm in losses since average cost at such an output would be greater than price. If the long-run average cost curve lies below the demand curve for any range of outputs, pure profits can be made by any firm that builds the correct scale of plant for any one of those outputs. New firms will enter until profits are eliminated. Profit possibilities are eliminated when individual firm long-run average cost curves are tangent to the demand curves faced by them. Losses are incurred when the long-run average cost curve lies above the demand curve for all outputs. Exit of firms from the industry will continue until the long-run average cost curve for each firm is again tangent to the demand curve faced by it. In long-run equilibrium the output at which losses are avoided by the firm ($SMC = LMC = MR$) is the output at which the average cost curves are tangent to the demand curve. Since the demand curve faced by the firm is downward sloping, the average cost curves must be downward sloping also at their point of tangency with the demand curve. Thus, with easy entry into the industry, individual firms will build a less than optimum scale of plant, such as SAC_1 in Figure 12–3, and they will operate at less than the optimum rate of output.

Some overcrowding with regard to the number of firms in the industry and some excess plant capacity may occur when entry is easy. Since each firm builds a less than optimum scale of plant, there is room for more firms to exist than there would be if all were building an optimum scale of plant. Also, since each firm tends to operate the scale of plant it does build at less than the optimum rate of output, it follows that excess plant capacity may exist. Empirical examples of both situations are not hard to find. The various industries of the textile group illustrate both an excess of firms in an industry and excess capacity for individual firms.

The inefficiencies of the firm pointed out above should not be overemphasized, nor is the foregoing paragraph an argument for restriction of entry into monopolistically competitive industries. The demand curve faced by the firm is highly elastic, and the more elastic it is the nearer the firm will come to building an optimum scale of plant to operate near the optimum rate of output. Free entry into the industry will cause total industry output to be greater than it would be if entry were restricted, and it will cause prices to be correspondingly lower.

When entry is restricted the firm will build the appropriate scale of plant to produce the output at which long-run marginal cost equals marginal revenue. There is no necessity or inducement for the firm to build an optimum scale of plant. The scale of plant built will be optimum only in the event that the firm's marginal revenue curve passes through the minimum point on its long-run average cost curve. Such an occurrence would be purely accidental.

Sales Promotion

Some waste advertising or design changes may occur under monopolistic competition. Efforts on the part of individual firms to expand their markets in this way may be counteracted by similar efforts on the part of the others, and the resources so used merely add to costs of production. Any such wastes of resources will be much smaller under monopolistic competition than they will be under oligopoly. Under oligopoly efforts on the part of one to expand his share of the market *induces* others to put forth similar efforts to prevent it. Such rivalries do not exist under monopolistic competition. Advertising done by one firm induces no retaliatory action by others. When the advertising done by one is counteracted by that of others, the counteraction is simply the result of all trying to do the same thing — expand their own markets. None are reacting to encroachments of others on their particular markets.

Range of Products Available

Consumers will have a broad range of types, styles, and brands of particular products from which to choose in market situations of monopolistic competition. The consumer can choose the type, style, or color of package that most nearly suits his fancy and his pocketbook.

A warning note may be sounded here, however. The different kinds of a particular product may be so numerous that they prove confusing to the consumer, and problems of choice may become more complicated. Ignorance with regard to actual quality differences results in a willingness to pay higher prices for particular brands which in reality are not superior to lower priced brands of the same product. What housewife can possibly be familiar with the comparative qualities of the many different brands of soaps and detergents, floor waxes, electric irons, and so on?[3]

SUMMARY

In a market situation of monopolistic competition there are enough sellers of differentiated products so that the activities of each have no effect on others and their activities have no effect on him. The demand curve faced by the firm has some downward slope because of product differentiation and attachment of consumers to particular brand names. However, it is highly elastic within the relevant price-output range.

---

[3] For a partial solution to the problem see Eugene R. Beem and John S. Ewing, "Business Appraises Consumer Testing Agencies," *Harvard Business Review,* XXXII (March-April 1954), 113–126.

Short-run profit maximization by the firms in the industry will occur at the prices and outputs at which each is equating his marginal cost to his marginal revenue. There is no single industry price. There will be a cluster of market prices reflecting consumer opinions of comparative qualities of product.

In the long run the nature of the adjustment of firms and the industry to a position of equilibrium will depend upon whether entry into the industry is blocked or is easy. With entry blocked, individual firms will produce the output and sell at the price at which long-run marginal cost equals marginal revenue. It will build the appropriate scale of plant for that output and with the appropriate scale of plant short-run marginal cost will also equal marginal revenue.

With entry easy, the existence of profits will induce new firms to enter, decreasing the demand curve faced by the firm and shifting the cost curves upward if the industry is one of increasing costs. Entry will continue until profits are squeezed out. The long-run average cost curve and the short-run average cost curve for each firm will be tangent to the demand curve faced by it at the appropriate output. Long-run marginal costs and short-run marginal costs will equal marginal revenue.

Some effects of monopolistic competition in the long run are these: (1) output may be restricted and prices increased somewhat; (2) price will exceed average costs only if entry is blocked; (3) there will be some inefficiency in individual firm operations; (4) there may be some advertising wastes; and (5) there will be a broader range of products among which consumers may choose than will occur in the other three market situations.

SUGGESTED READINGS

CHAMBERLIN, EDWARD H. *The Theory of Monopolistic Competition.* 8th ed; Cambridge, Mass.: Harvard University Press, 1962, chaps. IV and V.

MACHLUP, FRITZ. *The Economics of Sellers' Competition.* Baltimore: The Johns Hopkins Press, 1952, chaps. 5–7, 10.

Pricing and Employment of Resources: Pure Competition[1]

13

IN THIS CHAPTER we turn from the prices of consumer goods to the prices of the resources used in producing them. Resource prices play a key role in the operation of a free enterprise economy. They are important in determining the employment levels of resources and, as we shall see in Chapter 15, they allocate resources among different uses, guiding them away from less important uses toward more important ones. They guide individual firms toward the use of more efficient resource combinations. Also, since all of us are resource owners, resource prices and employment levels affect us personally. They determine our incomes and the share of the economy's output that each of us receives. We shall consider distribution of the economy's output in Chapter 16.

The principles underlying resource pricing and employment will be developed in this chapter in terms of pure competition both in product markets and in resource markets.[2] Pure competition in resource markets implies several things. No one firm takes enough of any given resource to be able to influence its price. No one resource supplier can place enough of a given resource on the market to be able to influence its price. Variable resources are mobile as among different employments, and their market prices are flexible. Using these assumptions, we shall analyze first the simultaneous employment of several variable resources by the firm. Next, we shall turn to the pricing and employment of any given variable resource.

---

[1] The material covered in this chapter leans heavily on that of Chapter 7. Unless the reader is thoroughly familiar with the principles of production, a rereading of that chapter should prove worth while.

[2] A simple definition of the market for a resource will suffice for most purposes. The market for a resource is the area within which the resource is free to move (or is mobile) among alternative employments. The extent of the market for a given resource will vary depending upon the time span under consideration. The longer the period of time the broader will be the market.

SIMULTANEOUS EMPLOYMENT OF SEVERAL VARIABLE RESOURCES

Up to this point, profit maximization by the firm has been considered in terms of product outputs and sales with little specific attention given to resource inputs. In this section, profit maximization will be viewed in terms of resource inputs and least-cost resource combinations. Second, marginal physical products of resources and resource prices will be converted into product marginal costs.

Profit Maximization and Least-Cost Combinations

The least-cost combination of variable resources for a given output was discussed in Chapter 7.[3] Resources must be so combined that the marginal physical product per dollar's worth of one is equal to the marginal physical product per dollar's worth of each of the other resources used if such a combination is to be achieved. However, the given output is not necessarily the profit-maximizing output of the firm. Suppose in Figure 13–1 that the firm produces an output of x_0 and uses two variable

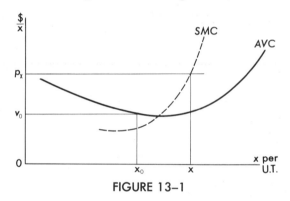

FIGURE 13–1

resources, A and B. To produce output x_0, resources A and B must be combined so that MPP_a/p_a equals MPP_b/p_b if average variable costs are to be kept down to v_0. If product price is p_x, the firm's output is too small for profit maximization. Although A and B are used in proper proportions, not enough of either is being used.

To maximize profits the firm's output must be increased to x. Additional output can be obtained by using more of both resource A and resource B. To keep average variable cost as low as possible as output is increased, increases in the quantities of resources A and B must be in such relationship to each other that the marginal physical product per

---

[3] Note, particularly, footnote 7, page 107.

dollar's worth of A continues to equal the marginal physical product per dollar's worth of B. When output x is reached, the firm will be using the resources not only in the least-cost combination but also in correct absolute quantities.

Marginal Physical Products and Marginal Cost

The least-cost combination conditions for resources A and B — MPP_a/p_a equals MPP_b/p_b — can be translated into terms of marginal cost of product X. Consider resource A first. Any one unit of resource A contributes an amount to the firm's total costs equal to p_a. It adds an amount to the firm's total product equal to MPP_a. Thus the fraction p_a/MPP_a should be read as "the change in the firm's total costs per unit change in product." This is the same thing as the marginal cost of product X; hence we can state that MC_x equals p_a/MPP_a. Likewise, MC_x equals p_b/MPP_b. Since MPP_a/p_a equals MPP_b/p_b when the firm is using a least-cost combination of A and B we can state that

$$\frac{MPP_a}{p_a} = \frac{MPP_b}{p_b} = \frac{1}{MC_x}$$

Or we can consider the reciprocals of the foregoing terms and state that

$$\frac{p_a}{MPP_a} = \frac{p_b}{MPP_b} = MC_x$$

The last statement means that at whatever output the firm is producing, if it uses the least-cost combination of resources, the amount of A or the amount of B or the combined amounts of both necessary to add a single unit to the firm's output will add the same amount of money to the firm's total costs. Suppose the product is men's suits and the variable resources used are labor, machines, and materials. The last one-unit increment in quantity produced per unit of time should increase total cost of the firm by the same amount regardless of whether the increment in product were obtained by increasing the ratio of labor to materials and machines, materials to labor and machines, or machines to labor and materials. Or total cost should be increased by the same amount if the increment in product were obtained by simultaneous increases in the quantities of all three resources. When resources are used in the correct combination they are equally efficient at the margin. The last dollar outlay on one resource adds the same amount to total product as the last dollar outlay on any other resource. And the increment in cost necessary to bring about the last unit increase in product output per unit of time is the marginal cost of the product.

Suppose we consider profit maximization by the firm again in terms of the quantities of resources that should be used. With reference to Figure 13–1 at output x_0, MC_x is less than p_x; or

$$\frac{MPP_a}{p_a} = \frac{MPP_b}{p_b} = \frac{1}{MC_x} > \frac{1}{p_x}$$

This means that the firm is using the resources in correct proportions to produce output x_0; however, output x_0 is too small for profit maximization since MC_x is less than p_x. In the pursuit of maximum profits the firm will increase output by increasing the inputs of A and B. Additional quantities of A and B used with the constant quantities of fixed resources cause the marginal physical product of each to decrease. The price of A and the price of B remain constant since the firm purchases them under conditions of pure competition; consequently, MPP_a/p_a and MPP_b/p_b decrease as does $1/MC_x$. Decreases in $1/MC_x$ are the same thing as increases in MC_x. Thus, decreases in the marginal physical products of A and B are the same thing as increases in the marginal cost of product X. Larger quantities of A and B will be employed to expand the firm's output up to the point at which

$$\frac{MPP_a}{p_a} = \frac{MPP_b}{p_b} = \frac{1}{MC_x} = \frac{1}{p_x}$$

or up to the point at which the firm's marginal cost equals its marginal revenue or product price. At the profit-maximizing output the firm will be using its variable resources both in the correct combination and in the correct absolute amounts.

PRICING AND EMPLOYMENT OF A GIVEN VARIABLE RESOURCE

Demand and supply analysis can be used to advantage in the determination of the market price and employment level of a given resource. Our task is largely that of constructing the individual firm demand curve, the market demand curve, and the market supply curve for the resource. Once we have accomplished these objectives we can determine the market price, the firm's employment level, and the market level of employment of the resource. We must then consider several special points with regard to the pricing of particular resources.

The Demand Curve of the Firm: One Resource Variable

The demand curve of a firm for a given variable resource should show the different quantities of it which the firm will take at various possible prices. But the factors influencing the quantities that a firm will take when confronted by various alternative prices of the resource differ when the given resource is the only variable resource used by the firm from those which prevail when the given resource is one of several variable resources used by the firm. Assume for the present that the given resource is the only variable one used by the firm; that is, the quantities of all other resources employed remain constant.[4] Assume also that the firm's objective is to maximize its profits.

The firm will eye different quantities of the resource — suppose we call it resource A — with regard to their effects on its total receipts and its total costs. If larger quantities of A per unit of time will add more to the firm's total receipts than to its total costs, those quantities will increase profits (or decrease losses). On the other hand, if larger quantities of A will add more to the firm's total costs than to its total receipts, they will cause profits to decrease (or losses to increase). The firm should employ that quantity of the resource at which the contribution of a unit of it to total receipts equals the contribution of a unit of it to total cost if profits are to maximized.[5]

VALUE OF MARGINAL PRODUCT • The market value of a firm's increment in product when it increases the employment level of resource A (or any other resource) by one unit per unit of time is called the *value of marginal product* of the resource, or MVP_a. In computing the value of marginal product of resource A, we note first that a one-unit increase in its employment level adds a certain amount (MPP_a) to the firm's total output. The additional output can be sold at its market price (p_x). Thus the extra product produced multiplied by the price per unit at which it can be sold is the value of the marginal product of a unit of resource A; that is, VMP_a is the same thing as $MPP_a \times p_x$ when the quantity of re-

---

[4] The assumption is the same as that made in defining the law of diminishing returns.

[5] Consider the case of a major integrated oil company employing pipeline riders. Intelligent decisions regarding how many riders to employ will turn on the stated conditions. The company must estimate the value of waste avoided by hiring an additional rider per unit of time and must weigh the value of the waste avoided against the additional expense incurred by hiring the rider. If the value of waste avoided exceeds the wages of the additional rider, it pays to hire him. Pipeline riders should be added up to the point at which the marginal contribution of any one rider to the firm's total receipts is just equal to the extra expense incurred in hiring him.

TABLE 13–1

(1) QUANTITY OF A	(2) MARGINAL PHYSICAL PRODUCT (MPP_a)	(3) PRODUCT PRICE (p_x)	(4) VALUE OF MARGINAL PRODUCT (VMP_a)	(5) RESOURCE PRICE (p_a)
4	7	$2	$14	$4
5	6	2	12	4
6	5	2	10	4
7	4	2	8	4
8	3	2	6	4
9	2	2	4	4
10	0	2	0	4

source A used is increased by one unit. In Table 13–1, which represents Stage II for resource A, column 2 lists the marginal physical product of A when various quantities of it are used with constant quantities of other resources. Price per unit of the final product of the firm is shown in column 3. Value of marginal product of resource A is shown in column 4. For the purely competitive seller of product, one-unit increases in the level of employment of a resource will add amounts to the firm's total receipts equal to the value of marginal product of the resource.

In Stage II for resource A, value of marginal product decreases as larger amounts of A per unit of time are employed. This is caused by operation of the law of diminishing returns. In Stage II for resource A, the marginal physical product of A declines as larger quantities of it are employed. Thus A's value of marginal product declines even though the price at which the final product is sold remains constant.

LEVEL OF EMPLOYMENT • A one-unit increase in the employment level of a resource adds an amount equal to its price to the firm's total cost when resources are purchased under conditions of pure competition. One firm takes such a small proportion of the total supply of the resource that by itself it cannot affect resource price. If the price of the resource (p_a) is $4 per unit, each one-unit increase in the amount of A employed adds $4 to the firm's total cost. This is shown in column 5 of Table 13–1.

The profit-maximizing level of employment of A by the firm is that level at which the value of the marginal product of A is equal to the price per unit of the resource. Refer to Table 13–1. A fourth unit of A per unit of time adds $14 to the firm's total receipts but adds only $4 to the firm's total cost. Therefore, it adds $10 to the firm's profits. A fifth, sixth, seventh, and eighth unit of A each adds more to total receipts than to total costs and, consequently, makes a net addition to profits. A ninth unit of A adds the same amount to both total receipts and total costs. A tenth unit of A, if employed, will decrease profits by $4. Hence when p_a is $4, profits are maximized with respect to resource A at an employment level of nine units. We can write the profit-maximizing condition in either of the following forms:

$$VMP_a = p_a$$

or

$$MPP_a \times p_x = p_a$$

The second form is simply an elaboration of the first.

THE DEMAND CURVE • The value of marginal product schedule for resource A, as listed in columns 1 and 4 of Table 13–1, is the firm's demand schedule for A if A is the only variable resource employed. It shows the different quantities which the firm will take at different possible prices. If p_a were $10 per unit, six units would be employed. If p_a were $14 per unit, four units would be employed.

The demand curve of the firm for the resource is the demand schedule or the value of marginal product schedule plotted. Figure 13–2 shows such a curve. With reference to the quantity axis, it occupies Stage II for resource A. With reference to the dollars per unit axis, the value of marginal product at each quantity of A is found by multiplying marginal physical product by the price per unit at which the final product is sold.

It may be instructive to consider profit maximization by the firm with respect to resource A again — this time in terms of the demand curve or value of marginal product curve. If the price of A in Figure 13–2 were

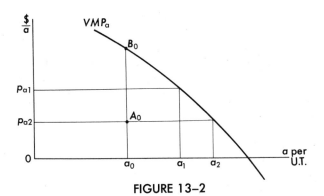

FIGURE 13–2

p_{a2}, the firm would maximize profits by using quantity a_2. If the firm were to use quantity a_0, the a_0 unit would add $a_0 A_0$ to the firm's total cost, but would add $a_0 B_0$ to the firm's total receipts. It would add $A_0 B_0$ to the firm's profits. Additional quantities of A up to a_2 add more to total receipts than to total costs and therefore increase profits. Beyond a_2 larger quantities add more to the firm's total cost than to its total receipts and cause profits to decrease. If the price of A were p_{a1}, the firm would maximize profits by using quantity a_1. At each of various prices of A the firm would maximize profits by using that quantity at which the value of marginal product of A equals its price per unit.

The Demand Curve of the Firm: Several Resources Variable

When a firm uses several variable resources, its demand curve for any one of them is no longer the value of marginal product curve of the resource. When several variable resources are used by the firm, a change in the price of one, assuming the prices of the others remain constant, will bring about changes in the quantities used of the other resources; and these changes will in turn affect the utilization of the one as the firm attempts to maximize profits and to reestablish a least-cost combination of resources. Suppose we call such changes the *firm* or *internal* effects of a change in the price of a resource.

To illustrate the internal firm effects, suppose that we want to derive the firm's demand curve for resource A, which is one of several variable resources. Suppose that initially the firm is producing the profit-maximizing output of product X and is using the appropriate least-cost combination of variable resources. As shown in Figure 13–3, the price

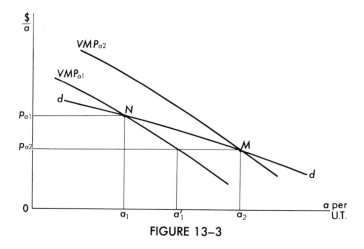

FIGURE 13–3

of A is p_{a1} and the quantity employed is a_1. The VMP_{a1} curve shows value of marginal product of A when the quantity of A, only, is varied.

Now suppose that for some reason the price of A falls to p_{a2}. Since $VMP_a > P_a$, the firm will tend to expand employment of A toward a_1'. However, the increased utilization of A will shift the marginal physical product and value of marginal product curves of variable resources complementary to A to the right. The corresponding curves of substitute resources will be shifted to the left. Since prices of other resources remain constant, utilization of complementary resources will increase while that of substitute resources will decrease. Such changes in the utilization of other resources will shift the marginal physical product and value of marginal product curves of A to the right. Each different level of utilization of each other variable resource will result in a different marginal physical product curve and value of marginal product curve for A. When these and higher order complementary and substitute effects have worked themselves out, the firm will be on some such value of marginal product curve as VMP_{a2} and will be employing that quantity of A at which its value of marginal product equals its price; that is, quantity a_2.[6] The employment levels of other variable resources will also be such that for each one its value of marginal product equals its price when the firm is again maximizing profits and using the appropriate least-cost combination.

Points N and M are points on the firm's demand curve for resource A. These points show the quantities of A that the firm would take at alternative prices of A when the prices of other resources are held constant and the quantities of all other resources are adjusted appropriately for each price of A. Other points on the firm's demand curve for A can be established in a similar fashion and would trace out such a curve as dd. Ordinarily the firm's demand curve for a resource will be more elastic than will any single value of marginal product curve of the resource. The better the substitutes available for a resource the more elastic its demand curve will be.

The Market Demand Curve

A first approximation to the market demand curve for a resource is the horizontal summation of individual firm demand curves for it. However, a straightforward horizontal summation leaves out of account

---

[6] The increasing ratios of resource A to fixed resources of the firm will insure that marginal physical product and value of marginal product of A decline even though the changing utilization of other variable resources tends to shift the curves for A to the right.

what we shall call the *market* or *external* effects of changes in the price of a resource.

In a purely competitive world an individual firm is small enough relative to the markets in which it operates to anticipate that its actions will have no effect on the price of anything it buys or sells. Consequently, the firm's demand curve for a resource should show the different quantities that the firm would take at various alternative resource prices when the firm anticipates that its actions will have no effect on the price of whatever product the firm sells. The firm considers the *firm* or *internal* effects, only, of resource price changes.

The *market* or *external* effects come about as a result of simultaneous expansion or contraction of industry outputs of products by all firms using a given resource as the price of the resource changes. If industry X is one of the industries using resource A, a decrease in the price of resource A will cause all firms using A to increase their employment of it. Although no one firm's increase in output is sufficient to cause a decrease in the price of X, the simultaneous increases in output of all firms may cause such a price decrease to come about. Each such decrease in the price of X will cause shifts to the left or decreases in the whole family of individual firm value of marginal product curves and, consequently, shifts to the left or decreases in individual firm demand curves for resource A.

The external effects of changes in the price of a resource and construction of the market demand curve for the resource are illustrated in Figure 13–4. Suppose that the firm of the diagram and every other firm which uses resource A is in equilibrium and the price of A is p_{a1}. The firm's demand curve for A is $d_1 d_1$ and the firm is employing a_1 of A. By summing the amounts which all firms employ at price p_{a1}, the total

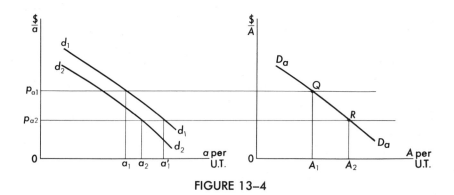

FIGURE 13–4

amount taken off the market at that price is A_1. Thus, Q is a point on the market demand curve for A.

Now suppose the price of A falls to p_{a2}. Each firm will expand its employment of A. But as the firms in each industry which uses A expand employment of it and, consequently, industry outputs of product, market prices of products decrease. Individual firm demand curves for resource A shift to the left toward positions such as d_2d_2. Thus, the individual firm employment levels of A will increase toward such quantities as a_2 rather than toward such quantities as a_1'. Restricted expansion in the employment of A results from the market or external effect of the decrease in resource price. When each individual firm has made the necessary adjustments to achieve a least-cost combination of resources and a profit-maximizing product output and each firm's level of employment is some such level as a_2, the amounts which all firms together employ at price p_{a2} can be totaled to obtain quantity A_2 and R is a second point on the market demand curve for A. Other points on the market demand curve can be found in a similar way to trace out the market demand curve D_aD_a.

The Market Supply Curve

The market supply curve for resource A, or for any other resource, shows the different quantities per unit of time that its owners will place on the market at different possible prices. Generally it will be upward sloping to the right, indicating that at higher prices more of it will be placed on the market than at lower prices. If resource A were a certain kind of labor, higher wage rates tend to induce more workers to enter the occupation. Also, higher wage rates in a given occupation tend to induce workers qualified for that occupation, but who have been working in other occupations, to reenter it. In the case of non-human resources, parallel forces are at work. In the petroleum industry, for example, increases in crude oil prices lead to a more rapid rate of recovery and vice versa. The precise shape of resource supply curves is not of paramount importance for our purposes, although for certain types of economic problems it will be. For our purposes, it may be upward sloping to the right, it may be absolutely vertical, or it may bend back on itself at high prices. The basic analysis will be the same in each case.

Resource Pricing and the Level of Employment

The conditions of market demand and the conditions of market supply, as summed up in the market demand curve and the market

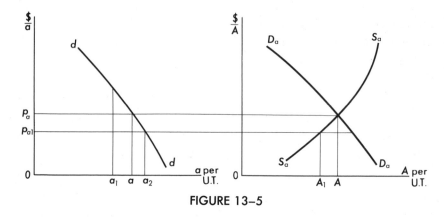

FIGURE 13–5

supply curve, determine the market price of the resource. Its equilibrium price will be that at which resource buyers are willing to take the same quantity per unit of time that sellers want to sell. In Figure 13–5 the market demand curve and the market supply curve are D_aD_a and S_aS_a, respectively. Resource A will be priced at p_a. At a higher price sellers will want to sell more than buyers will want to employ at that price. Some unemployment will occur and the owners of unemployed units will undercut each other to secure full employment of their particular supplies. Thus the price will be driven down to the equilibrium level of p_a. At prices lower than p_a there will be a shortage of the resource. Resource buyers will bid against each other for the available supply, driving the price up to the equilibrium level.

In the economy with which we are working determination of the equilibrium market price for a given resource will tend to occur as we have described it, but it may be well to reiterate the assumptions underlying that economy. We have assumed that the economy is a stable one — free of major fluctuations up and down — and that high levels of resource employment exist. To put it in a slightly different way, we assume that fiscal-monetary policies of the federal government are such that national income is stabilized at high levels of resource employment.

In a free enterprise economy in which stability is not assured, determination of resource prices and employment levels is more complex. Resource supplies and resource demands are not independent. In the Great Depression of the 1930s, for example, decreasing demand for products and for resources created unemployment and lowered resource prices. But resource employment levels and prices determine individual incomes. Hence individual incomes dropped, decreasing demand for products and for resources still more. Demand curves for resources in the unstable economy thus depend in some degree upon the levels of unemployment and prices of resources. Additionally, in a contracting economy fear of unemployment and declining incomes may induce resource owners to offer larger quantities at particular prices; that is, may shift resource supply curves to the right, augmenting the problem of unemployment. We need not pursue this line of reasoning since it lies outside the scope of our analysis. It does, however, point up the intricate relationships between macroeconomics and microeconomics, as well as show that the theory of price developed in terms of a stable economy has certain limitations.

Returning to the stable economy, an individual firm, purchasing resource A competitively, can get as much as it wants at a price of p_a per unit. The single construction firm in Chicago will not be able to influence the market price of steel. Thus the supply curve of the resource from a single firm's point of view is shown in Figure 13–5 as a horizontal line at the equilibrium market price. The dollars per unit axes on the firm and market diagrams are identical. The scale of the quantity axis of the market diagram is greatly compressed as compared with that of the single firm. The level of employment of the resource by the single firm is quantity a, assuming that dd is the demand curve of the firm associated with price p_a, and at that quantity value of marginal product is equal to its price per unit. The market level of employment of the resource is the summation of the quantities employed by the individual firms and is shown as quantity A in the market diagram.

The belief that resources are often paid lower than equilibrium prices is widespread enough to warrant consideration of such a situation in some detail. Suppose in Figure 13–5 that resource A is priced at p_{a1}. At that price individual firms want quantity a_2 in order to maximize their profits with respect to the resource. All firms cannot get as much as they desire, since the entire quantity placed on the market at that price is A_1. In fact, many or perhaps all firms will each get some quantity even less than a — say, a_1. For such firms the value of marginal product of A is greater than the resource price. These firms desire to expand employment of the resource in order to increase profits. Each firm believes that by offering a slightly higher price than p_{a1} it will be able to get as much of the resource as it desires. In the absence of collusion among the firms employing the resource — and in pure competition there is no collusion — each attempts the same thing. No firm succeeds in getting as much as it wants until the price has been driven up to p_a. Under pure competition in resource buying, independent action on the part of each firm and the desire to maximize profits preclude the permanent location of price below the equilibrium level.

It is worth noting that under pure competition a particular resource receives a price per unit equal to the value of its marginal product. Thus a unit of resource A is paid just what it contributes to the value of the economy's product. The market demand curve for A shows the value of marginal product for A in all its uses combined. The market demand curve, together with the market supply curve, determines price; hence the resource price is equal to its value of marginal product in any one or in all of the firms which use the resource. Any one firm takes the market price as given and adjusts the quantity of the resource employed in such a way that the value of its marginal product in that firm is equal to the market price of the resource.[7]

The conditions set out in the first part of the chapter for employing the correct amounts and correct proportions of several resources simultaneously to maximize the firm's profits can also be reached by considering resources one by one. Suppose the firm uses two resources, A and B. To maximize profits with respect to A, it should employ it up to the point at which

$$MPP_a \times p_x = p_a, \text{ or } \frac{MPP_a}{p_a} = \frac{1}{p_x} \qquad (13.1)$$

Likewise, B should be employed up to the point at which

$$MPP_b \times p_x = p_b, \text{ or } \frac{MPP_b}{p_b} = \frac{1}{p_x} \qquad (13.2)$$

Equations (13.1) and (13.2) can then be combined as follows:

$$\frac{MPP_a}{p_a} = \frac{MPP_b}{p_b} = \frac{1}{p_x} \qquad (13.3)$$

Since MPP_a/p_a and MPP_b/p_b are the same as $1/MC_x$, then

$$\frac{MPP_a}{p_a} = \frac{MPP_b}{p_b} = \frac{1}{MC_x} = \frac{1}{p_x} \qquad (13.4)$$

When the firm employs each of its variable resources in the correct absolute amount for profit maximization, it necessarily will be using them in the correct combination.

---

[7] This is frequently misconstrued. A firm is said to pay a resource a price equal to the value of its marginal product — implying that the firm determines the value of the marginal product of the resource, then pays it accordingly. This implication misrepresents the nature of marginal productivity theory under pure competition. The firm has nothing to say about price. It must pay the market price, but it adjusts quantity taken to the point at which value of marginal product equals that price.

Alternative Costs Reconsidered

The alternative cost doctrine, which we met in Chapter 8, can be restated in terms of the value of marginal product of any given resource. Under pure competition, each firm using a given resource employs that quantity of it at which its value of marginal product equals its price. Any discrepancy in resource prices offered by different firms induces units of it to move from the lower paying to the higher paying uses until a single price prevails throughout the market. Thus, the resource price, or its cost to any firm, will be equal to the value of its marginal product in its alternative employments.

Economic Rent

Perfect mobility of all resources does not occur in the short run even under conditions of pure competition. Those resources constituting the firm's scale of plant are not mobile — they are fixed in quantity for particular uses or users. The longer the time period under consideration the fewer will be the fixed resources.

The returns received by fixed resources are not determined according to the principles set out above. Since those resources are not free to move into alternative employments, their short-run remuneration will be whatever is left over after the mobile resources have been paid whatever it takes to hold them to the particular firm. The mobile resources must be paid amounts equal to what they can earn in alternative employments; that is, amounts equal to the values of their marginal product in alternative employments. The residual left for the fixed resources is called economic rent.[8]

A short-run cost-price diagram for an individual firm will help us understand the nature of economic rent. In Figure 13–6 the short-run average cost curve, average variable cost curve, and marginal cost curve are drawn. Suppose the market price of the product is p. The firm's output will be x. Total cost of the variable (mobile) resources is $OvAx$. This is the outlay necessary if the firm is to hold its variable resources. Should the firm attempt to reduce the payments made to variable resources, some or all of them would move into alternative uses where their values of marginal product and remunerations are greater. Thus the average variable cost curve shows the necessary outlays per unit of product output that the firm must make for variable resources. The fixed resources get whatever is left from the firm's total receipts; that is, they receive economic rent. Total rent for the fixed resources is $vpBA$.

---

[8] These returns are sometimes called quasi rents. The term *quasi rent*, introduced by Alfred Marshall, is used so ambiguously in economic literature that we shall avoid it altogether.

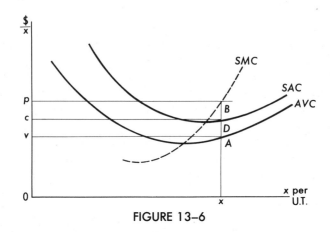

FIGURE 13-6

The lower the market price of the product, the less the rent will be. The higher the market price of the product, the higher is the economic rent.

A problem now arises with regard to the nature of the *SAC* curve. What does it show? To get at the problem suppose we lump the fixed resources together and call them investment in the firm. The rent represents the return on investment in the firm. Only that part of rent that represents a return on investment equal to what that amount of investment could earn elsewhere in the economy (or in alternative uses) constitutes fixed cost for the firm. Thus the part of rent represented by *vcDA* is fixed costs for the firm. The rest of the rent we have defined previously as pure profits. Average cost at any output is equal to average fixed cost plus average variable cost at that output.

Economic rent may be equal to, greater than, or less than enough to cover the firm's fixed costs. When investment in the firm yields a higher rate of return than investment on the average elsewhere in the economy, rents are greater than total fixed costs and we say that the firm is making pure profits. The firm's profits are zero when rents equal total fixed cost; that is, when investment in the firm yields the same rate of return as investment elsewhere. When product price is not sufficient for rents to equal total fixed costs, or when investment elsewhere in the economy yields a higher rate of return than it does for the firm, we say that the firm is incurring losses.

SUMMARY

This chapter applies the principles of production to the pricing and employment of resources under conditions of pure competition both in product selling and in resource buying. First, the principles underlying employment of several variable resources by a firm were established. Second, the principles underlying pricing and employment of any given variable resource were determined.

When several variable resources are used by the firm, two problems are solved simultaneously by the firm in the process of maximizing its profits. It must use resources in the correct (least-cost) combination and it must use the absolute amounts necessary to produce that quantity of product which maximizes profits. Use of resources in the correct absolute amounts means that they are used in the correct combination, also. The firm should employ those amounts of resources and produce that amount of product at which

$$\frac{MPP_a}{p_a} = \frac{MPP_b}{p_b} = \cdot \quad \cdots \quad \cdot = \frac{MPP_n}{p_n} = \frac{1}{MC_x} = \frac{1}{p_x}$$

The individual firm demand curve, the market demand curve, and the market supply curve for a resource are necessary for determining market price, individual firm level of employment, and market level of employment of the resource. When the firm employs one variable resource, only, the value of marginal product curve for the resource is the firm's demand curve for it. If the firm employs several variable resources, the firm's demand curve for a given resource shows the different quantities that the firm would take at various alternative prices when prices of other resources are held constant and at each price of the given resource the firm makes all the adjustments necessary in the quantities of all resources used in order to maximize its profits. The market demand curve is obtained by summing the quantities that all firms in all industries using the resource will take at each possible resource price. The market supply curve shows the quantities of the resource that its owners will place on the market at various possible prices. Once market price is established the firm will employ a quantity of the resource at which its value of marginal product is equal to its market price. The market level of employment is the summation of individual firm levels of employment.

SUGGESTED READINGS

HICKS, JOHN R. *Value and Capital.* 2d ed.; Oxford, England: The Clarendon Press, 1946, chaps. VI, VII, and VIII.

ROBERTSON, DENNIS H. "Wage Grumbles," *Economic Fragments.* London: R. S. King & Son, Ltd., 1931, 42–57. Reprinted in *Readings in the*

Theory of Income Distribution. Philadelphia: The Blakiston Company, 1946, 221–236.

SCITOVSKY, TIBOR. *Welfare and Competition.* Chicago: Richard D. Irwin, Inc., 1951, chap. VII.

STIGLER, GEORGE J. *The Theory of Price.* Rev. ed.; New York: The Macmillan Company, 1952, chap. XI.

Pricing and Employment of Resources: Monopoly and Monopsony

14

THE ANALYSIS OF THE PRECEDING chapter can be modified to apply to situations other than pure competition. The present chapter will center around (1) firms that sell products as monopolists while buying resources under conditions of pure competition, and (2) firms that buy resources as monopsonists while selling products either as pure competitors or as monopolists. The primary modification necessary to take product monopoly into account is that of redefining the firm's demand curve for a resource. The analysis so modified will include product markets of monopolistic competition and oligopoly as well as those of pure monopoly. To take monopsony into account a modified view of the resource supply curve facing the firm will be necessary. The modification also includes cases of oligopsony and monopsonistic competition. Monopoly and monopsony will be considered in turn.

MONOPOLY IN THE SELLING OF PRODUCTS

Simultaneous Employment of Several Variable Resources

The first concern of the monopolist who uses several variable resources is that of determining the proper combinations of resources to produce alternative outputs at the least possible costs. He faces the same situation as that faced by a pure competitor. The least-cost combination for a given output is that at which the marginal physical product per dollar's worth of one variable resource is equal to the marginal physical product per dollar's worth of every other variable resource used. If A and B are two such resources, they should be combined so that

$$\frac{MPP_a}{p_a} = \frac{MPP_b}{p_b}$$

To maximize profits the monopolist must do more than determine least-cost combinations of variable resources. He must use enough of

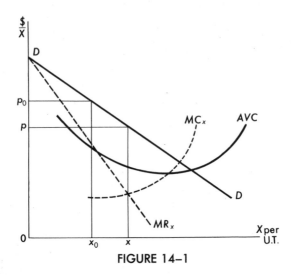

FIGURE 14–1

each to produce the product output at which marginal revenue from his product sales and marginal cost of his product output are equal. With reference to Figure 14–1, suppose he uses the least-cost combination for production of x_0 units of product. Marginal cost of the product is less than marginal revenue from it. Output of X and quantities used of resources A and B are all too small. These conditions can be summarized as follows:

$$\frac{MPP_a}{p_a} = \frac{MPP_b}{p_b} = \frac{1}{MC_x} > \frac{1}{MR_x}$$

The monopolist can increase output by increasing the quantities of A and B used in combination with his fixed resources. Marginal physical product of both A and B will decrease, causing marginal cost of the product to rise. The larger output and sales of the monopolist cause marginal revenue from the product to fall. Quantities of A and B, together with the firm's output, will be increased until marginal cost and marginal revenue are equal. At output x and price p profits will be maximized. Variable resources will be used in the least-cost combination as well as in the correct absolute quantities. The profit maximizing conditions with respect to resource purchases, resource combinations, and product output can be summarized as follows:

$$\frac{MPP_a}{p_a} = \frac{MPP_b}{p_b} = \frac{1}{MC_x} = \frac{1}{MR_x}$$

These principles of profit maximization apply to all types of sellers' markets — pure competition, pure monopoly, oligopoly, and monopolistic competition — as long as pure competition prevails in the buying of resources.[1]

Pricing and Employment of a Given Variable Resource

Determination of the price and employment level of a given variable resource when resource purchasers are monopolistic sellers of product is very similar to that when resource purchasers are purely competitive product sellers. The monopolist's demand curve for a resource, while defined in the same way as that of the pure competitor, is computed in a slightly different manner. As in the purely competitive market, we must differentiate between the case in which the given resource is the only variable one employed by the firm and the case in which it is one of several variable resources employed.

THE DEMAND CURVE OF THE FIRM: ONE RESOURCE VARIABLE • To maximize profits with respect to a single variable resource the monopolist must employ that quantity at which a one-unit change in the quantity employed per unit of time changes total revenue and total cost in the same direction by the same amount. Using the procedure of the last chapter, the effects of one-unit changes in the quantity employed on total receipts and on total costs can be determined. Then the quantities that will be purchased at different resource prices can be derived.

TABLE 14–1

(1) QUANTITY OF A	(2) MARGINAL PHYSICAL PRODUCT (MPP_a)	(3) TOTAL PRODUCT	(4) PRODUCT PRICE (p_x)	(5) TOTAL REVENUE	(6) MARGINAL REVENUE PRODUCT (MRP_a)
4	8	28	$10.00	$280.00	
5	7	35	9.80	343.00	$63.00
6	6	41	9.60	393.60	50.60
7	5	46	9.50	437.00	43.40
8	4	50	9.40	470.00	33.00

Changes in the firm's total receipts and the forces underlying those changes are shown in Table 14–1. Columns 1 and 2 show a portion of the marginal physical product schedule for resource A lying in Stage II for that resource. Resource A is the only variable resource used by

---

[1] The only difference between this and the similar purely competitive situation of the preceding chapter is that p_x in the competitive case is replaced by MR_x in the monopolistic case. Since p_x and MR_x are the same for the competitive firm, the conditions stated here hold for a competitive firm as well as for the monopolistic firm.

the firm; the quantities of all other resources are fixed. Columns 3 and 4 show the portion of the product demand schedule of the monopolist corresponding to the quantities of A shown in column 1.

Column 6 is the important one for the present. It shows the additions to the firm's total receipts made by one-unit increments in the quantity of A employed per unit of time and is called the *marginal revenue product* of resource A. The marginal revenue product of a given quantity of A can be computed directly from column 5, but in a fundamental sense it is the marginal physical product of A at that quantity multiplied by the marginal revenue obtained from sale of the final product. Marginal revenue product of A, or MRP_a, when, say, five units are employed, equals marginal physical product of A at that point multiplied by the marginal revenue from each of the additional units of sales.[2]

Increases in the level of employment of A by the monopolist cause marginal revenue product of A to decrease for two reasons. First, they cause marginal physical product of A to decline, because of the operation of the law of diminishing returns. Second, marginal revenue for the monopolist ordinarily will decrease as he markets larger quantities of product.

The marginal revenue product curve is the monopolist's demand curve for A when the monopolist buys the resource competitively and

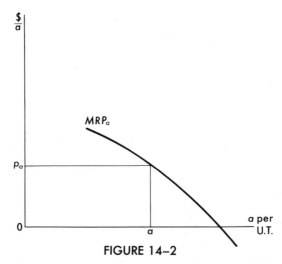

FIGURE 14–2

---

[2] A fifth unit of A per unit of time increases output and sales of X from 28 units to 35 units, and total receipts of the firm from \$280 to \$343. The increment in revenue per unit increment in sales, or MR_x, equals \$63 ÷ 7 or \$9 per unit for each of the 7 units. Marginal revenue product of A, then, when five units are employed must equal $MPP_a \times MR_x$; that is, $7 \times \$9 = \$63$.

when resource A is the only variable resource used by the firm. The monopolist will buy that quantity of A at which the additions made to total receipts by a·one-unit increment are equal to the additions made to total cost by the increment. Since the resource is purchased competitively, the additions to total cost made by each additional unit of A purchased per unit of time are the same as the price per unit of A. Thus, in Figure 14–2, if MRP_a is the monopolist's marginal revenue product curve for A and p_a is the price per unit of A, the monopolist will use quantity a. The profit-maximizing conditions can be written as:

$$MRP_a = p_a$$

or $$MPP_a \times MR_x = p_a$$

At different possible prices of A the marginal revenue product curve shows the different quantities which the monopolist will purchase per unit of time.

THE DEMAND CURVE OF THE FIRM: SEVERAL RESOURCES VARIABLE • The procedure for establishing the monopolist's demand curve for a given resource when several variable resources are employed is very little different from that used in the purely competitive case. Assuming that the prices of all other resources remain constant, changes in the price of the given resource will give rise to the same sort of *firm* or *internal* effects.

These effects are shown in Figure 14–3, in which A is the given variable resource. Suppose that the initial price of A is p_{a1}; the firm is

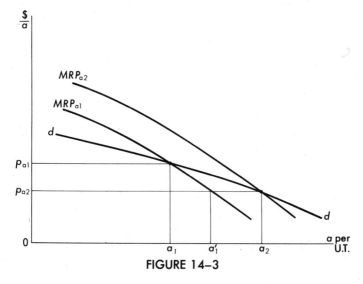

FIGURE 14–3

using a least-cost combination of variable resources and is producing the profit maximizing quantity of product X. The quantity of A employed is a_1. The curve MRP_{a1} is valid for changes in the quantity of A, only.

A decrease in the price of A to p_{a2} will provide an incentive for the monopolist to increase employment of the resource toward a_1'. But as employment of A is expanded, the marginal physical product curves and marginal revenue product curves of complementary resources will be shifted to the right, causing larger quantities of these resources to be used at their given prices. The corresponding curves of substitute resources will be shifted to the left by the greater utilization of A, and smaller quantities of substitute resources will be employed at their given prices by the monopolist. Both effects will shift the marginal physical product curve and the marginal revenue product curve of resource A to the right. When the monopolist has again established a least-cost profit maximizing combination of variable resources, the marginal revenue product curve for A will be in some such position as MRP_{a2} and the quantity of A employed will be a_2. Thus the firm's demand curve for resource A will consist of points tracing out a curve such as dd.

THE MARKET DEMAND CURVE AND RESOURCE PRICING • If all purchasers of resource A were purely monopolistic sellers of product, the market demand curve for A would be the horizontal summation of all individual firm demand curves for it. There would be no external or industry effects resulting from a decrease in the price of A, since each monopolist is the sole supplier of product for his industry. The effect of a decrease in the price of A on the quantity of product produced in any given industry and, consequently, on the price of that product has already been taken into account in the marginal revenue product curves and in that monopolist's demand curve for the resource.

If the purchasers of resource A are oligopolists or monopolistic competitors, the market demand curve for the resource is no longer the horizontal summation of individual firm demand curves for it. A change in the price of A changes not only the output that any single firm in a given industry will produce but the outputs of all the firms in the industry as well. This will be so in every such industry that uses the resource. As in the purely competitive case of the last chapter, changes in product outputs of other firms in the industry will shift the product demand curve facing any given firm and, consequently, the firm's demand curve for resource A. Thus, at any given price of A the quantities employed by all firms in all industries using A when each firm is maximizing its profits must be totaled to locate a point on the market demand curve for A. Other points on the market demand curve can be obtained in the same fashion.

The procedure just outlined is applicable for establishing the market demand curve for a resource regardless of the type of product market in which the firms using the resource sell. The usual case will be that some of the firms using resource A will sell in one type of product market and some will sell in other types. The only market structure requirement which must be met is that all firms purchase the resource competitively.

With regard to market supply, resource pricing, and resource employment, monopoly in the product market adds nothing new to the analysis presented in the preceding chapter. The market supply curve for resource A again shows the different quantities of it which its owners will place on the market at various alternative prices. The market price of the resource moves toward the level at which firms are willing to employ the quantity per unit of time that its owners are willing to place on the market.

The market price of A determines its level of employment. The monopolist, like a firm selling under conditions of pure competition, is faced with a horizontal supply curve for resource A at a level equal to its market price. The monopolist will employ the resource up to the point at which it is maximizing its profits with respect to it. At this point, marginal revenue product of the resource is equal to its price. The market level of employment of the resource is the summation of all individual firm employment levels, whether those firms be monopolists, pure competitors, oligopolists, or monopolistic competitors.

When the monopolist is maximizing profits with respect to each variable resource used, those resources will necessarily be used in a least-cost combination. Suppose that A and B are the only two variable resources used by a monopolist producing product X. When profits are maximized with respect to A, then

$$MPP_a \times MR_x = p_a \qquad (14.1)$$

Similarly, maximization of profits with respect to B means

$$MPP_b \times MR_x = p_b \qquad (14.2)$$

Consequently

$$\frac{MPP_a}{p_a} = \frac{MPP_b}{p_b} = \frac{1}{MC_x} = \frac{1}{MR_x} \qquad (14.3)$$

Monopolistic Exploitation of a Resource

Monopoly in a product market is said to result in exploitation of resources used by the monopolist. In this respect exploitation means that units of a resource are paid less than the value of the product that they add to the economy's output. A monopolist employs that quantity of a resource at which its price equals its marginal revenue product — marginal physical product multiplied by marginal revenue from the sale of the product. But the value of product added to the economy's output by a unit of the resource is its value of marginal product — marginal physical product multiplied by price per unit at which the product is sold. Marginal revenue product of the resource to a particular firm facing a downward sloping product demand curve is less than value of marginal product of the resource since marginal revenue is less than product price in such cases. Hence, the prices paid resources used by monopolistic firms are less than the values of the products which they add to the economy's output.

Nevertheless, the price paid a resource must be equal to what it can earn in alternative employments. Exploitation does not mean that the monopolist pays units of the resource less than do competitive firms hiring units of the same resource. Exploitation under monopoly occurs because the monopolist, faced by the market price of the resource, stops short of the employment level at which value of marginal product of the resource equals resource price. Units of the resource contribute more to the value of the economy's output when employed by the monopolist than they do when employed by the purely competitive firm, but they are paid the same price in each market situation. Thus, market forces will not induce resources to move into their more valuable uses.

MONOPSONY IN THE BUYING OF RESOURCES

A resource market situation in which there is a single buyer of a particular resource is called one of *monopsony*.[3] A monopsonistic situation contrasts directly with the situation of pure competition among resource buyers which we have heretofore assumed exists. Two additional resource market situations can be distinguished. The first is oligopsony, in which there are a few buyers of a particular resource which may or may not be differentiated. One buyer takes a large enough proportion of the total supply of the resource to be able to influence the market price of the resource. The second situation is one of monopsonistic competition. Here, there are many buyers of a particular kind of resource, but there is differentiation within the resource category which causes particular buyers to prefer the resource of one seller to that of another. Our

---

[3] The term *monopsony* is applied also to cases in which there is a single buyer of a particular product; however, our discussion will be confined to monopsony in resource markets.

analysis will center around monopsony — one buyer of a particular resource — but it may be applied also to oligopsony and to monopsonistic competition.

Resource Supply Curves and Marginal Resource Costs

As the only buyer of a particular resource, the monopsonist faces the market supply curve for the resource. This means that ordinarily the monopsonist faces an upward sloping supply curve for the resource. A producer who furnishes virtually the entire source of employment in an isolated area would be in this position — in the short run, at least. Contrast this with the resource supply curve faced by the firm that buys a resource under conditions of pure competition. Under pure competition the firm can get as many units of the resource per unit of time as it desires at the going market price; hence it is faced with a horizontal or perfectly elastic resource supply curve even though the market supply curve may be upward sloping to the right or less than perfectly elastic.

The upward slope of the resource supply curve faced by the monopsonist gives monopsony the characteristics that distinguish it from pure competition. To obtain larger quantities of the resource per unit of time, the monopsonist must pay higher prices per unit. Columns 1 and 2 of Table 14–2 present a portion of a typical resource supply schedule illustrating this situation. Column 3 shows the total cost of resource A to the firm for different quantities purchased. Column 4 shows marginal resource cost of A to the firm.

Marginal resource cost is defined as the change in the firm's total cost resulting from a one-unit change in the purchase of the resource per unit of time. When the resource supply curve faced by the firm is upward sloping to the right, marginal resource cost will be greater than the resource price for any quantity purchased by the firm. This can be explained with reference to Table 14–2. Suppose the firm increases the

TABLE 14–2

(1) QUANTITY OF A	(2) RESOURCE PRICE (p_a)	(3) TOTAL RESOURCE COST (TC_a)	(4) MARGINAL RESOURCE COST (MRC_a)
10	$0.60	$6.00	——
11	0.65	7.15	$1.15
12	0.70	8.40	1.25
13	0.75	9.75	1.35

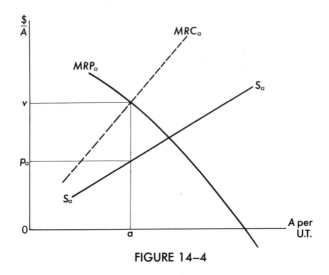

FIGURE 14–4

quantity of *A* which it purchases from ten units to eleven units. The eleventh unit costs the firm $0.65. However, in order to obtain eleven units per unit of time the firm must pay $0.65 per unit for *all eleven units*. Therefore the cost of obtaining the other ten units has increased from $0.60 to $0.65 per unit. An additional cost of $0.50 is incurred on the ten. Add this to the $0.65 which the eleventh unit costs and the increase in the firm's total cost is $1.15. The marginal resource cost of the twelfth and thirteenth units can be computed in a similar way.[4]

A graphic illustration of the resource supply curve and the marginal resource cost curve faced by a monopsonist is shown in Figure 14–4. The market supply curve for resource *A* is S_aS_a. The marginal resource cost curve is MRC_a and lies above the supply curve. It may be helpful to note that the marginal resource cost curve bears the same relationship to the supply curve that a marginal cost curve bears to an average cost curve. In fact, the market supply curve of resource *A* is the average cost curve of resource *A* alone and the marginal resource cost curve is the marginal cost curve of resource *A* alone. Obviously then, if the supply (average cost) curve of *A* is increasing, the marginal resource cost (marginal cost) curve must lie above it.[5]

---

[4] Marginal resource cost to the firm buying under conditions of pure competition is equal to the price of the resource. Since the firm can purchase as much as it desires at a constant price per unit, each additional unit adds an amount to the firm's total cost equal to the resource price.

[5] See pages 139–140.

Pricing and Employment of a Single Resource

Profit maximization with respect to resource A follows the same general principles for the monopsonist as for firms buying resources competitively. Larger quantities of A per unit of time will be purchased if they add more to the firm's total receipts than to its total costs. Additions to the monopsonist's total receipts as more A is employed are shown by the curve MRP_a in Figure 14–4. Additions to total cost are shown by the marginal resource cost curve. Profits are maximized when quantity a of the resource is employed. Larger quantities of A would add more to total cost than to total receipts and would cause profits to decline. We can state the profit-maximizing conditions in equation form. When the monopsonist's profits are maximized, he employs that quantity of A at which

$$MRP_a = MRC_a$$

or

$$MPP_a \times MR_x = MRC_a$$

The monopsonist deviates from the competitive buyer of resources with respect to the price paid for the resource at the profit maximizing level of employment. For quantity a of the resource it is necessary for the monopsonist to pay a price of p_a only, although the marginal revenue product of the resource at that level of employment is v. Should the monopsonist employ that quantity of A at which its marginal revenue product is equal to its price — as does the competitive resource buyer — he would make less profit. To maximize his profits he restricts the quantity of the resource used and pays it a price per unit less than its marginal revenue product. The important consideration for profit maximization is the employment of that quantity at which marginal resource cost equals marginal revenue product — and for the monopsonist resource price is less than marginal resource cost. Monopsony profits, resulting from the excess of the marginal revenue product of the resource over its price per unit, are equal to $p_a v \times a$.

Simultaneous Employment of Several Variable Resources

The conditions that must be met by the monopsonist if he is to employ least-cost combinations of variable resources for given outputs differ somewhat from those applying to purely competitive resource buyers. As before, the least-cost combination for the monopsonist is that combination at which the marginal physical product per dollar's worth of one resource is equal to the marginal physical product per

dollar's worth of every other resource. The difference between the monopsonistic and the competitive buyer rests upon what constitutes the
marginal physical product per dollar's worth of a resource.

An illustration should clear the air. Suppose a coal-mining firm
buys miners' labor monopsonistically. At the current level of employment a single miner's labor adds a ton of coal per day to the firm's output. This is the marginal physical product of the miner's labor. It adds
$20 to the firm's total costs. This is the marginal resource cost of the
miner's labor, and it exceeds the daily wage rate. The addition made to
the firm's total product per additional dollar's expenditure on labor is
1/20 of a ton of coal, or is equal to MPP_l/MRC_l. The same calculation
applies to any other resource purchased monopsonistically. The marginal
physical product per dollar's worth of any resource is found by dividing
its marginal physical product by its marginal resource cost.

If a firm purchases variable resources A and B monopsonistically,
to achieve the least-cost combination for a given output it must use them
in such proportions that

$$\frac{MPP_a}{MRC_a} = \frac{MPP_b}{MRC_b}$$

The reciprocal of either or both of the fractions in the equation represents marginal cost of the product at whatever output the firm is producing. A unit of A used adds an amount MRC_a to total cost and an
amount MPP_a to total product. Therefore the addition to total cost per
unit increase in output is MRC_a/MPP_a. Similarly, marginal cost of the
product in terms of resource B is MRC_b/MPP_b.

Suppose that initially the monopsonist is using too little of A and
B for profit maximization but is using the least-cost combination for the
product output he is producing. Marginal cost of the product is less than
marginal revenue from its sale. These conditions can be summed up as
follows:

$$\frac{MPP_a}{MRC_a} = \frac{MPP_b}{MRC_b} = \frac{1}{MC_x} > \frac{1}{MR_x}$$

Profit maximization requires employment of greater quantities of the
variable resources per unit of time. This will increase output and decrease
marginal revenue received from the product. Additional quantities of A
and B cause the marginal physical products of both resources to decline.
At the same time marginal resource costs of A and B increase. Thus

marginal cost of the product to the firm rises as a result of two forces working simultaneously — declining marginal physical products and rising marginal resource costs. Additional quantities of A and B will be employed per unit of time until marginal cost equals marginal revenue. At this point the resources are used in the correct absolute quantities as well as in the least-cost proportions. The conditions necessary for profit maximization can be stated as follows:

$$\frac{MPP_a}{MRC_a} = \frac{MPP_b}{MRC_b} = \frac{1}{MC_x} = \frac{1}{MR_x}$$

The conditions necessary for profit maximization by the monopsonist also can be established from consideration of resources A and B individually. Resource A should be used up to the point at which

$$MPP_a \times MR_x = MRC_a, \quad \text{or} \quad \frac{MPP_a}{MRC_a} = \frac{1}{MR_x} \qquad (14.4)$$

Likewise, resource B should be used up to the point at which

$$MPP_b \times MR_x = MRC_b, \quad \text{or} \quad \frac{MPP_b}{MRC_b} = \frac{1}{MR_x} \qquad (14.5)$$

From (14.4) and (14.5) we can write

$$\frac{MPP_a}{MRC_a} = \frac{MPP_b}{MRC_b} = \frac{1}{MC_x} = \frac{1}{MR_x} \qquad (14.6)$$

The profit-maximizing conditions set forth above for the monopsonist are general enough to apply to all classifications of both product sellers' markets and resource buyers' markets. Under conditions of pure competition in resource buying, MRC_a and MRC_b become P_a and P_b, respectively. Under conditions of pure competition in product selling, MR_x becomes P_x.

Conditions Giving Rise to Monopsony

Monopsonistic situations result from either or both of two basic causes. First, monopsonistic purchases of a resource may occur when units of the resource are specialized to a particular user. This means that marginal revenue product of the resource in the specialized use is enough higher than it is in any alternative employments in which it conceivably can be used to eliminate the alternative employments from the consideration of resource suppliers. Thus, the resource supply curve facing the monopsonist will be the market supply curve of the resource and usually will be upward sloping to the right. The more he is willing to pay for the resource the greater will be the quantity placed on the market.

A situation of the kind described may occur when a special type of skilled labor is developed to meet certain needs of a particular firm. The higher the wage rate offered for the special category of labor, the more individuals there will be who are willing to undergo the necessary training to develop it. No other firm utilizes labor with this or similar skills; consequently, once trained, the alternatives facing the workers are to work for the particular firm or to work elsewhere at jobs where their marginal revenue products and their wage rates are significantly lower.

Specialization of resources to a particular user is not confined to the labor field. A large aircraft or automobile manufacturer may depend upon a number of suppliers to furnish certain parts used by no other manufacturer. In the tightest possible case, such suppliers sell their entire outputs to the manufacturer, and complete monopsony by the manufacturer exists. Given time, the suppliers may be able to convert production facilities to supply other types of parts to other manufacturers, and the degree of monopsony enjoyed by the one may be decreased correspondingly.

Special monopsonistic cases occur in the field of entertainment. Performers are placed under contract by particular users and are then no longer free to work for alternative employers. Major league baseball players fall in this category. Under the well-known reserve clause, once signed to play for a particular team, a player either accepts the best salary terms he can get from that employer or he is not allowed to play in the major leagues at all. He cannot transfer from one major league team to another of his own volition, although his contract can be sold by his employer to another team.

The second condition from which monopsony may stem is lack of mobility on the part of certain resources. It is not necessary that resources in general be immobile. It is only necessary that mobility out of certain areas or away from certain firms be lacking, creating particular monopsonistic situations. Various forces may hold workers in a particular community or to a particular firm. Among these are emotional ties to community and friends, together with a fear of the unknown. Ignorance regarding alternative employment opportunities may exist. Funds may not be sufficient to permit job seeking in and movement to alternative job areas. Seniority and pension rights accumulated with a particular firm may make workers reluctant to leave. Specific cases of immobility among firms within a given geographic area may result from agreements among employers not to "pirate" each other's work forces.

Monopsonistic Exploitation of a Resource

Monopsony in the purchase of a resource also is said to result in exploitation of that resource. Monopsonistic exploitation can be understood best by comparison of monopsony with pure competition in resource buying. Under a purely competitive situation each firm will add to its profits by taking larger quantities of the resource up to the point at which the marginal revenue product of the resource is equal to the resource price. The resource receives a price per unit equal to what any one unit of it contributes to the firm's total receipts.[6]

In contrast, the monopsonist maximizes profits by stopping short of the resource employment level at which marginal revenue product of the resource is equal to its price per unit. This is shown in Figure 14-4. The profit-maximizing level of employment is that at which marginal revenue product equals marginal resource cost. Since marginal resource cost exceeds resource price, so does marginal revenue product of the resource. Hence units of the resource are paid less than what any one of them contributes to the total receipts of the firm. This is called monopsonistic exploitation of the resource. The monopsonist restricts the quantity of the resource used and holds down its price.

Measures to Counteract Monopsony

What can be done to counteract monopsonistic exploitation of resources? Two alternatives will be considered. First, administered or fixed minimum resource prices can be used. Second, measures successful in increasing resource mobility will reduce the monopsonistic power of particular resource users.

MINIMUM RESOURCE PRICES • Minimum resource prices can be established by the government or by organized groups of resource suppliers. The typical monopsonistic situation is pictured in Figure 14–5. The level of employment of resource A is quantity a. Its price per unit is p_a; however, marginal revenue product is v and the resource is being exploited. Suppose a minimum price is set at p_{a1} and that the firm must pay a price of at least p_{a1} per unit for all units purchased. Should the firm want more than a_1 units, it faces the mn sector of the resource supply curve. The entire supply curve now faced by the firm will be $p_{a1}mn$.

---

[6] Monopolistic exploitation will occur if the resource-buying firms face downward sloping product demand curves, but there is no monopsonistic exploitation.

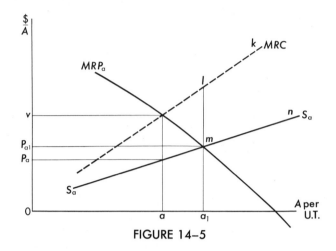

FIGURE 14–5

The alteration in the resource supply curve facing the firm alters also the marginal resource cost curve. For quantities between zero and a_1, each additional unit of A employed per unit of time will add an amount equal to p_{a1} to the firm's total costs. The new marginal resource cost curve coincides with $p_{a1}m$, the new supply curve, out to quantity a_1. For quantities greater than a_1, the regular supply curve mn is the relevant one and the corresponding sector of the marginal resource cost curve becomes lk. The altered marginal resource cost curve is $p_{a1}mlk$. At quantity a_1 it is discontinuous between m and l.

The quantity of A that the firm should use now to maximize profits will differ from the quantity used before the minimum price was set. The firm should use quantity a_1 at which the new marginal resource cost is equal to marginal revenue product of A. The minimum price not only eliminates monopsonistic exploitation of the resource; it increases the level of employment in the process.

The above analysis assumes that the minimum price of resource A is set at just the correct level to counteract monopsony completely. Such precision may or may not be accomplished. However, any minimum price between p_a and p_{a1} will counteract monopsony to some extent. The nearer to p_{a1} the price is set the more nearly will exploitation be eliminated. Prices set between p_{a1} and v will counteract exploitation also, but the counteraction will be at the expense of employment. Unemployment will occur, since at any price level above p_{a1} resource sellers will want to put more on the market than buyers are willing to buy.

Counteraction of monopsony by price regulation will at best be a difficult job. The precise price level at which monopsony is offset completely will be hard to determine. In the labor field — where monopsony is most publicized — minimum-wage laws may be the counteracting device used. However, different degrees of monopsony for different kinds of labor and for different situations make blanket price fixing of this type impractical as an over-all monopsonistic offset. Collective bargaining on a firm-by-firm basis could more nearly meet and offset individual monopsonistic cases. Even here the problem of determining — leaving aside the difficulty of obtaining — the "correct" minimum price for the resource remains.

MEASURES TO INCREASE MOBILITY • Measures to increase resource mobility among alternative employments get at the causes of monopsony. Immobility of resources is thought by many economists to be most serious in labor markets; hence our discussion will be centered upon the labor resource. We shall present a few general lines of approach rather than specific and detailed programs. With regard to the labor resource, mobility among geographic areas and firms, horizontal mobility among occupations at the same skill level, and vertical occupational mobility to higher skill classifications will be of value.

An efficient system of federal employment exchanges should provide one avenue of attack on labor immobility. An important function of such a system would be collection and dissemination of information regarding alternative employment opportunities. It should make available to the entire labor force — including those in now isolated communities — data with regard to high-wage, scarce-labor-supply areas including descriptions of the requisite skills for obtaining employment in such areas. In addition, the system should perform the more common function of bringing together job opportunities and workers seeking alternative jobs.

The educational system offers a second avenue of attack. It can increase both the vertical mobility and the horizontal mobility of labor resources. With regard to vertical mobility, the availability and use of educational opportunities can channel larger numbers of the younger generation toward the higher paying, higher level occupations. Through such devices as night schools the educational system can provide older workers with the training necessary for upward movement through skill classifications. With regard to horizontal mobility, vocational guidance can assist in steering the potential labor force away from lower paying occupations toward those providing higher remuneration. Additionally, adult education programs can furnish the retraining necessary to escape from particular low-paying occupations.

Still a third line of attack is that of a limited amount of subsidization of worker migration out of areas characterized by monopsony, since one of the causes of immobility is lack of funds needed to move into alternative employment areas. Subsidization of migration may occur in the form of government loans or outright grants of funds to assist in worker relocation. Such a system could, of course, be subject to considerable abuse unless adequate safeguards were developed.

The Concept of Mobility

A few observations regarding the meaning of mobility are in order lest we obtain a wrong impression with regard to it. To some people, reference to a mobile labor force may imply reference to a drifting labor force — an undesirable social situation. Mobility, as the term is used in economics, does not mean a complete lack of ties to particular communities and social institutions, nor does it mean that all workers must be ready to pack up and move at the slightest provocation. The amount of actual movement necessary to prevent monopsony from occurring usually will be quite small. The possibility or the likelihood of migration is the important factor. Also, there is at all times considerable change and turnover of the labor force — workers changing jobs, new workers entering the labor force, and old workers retiring from the labor force. This constitutes mobility. The primary problem is that of directing the mobility which already exists into economically desirable channels.

SUMMARY

Analysis of resource pricing and employment in situations other than pure competition requires modification of the principles established in the preceding chapter. Monopoly in product markets alters the nature of individual firm demand curves for resources. Monopsony in the purchase of resources alters the nature of the resource supply curve faced by the firm.

The monopolistic firm employing several variable resources must determine the least-cost resource combinations for various possible outputs and must determine the profit-maximizing quantities of variable resources to use. The least-cost combination for a given product output is the one at which the marginal physical product per dollar's worth of one resource is equal to the marginal physical product per dollar's worth of every other resource used. To maximize profits the firm must use both a least-cost combination and the correct absolute amounts of each resource. Resources must be used so that

$$\frac{MPP_a}{p_a} = \frac{MPP_b}{p_b} = \cdots\cdots\cdots = \frac{MPP_n}{p_n} = \frac{1}{MC_x} = \frac{1}{MR_x}$$

Monopoly in product markets is said to result in monopolistic exploitation of resources, since resource price equals its marginal revenue product for the firm and is less than the value of its marginal product for the economy as a whole.

Market price and the employment level of a resource are determined simultaneously. Where monopoly occurs in product markets, marginal revenue product of each variable resource used must be equal to its price if profits are to be maximized. If the monopolist uses only one variable resource, the marginal revenue product curve of the resource is the firm's demand curve for it. If several variable resources are used, internal or firm effects of price changes in any given resource must be taken into account in determining the firm's demand curve for it. The market demand curve for a resource is obtained by summing the quantities of it that all firms will employ at each possible price, whether those firms operate as monopolists or as pure competitors in selling products. Resource price is determined by the conditions of market demand and market supply. As market price is established, the firm adjusts employment of the resource to the level at which marginal revenue product equals the resource price. The market employment level is the summation of individual firm employment levels.

Monopsony means a single buyer of a particular resource; hence the monopsonist faces a resource supply curve that slopes upward to the right. He also faces a marginal resource cost curve that lies above the supply curve. He maximizes profits by employing that quantity of the resource which equates its marginal revenue product to its marginal resource cost. Marginal resource cost and marginal revenue product of the resource exceed the resource price at the profit-maximizing level of employment, thus resulting in monopsonistic exploitation of the resource.

To maximize profits with several variable resources purchased monopsonistically, the firm must employ the correct resource combination and the correct absolute quantities of those resources. The necessary conditions can be stated as follows:

$$\frac{MPP_a}{MRC_a} = \frac{MPP_b}{MRC_b} = \cdots\cdots\cdots = \frac{MPP_n}{MRC_n} = \frac{1}{MC_x} = \frac{1}{MR_x}$$

These conditions apply to profit maximization under all classifications of both product and resource markets.

Monopsony stems from two basic causes: (1) specialization of resources to particular users, and (2) immobility of resources employed in certain localities and by particular firms. Monopsony can be counteracted in either of two ways. First, establishment of minimum prices for the resource above the monopsonistic price will bring marginal revenue product and the resource price closer to each other. Second, measures designed to increase mobility of resources from monopsonistic areas and firms may assist in breaking down those monopsonistic situations.

SUGGESTED READINGS

Nicholls, William H. *Imperfect Competition within Agricultural Industries*. Ames: The Iowa State College Press, 1941, Introduction and chaps. 1–3.

Robinson, Joan. *The Economics of Imperfect Competition*. London: Macmillan & Co., Ltd., 1933, chaps. 25 and 26.

Resource Allocation | 15

AN IMPORTANT FUNCTION performed by resource prices in a free enterprise economy is that of allocating resources among different uses and different geographic areas. Ordinarily this will be done in such a way as to increase the efficiency of the economy. If a high level of want satisfaction is to be attained in the economy, constant reallocation of resources must occur in response to changes in human wants, changes in the kinds and quantities of resources available, and changes in available techniques of production. In developing the principles of resource allocation we shall discuss first the concept of resource markets. Next we shall consider the conditions of resource allocation leading to maximum efficiency in resource use. Third, we shall examine certain factors that prevent resources from being correctly allocated.

RESOURCE MARKETS

The extent of a resource market depends upon the nature of the resource under consideration and upon the time span relevant to the problem at hand. Within a given time span some resources are more mobile than others and, consequently, their markets tend to be larger. Mobility depends upon a number of things — shipping costs, perishability, social forces, and the like — and resources differ with respect to these characteristics.

Ordinarily, the mobility of any given resource depends upon the time span under consideration. Over a short period of time its mobility will be more limited than will be the case over a longer period of time. Labor of a certain kind — say, machinists — will furnish as clear an example as any. Over a short time period of a few months, or perhaps of a year, machinists of the United States will not move freely from one geographic area to another, although they may be fairly free to move from one employer to another within a single locality. The longer the period of time under consideration the larger the geographic area within which they are free to move. Over a period of twenty-five years they may be fairly mobile through the entire economy.[1]

For short periods of time all the machinists or all the units of any other resource in the economy do not necessarily operate in the same market. We can divide the economy into a number of submarkets, each submarket being the area within which a certain group is mobile in the given time span. The longer the time span considered, the greater the interconnections among the submarkets. Over a sufficiently long period the submarkets tend to fuse into a single market.

The submarkets for a resource tend to be conceptual rather than real in the sense that boundaries between submarkets are blurred. Each submarket overlaps others. But if we think of them as being separate and apart from each other, we can make better progress with the analysis of resource allocation. Also, in place of the whole continuum of time periods we shall act as though there were only two: (1) a short period during which the submarkets for a given resource are separate, and (2) the long period in which resources have sufficient time to move freely among the submarkets and the submarkets in reality are fused into a single market.

THE CONDITIONS OF MAXIMUM EFFICIENCY

Since maximum efficiency in resource use would tend to occur in purely competitive product markets and resource markets, we shall assume for the present that pure competition prevails. The allocation of any given resource that provides greatest efficiency in its use will be called the correct allocation. When resources are not correctly allocated, net national product is below its potential maximum. This malallocation automatically sets in motion the forces necessary to reallocate resources in such a way that net national product and the efficiency of the economy are increased. First we shall discuss short-period allocation of a resource within a given submarket. Then we shall expand the discussion to include long-period allocation among submarkets or over the entire economy.

Allocation within a Given Submarket

When units of a resource are so allocated that the value of marginal product in one use is greater than it is in other uses, the allocation is incorrect from the point of view of economic efficiency. They would be more valuable to society in the higher value of marginal product use,

---

[1] Mobility does not require the physical transference of a machinist from one area to another or even from one employer to another. As old machinists retire from the work force and as new machinists enter, mobility can exist. In certain areas the retiring machinists may not be replaced. In other areas the number of entrants to the trade may exceed retirements. This constitutes mobility.

and if units were transferred from the lower to the higher value of marginal product uses the total value of the economy's output would be increased. Suppose, for example, that any one tractor used on a farm contributes $2000 worth of farm products per year to the economy's output, and that the same tractor used in construction can increase other products produced by $3000 worth per year. The economy would gain $1000 worth of product if a tractor were switched from farming to construction work, and a better allocation of tractors would therefore exist.

Resource prices furnish the mechanism for reallocation when resources are incorrectly allocated. Firms in which the value of marginal product of a given resource is lower are not willing to pay more for it than its value of marginal product. On the other hand, firms in which its value of marginal product is higher can increase profits by expanding the quantity employed. The latter firms bid the resource price above its value of marginal product in the former firms, and resource owners, seeking maximum income, transfer resource units from the lower-paying to the higher-paying uses.[2] As units of the resource are transferred, its value of marginal product decreases in the employments to which it is transferred and increases in the employments from which it is transferred. The transfer continues until its value of marginal product is equalized in all its uses and all firms in the submarket pay a price per unit equal to its value of marginal product. At this point, the resource is correctly allocated and, within the submarket, makes its maximum contribution to net national product.

To illustrate in more detail the role of resource prices in allocating resources among different uses, suppose firms of two different industries, producing X and Y, in the same submarket use a particular resource A. Suppose initially that units of A are correctly allocated among firms of the two industries. The value of marginal product of A in firms of the industry producing X (V of MP_{ax}) is equal to the value of marginal product of A in firms of the industry producing Y (V of MP_{ay}). Suppose further that there is neither a surplus nor a shortage of A on the market, so that

$$V \text{ of } MP_{ax} = V \text{ of } MP_{ay} = p_a$$

or

$$MPP_{ax} \times p_x = MPP_{ay} \times p_y = p_a$$

where p_a is the price per unit of resource A, and p_x and p_y are the respective prices of product X and product Y.

---

[2] New resource units just entering the market — say, college graduates — may be attracted to the jobs offering the higher pay. This, together with the failure to replace resource units retired from the market in the lower paying employments, provides an important method of transfer.

Suppose an increase occurs in the market demand for commodity X while demand for commodity Y remains unchanged. The level of aggregate demand remains constant, and the increase in demand for X is offset by decreases in demand for commodities other than X and Y. The price of X rises, thereby increasing V of MP_{ax}. Resource A has become more valuable to society in the production of X than it is in the production of Y. At price p_a for the resource, employers in the industry producing X find that a shortage of A exists. Consequently, they will bid up the price of A enough to cause owners of A to transfer units of it from the industry producing Y to the industry producing X. As the quantity of A employed by firms in the industry producing X increases relative to the quantities of other resources employed, MPP_{ax} declines. As the output of X increases, p_x declines. Thus, V of MP_{ax} declines.

Changes within the industry producing Y will accompany the changes in the industry producing X. As units of A are transferred from the production of Y to X the proportions of A to other resources used by firms in the industry producing Y decrease and MPP_{ay} increases. Smaller amounts of Y are produced and sold; consequently, p_y rises. Increases in MPP_{ay} and in p_y increase V of MP_{ay}.

Reallocation of A from the production of Y to X continues until units of the resource are again correctly distributed between the two industries. Units of A move from the industry producing Y to the industry producing X until the V of MP_{ax} has gone down enough and the V of MP_{ay} has gone up enough for the two to be equal. The new price per unit of A will be somewhat higher than the old price since its value of marginal product is now higher in both industries than it was previously.

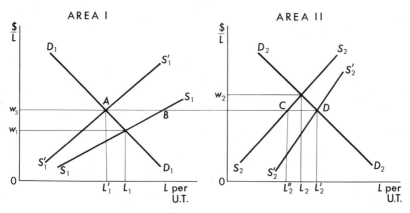

FIGURE 15–1

In bidding against each other for the available supply of A, firms in both industries have raised the price of A to the level of its value of marginal product in both uses.

Resource A again will be making its maximum contribution to net national product. When V of MP_{ax} was greater than V of MP_{ay}, every movement of a unit of A from the industry producing Y to the industry producing X increased A's contribution to net national product. Withdrawal of a unit of A from the industry producing Y decreased A's contribution to net national product by an amount equal to V of MP_{ay}. Placing the unit of A to work in the industry producing X increased A's contribution to net national product by V of MP_{ax}. Hence a net gain in A's contribution to net national product resulted from such transfers until A's value of marginal product was once more equalized among firms in the two industries.

Allocation among Submarkets

The analysis can be extended by increasing the time span under consideration and by joining short-period with long-period analysis. By way of simplification we shall limit ourselves to two resources: (1) a certain kind of labor, and (2) capital. The total supply of the kind of labor involved is a small proportion of the economy's total supply of all kinds of labor, and all units of it are homogeneous. Capital is fixed in specific forms and is immobile for the short period, but over the long period it is mobile, can change its form, and can be reallocated from one use to others.[3]

ALLOCATION OF LABOR • Suppose that Area I and Area II constitute separate and almost identical short-period submarkets initially. The products produced in the two submarkets are the same, capital facilities are the same, and their labor demand curves, D_1D_1 and D_2D_2 in Figure 15–1, are the same. However, labor supplies for the two areas differ.

---

[3] Capital is usually thought of in two contexts: (1) as concrete agents of production, and (2) as a fluid stock of productive capacity. The first context is a short-run concept with capital taking such specific forms as buildings, machinery, wheatland, and so on. The second is a long-run concept. Concrete pieces of equipment have time to wear out and be replaced. But replacement of the same kind and in the same place does not necessarily occur. Replacement can take place in the form of new and different kinds of concrete agents. In agriculture, horse-drawn machinery was allowed to depreciate as the use of tractors became widespread and special machinery adapted to the tractor gradually took its place. Or capital may flow from one industry to another and from one location to another through depreciation in the one and the building of new equipment in the other. Thus while capital may be almost completely immobile in the short run, in the long run it becomes quite mobile. See Frank H. Knight, *On the History and Method of Economics* (Chicago: The University of Chicago Press, 1956), pp. 56–57.

Area I has a larger labor supply than Area II; so the labor supply curve S_1S_1 of Area I lies farther to the right than that of Area II.

Labor is malallocated and its maldistribution causes its value of marginal product and its price to differ between the two areas. The price of labor, or the wage rate, in Area I will be w_1, and in Area II it will be w_2. The level of employment in Area II is L_2 while that in Area I is higher at L_1. The higher ratio of labor to capital in Area I causes the marginal physical product and value of marginal product of labor to be lower in that area. The reverse holds in Area II. The ratio of labor to capital is smaller; consequently, the marginal physical product and value of marginal product of labor are higher.

The disparate submarket prices for labor furnish the incentive for long-period movement or reallocation of labor from Area I to Area II, and reallocation tends to eliminate the wage differential. As workers leave Area I, the short-period supply curve for that submarket shifts to the left. As they enter Area II, its short-period supply curve shifts to the right. As the ratio of labor to capital declines in Area I, labor's value of marginal product and the wage rate increase. In Area II the increasing ratio of labor to capital decreases labor's value of marginal product and the wage rate. Reallocation continues until wage rates of the two submarkets are equal at w_3. The labor supply curve of Area I is now $S_1'S_1'$ and that of Area II is $S_2'S_2'$.

The reallocation of labor between Area I and Area II increases net national product. Before movement began, the value of marginal product of labor in Area I was w_1. In Area II it was substantially higher at w_2. The movement of a unit of labor from Area I to Area II causes a loss of w_1 dollars' worth of product in Area I and a gain of almost w_2 dollars' worth of product in Area II. The gain in Area II more than offsets the loss in Area I and creates a net increase in total value of product produced in the economy. Each transfer of a unit of labor from Area I to Area II brings about such a net increase until the values of marginal product and the wage rates of labor are the same in the two areas. Labor is then correctly allocated between the two areas. No further transfer of labor in either direction can increase net national product, but will decrease it instead. Also, equalization of the wage rates will have removed the incentive for labor migration to occur.

ALLOCATION OF CAPITAL • The entire burden of adjustment will not be thrown on labor in the long period as the foregoing analysis suggests, but will be partly absorbed by reallocation of capital. The high ratio of labor to capital in Area I amounts to the same thing as a low ratio of capital to labor. Likewise, the low ratio of labor to capital in Area II means a high ratio of capital to labor. Therefore we would expect the value of marginal product of capital in Area I to exceed that in Area II. Differing productivities of capital and returns on investment between the two areas furnish the incentive for capital to migrate from Area II to Area I.

Long-period capital migration affects the short-period labor demand curves and the wage rates of the two areas. As units of capital leave Area II the demand curve (value of marginal product curve) for labor in that area shifts to the left, augmenting the decline in wage rates caused by the increasing labor supply. As units of capital enter Area I the demand curve for labor in Area I increases. The increases in demand join the decreases in supply in raising the wage rates of Area I. When the reverse migrations of labor and capital have been sufficient to equalize wage rates between the two areas and returns on investment between the two areas, both labor and capital will be correctly allocated. Further transfers of either resource in either direction will reduce the total value of product produced by the two submarkets combined.

FACTORS PREVENTING CORRECT ALLOCATION

A number of forces in the real world prevent the correct allocation of given resources from occurring. Even with the price system free to operate and with resource prices free to guide resource allocation, three important causes of incorrect allocation can be cited. These are monopoly in product markets, monopsony in resource markets, and certain nonprice impediments to resource movements. Additionally, direct interference with the price mechanism by the government or by private groups of resource owners and resource purchasers constitutes a cause of incorrect allocation. We shall consider the causes in turn. The term monopoly is used in a broad context to include pure monopoly, oligopoly, and monopolistic competition — all cases in which individual firms face downward sloping product demand curves. Similarly, the term monopsony is used broadly. Complete monopsony in resource purchases precludes any reallocation whatsoever. With less than complete monopsony, units of a given resource may be free to move among a limited number of buyers, any one of which can influence market price of the resource.

Monopoly

Monopoly in product markets may not affect all resource movements directly. Some resources may be free to move among alternative employers even though some of the firms employing them enjoy a degree of product monopoly. Steel, common labor, certain raw materials. and other resources are employed by many firms and may be free to flow from one to another without regard to the types of product market in which individual firms sell. Where price discrepancies for any such resource exist within or among submarkets, long-period reallocation of the resource tends to occur to the extent necessary to eliminate the discrepancies. Every firm in every submarket tends to employ that quantity of the resource at which its marginal revenue product equals the resource price. Reallocation tends to occur until the marginal revenue product and the price of the resource are the same in all its alternative employments.

Partially or completely blocked entry into monopolistic industries may prevent other resources from being so allocated that their respective marginal revenue products and prices are equalized as within and among submarkets. We can think of such resources as being inseparable from the existence of individual firms — they are certain ones of the short-run "fixed" resources. They can enter industries only in the form of plant for new firms. The existence of long-run profits for the firms in an industry indicates that the marginal revenue products of such resources are greater in that industry than they are elsewhere in the economy.

When some degree of product monopoly exists, net national product would not be maximized even though all resources were so allocated that the marginal revenue product of each is the same in all its alternative employments. Individual firms face downward sloping product demand curves and for each firm marginal revenue is less than product price. Thus for any given resource, value of marginal product in each of its uses would exceed marginal revenue product. But discrepancies would occur among the values of marginal products of the resource in its various uses even though its marginal revenue product were the same in all of them. This will be the case because of differing demand elasticities of the various products that the resource aids in producing. Differing demand elasticities mean that product prices and corresponding marginal revenues are not proportional to each other among the different products. Hence values of marginal products of the resource in its various uses are not proportional to its marginal revenue products. When the latter are equal the former will be unequal. Inequalities among values of marginal product of a resource in its various uses show that net national product could be increased by transferring units of the resource from lower value of marginal product uses to higher value of marginal product uses.

It is the *value of marginal product* of a resource that measures the contribution of a unit of it to the value of the economy's output — its marginal physical product multiplied by price of the final product. *Marginal revenue product* shows the contribution that a unit of the resource makes to the total receipts of a single firm, but where monopoly exists this is less than the value of the product added to the economy's output by the resource unit. Thus, when a resource is so allocated that its marginal revenue product is equalized in all alternative uses and when its price equals its marginal revenue product, the price system is through with its job. Even though further reallocation from lower value of marginal product uses to higher value of marginal product uses will increase net national product, there is no automatic motivation to make it occur.

Suppose that machinists in Detroit work both for firms selling as oligopolists and for firms selling as pure competitors. An automobile manufacturer furnishes an example of the former type of firm, whereas any one of the many small independent machine shops is an example of the latter. Suppose an equilibrium allocation of machinists exists — they are paid $2 per hour in all alternative employments. The small machine shop hires that quantity at which the value of marginal product of machinists is $2 per hour. The automobile manufacturer hires that quantity at which marginal revenue product equals $2 per hour. But since the automobile manufacturer faces a downward sloping product demand curve, value of marginal product of machinists employed by him exceeds their marginal revenue product. Value of marginal product may be $3 per hour. Society would gain in terms of net national product if some machinists would transfer from the small independent machine shops to automobile manufacturers. However, since both pay $2 per hour, the price system will not motivate the transfers.

Monopsony

The existence of monopsony in resource purchases also may prevent the correct allocation of given resources from occurring. Where some degree of monopsony is present, an individual firm purchases that quantity of the resource involved at which its marginal revenue product equals its marginal resource cost. When the resource supply curve to the firm slopes upward to the right, marginal resource cost exceeds the price which the firm pays the resource. Thus, when equilibrium for any single firm in the purchase of the resource is reached, the price paid the resource is below its marginal revenue product.

Differential prices of the resource guide its allocation among the few firms using it just as they did in the previous analysis. Voluntary reallocation of the resource will cease when its price is the same in its alternative uses. Resource owners will have no incentive to transfer units of it from one employment to another and an equilibrium allocation will have been achieved.

Even though an equilibrium allocation may be achieved and all firms pay the same price for the resource, it will not be making its maximum contribution to net national product. To the extent that the supply curves of the resource facing different firms have differing elasticities, marginal resource costs and marginal revenue products of the resource as among different firms will not be equal. Some degree of monopoly in product markets creates further distortions in the pattern of values of marginal products. Hence there is no reason for believing that the values of marginal products of the resource will be the same among its alternative employments even though it is everywhere paid the same price. About the most we can say on this point is that resource transfers from lower value of marginal product uses to higher value of marginal product uses would increase net national product, but since the resource price is the same in its alternative employments, resource owners will not make such transfers voluntarily.

Nonprice Impediments

IGNORANCE • Lack of knowledge on the part of resource owners may prevent resources from moving from lower-paying to higher-paying uses. In the most obvious case resource owners may lack information concerning the price patterns of the resources that they own over the economy as a whole. Bricklayers may not be aware of the areas and firms paying the highest wages for bricklayers. Farmers may sell products at unnecessarily low prices when they are not aware of higher prices which can be obtained elsewhere. Investors make mistakes when they lack knowledge of alternative investment opportunities throughout the economy.[4]

Lack of knowledge also may prevent potential resources from being channeled into the resource supply categories in which they will contribute most to net national product. Various kinds of labor resources will illustrate the point. For what trade or profession should potential entrants to the labor force be trained? Do those responsible for influencing or selecting the vocation possess full knowledge of the future returns to be derived from alternative vocations? Usually they do not. Sons may follow fathers as sharecroppers, or coal miners, when alternative occupations would be more lucrative. Or where sons do not follow fathers'

---

[4] The classic examples here are the many single proprietorships which fail in such fields as neighborhood grocery stores, eating and drinking establishments, and filling stations.

occupations, the information on which decisions are made is often sketchy. Frequently the potential entrant and his advisers do not discover until the training program is well advanced or completed that the choice of occupation has been an unfortunate one economically — and at this point it may be too late to change.

SOCIOLOGICAL AND PSYCHOLOGICAL IMPEDIMENTS • Sociological and psychological factors may throw blocks in the way of the allocation of resources that will maximize net national product.[5] They include those ties to particular communities, to friends, and to the family that restrict mobility regardless of the monetary incentives to move. Or the virtues of a particular occupation, community, or way of living may be so extolled by various social groups that mobility is restricted. Glorification of the family farm, or of southern California, or of the teaching profession may be cases in point.

INSTITUTIONAL FACTORS • Various institutional barriers to reallocation of resources are evident in the economy. In the industrial world workers accumulate rights of various kinds with particular firms. These include pension rights and seniority rights. In some cases labor unions may restrict entry directly into particular occupations. Patent rights held by one firm or a group of firms in an industry may block the entry of new firms into the industry and thus condemn quantities of certain resources to other occupations in which their values of marginal products and rates of pay are lower. The list can be extended considerably, but these serve to illustrate the point.

Interferences with the Price Mechanism

Sometimes the price mechanism is not allowed to perform its function of signaling the spots where quantities of certain resources should be transferred in or out. Some resource prices are fixed or controlled by the government. Control may be exercised through such devices as minimum-wage legislation, agricultural price supports, or the general price and wage controls so common during times of war. Some resource prices may be partially or completely controlled by organized private groups of resource owners and resource purchasers. Some labor unions fall within this category, as do certain farm marketing cooperatives and some employer associations. The hypothetical examples of this subsection illustrate some of the effects of controlled resource prices on the

---

[5] This is not to say that such blocks constitute mistakes on the part of society. The "good life" is not necessarily achieved through maximization of net national product. It may be desirable to sacrifice some product, in some instances, for the achievement of other objectives or values.

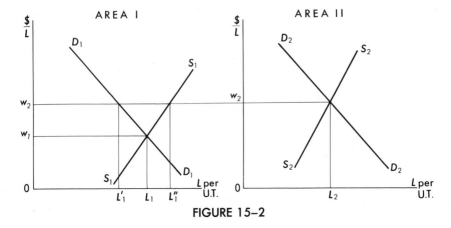

FIGURE 15–2

equilibrium allocation of resources and on net national product. We shall assume that in the absence of control pure competition would exist; however, even if some degree of monopoly in product markets were to exist, the results would be approximately the same.

Two submarkets for a given resource are shown in Figure 15–2. As a matter of convenience we shall call the resource labor. The two submarkets are essentially alike except for the initial distribution of labor. They produce the same products and have identical supplies of capital. The demand curves for labor are the same for each submarket. Since Area I has a greater labor supply than Area II, the short-period price of labor will be lower in Area I and the employment level will be higher. We shall consider three possible cases.

CASE I • Assume first of all that the workers of Area II are organized and that those of Area I are unorganized. In Figure 15–2 the initial labor demand and labor supply situations are shown. The equilibrium wage rate and employment level in Area I are w_1 and L_1, respectively. In Area II they are w_2 and L_2, respectively. Assume, further, that the organized workers, through collective bargaining, succeed in securing a wage rate of w_2 in Area II.

The immediate or short-period effects of the minimum-wage rate of w_2 in Area II will be nil. Since w_2 is initially the equilibrium wage rate in Area II, the union should have little difficulty in obtaining it. At that wage rate, employers of Area II are willing to employ as much labor as is willing to go to work. The wage differential between the two areas continues to reflect the existence of the initial maldistribution of labor.

The effects of the minimum-wage rate set in Area II are felt in the long period. The wage differential creates an incentive for workers to migrate from Area I to Area II. However, if additional workers were hired in Area II, the ratio of labor to capital would increase, the marginal physical product of labor would decrease, and the value of marginal product of labor would decrease. Since the wage rate of such additional workers would be w_2, and would exceed their values of marginal product, they would not be hired. Any workers migrating from Area I to Area II would find themselves unemployed and this prospect would keep migration from occurring. Employment in Area I at the lower wage rate of w_1 will be preferable to no employment at all in Area II, regardless of how high wage rates are in Area II. Labor will remain poorly allocated between the two areas and net national product will be held at a lower level than it would be otherwise.

This situation sets the stage for interesting repercussions with regard to capital. An incentive for capital to migrate in the long period will be present in this case, also. In fact, capital migration is the only adjustment in resource allocation which can occur. As capital migrates from Area II to Area I, demand for labor will decrease in Area II and will increase in Area I. This will increase wage rates and employment in Area I. However, unemployment will develop among the organized workers of Area II, and net national product will still be below its maximum potential level.[6]

CASE II • Assume that the organized workers of Area II suceed in extending their organization to Area I. Once Area I is organized assume that workers of the two areas can bring wage rates in Area I up to w_2 (Figure 15–2). Immediate short-period effects occur. There will be no effect on the employment level in Area II, initially. However, in Area I, unemployment amounting to $L_1'L_1''$ will occur. In Area I, at the old wage level of w_1, employment level L_1 equated value of marginal product of labor to the wage rate. The minimum-wage rate of w_2 makes the wage rate greater than the value of marginal product of labor at the old employment level of L_1. Employers find that a reduction in employment will decrease their total receipts by less than it reduces their total costs; hence workers are laid off. The decreasing ratio of labor to capital increases the value of marginal product of labor until, when only L_1' workers are employed, their value of marginal product is again equal to the wage rate. Here the layoffs will stop.

---

[6] The women's full-fashioned hosiery industry furnishes an excellent example of the migration of capital from high-cost union areas to low-cost nonunion areas. See Sumner H. Slichter, *Union Policies and Industrial Management* (Washington, D.C.: The Brookings Institution, 1941), pp. 353–360.

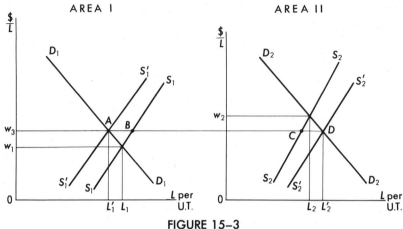

FIGURE 15-3

The long-period effects of the minimum-wage rate of w_2 will be approximately the same as the immediate effects. Since the wage differential is eliminated, there is no incentive for employed workers of Area I to migrate to Area II. Employers of Area II will not find it profitable to employ more workers than L_2 at a wage rate of w_2; hence unemployed workers of Area I will not find migration to Area II of any benefit.

With regard to capital, the minimum-wage rate of w_2 in Area I and the reduced ratio of labor to capital (increased ratio of capital to labor) eliminate the incentive for capital to migrate to Area I in the long period. The ratio of capital to labor in Area I is increased sufficiently by the worker layoffs to make the value of marginal product of capital in Area I equal to that in Area II.[7] Thus the minimum-wage rate of w_2 extended to both cities prevents the effects of the initial malallocation of resources from being alleviated by either labor migration or capital migration.

CASE III • A third possibility in which controlled resource prices may not affect resource allocation adversely deserves some consideration. Assume that both areas are organized or, alternatively, that the government sets a minimum-wage rate applicable to both. The wage rate is set through collective bargaining or by the government at level w_3 in Figure 15-3, that is, at precisely the level which would prevail in free markets in the long period after workers have had sufficient time to migrate. The

---

[7] Since the initial capital facilities and products produced in the two areas were assumed to be the same, the labor demand curves are also the same. At wage rate w_2 each market employs the same quantity of labor; i.e., L_1' units of labor equals L_2 units of labor in Figure 15-2. Consequently ratios of labor to capital in the two areas, when the wage rate for both is w_2, will be the same and so will the value of marginal product of capital.

initial demand and supply relationships are D_1D_1 and S_1S_1, respectively, in Area I. In Area II they are D_2D_2 and S_2S_2, respectively. In Area I the minimum wage rate of w_3 will cause unemployment equal to AB. In Area II, a labor shortage equal to CD would occur at wage rate w_3, so the wage rate in that submarket will rise to w_2.

Unemployment will assist the price system in reallocating labor from Area I to Area II in the long period. The unemployed and the lower paid workers of Area I will seek the higher paying jobs of Area II. The supply curve for labor in Area I will shift leftward to $S_1'S_1'$ and that of Area II will shift rightward to $S_2'S_2'$. Labor will be reallocated so that its value of the marginal product is equalized between the two submarkets and so that labor is making its maximum contribution to net national product.

Again some migration of capital from Area II to Area I may occur in the long period. At wage rate w_3 the initial employment level is L_1' in Area I and is greater than the initial employment level of L_2 in Area II. Therefore the ratio of capital to labor is smaller and the marginal revenue product of capital is greater in Area I than in Area II. Capital migration will reduce the demand for labor in Area II and will increase the demand for labor in Area I, thus reducing the amount of labor migration necessary to secure full employment and maximum net national product.

SUMMARY

Resource prices serve the function of allocating resources among different uses and different geographic areas. Resources are correctly allocated when they make their maximum contributions to net national product. In the long period, resources are more mobile among different employments and different geographic areas than they are in the short period.

Only if pure competition in product markets and resource markets were to prevail would resources be automatically allocated to maximize net national product. Under pure competition malallocation of any given resource causes its values of marginal products in different employments to differ from each other. Consequently, employers for whom its value of marginal product is higher bid resources away from those for whom its value of marginal product is lower. Transfers of resource units from lower to higher value of marginal product uses increase the contributions of the resource to net national product. Its maximum contribution occurs when value of marginal product of the resource is the same in all its possible uses. Price of the resource will also be the same in all its alternative uses; therefore no incentive will exist for further transfers to be made.

With some degree of monopoly in product markets a resource will be reallocated among its alternative uses until its price is the same in all of them. However, where employers are monopolists in some degree they employ those quantities of the resource at which its marginal revenue product equals its price. The marginal revenue products of the resource will be the same in alternative employments. Differing product demand elasticities cause values of marginal products of the resource to differ in the alternative employments. Thus, the resource does not make its maximum contribution to net national product.

Where employers have some degree of monopsony, but there is no resource differentiation a resource will again be reallocated until its price is the same in alternative employments. But a monopsonist employs the resource up to the point at which marginal revenue product equals marginal resource cost. The different monopsonists may face resource supply curves of differing elasticities and, if so, marginal resource cost will be different for each even though all pay the same price per unit for the resource. With the equilibrium allocation of the resource achieved, marginal revenue products differ. The usual case will be that differences in values of marginal product also occur, and the resource will not be making its maximum contribution to net national product.

Nonprice impediments to correct allocation of resources include ignorance, sociological and psychological factors, and institutional restrictions. In some instances the achievement of noneconomic values may be of more importance to society than correct resource allocation.

Direct interferences with the price mechanism by the government and by private groups may prevent resources from being correctly allocated in some cases. In other cases they may not lead to adverse effects.

SUGGESTED READINGS

CLARK, JOHN BATES. *The Distribution of Wealth.* New York: The Macmillan Company, 1923, chap. XIX.

PIGOU, A. C. *The Economics of Welfare.* 4th ed.; London: Macmillan & Co., Ltd., 1932, pt. III, chap. IX.

Product Distribution | 16

OF THE FOUR FUNCTIONS of an economic system with which we are concerned, we have yet to consider the distribution of the economy's product. In a free enterprise economy, product distribution depends upon income distribution and, since all of us tend to be preoccupied with our income shares, it is probably a matter closer to us as individuals than are the other three functions. The share of net national product that each individual can claim depends upon his income relative to those of other individuals in the economy. The principles of product distribution, then, are really the principles of income distribution. The chapter is divided into four parts — individual income determination, personal distribution of income, causes of income differences, and mitigation of income differences.

INDIVIDUAL INCOME DETERMINATION

The generally accepted principles of individual income determination and of income distribution are provided by marginal productivity theory. These principles have been met in previous chapters, but we shall draw them together and summarize them in this section. A distinction will be made among conditions of pure competition, both in product markets and in resource markets — monopoly in product markets, and monopsony in resource markets. First we shall note certain criticisms levied against marginal productivity theory; then we shall discuss its role in the determination of individual incomes.

Criticisms of Marginal Productivity Theory

Marginal productivity theory is sometimes criticized on two counts. In the first place, some refuse to accept it because they believe it attempts to justify or approve the existing income distribution — and they do not like the existing distribution. However, observation of how a free enterprise economy does in fact distribute income in no sense constitutes justification or approval of that distribution. If marginal productivity principles furnish the best available explanation of income determination and income distribution in a free enterprise economy, we should understand their operations whether or not we like their results. A clear understanding of how distribution occurs necessarily precedes any intelligent modification of it.

The second criticism is more serious. Some maintain that marginal productivity is not an adequate basis for income determination and distribution theory — that there is no close correlation between the remunerations received by resource owners and the values of marginal product or the marginal revenue products of the resources which they own. If these critics are correct, and can produce the evidence substantiating their criticisms, then marginal productivity must go by the board — as must most of the rest of the marginal analysis of economic activity. To date the necessary evidence has not been forthcoming and marginal productivity continues to occupy the center of distribution theory.

Income Determination

The principles of income determination where pure competition prevails, both in product markets and in resource markets, were developed in Chapter 13. The owner of a given resource is paid a price per unit for the units employed equal to the value of marginal product of the resource. However, the price of the resource is not determined by any single employer or by any single resource owner. It is determined by the interactions of all buyers and all sellers in the market for the resource.

If for some reason the price of a resource should be less than the value of its marginal product, a shortage will occur. Employers want more of it at that price than resource owners are willing to place on the market. Employers, bidding against each other for the available supply, will drive the price up until the shortage disappears and each is hiring (or buying) that quantity of the resource at which its value of marginal product equals its price.

A price high enough to create a surplus of the resource will set forces in motion to eliminate the surplus. Employers take only those quantities sufficient to equate its value of marginal product to its price. Resource owners undercut each other's prices to secure employment for their unemployed units. As price drops, employment expands. The undercutting continues until employers are willing to take the quantities that resource owners want to place on the market.

Where some degree of monopoly[1] exists in product markets, the foregoing principles will be altered to some extent. Monopolistic firms employ those quantities of the resource at which its marginal revenue product is equal to its price. Thus the price per unit received by owners of the resource is less than its value of marginal product, and the resource is exploited monopolistically.

Some degree of monopsony in the purchase of a given resource will cause it to be paid still less than its marginal revenue product. The monopsonist, faced with a resource supply curve sloping upward to the right, employs that quantity of the resource at which its marginal revenue product is equal to its marginal resource cost. Marginal resource cost is greater than the price paid for the resource. Monopsonistic exploitation of the resource occurs to the extent that its marginal revenue product exceeds its price. If the resource purchaser is also a monopolist, marginal revenue product of the resource in turn will be less than its value of marginal product, and the resource will be exploited monopolistically as well as monopsonistically.

As we noted in Chapter 2, an individual's income per unit of time is the sum of the amounts earned per unit of time by the various resources which he owns. If he owns a single kind of resource, his income will be equal to the number of units placed in employment multiplied by the price per unit which he receives for it. If he owns several kinds of resources, the income from each can be computed in the same manner. These can be totaled to determine his entire income.

PERSONAL DISTRIBUTION OF INCOME

Personal distribution of income refers to income distribution among spending units of the economy. We shall survey first the distribution of income by income sizes and then we shall point up certain problems involved in discussing income differences and income equality.

Distribution among Spending Units

Table 16–1 shows a simple picture of the distribution of income in the United States. It is not a refined picture, but it does give us in broad outline the spread of incomes over different income ranges and it shows us the income ranges within which the largest concentrations of spending units and money incomes occur. The lowest 11 percent of spending units received 2 percent of total income earned, and earned less than

---

[1] Again we use the term to refer to all cases in which the firm faces a downward sloping product demand curve. They include cases of pure monopoly, oligopoly, and monopolistic competition.

TABLE 16–1
DISTRIBUTION OF SPENDING UNITS AND TOTAL MONEY INCOME BEFORE TAXES, 1963

FAMILY PERSONAL INCOME	PERCENT OF FAMILIES	PERCENT OF INCOME
Under 2,000	11	2
2,000-3,999	18	7
4,000-5,999	20	13
6,000-7,999	18	17
8,000-9,999	12	14
10,000-14,999	13	21
15,000 and over	8	26
All Cases	100	100

SOURCE: U.S. Department of Labor, *Survey of Current Business* (April 1964), 4.

$2000 each in 1963. The highest 8 percent of spending units received 26 percent of the economy's income. Their incomes exceeded $14,999 each. But note the large proportions of spending units and income in the ranges between $4000 and $15,000 per year. Sixty-three percent of the spending units were within these ranges and received 65 percent of total 1963 income.

Income Equality and Income Differences

Any discussion of income distribution inevitably raises questions of justice or fairness. Questions of justice and fairness frequently are confused with questions of income equality or income differences. We shall side-step the issues of justice and fairness since these are ethical concepts not subject to objective measurement. They mean different things to different individuals, depending upon individual predilections and value judgments. However, it does appear offhand that equality or differences in incomes are subject to objective measurement.

Several methods have been devised for showing the degree of equality achieved in personal income distribution,[2] but usually these measure the degree of equality among spending units only. Spending units differ in size and composition; hence equality among spending units does not mean equality among individual persons.

[2] See Mary Jean Bowman, "A Graphic Analysis of Personal Income Distribution in the United States," *American Economic Review*, XXV (September, 1945), 607–628, reprinted in *Readings in the Theory of Income Distribution* (Philadelphia: The Blakiston Company, 1946), pp. 72–99.

With regard to size, spending units are composed either of unattached single individuals or of families. Family units vary in size from two persons up. Usually they include relatives living as members of the same household.

Differences in the compositions of spending units lead to further complications in assessing the extent of income differences. Variations in the ages of members occur among different spending units. Cultural differences exist. Differences in regional locations occur. These and other differences of a similar nature lead to differences in tastes and preferences among spending units and to differences in capacities to enjoy product consumption.

The difficulties encountered in trying to define and measure income equality or income differences will not be of major importance for our purposes. We are interested in the causes of differences rather than in their ethical implications. We shall have occasion to refer to "movements toward greater equality," but this should be accepted for what it is — a loose statement meaning some mitigation of income differences among heterogeneous spending units. It means some lopping off of the incomes at the top and some augmenting of incomes at the bottom. It does not mean that we can state with any precision the point at which income distribution will be "equalized."

CAUSES OF INCOME DIFFERENCES

With reference to the determinants of individual[3] incomes, it becomes clear that differences in incomes, arise from two basic sources: (1) differences in the kinds and quantities of resources owned by different individuals, and (2) differences in prices paid in different employments for units of any given resource. The former are the more fundamental. The latter arise from various types of interference with the price system in the performance of its functions and from any resource immobility which may occur.

It will be convenient to discuss labor resources and capital resources separately. To enable us to see in perspective the importance of each it should be worth while to note the *functional distribution* of income in the United States; that is, distribution according to the resource classes into which resources are divided. In Table 16–2, compensation of employees represents income received by the owners of labor resources for the listed years, while corporate profits, interest, and rental income rep-

---

[3] The term *individual* will be used throughout the rest of the chapter to refer to a spending unit regardless of its size or composition.

TABLE 16–2
NATIONAL INCOME BY TYPE OF INCOME
1939–1964

TYPE OF INCOME	1939		1949		1959		1964[a]	
	Income billions of dollars	Percent of income	Income billions of dollars	Percent of income	Income billions of dollars	Percent of income	Income billions of dollars	Percent of income
Compensation of employees	48.1	66.3	140.8	64.7	278.5	69.6	361.7	70.9
Business and professional proprietors' income	7.3	10.0	22.7	10.4	35.1	8.8	39.3	7.7
Farm proprietors' income	4.3	5.9	12.9	5.9	11.4	2.8	12.7	2.5
Rental income	2.7	3.7	8.3	3.8	11.9	3.0	12.4	2.4
Net interest	4.6	6.3	4.8	2.2	16.4	4.1	26.8	5.3
Corporate profits (before taxes)	5.7	7.9	28.2	13.0	47.2	11.8	57.0	11.2
Total	72.8	100.0	217.7	100.0	400.5	100.0	509.8	100.0

[a]Preliminary figures.
SOURCE: *Economic Report of the President*, Washington, D. C.: Government Printing Office, 1965, p. 203.

resent income received by capital owners. All are understated substantially because proprietors' income includes both income from labor and income from capital. However, since accounting records for such enterprises often do not differentiate between returns to labor and returns to capital, we cannot split the item into categories labeled capital and labor. We can guess roughly that labor resources account for 75 to 80 percent of national income and that capital resources account for some 20 to 25 percent.

In this section we shall consider, first, differences in kinds and quantities of labor resources owned by different individuals. Next, differences in capital resources owned will be discussed. Last, we shall examine the effects on income distribution of certain interferences with the price mechanism.

Differences in Labor Resources Owned

The labor classification of resources is composed of many different kinds and qualities of labor. These have one common characteristic — they are human. Any single kind of labor is a combination or complex of both inherited and acquired characteristics. The acquired part of a man's labor power is sometimes referred to as human capital; however, separation of innate ability from the results of investment in the human agent, if we were able to accomplish it, would be of little value to us.

Labor can be subclassified horizontally and vertically into many largely separate resource groups. Vertical subclassification involves grading workers according to skill levels from the lowest kind of undifferentiated manual labor to the highest professional levels. Horizontal subclassification divides workers of a certain skill level into the various occupations requiring that particular degree of skill. An example would be the division of skilled construction workers into groups — carpenters, bricklayers, plumbers, and the like. Vertical mobility of labor refers to the possibility of moving upward through the vertical skill levels. Horizontal mobility means the ability to move sideways among groups at a particular skill level.

HORIZONTAL DIFFERENCES IN LABOR RESOURCES • At any specific horizontal level, individuals may receive different incomes because of differences in demand and supply conditions for the kinds of labor which they own. A large demand for a certain kind of labor relative to the supply of it available will make its marginal revenue product and its price high. On the same skill level, a small demand for another kind of labor relative to the supply available will make its marginal revenue product and its price low. The difference in prices tends to cause differences in incomes for owners of the two kinds of labor. Suppose, for example, that initially bricklayers and carpenters earn approximately equal incomes. A shift in consumer tastes occurs from wood construction to brick construction in residential units. The incomes of bricklayers will increase while those of carpenters will decrease because of the altered conditions of demand for them. Over a long period of time horizontal mobility between the two groups tends to decrease the income differences thus arising.

Quantitative differences in the amount of work performed by individuals owning the same kind of labor resource may lead to income differences. Some occupations afford considerable leeway for individual choice of the number of hours to be worked per week or per month. Examples include independent professional men such as physicians, lawyers, and certified public accountants, along with independent proprietors such as farmers, plumbing contractors, and garage owners. In other occupations, hours of work are beyond the control of the individual. Yet in different employments of the same resource, differences in age, physical endurance, institutional restrictions, custom, and so on, can lead to differences in hours worked and to income differences among owners of the resource.

Within a particular labor resource group, qualitative differences or differences in the abilities of the owners of the resource often create income differences. Wide variations occur in public evaluation of different dentists, or physicians, or lawyers, or automobile mechanics. Consequently, within any one group, variations in prices paid for services and in quantities of services which can be sold to the public will lead to income differences. Usually a correlation exists between the ages of the members of a resource group and their incomes. Quality tends to improve with accumulated experience. Data reported by Friedman and Kuznets suggest, for example, that incomes of physicians tend to be highest between the tenth and twenty-fifth years of practice, and incomes of lawyers tend to be highest between the twentieth and thirty-fifth years of practice.[4]

VERTICAL DIFFERENCES IN LABOR RESOURCES • The different vertical strata themselves represent differences in labor resources owned and give rise to major labor income differences. Entry into high-level occupations such as the professions or the ranks of business executives is much more difficult than is entry into manual occupations. The relative scarcity of labor at top levels results from two basic factors. First, individuals with

---

[4] Milton Friedman and Simon Kuznets, *Income from Independent Professional Practice* (New York: National Bureau of Economic Research, 1945), pp. 237–260.

the physical and mental characteristics necessary for performance of high-level work are limited in number. Second, given the necessary physical and mental characteristics, many lack the opportunities for training and the necessary environment for movement into high-level positions. Thus limited vertical mobility keeps resource supplies low relative to demands for them at the top levels and it keeps resource supplies abundant relative to demands for them at the low levels.

Differences in labor resources owned because of differences in innate physical and mental characteristics of individuals are accidents of birth. The individual has nothing to do with choosing them. Nevertheless they account partly for restricted vertical mobility and for income differences. The opportunities of moving toward top positions and relatively large incomes are considerably enhanced by the inheritance of a strong physical constitution and a superior intellect; however, these by no means ensure that individuals so endowed will make the most of their opportunities.

Opportunities for training tend to be more widely available to individuals born into wealthy families than to those born into families in the lower-income groups. Some of the higher-paying professions require long and expensive university training programs — often beyond the reach of the latter groups. The medical profession is a case in point. However, the advantages that the wealthy have should not be overemphasized. Every day we see individuals who have had the initial ability, the drive, and the determination necessary to overcome economic obstacles thrown in the way of vertical mobility.

Differences in social inheritance constitute another cause of differences in labor resources owned. These will be closely correlated with differences in material inheritance. Frequently, individuals born on the wrong side of the tracks face family and community attitudes that sharply curtail their opportunities and their desires for vertical mobility. Others, more fortunately situated, acquire the training necessary to be highly productive and to obtain large incomes because it is expected of them by the social groups in which they move. Their social position alone, apart from the training induced by it, may be quite effective in facilitating vertical mobility.

Differences in Capital Resources Owned

In addition to inequalities in labor incomes, large differences occur in individual incomes from differences in capital ownership. Different individuals own varying quantities of capital — corporation or other business assets, farm land, oil wells, and property of various other forms. We shall examine the fundamental causes of inequalities in capital holdings.

MATERIAL INHERITANCE • Differences in the amounts of capital inherited or received as gifts by different individuals create large differences in incomes. The institution of private property on which free enterprise rests usually is coupled with inheritance laws allowing large holdings of accumulated property rights to be passed on from generation to generation. The individual fortunate enough to have selected a wealthy father inherits large capital holdings, his resources contribute much to the productive process, and he is rewarded accordingly. The son of the southern sharecropper, who may be of equal innate intelligence, inherits no capital, contributes less to the productive process, and receives correspondingly a lower income.

FORTUITOUS CIRCUMSTANCES • Chance, luck, or other fortuitous circumstances beyond the control of individuals constitute a further cause of differences in capital holdings. The discovery of oil, uranium, or gold on an otherwise mediocre piece of land brings about a large appreciation in its value or its ability to yield income to its owner. Unforeseen shifts in consumer demand increase the values of certain capital holdings while decreasing the values of others. National emergencies such as war lead to changes in valuations of particular kinds of property and, hence, to differential incomes from capital. Dalton cites an example of the stockholders in a concern which made mourning weeds. As the casualty lists grew during World War I, their capital holdings appreciated in value.[5] Fortuitous circumstances can work in reverse, also, but even so their effects operate to create differences in the ownership of capital.

PROPENSITIES TO ACCUMULATE • Differing psychological propensities to accumulate and differing abilities to accumulate lead to differences in capital ownership among individuals. On the psychological side a number of factors influence the will to accumulate. Stories circulate of individuals determined to make a fortune before attainment of a certain age. Accumulation sometimes occurs for purposes of security and luxury in later life. It sometimes occurs from the desire to make one's children secure. The power and the prestige accompanying wealth provide the motivating force in some cases. To others, accumulation and manipulation of capital holdings is a gigantic game — the activity involved is fascinating to them. Whatever the motives, some individuals have them

---

[5] Hugh Dalton, *The Inequality of Incomes* (London: Routledge & Kegan Paul, Ltd., 1925), p. 273.

and others do not. In some instances the will to accumulate may be negative and the opposite of accumulation occurs.

The ability of an individual to accumulate depends largely upon his original holdings of both labor resources and capital resources. The higher the original income the easier saving and accumulation tend to be. The individual possessing much initially in the way of labor resources is likely to accumulate capital with his income from labor — he invests in stocks and bonds, real estate, a cattle ranch, or other property. Or the individual possessing substantial quantities of capital initially — and the ability to manage it — receives an income sufficient to allow saving and investment in additional capital. In the process of accumulation, labor resources and capital resources of an individual augment each other in providing the income from which further accumulation can be accomplished.

Restrictions Placed on the Price Mechanism

Various groups of resource owners throughout the economy, dissatisfied with their current shares of national income, seek to modify income distribution through manipulation or fixing of the prices of the resources which they own or the prices of the product which they produce and sell. Certain groups of farmers — wheat farmers, cotton farmers, dairy farmers, and others — have been able to obtain government-enforced minimum prices for the products which they sell. Certain groups of retailers have been able to secure state laws forbidding product selling prices below a fixed percentage markup over cost. Labor organizations seek to increase — or in some cases to maintain — their shares of national income by fixing wages through the collective bargaining process. Social-minded people all over the economy, concerned with the small distributive shares of low-paid workers, support minimum-wage legislation. We shall examine typical cases of administered prices[6] in an attempt to assess their effects upon income distribution. In each case we shall assume that the particular resource concerned constitutes a small proportion of the economy's total resources.

ADMINISTERED PRICES: PURE COMPETITION • Suppose that owners of a given resource, dissatisfied with their shares of national income, seek and obtain a higher administered price for their resource. Will the incomes of the resource owners involved increase relative to the incomes of the owners of the other resources? In other words, will the owners of

---

[6] Administered prices are prices fixed by law, fixed by groups of sellers, fixed by groups of buyers, or fixed by collective action of buyers and sellers. They are the antithesis of free market prices established by free interactions of buyers and sellers in the market places.

the given resource receive a larger share of the economy's product? Equally important, what will happen to the share of the total earnings of the resource received by each of its owners? Third, what will be the effects on the efficiency of the economy's operation?

Assuming that demand for the given resource remains constant,[7] the effect of the administered price upon total income earned by the resource will depend upon the elasticity of demand. If elasticity is less than one, total income will increase and owners of the resource as a group will have increased their distributive share. If elasticity equals one, no change in total income will occur. However, if elasticity is greater than one, total income and the distributive share of owners of the resource as a group will decline.

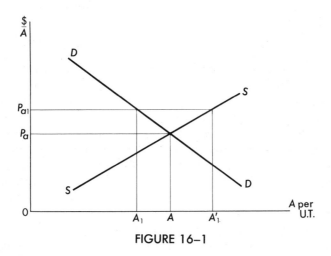

FIGURE 16–1

Reference to Figure 16–1 will assist us in answering the second question — the effects of the administered price upon the distribution of total income earned by the resource among its owners. The demand curve and supply curve for resource A are DD and SS, respectively. The equilibrium price is p_a and the level of employment is quantity A. Sup-

---

[7] There seems to be no valid reason for assuming that demand will not remain constant if the resource concerned constitutes a small proportion of the economy's total supplies of resources — and this is usually the case for any given resource. Even if the administered price raises the total income of the resource owners involved, it seems unlikely that demand for the products which the resource assists in producing will be increased to any significant degree. In a stationary economy, particularly, the assumption of independence between resource price changes and consequent changes in demand for the resource appears to be the logical one to make.

pose now an administered price of p_{a1} is set for the resource — none can be sold for less. Whether the administered price is set by the government, through bargaining between organized groups of buyers and sellers, or through unilateral action on the part of either resource buyers or resource sellers, is of no consequence. The effects will be the same. Confronted by the higher price, each firm using resource A finds that if it employs the same quantity as before, value of marginal product for the resource will be less than its price. Consequently, each firm finds that reductions in the quantity of the resource used will reduce total receipts less than they decrease total costs and will increase the firm's profits. When all firms have reduced employment sufficiently for the value of marginal product of the resource in each to equal p_{a1}, they will again be maximizing profits. The market level of employment will have dropped to A_1.

The administered price p_{a1} may create unemployment, thus causing income differences between those whose resources are employed and those whose resources are unemployed.[8] At price p_{a1} employers will take quantity A_1, but quantity A_1' of the resource seeks employment. Unemployment amounts to A_1A_1'. Those whose units of the resource remain employed gain greater distributive shares of the economy's product; however, those owning unemployed units now receive nothing. Units of the resource still are paid according to their marginal contributions to the value of the economy's output. The employed units have a greater value of marginal product than formerly because of the reduction in the ratio of resource A to other resources used by individual firms. The value of marginal product of the unemployed units is zero.

The unemployed units of resource A may seek employment in another resource classification. Suppose, for example, that units of resource A are carpenters. Carpenters denied employment in that skill category, at a wage rate of p_{a1}, may seek employment as common laborers rather than remain as unemployed carpenters. However, their value of marginal product and their wage rate will be lower in the lower skill classification. The administered wage rate increases income differences in two ways: (1) employed carpenters receive higher wage rates and incomes than they would otherwise receive, and (2) the wage rates and incomes of common labor are lower than they would otherwise be as unemployed carpenters join the ranks and increase the supply of common labor.

The effects of the administered price on economic efficiency or the total output of the economy are clear. The unemployed units of A contribute nothing to the value of the economy's output, or to the extent

---

[8] Unless, of course, the unemployment is shared equally by all owners of the resource.

that they shift into lower productivity classifications they contribute less than they would have otherwise. If the resource price were allowed to drop to its equilibrium level, greater employment in the higher value of marginal product uses would raise the value of the economy's output — and at the same time would contribute toward greater income equality among owners of the resource.

SUPPLY RESTRICTIONS: PURE COMPETITION • Resource prices in particular employments may be increased indirectly through restriction of the resource supplies that can be used in those employments. Examples are furnished by governmental acreage restrictions placed on cotton farmers and wheat farmers. Or the same result may be obtained by labor union activity. For example, the milk wagon drivers' union in a large city may succeed in making union membership a condition of employment while at the same time it restricts entry into the union.

The effects on income distribution and total output of the economy are about the same as those resulting frqm directly administered prices. The employment level of the resource in its restricted use is decreased, leaving some of the resource units either unemployed or seeking employment in alternative uses. Land excluded from cotton and wheat farming may be switched to the production of other products. Light-truck drivers excluded from driving milk wagons may secure such alternative employments as delivery truck or taxi driving. Value of marginal product and price of resource units in the restricted use increase[9] while value of marginal product and price of those placed in other employments decrease. This leads to differential prices for the resource and to greater income differences. At the same time it leads to net national product smaller than the economy is capable of producing.

ADMINISTERED PRICES: PRODUCT MONOPOLY • Do administered resource prices, when resource buyers sell product as monopolists, offset monopoly? The argument is frequently made that they do, and that

---

[9] In the case of wheat land or cotton land, the ratio of land to other resources is decreased both through decreased acreage allowances and through more intensive application of labor and fertilizer. Greater marginal physical product of the land and possibly higher prices for smaller crops increase the value of marginal product of land.

About the same thing happens with regard to milk wagon drivers. Firms faced with restricted supplies attempt to make each driver as productive as possible. Slightly larger trucks may be used to minimize the number of trips back to the plant for reloading. Trucks may be made more convenient to get into, to get out of, and to operate. Idle truck time is avoided through better maintenance and repair facilities for trucks. Such measures increase the marginal physical product of the drivers. Additionally, the employment of fewer drivers may lead to smaller milk sales and higher milk prices. Thus the value of marginal product of milk wagon drivers will be higher than before.

the advance in resource prices comes from the monopolists' profits. Suppose that initially the equilibrium price for a given resource prevails. Firms with some degree of monopoly in product markets buy the resource, and it is so allocated that its price is the same in its alternative uses. However, since the resource price equals its marginal revenue product in its various employments, rather than the value of its marginal product, the units of the resource are exploited monopolistically — they receive less than they contribute to the value of the economy's output.

Will an administered resource price above its equilibrium price regain what is lost by resource owners from monopolistic exploitation? Suppose such an administered price is obtained. Marginal revenue product of the resource for individual firms would be less than the administered price if firms were to continue hiring the same quantities as before. Consequently, each firm cuts employment of the resource to the level at which its marginal revenue product equals the administered price. But note that it is still *marginal revenue product* and not *value of marginal product* of the resource that equals its price. Despite the administered price, monopolistic exploitation of the resource continues to occur.[10]

When firms have some degree of product monopoly the effects of the administered resource price increases will be the same as those which occur when firms sell products under conditions of pure competition. At the higher price the firms employ fewer units of the resource. More units seek employment. Unemployment and differences in income among owners of the resource occur. If the unemployed units then find employment in lower marginal revenue product resource classifications or uses, income differences are mitigated to some extent but they still occur.

ADMINISTERED PRICES: MONOPSONY • In monopsonistic cases, administered resource prices can offset monopsonistic exploitation of a resource. The employment level of the resource can be increased at the same time that its price is raised above the market level. The income and the distributive shares of the owners of the resource are increased relative to those of other resource owners in the economy.

Detailed explanation of how an administered resource price offsets monopsonistic exploitation was presented in Chapter 14. To recapitulate the analysis, an administered price set above the market price makes the resource supply curve faced by the firm horizontal at that price. For prices higher than the administered price, the original supply curve is

---

[10] Thus measures to offset monopolistic exploitation of resources must attack the monopolistic product demand situation. They must eliminate the difference between marginal revenue and price for the monopolist and, hence, between marginal revenue product and value of marginal product of resources.

the relevant one. For the horizontal section of the resource supply curve, marginal resource cost and resource price will be equal. By judicious setting of the administered price the firm can be induced to employ that quantity of the resource at which marginal revenue product equals resource price. Without the administered price the firm restricts employment and pays units of the resource less than their marginal revenue product.

PRICE INCREASES ACCOMPANYING DEMAND INCREASES • The effects of administered resource price increases when demand for the resource remains constant are often confused with the effects of resource price increases which accompany increases in demand for the resource. Suppose demand for a given resource is increasing while, simultaneously, resource owners organized as a group succeed in bargaining out a series of price increases with the buyers of the resource. Suppose further that the contract prices at no time exceed the rising equilibrium price. No adverse distributive effects for the owners of the resource arise. Their positions are continuously improving as individual resource owners and as a group. However, it is erroneous to conclude from situations of this kind that administered resource price increases will in general have no adverse effects on total income of the owners of the resource in question or on the distribution of income within the group. We must distinguish carefully between those administered price increases which are accompanied by increases in demand for the resource and those which are not. Although the former may have no adverse effects on total income of the owners of the resource or on the distribution of income among owners of the resource, adverse effects — except in the case of monopsony — are likely to arise from the latter.

A GREATER MEASURE OF EQUALITY

For various reasons — economic, ethical, and social — many people favor some mitigation of income differences. The causes of differences should furnish the clues for measures leading toward their mitigation — if movement toward greater equality is thought by society to be desirable. Thus equalizing measures may be (and are) attempted via the price system or they may be (and are) attempted through redistribution of resources among resource owners. We shall consider each of these in turn.

Via Administered Prices

Equalizing measures attempted via the price system are likely to miss their mark except in monopsonistic cases. Where competitive and monopolistic conditions prevail in product markets and where competitive conditions prevail in the purchase of a given resource, the equilibrium price of the resource tends to be equal to its value of marginal product or its marginal revenue product, as the case may be. Additionally, the resource tends to be so allocated that its price is the same in its alternative employments. Successful administered price increases are likely to result in unemployment and malallocation of the resource and this in turn contributes toward greater rather than smaller income differences. As we have observed before, administered resource prices in monopsony cases can offset monopsonistic exploitation of a resource by increasing both its price and its level of employment.

Via Redistribution of Resources

The major part of any movement toward greater income equality must consist of redistribution of resources among resource owners, since here is the major cause of income differences. Redistributive measures can take two forms: (1) redistribution of labor resources, and (2) redistribution of capital resources.

LABOR RESOURES • Labor resources can be redistributed through measures designed to increase vertical mobility. Greater vertical mobility will increase labor supplies in the top vocational levels and decrease labor supplies in the lower levels. Greater supplies at the top will decrease values of marginal product or marginal revenue products and consequently will reduce the top incomes. Smaller supplies at the lower levels will increase values of marginal product or marginal revenue products, thereby increasing incomes at the lower occupational levels. The transfers from lower to higher occupations will mitigate income differences and will increase net national product in the process.

At least three methods of increasing vertical mobility can be suggested. First, there are possibilities of providing greater equality in educational and training opportunities for capable individuals. Second, to the extent that differences in capital ownership are reduced, greater equality in the economic opportunities for development of high-grade labor resources will tend to occur. Third, measures may be taken to reduce those barriers to entry established by associations of resource owners in many skilled occupations.[11]

Measures to increase horizontal mobility also can serve to decrease income differences. These include the operation of employment exchanges, perhaps some subsidization of movement, vocational guidance,

---

[11] An example of such a barrier is provided by the professional association which controls licensing standards when prospective entrants must be licensed in order to practice the profession.

adult education and retraining programs, and other measures of a similar nature. The argument here is really one for better allocation of labor resources, both among alternative jobs within a given labor resource category, and among the labor resource categories themselves. Greater horizontal mobility, as well as greater vertical mobility, will increase net national product at the same time that it decreases income differences.

CAPITAL RESOURCES • Redistribution of capital resources meets considerable opposition in a free enterprise economy. Many vociferous advocates of movement toward greater income equality will protest vigorously measures designed to redistribute capital ownership — and these are the measures which will contribute most toward that objective. The opposition centers around the rights of private property ownership and stems from a strong presumption that the right to own property includes the right to accumulate it and to pass it on to one's heirs.

Nevertheless, if income differences are to be mitigated, some means of providing greater equality in capital accumulation and capital holdings among individuals must be employed. The economy's system of taxation may move in this direction. In the United States, for example, the personal income tax, the capital gains tax, and estate and gift taxes — both federal and state — already operate in an equalizing manner.

The personal income tax by its progressive nature serves to reduce income differences directly and in so doing it reduces differences in abilities to accumulate capital. But the personal income tax alone cannot be expected to eliminate those differences without seriously impairing incentives for efficient employment of resources and for reallocation of resources from less productive to more productive employments.

The capital gains tax constitutes either a loophole for escaping a part of the personal income tax, or a plug for a loophole in the personal income tax, depending upon one's definition of income. The capital gains tax is applied to realized appreciation and depreciation in the value of capital assets. Those who can convert a part of their income from capital resources into the form of capital gains have that part of their remuneration taxed as capital gains at a rate ordinarly below the personal income tax rate. For them the capital gains tax provides a loophole through which personal income taxes can be escaped. On the other hand, if certain capital gains would escape taxation altogether under the personal income tax, but are covered by the capital gains tax, the latter can be considered a supplement to the personal income tax. In either case the capital gains tax allows some remuneration from capital resources to be taxed at rates below the personal income tax rates and, if differences in opportunities to accumulate capital are to be mitigated, it must be revised to prevent individuals from taking undue advantage of its lower rates.

Estate and gift taxes will play the major roles in any tax system designed to reduce differences in capital ownership. The estate taxes in such a system would border on the confiscatory side above some maximum amount in order to prevent the transmission of accumulated capital resources from generation to generation. Gift taxes would operate largely to plug estate tax loopholes. They would be designed to prevent transmission of estates by means of gifts from the original owner to heirs prior to the death of the original owner.

REDISTRIBUTION AND THE PRICE SYSTEM • Redistribution of labor resource and capital resource holdings can be accomplished within the framework of the price system and the free enterprise economic system if movement toward greater income equality is thought by society to be desirable. Redistribution measures such as those sketched out above need not seriously affect the operation of the price mechanism. In fact, the price mechanism can act as a positive force assisting the measures to reach the desired objectives. Some of the fundamental measures — educational opportunities, progressive income taxes, gift and estate taxes — are already in existence, although their effectiveness could be increased greatly. Redistribution measures can be thought of as rules of the free enterprise game — along with a stable monetary system, monopoly control measures, and other rules of economic conduct.

SUMMARY

Individual claims to net national product depend upon individual incomes; thus, the theory of product distribution is really the theory of income distribution. Marginal productivity theory provides the generally accepted principles of income determination and income distribution. Resource owners tend to be remunerated according to the marginal revenue products of the resources which they own except in cases where resources are purchased monopsonistically.

Incomes are unequally distributed among spending units in the United States. Income differences stem from three basic sources: (1) differences in labor resources owned, (2) differences in capital resources owned, and (3) restrictions placed on the operation of the price mechanism. With regard to labor resources, different individuals own different kinds of labor at the same general skill level. These we call horizontal differences in labor resources. Different individuals also own different kinds of labor graded vertically from undifferentiated manual labor to the top-level professions. Differences in capital resources owned result from differences in material inheritance, fortuitous circumstances, and differences in propensities to accumulate. Administered prices for a given resource often lead to unemployment or malallocation of some units of the resource and hence to differences in incomes among owners of the resource. The case of monopsony provides an exception. Under monopsony, administered resource prices can offset monopsonistic exploitation of the resources involved.

Attacks on income differences, if society desires to mitigate those differences, should be made by way of redistribution of resources among resource owners. Attacks made by way of administered prices are not likely to accomplish the task. Redistribution of labor resources can be accomplished through measures designed to increase both horizontal and vertical mobility. These will in turn increase net national product. The tax system offers the means of effecting redistribution of capital resources. Estate and gift taxes will bear the major burden of redistribution and should be supplemented by adequate personal income and capital gains taxes. Redistribution of resources can be accomplished within the framework of the price system and the free enterprise economy.

SUGGESTED READINGS

DALTON, HUGH. *The Inequality of Incomes.* 2d ed.; London: Routledge & Kegan Paul, Ltd., 1925, pt. IV, pp. 239–353.

PIGOU, A. C. *The Economics of Welfare.* 4th ed.; London: Macmillan & Co., Ltd., 1932, ·pt. IV, chap. V.

Equilibrium | **17**

THE CONCEPT OF EQUILIBRIUM furnishes a focal point for drawing together the principles of price theory and resource allocation. Equilibrium concepts have been used throughout the book, but no distinction has been drawn between particular equilibrium analysis and general equilibrium analysis. We are in a position now to expand our concept of equilibrium and then to use it in summarizing the operation of a free enterprise economy.

THE CONCEPT OF EQUILIBRIUM

Equilibrium means a state of rest — the attainment of a position from which there is no incentive nor opportunity to move. A consumer is in equilibrium when his expenditures on different goods and services yield maximum satisfaction. No move on his part can increase his satisfaction but, rather, will decrease it. Similarly, a business firm is in equilibrium when its resource purchases and its output are such that it maximizes its profits, if profit maximization is its objective. Any change on its part will cause profits to decrease. A resource owner is in equilibrium when the resources which he owns are placed in their highest paying employments and the income of the resource owner is maximized. Any transfers of resource units from one employment to another will cause his income to decrease.

Equilibrium concepts are important, not because equilibrium is ever in fact attained but because they show us the directions in which economic changes proceed. Economic units in disequilibrium usually move toward equilibrium positions. Economic disturbances of various kinds — changes in consumer tastes and preferences, technological developments, changes in resource supplies, and so on — change the equilibrium positions and motivate the various economic units to move toward the new positions until further disturbances occur. Generally

327

movements toward equilibrium are at the same time movements toward greater economic efficiency.

Particular Equilibrium

A large part of the analytical structure that we have built up is called particular or partial equilibrium analysis. It has been concerned with movements of particular economic units or particular industries toward equilibrium positions in response to the given economic conditions confronting them. Thus, the consumer, with his given tastes and preferences, is confronted with a given income and with given prices of goods and services. He adjusts his purchases accordingly to move toward equilibrium. The business firm, faced with given product demand situations, a given state of technology, and given resource supply situations, moves toward an equilibrium adjustment. The resource owner has given quantities of resources to place in employment. He faces given alternative employment possibilities and resource price offers. His equilibrium adjustment is made on the basis of the given data. The conditions of demand and the conditions of cost in a particular industry cause profits or losses to be made, and these motivate entry of new firms (if entry is possible) or exit of existing firms, thus leading toward equilibrium for the industry. Changes in the given data facing economic units and industries change the positions of equilibrium which each is attempting to reach and motivate movements toward the new positions.

Particular equilibrium is especially suitable for analysis of two types of problems, both of which we met time and again throughout the book. Problems of the first type are those arising from economic disturbances that are not of sufficient magnitude to reach far beyond the confines of a certain industry or sector of the economy. Problems of the second type are concerned with the first-order effects of an economic disturbance of any kind.

As an illustration of the first type of problem, suppose the production workers of a small manufacturer of plastic products go on strike. Suppose further that the plant is located in a large city and that the workers are fairly well dispersed among the residential areas of the city. The effects of the strike will be limited largely to the company and to the employees concerned. Particular equilibrium analysis will provide the relevant answers to most of the economic problems arising from the strike.

As an example of the second type of problem, suppose a rearmament program increases the demand for steel suddenly and substantially. Partial equilibrium analysis will provide answers to the first-order effects on the steel industry — what happens to its prices, its output, its profits, its demands for resources, resource prices, and resource employment levels. However, the first-order effects by no means end the repercussions from the initial disturbance.

General Equilibrium

As individual economic units and industries seek their particular equilibrium adjustments to what appear to be given facts, their actions change the facts which they face. If some units were in equilibrium and others were not, those in disequilibrium would move toward equilibrium. Their activities would change the facts faced by units in equilibrium and would throw the latter into disequilibrium. General equilibrium for the entire economy could exist only if all economic units were to achieve simultaneous particular equilibrium adjustments. The concept of general equilibrium stresses the interdependence of all economic units and of all segments of the economy on each other.

A line of demarcation between particular equilibrium analysis and general equilibrium analysis is hard to draw. Instead of establishing a dichotomy, it will be preferable to think in terms of moving along a continuum from particular into general equilibrium, or from first-order effects of a disturbance into second-, third-, and higher-order effects. For example, in discussing pricing and output under market conditions of pure competition, we were concerned first with particular equilibrium — equilibrium of the individual firm. Next we extended the analysis to an entire industry and observed the impacts of individual firm actions upon each other. Last, we observed how productive capacity is organized in a purely competitive free enterprise economy according to consumer tastes and preferences. This represents progressive movement from the application of particular equilibrium analysis to the application of general equilibrium analysis.

OBJECTIVES OF GENERAL EQUILIBRIUM THEORY • General equilibrium theory provides the analytical tools for accomplishing two objectives. First, from the standpoint of pure theory, it provides the means of viewing the economic system in its entirety — the means of seeing what holds it together, what makes it work, and how it operates. The second objective — and this is really an application of the first — is the determination of the second-, third-, and higher-order effects of an economic disturbance. When the impact of an economic disturbance is of sufficient magnitude to have repercussions throughout most of the economy, general equilibrium analysis provides the more relevant answers regarding its ultimate effects. First comes the big splash from the disturbance. Particular equilibrium analysis handles the splash. But waves and then ripples are set up from it, affecting one another and affecting the area of the splash. The ripples run farther and farther, becoming smaller and smaller, until eventually they dwindle away. The tools of general equilibrium are required for analysis of the entire series of readjustments.

Suppose the higher-order repercussions from the increase in demand for steel are to be examined. The first-order or particular equilibrium effects are higher prices, larger outputs, with given facilities, larger profits, and larger payments to the owners of resources used in making steel. But these generate additional disturbances. Higher incomes for the resource owners concerned increase demand for other products setting off disturbances and adjustments in other industries. Demands increase for steel substitutes, generating another series of disturbances and adjustments. Productive capacity will be diverted from other activities toward the making of steel. Eventually, effects will be felt over the entire economy. If the full impact of such a disturbance is to be determined, general equilibrium analysis must provide the tools to do the job.

VARIANTS OF GENERAL EQUILIBRIUM THEORY • Since general equilibrium analysis covers the interrelationships of all parts of the economy, it necessarily becomes exceedingly complex. There are two principal variants of it. Following Walras, most economists find it convenient to discuss general equilibrium in mathematical terms. The interdependence of economic units is shown through a system of simultaneous equations relating the many economic variables to each other. It can be demonstrated that there are as many variables to be determined as there are equations relating them. Solving the system of equations establishes those values of the variables that are consistent with general equilibrium for the economic system.[1] The Walrasian version of general equilibrium provides essentially the theoretical apparatus for understanding the interrelationships of the various sectors of the economy.

The second and newer variant is Wassily W. Leontief's input-output analysis which is still in the process of development.[2] The input-output approach is an empirical descendant of the abstract Walrasian approach. It divides the economy into a number of sectors or industries, including households and the government as "industries" of final demand. Each industry is viewed as selling its output to other industries —

[1] See George J. Stigler, *The Theory of Price* (rev. ed.; New York: The Macmillan Company, 1952), pp. 290–295.

[2] For an excellent survey and analysis of this approach see Robert Dorfman, "The Nature and Significance of Input-Output," *Review of Economics and Statistics,* XXXVI (May 1954), 121–133.

these outputs become inputs for the purchasing industries. Likewise, each industry is viewed as a purchaser of the outputs of other industries. Thus the interdependence of each industry on the others is established. Statistical data gathered around the basic framework of the system provide an informative and useful picture of the interindustry flows of goods, services, and resources. The input-output approach shows promise for analyzing and measuring statistically the effects of major economic disturbances as well as for mobilizing an economy in periods of national emergency.

THE OPERATION OF THE ECONOMY

The particular and general equilibrium viewpoints will be helpful in reviewing the operation of a free enterprise economy. The general equilibrium approach which we shall use is a verbal — and therefore limited — version of the mathematical approach. But it will assist us in summarizing and binding together the major principles which we have covered. The summary will be in terms of the three major functions of an economic system — determination of what is to be produced, organization of production, and distribution of the product.

Determination of What Is to Be Produced

Determination of what is to be produced is essentially the problem of valuation of goods and services. Suppose that individual consumer tastes and preferences are given, individual consumer incomes per unit of time are given, supplies of goods available per unit of time are given,[3] and the initial price pattern is not an equilibrium pattern.

PARTICULAR EQUILIBRIUM • Individual consumers seek to maximize satisfaction. In terms of classical utility analysis, each consumer, faced with given product prices, seeks to allocate his income among the products available in such a way that the marginal utility per dollar's worth of one will be equal to the marginal utility per dollar's worth of every other product. In terms of indifference curve analysis, each consumer seeks that combination of goods with his given income at which the marginal rate of substitution between any two equals the ratio of their prices.[4]

---

[3] The assumption of given supplies makes the function of very short-run rationing an integral part of the function of valuing goods and services.

[4] The discussion of consumer equilibrium will be built around utility analysis. It could easily be put in terms of indifference curve analysis. In place of marginal utilities per dollar's worth of different commodities we would use the relationships of marginal rates of substitution to price ratios.

GENERAL EQUILIBRIUM • With the initial price pattern the prices of some goods will be below their equilibrium level. Consumers in the aggregate will want more than are available, and shortages of those commodities will exist. Some consumers — call them Group A — may have succeeded in obtaining enough of the short goods at those prices to equate marginal utilities per dollar's worth of all goods purchased, but for other consumers — Group B — the marginal utilities per dollar's worth of the goods in short supply will exceed those of other goods. Consumers of Group B want to expand their purchases of the short goods and to contract their purchases of other goods; that is, they want to exchange other goods for the short goods. Consumers bid against each other for the short supplies — each attempting to obtain larger quantities — and their prices rise.

As the prices of the short goods rise, Group A consumers, who had been in equilibrium, now find themselves in disequilibrium. Marginal utilities per dollar's worth of the short goods fall relative to those of other goods and they become willing to trade short goods for other goods since they can gain satisfaction by so doing. Exchanges between consumers of the two groups occur; but as long as the marginal utility per dollar's worth of any short commodity is higher than that of other goods for any consumer of Group B, further price rises for that good and further exchanges will occur. Price increases for the short goods and exchanges among consumers will stop when two sets of conditions are met. First, prices of the short goods must have risen enough to cause consumers in the aggregate to limit their purchases to the available supplies; that is, the shortages no longer exist. Second, each consumer in the economy must be obtaining those quantities of various goods with his income at which the marginal utility per dollar's worth of one good equals the marginal utility per dollar's worth of every other good.

The initial prices of other goods will be above their equilibrium levels and surpluses of such goods will occur. Consumers succeed in maximizing satisfaction before the entire supplies are taken off the market. All consumers may be in equilibrium even though the surplus exists.

Sellers constitute the disturbing force as they undercut each other's prices to get their surplus goods moving. As prices of the surplus goods decrease, their marginal utilities per dollar's worth to consumers increase relative to those of other goods. Disequilibrium for consumers results and they expand their purchases of the surplus goods.

Whether or not total expenditures on particular surplus goods increase, decrease, or remain constant as their prices fall and consumption of them is increased depends upon their respective elasticities of demand. To the extent that total expenditures on surplus goods in the aggregate increase, expenditures on certain other goods decrease, which in turn causes their prices to decrease. However, if total expenditures on surplus goods in the aggregate decrease as their prices fall, larger purchases and higher prices of certain other goods will occur.

Equilibrium for each consumer and for consumers as a group will be attained when the prices of the surplus goods have fallen enough for the surplus to have disappeared. Price adjustments and purchases of other goods will have been realigned so that no shortages or surpluses exist. For each consumer, the marginal utility per dollar's worth of one good will equal the marginal utility per dollar's worth of every other good available. No one will have any desire to exchange units of one good for units of another at the prevailing prices.

General equilibrium exists for consumers. With the given tastes and preferences of consumers, the given distribution of income, and the given supplies of products, individual consumers and consumers in the aggregate are maximizing satisfaction. No consumer has any incentive to alter the quantities of his purchases. All prices are equilibrium prices and reflect social or group valuations of the marginal units of each. Since there is neither a shortage nor a surplus of any commodity, no incentive exists for alterations of any price.

EFFECTS OF DISTURBANCES • Changes in any of the given circumstances — in consumer tastes and preferences, in income distribution, or in supplies of goods available — would touch off a chain reaction among consumers. Disequilibrium would occur. Shortages and surpluses for particular commodities at the existing prices would come into being and movement back toward general equilibrium would occur much in the manner that we have described. A new price pattern for goods and services would emerge corresponding to the new set of given circumstances.

INTERPERSONAL COMPARISONS OF UTILITY • Conditions of general equilibrium for consumers state nothing about whether the marginal utility per dollar's worth of one commodity is the same for one consumer as it is for another. They state only that each consumer must equate for himself the marginal utilities per dollar's worth of the various commodities available. It is entirely possible that for the rich man the marginal utility of a dollar's worth of each good is lower than it is for the poor man. Both would be maximizing satisfaction and neither could gain from an exchange. If interpersonal comparisons of marginal utilities could be made, they would be of no assistance in establishing the conditions necessary for maximization of individual and aggregate consumer satisfaction under the assumed given circumstances.[5]

The Organization of Production

Suppose we consider the planning on the part of business firms which occurs in response to consumer valuations of goods and services. We shall assume that resource supplies are fixed in quantities, that the range of productive techniques available is given for each industry, that the initial pattern of resource prices is not an equilibrium pattern, that the distribution of firms among industries is random, and that initially these firms are producing the fixed supplies assumed in the preceding subsection.

THE SHORT RUN • In the short run, individual firms seek to maximize profits or minimize losses. Each is faced with given product prices or, in the event that some degree of monopoly occurs, with given estimated demand situations. Each firm faces the initial prices of variable resources or, in case some degree of monopsony exists, estimated resource supply situations. The scale of plant is fixed for each firm. Available techniques of production and resource prices determine individual firm costs. Losses are incurred by firms in some industries and profits are made by firms in others. No firm operates unless the price of its product exceeds its average variable costs.

At the initial resource prices, marginal revenue products of some resources employed by some firms — suppose we call them Group A firms — will exceed their prices and shortages of those resources will occur. Consumer valuations of the products that those resources contribute to production exceed the costs of the resources used in producing them. In other firms — Group B firms — enough of the same resources may be secured to equate marginal revenue products to resource prices.

Group A firms stand to increase profits or to reduce losses by expanding employment of the short resources. Consequently, they offer higher prices for them in order to secure larger quantities. Resources move from Group B firms to Group A firms, that is, they move from uses in which their marginal revenue products are lower into uses in which

---

[5] If interpersonal comparisons of utility could be made and if it were found that the marginal utility of money to the rich man is less than it is for the poor man, shifts in the distribution of income from the rich toward the poor would increase aggregate consumer satisfaction. A dollar taken away from the rich man under such circumstances would cause a decrease in his total satisfaction smaller than the increase in the total satisfaction brought about by giving the dollar to the poor man. This is the common argument for progressive taxation. The issue of interpersonal comparisons of utilities has been the center of much debate among students of welfare economics.

their marginal revenue products are higher. Generally, such movements provide consumers with more of the goods they value highly at the expense of goods on which they place lesser values.[6]

As resources are transferred from Group B to Group A firms, their marginal revenue products decrease in Group A firms and increase in Group B firms. As larger quantities are employed in Group A firms, their marginal physical products decline because of the operation of the law of diminishing returns. At the same time, larger supplies of Group A products serve to reduce their prices or consumers' valuations of them. The opposite is happening to Group B products.[7]

Reallocation of the short resources will stop when their prices have increased sufficiently for the shortages to have disappeared and when the marginal revenue product of each resource in each of its uses is equal to its price. The price (or cost) of any resource to any single firm is equal to the amount it could earn in its best alternative use.[8]

The initial prices of other resources will be so high that when firms employ sufficient quantities of them to equate their marginal revenue products to their prices, some units will still remain unemployed; that is, surpluses occur. The owners of unemployed units will cut prices in order to secure employment for them. Thus it becomes profitable for firms using those resources to expand the quantities employed until marginal revenue products equal the new lower prices. The resource price decreases will continue until they are low enough for the resources in question to be fully employed.[9] For all firms using them, marginal revenue products equal prices and again the price or cost of each resource to any one firm is equal to what it could earn in its best alternative employments.

We have considered independently the adjustments in prices and employment of the resources initially in short supply and those of

[6] This will always be the case where pure competition exists in product markets. It will usually be the case where some degree of product monopoly occurs. However, where some degree of product monopoly exists, there is a possibility that resource transfers from lower to higher *marginal revenue product uses* will at the same time be from higher to lower *value of marginal product uses*. Such transfers will decrease consumer satisfaction.

[7] Changing supplies of goods bring about disequilibrium for consumers, setting off a whole chain of consumer readjustments toward a new position of consumer equilibrium. The new consumer equilibrium position will, of course, involve greater consumption of Group A goods at lower prices and lesser consumption of Group B goods at higher prices.

[8] If pure competition in product markets and resource markets exists, the resource will be making its maximum (short-run) contribution to consumer satisfaction.

[9] As employment levels of surplus resources are increased, product outputs of the industries employing them increase. Consumer disequilibrium results and consumers move toward new equilibrium positions involving lower prices and greater consumption of those products.

resources for which some unemployment existed initially. Actually the increases in the prices of the short resources will encourage employment of those for which surpluses exist. Decreases in the prices of surplus resources will discourage use of the short resources. These tendencies arise from attempts by individual firms to use variable resource combinations such that the marginal physical product per dollar's worth of one is equal to the marginal physical product per dollar's worth of every other variable resource employed. Rising prices of the short resources decrease their respective marginal physical products per dollar's worth while falling prices of surplus resources increase their respective marginal physical products per dollar's worth. Consequently firms are induced to substitute units of surplus resources for units of short resources. The price changes and substitutions continue until the short resources are no longer short and the surplus resources are no longer surplus.

We have reached a position of short-run general equilibrium for the economy as a whole. Each product is priced so that neither shortages nor surpluses appear. Each consumer has adjusted product consumption so that the marginal utility per dollar's worth of one product equals the marginal utility per dollar's worth of every other product available. Each variable resource is priced so that no shortages or surpluses occur. Marginal revenue product of each variable resource in each of its employments equals its price and this in turn means that each individual firm must be employing variable resources in combinations such that the marginal physical product per dollar's worth of one equals the marginal physical product per dollar's worth of every other resource which it can use. Also, if resource marginal revenue products are equal to resource prices, then marginal cost of the product produced by each firm must equal marginal revenue received from it. Nevertheless, since sufficient time for reallocation of fixed resources has not been allowed, some firms will be making profits and others will be incurring losses.

The returns to fixed resources in the short run are in the nature of economic rent. Where losses occur, economic rent is less than the (long-run) opportunity costs of the fixed resources. Profits mean that the rents of the fixed resources exceed their (long-run) opportunity costs.

THE LONG RUN • In the long run those resources that were fixed in the short run become variable.[10] These are the resources that constitute the plants of individual firms. As they become variable, it becomes pos-

---

[10] In our discussion of the long run we shall continue to distinguish between "fixed" resources and "variable" resources even though all are variable. This will enable us to keep those resources that constitute scale of plant separate from those that do not, and will facilitate the discussion.

sible for individual firms to change scale of plant, for firms to exit from those industries in which losses occur, and for firms to enter those industries which make profits — provided entry is easy, as it is under conditions of pure and monopolistic competition.

As "fixed" resources are channeled into profitable industries, marginal physical products and marginal revenue products of "variable" resources will increase in those employments because of the higher ratios of the "fixed" to the variable resources. At the same time, marginal physical products and marginal revenue products of "variable" resources will decrease in the industries from which "fixed" resources are transferred. Thus the short-run equilibrium allocation of "variable" resources is disturbed and price differentials in the different employments for any one of them develop. Reallocation of "variable" resources from the loss-incurring industries to the profitable industries supplements the similar reallocation of fixed resources. More of the products that consumers value highly in relation to their costs are produced, while production of products valued less by consumers in relation to their costs declines.

The changes in product supplies again cause disequilibrium for consumers, but the disequilibrium and the consequent movement toward a new equilibrium position increase consumer satisfaction. Consumers value the product contribution of a given resource unit in a profitable industry more than they value its contribution in a loss-incurring industry.[11] Consequently, resource transfers from the latter to the former must increase consumer satisfaction. But as more of the higher-valued goods are produced, consumption of them increases and consumer valuations of them decrease. As less of the lower-valued goods are produced, consumer consumption of them decreases and valuations of them increase. Consumer satisfaction will be maximized by resource transfers up to the point at which the marginal product contributions per unit of any given resource in all of its employments are valued alike by consumers.

Long-run equilibrium will be reached when *all* resources are so allocated that their respective marginal revenue products are equalized in all alternative uses. No shortages or surpluses occur for any resource; that is, the marginal revenue product of each is equal to its price. When the equilibrium allocation of resources is achieved, each firm will be using resources in the least-cost combination — the marginal physical product per dollar's worth of one will be equal to the marginal physical product per dollar's worth of every other resource used.

---

[11] In technical terms, its value of marginal product in the profitable industry exceeds its value of marginal product in the loss-incurring industry.

If entry into particular profitable industries is restricted or blocked, as it may be under conditions of pure monopoly or oligopoly, movement toward the long-run equilibrium allocation of resources referred to in the preceding paragraph will be stopped short of its goal. "Fixed" resources will not be able to move into those industries in sufficient quantities to eliminate the profits. Consequently, "fixed" resources already in those industries will be paid higher returns than those forced to remain in other employments. Firms will adjust their scales of plant in such industries to the extent necessary to equate long-run marginal cost to marginal revenue and will use least-cost resource combinations for the outputs which they produce.

Distribution of the Product

Distribution of the product, or income distribution, and its place in the general equilibrium picture have yet to be considered. Since we assume that the quantities of resources in existence and their distribution among the households of the economy are fixed, we shall be interested in the effects of resource pricing on incomes and in the effects of income changes on the economy as a whole.

EFFECTS OF RESOURCE PRICING ON INCOMES • As resource prices change from their initial pattern and as full employment of all resources is achieved, individual incomes change. The owners of those resources originally in short supply receive larger incomes as the prices of their resources increase. The owners of those resources that originally were not fully employed may find that their incomes decrease, remain the same, or increase.

Some of the owners of a given resource for which economy-wide surpluses occurred may have been able to find employment for their individual supplies at the initial prices. However, unemployment of units owned by others causes the market price of all units to decrease. Lower prices paid for given supplies placed in employment lead to lower incomes for the former group of resource owners.

Those who were unable to secure employment at the initial prices for all resource units owned are in a different situation. As prices decrease they are able to place more resource units in employment. For the owner of a single kind of resource, if the percentage increase in the quantity which he can place in employment exceeds the percentage decrease in its price, his income from the resource will increase. If the percentage increase in the quantity which he can place in employment equals the percentage decrease in its price, no change in income from it occurs. If the percentage increase in the quantity which he can place in employment is less than the percentage decrease in its price, his income from it will decrease. For those owning several such resources, different combinations of the foregoing possibilities may lead to individual income increases, constancy, or decreases.

EFFECTS OF INCOME CHANGES ON THE ECONOMY • Changes in consumer incomes will change individual consumer positions of equilibrium and demands for different products.[12] The changes in demands for products will have repercussions throughout the economy. Individual consumers move toward their new equilibrium positions. Prices of products move to reflect the new consumer valuations of goods. New possibilities of profit and prospects for loss occur for business firms causing reallocation of productive capacity to meet the new pattern of consumer tastes and preferences. Marginal revenue products of resources and resource prices will be higher in the production of those products toward which demand has shifted and lower in the production of those products away from which demand has shifted. Resources will be transferred from the lower-paying to the higher-paying uses, except to the extent that restricted entry into industries blocks their movements. And so the economy moves toward general equilibrium.

SUMMARY

If the economy could be and were one of pure competition throughout, and if the stationary assumptions of the present chapter were fulfilled, the attainment of general equilibrium would provide the greatest possible measure of consumer satisfaction that the given distribution of resource ownership would allow. No consumer could gain by exchanging quantities per unit of time of one product for another. No transfers of a resource from one employment to another could increase net national product since the value of marginal product for any given resource would be the same in its alternative uses. No profits or losses would occur. Average (and marginal) cost of production for any particular commodity would be equal to its price.

But this economic utopia will never be achieved. Various deviations from pure competition in both product and resource markets prevent the free enterprise system from allocating its resources perfectly among different uses. Many are inherent in the state of modern technological developments. Some arise from lack of knowledge — the scope

---

[12] Changes in market demands for particular products will be much less than changes in individual consumer demands for those products. Increases in some consumers' demands for a product may be partly or wholly offset by decreases in other consumers' demands for the same product, or vice versa.

and the complexities of the economic system are too great for perfect knowledge on the part of all economic units to be attained. Others, such as rigid rather than flexible prices, arise from the activities of particular private economic institutions or the government, or from the psychological make-up of particular economic units. Additionally, the real world is a dynamic one with changes occurring constantly in such basic factors as consumer tastes and preferences, the range of available productive techniques, the quantities of available resources, the kinds of resources available, and the distribution of resource ownership. All of these prevent the attainment of equilibrium positions. Nevertheless, it is the motivating forces supplied by equilibrium positions that perform the task of organizing and guiding a free enterprise economy toward more efficient operation.

SUGGESTED READINGS

DUE, JOHN F., and ROBERT W. CLOWER. *Intermediate Economic Analysis.* 4th ed.; Homewood: Richard D. Irwin, Inc., 1961, chap. 20.

HICKS, J. R. *Value and Capital.* 2d ed.; Oxford, England: The Clarendon Press, 1946, chaps. IV–VI, and VIII.

KNIGHT, FRANK H. "A Suggestion for Simplifying the Statement of the General Theory of Price," *Journal of Political Economy,* XXXVI (June 1928), 353–370.

SMITH, ADAM. *The Wealth of Nations.* Edwin Cannan, ed. New York: The Modern Library, 1937, chaps. VI and VII.

Linear Programming $\Big|$ 18

LINEAR PROGRAMMING is the simplest and most widely used of the mathematical programming techniques that have come into vogue since World War II. It is a technique for solving maximization and minimization problems confronting decision-making agencies subject to certain side conditions or constraints which limit what the agencies are able to do. Its development has been concurrent with and tremendously enhanced by the advent of electronic computers.

Linear programming techniques provide little information regarding the operation of the economy beyond that provided by the conventional theory of the firm. Their prime virtue is that they provide computational possibilities that are not present in conventional theory owing to the smooth, continuous and frequently nonlinear nature of conventional theory's production, cost, and revenue functions. The observable data confronting decision-making agencies are ordinarily not continuous and may not be amenable to marginal analysis or calculus techniques. From an assumption that relations among observable data are linear, straightforward solutions to complex maximization and minimization problems can be obtained through linear programming. Moreover, problems programmed for this sort of solution can make extensive use of electronic computers that are not yet able to perform the operations of the infinitesimal calculus. Sometimes the distortions resulting from the exclusive use of linear relationships may render worthless the solutions arrived at by means of the technique. But in many cases distortions of this kind may be more or less negligible. Like any other technique, if its results are to be useful it must be applied with good judgment and common sense.

This chapter presents the nature and method of linear programming. First, we shall establish the assumptions on which linear programming problems rest. Second, we shall formulate and solve graphically a general maximization problem involving one output and two inputs. Third,

341

we shall formulate and solve a maximization problem involving multiple outputs and multiple inputs. Fourth, we shall consider the dual solution to a maximization problem.

THE ASSUMPTIONS

The linear programming technique rests on several basic assumptions. In the first place, the decision making to which it is applied always involves constraints on the decision-making agency. In the second place, input and output prices are assumed to be constant. In the third place, the firm's[1] input-output, output-output, and input-input relations are presumed to be linear. These will be discussed in turn.

The Constraints

In linear programming problems, the firm is viewed as facing various limitations on its activities. There may be quantity limitations on particular kinds of inputs or facilities used by the firm. An automobile final assembly line, for example, can turn out some maximum number of automobiles per twenty-four-hour period. A firm's warehouse space contains a fixed number of square feet. A candy factory can wrap only so many bars per day. The firm's access to credit may be restricted. And so on.

The firm is viewed also as facing a limited number of alternative production processes. Any one process is defined in terms of a constant ratio of inputs. Suppose process A involves the use of one man of a given skill and one machine of a given kind and size. Production carried on with process A can be increased or decreased until input quantity limitations are reached but always will involve one man per machine regardless of the total number of machines used.

Constant Prices

Linear programming techniques make use of the purely competitive approach to prices. Output prices and input prices are assumed to be unaffected by the actions of any one individual firm. Output prices are the same whether the firm's output be large or small. Input prices are the same regardless of how much or how little of the inputs the firm uses. As sellers and as buyers firms are thought of as being price takers rather than price makers.

---

[1] As a matter of convenience the decision-making agency will be designated as a firm throughout the chapter. Linear programming techniques can be and are used by agencies other than firms, e.g., military procurement units.

Linear Relations

Linear programming techniques take advantage of the simplicity of linear relations. In many instances linear relations are found in fact. A firm purchasing an input at a constant price per unit faces a linear total cost curve for that input. The total revenue curve from sale of a product will be linear when the product sells at a constant price per unit. An isocost curve for two inputs will be linear, given the prices of the inputs. An isorevenue curve for two outputs will be linear, given the prices of those outputs.

In other cases relations among variables that may not actually be linear can be represented usefully by a series of (different) discrete linear relationships or by a single linear relationship. An isoquant, for example, is ordinarily a nonlinear constant product curve for two resources. The linear programming counterpart is a series of connected linear relations. Similarly, actual production functions may very well show nonlinear relations between inputs and output. In linear programming problems they are taken as being linearly homogeneous.

MAXIMIZATION PROBLEMS

Two maximization problems will be considered in this section. In the first we shall be concerned with the optimum use of inputs in the production of a single output. In the second we shall be concerned with the optimum output mix to be produced with particular inputs.

One Output, Two Inputs

COST OUTLAY CONSTRAINTS • Suppose that a firm producing one output X and using inputs A and B seeks to maximize output subject to a given cost outlay. This problem is familiar from our previous study of the theory of production and serves as a good introduction to linear programming. However, suppose that the possibilities of continuous substitution between A and B that characterize the usual theoretical presentation of the problem are absent. Instead suppose that there are only four processes (possible ratios of B to A) by which the firm can produce the product. The firm faces constant input prices and a constant output price.[2]

The nature of a process is illustrated in Figure 18–1. Units of input A per unit of time are measured along the horizontal axis and units of input B per unit of time are shown on the vertical axis. If process C — one of the four processes available to the firm — requires three units of input B to every one unit of input A, the process can be represented by

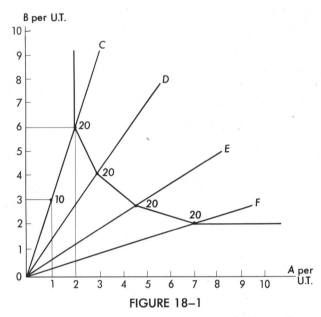

FIGURE 18–1

the linear ray OC. Ignore for the moment the scale numbers along OC. The various points making up the ray OC show the fixed ratio of B to A, but at different levels of utilization. Similarly process rays OD, OE, and OF can be drawn for the other three processes available to the firm. Each process ray shows a given ratio of B to A throughout its length. The ratio of B to A is different for each of the process rays.

The assumption that the production function is linearly homo-geneous enables us to measure product output along each of the process rays. A production function is of this type if when *all* inputs are increased in a given proportion, output is increased in the same proportion. Focus-ing for the moment on process ray OC, suppose that three units of B used with one unit of A will produce ten units of output X. The point on OC representing this combination of A and B can be marked off as ten units of X. Now if the inputs are doubled to six units of B and to two units of A, output is doubled to twenty units of X. The point on OC representing the new combination of A and B can be scaled as twenty units of X and will lie twice as far from the origin as does the point representing ten units of X. The output scale along OC is thus easily established.

Output scales can be established in a similar way along each of the

---

[2] The problem would not be changed if total revenue were stated as the quantity to be maximized. Since price per unit of output is given, maximization of output also maximizes total revenue.

other three process rays. However, the distance measuring twenty units of output (or any other given quantity of output) will not ordinarily be the same along one process ray as it will be along another. The technological efficiency of the other three processes are assumed to be such that the twenty-unit output marks on their respective process rays are those indicated in Figure 18–1.

The points on the various process rays representing any given quantity of output can be joined by a series of straight lines, as they are at the twenty-unit level in Figure 18–1. The resulting kinked curve can be called an isoquant, just as was its counterpart in traditional theory. A different isoquant can be drawn for each possible output level. The higher the output level, the farther from the origin the isoquant lies. The linear segment of an isoquant between any two process rays will always be parallel to the corresponding linear segment of any other isoquant.

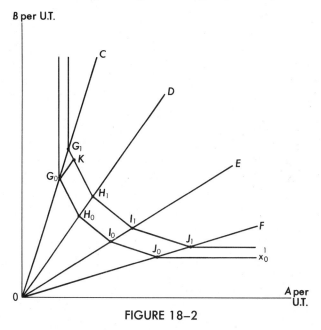

FIGURE 18–2

For example in Figure 18–2 the G_1H_1 segment of isoquant x_1 is parallel to the G_0H_0 segment of isoquant x_0.*

Any point such as K on isoquant x_1 represents the simultaneous use by the firm of two processes to produce a given amount of output.

---

* This must be so because the sides OG_1 and OH_1 of triangle G_1H_1O are cut into proportional segments by line G_0H_0; i.e. $OG_0/G_0G_1 = OH_0/H_0H_1$.

In this case the firm would be using process C and process D. The processes are assumed to be technologically independent of one another. The productivity of process C is unaffected by the level at which process D is used and vice versa. Quantity OG_0 of X is produced by means of process C. Quantity G_0K ($=H_0H_1$) of X is produced using process D. The output scale measuring G_0K (or H_0H_1) of X is different from that measuring OG_0 of X. The scale of process ray OD is used for the former while the scale of process ray OC is used for the latter.

In general we would expect isoquants to exhibit the shapes illustrated in Figures 18–1 and 18–2. In Figure 18–2 suppose that B is capital and that A is labor. Continuous substitution of one for the other is assumed to be impossible. Nevertheless, the same general type of reasoning as that used in discussing conventional isoquant shapes still applies. If the firm were using process F to produce a given amount of product, the ratio of labor to capital would be relatively high. Therefore, if the firm were to consider a process using smaller ratios of labor to capital, say, process E, it is likely that it could give up a rather large amount of labor to obtain the additional capital — the amount of output remaining constant. But as the firm moves to processes using relatively smaller ratios of labor to capital, say, processes D and C, the amounts of labor that could be given up to obtain additional units of capital, output remaining constant, would be expected to become smaller and smaller.

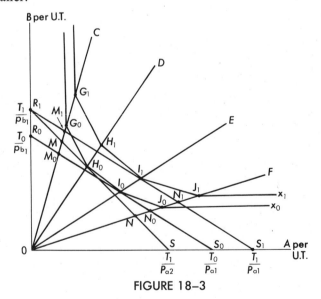

FIGURE 18–3

The cost constraint on the firm is represented by a conventional isocost curve. Its position and shape are determined by the fixed cost outlay and the fixed prices per unit of the firm's inputs. In Figure 18–3 suppose the cost outlay is T_1 while the prices of A and B are p_{a1} and p_{b1}, respectively. The cost outlay divided by the price of A, or T_1/p_{a1} establishes point S_1 which is the number of units of A that can be obtained if no B is purchased. Similarly, T_1/p_{b1} is the number of units of B that can be purchased if no A is taken; it is represented by point R_1. A straight line joining R_1 and S_1 is the isocost curve showing the combinations of A and B available with the cost outlay T_1. The isocost curve has a negative slope equal to $OR_1/OS_1 = T_1/p_{b1} \div T_1/p_{a1} = T_1/p_{b1} \times p_{a1}/T_1 = p_{a1}/p_{b1}$.*

The isocost curve and process rays OC and OF place limits on what the firm is able to do. Any point on or within the triangle OM_1N_1 is a possible combination of inputs A and B and will lie on some isoquant of the firm; that is, it will produce some specific level of output. The area bounded by OM_1N_1 is called the area of *feasible solutions* to the firm's problem. No production possibilities outside this area are open to the firm.

From the feasible solutions to the firm's problem the *optimal solution* must be found. This has already been postulated as the one that maximizes the firm's output subject to the cost outlay constraint. The optimal solution will occur at point I_1 at which the isocost curve touches the highest possible isoquant. Output x_1 is the highest output possible with the given cost outlay. The firm will use process E. Cost level T_1 expended on any of the other processes will not produce outputs as high as x_1.

A change in the cost constraint, with the prices of A and B remaining constant, will not affect the process used, but will affect only the level at which it is used. Changes in T will shift the position of the isocost curve but will not affect its slope. A reduction in the cost outlay to T_0 shifts the isocost curve to the left parallel to itself to R_0S_0. The area of feasible solutions is now bounded by OM_0N_0. The firm maximizes output by using process E at level I_0. The maximum output is x_0. Iso-

---

* The equation of the isocost curve will be

$$ap_{a1} + bp_{b1} = T_1$$

or,

$$b = \frac{T_1}{p_{b1}} - a\frac{p_{a1}}{p_{b1}}$$

for which $\dfrac{T_1}{p_{b1}}$ is the B axis intercept and p_{a1}/p_{b1} is the slope.

costs parallel to R_1S_1 will always touch those isoquant corners falling along process ray OE. This will be so because, due to the assumption that the production function is homogeneous, the corresponding segments of the various isoquants are parallel to each other.

On the other hand, if the price of A relative to the price of B were to increase enough, the firm would shift to a different process. Suppose the total cost outlay were to remain the same and the price of A were to rise to p_{a2}. The restricting isocost curve now becomes R_1S and the area OMN encloses the feasible solutions. To maximize output subject to the constraint the firm would use process D at level H_0. It is possible, too, that the price of A relative to that of B could change just enough to make the isocost curve coincide with a linear segment of an isoquant — say, a segment corresponding to G_1H_1. If this were the case process C and process D would be equally efficient. It would make no difference which the firm uses. Or any combination of the two processes shown by the linear isoquant segment G_1H_1 could be used.

Where the firm is faced by a single constraint, not more than one process is required to maximize whatever the firm is maximizing. In the case at hand, the process to be used will be determined by the ratio of input prices. Once the output-maximizing process has been identified, it becomes apparent that a considerable change in input price ratios may occur without inducing the firm to switch from one process to another.

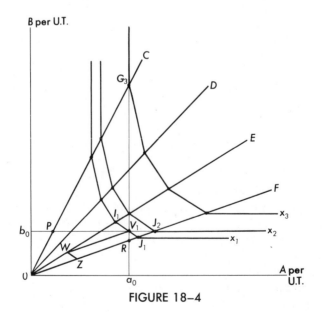

FIGURE 18–4

The extent to which input price ratios must change to induce a change in the input price used will depend upon the number of processes available and the measures of the angles formed by linear segments of the isoquants.

INPUT QUANTITY CONSTRAINTS • The optimal solution to the problem of output maximization is different if instead of being faced with a total cost outlay constraint, the firm is faced with quantity limitations per time period on one or more of its inputs. Common examples of this sort of thing are warehouse space, number of machines available, size of a drying kiln, and so on. We shall look first at a situation in which only one of two inputs is limited in quantity. Then we shall extend the constraint to include both of the inputs that the firm uses.

In Figure 18–4 we assume first that not more than b_0 of B is available to the firm and that A is available in unlimited quantities. The area of feasible solutions would be on or within triangle OPJ_2 — the area on or between process rays OC and OF and on or below the horizontal line extending to the right from b_0. There will be some isoquant the horizontal segment of which coincides with the horizontal line. This isoquant is designated x_2 in the diagram and represents the highest output level available with quantity b_0 of B. Process F used at level OJ_2 will maximize the firm's output.

On the other hand if A were limited to a_0 while B were unlimited in quantity, the area of feasible solutions would lie between process rays OC and OF and on or to the left of a vertical line extending upward from a_0. Output would be maximized by using process C at level OG_3 and would be x_3. In each of the two cases output maximization requires but a single process. In neither case is the ratio of input prices a determinant of the process to be used.

Turning now to the case in which both inputs are limited in quantity, assume in Figure 18–4 that the availability of input A is limited to a_0 while that of B is limited to b_0. Subject to these limitations, the area of feasible solutions is on or within the polygon OPV_1R. The solution lies at point V_1 and the maximum output of the firm is x_1. In the case illustrated process E and process F will both be used. Quantity OW will be produced using process E, and quantity WV_1 ($=ZJ_1$) will be produced using process F. Conceivably, if the available quantity of A were smaller and that of B were larger the solution to the problem could fall at an isoquant corner such as I_1. If this were the case, process E, only, would be required. Again the ratio of the price of A to the price of B plays no part in determining the process or processes to be used.

The problems discussed above illustrate a fundamental principle in linear programming techniques. No larger number of processes than the number of constraints placed on the firm will be required in whatever the firm is maximizing or minimizing. In the example in which total cost outlay was the only constraint, one process was required. In the example in which the constraint was the quantity of one input, no more than one process was required. When two inputs were limited in quantity, no more than two processes were required. Where there are more inputs limited in quantity more processes may be required, but these will not exceed the number of inputs for which there are effective limitations.

Multiple Outputs, Multiple Inputs

Moving now to a more complex problem, suppose that the objective of a firm is to maximize the excess of its total receipts over its total variable costs — that is, its total economic rent as defined in Chapter 13[3] — subject to limitations in the capacities of certain fixed facilities. Suppose the firm produces two kinds of output, X and Y. It has four kinds of facilities each of which is fixed in capacity. We shall designate these as facilities M, N, R, and S. These could be such things as paint shop capacity, final assembly capacity, packaging capacity, and the like.

Rent yielded per unit of X and per unit of Y will depend upon the prices received for each of the products and the average variable costs of each. We shall assume that given quantities of variable inputs are required per unit of X regardless of the amount of X produced; therefore average variable cost of X will be constant. The same assumption will be made for product Y. Rent yielded per unit of product X produced is equal to its price minus its average variable cost and thus will be a constant amount. Rent yielded per unit of product Y is computed in the same way. These can be designated as r_x and r_y, respectively.

If r_x and r_y were \$8 and \$6, respectively, the following *objective equation* could be established showing what it is that the firm wants to maximize:

$$8x + 6y = W \qquad (18.1)$$

Rent yielded per unit of X multiplied by the total amount of X produced will be total rent received from the production of X. Rent yielded per unit of Y multiplied by the quantity of Y produced will show total rent obtained from the production of Y. The sum of the two will be W, or total rent received by the firm.

---

[3] Maximization of rent also means that profit will be maximized, since profit is equal to rent minus total fixed costs. In the problem being formulated the firm's fixed costs will not be known. Thus rent can be computed but profit cannot.

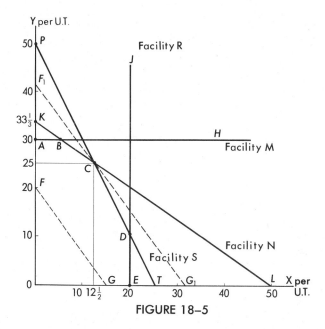

FIGURE 18-5

The objective equation is the equation for a family of *isorent curves* — one for every possible value of W. In Figure 18-5 the line FG is the isorent curve for W equals \$120. It shows all combinations of X and Y which will yield that amount of rent. Its slope is $-r_x/r_y$, or in this case $-8/6$. Isorent curves for higher values of W lie farther to the right but have the same slope. Those for lower values of W also have the same slope but lie farther to the left.

The constraints on the firm's activities are the fixed facilities M, N, R, and S. Suppose we designate the entire amount of each as unity. In Table 18-1, that part of each facility required in the production of one unit of X and that part of each required in the production of one unit of Y are shown.

TABLE 18-1

FACILITY	FACILITY INPUT PER UNIT OF OUTPUT	
	X	Y
M	0.0	0.033
N	0.02	0.03
S	0.04	0.02
R	0.05	0.0

Essentially, Table 18-1 defines the processes involved in the problem. There will be two processes used if both outputs are produced. The production of X requires one process — fixed proportions of facilities M, N, S, and R. Similarly the production of Y requires one process — fixed proportions of the four facilities but proportions that are different from those required to produce X.

From Table 18-1 we can construct a set of algebraic representations of the constraints placed on the production of X and Y by the fixed facilities. These are

$$0.033y \leq 1 \tag{18.2}$$
$$0.05x \leq 1 \tag{18.3}$$
$$0.02x + 0.03y \leq 1 \tag{18.4}$$

and

$$0.04x + 0.02y \leq 1 \tag{18.5}$$

in which

$$x \geq 0 \text{ and } y \geq 0$$

Inequality (18.2) sums up the constraint exercised by facility M. This facility is useful in the production of Y only. It is not useful in the production of X. The amount required in the production of one unit of Y is 0.033 of the entire facility. If we consider (18.2) as an equation, solving for y we find that the entire facility will permit the production of thirty units of Y per unit of time. It will, of course, permit the production of smaller quantities. Graphically the horizontal straight line AH in Figure 18-5 at thirty units of Y represents the limitations on production inherent in facility M.

Similarly, inequality (18.3) sums up the constraint exercised by facility R. Facility R is used only in the production of X and an amount 0.05 of the entire facility is required for each unit. The maximum quantity of X that facility R will permit is twenty units per time period. This is shown graphically by the vertical line EJ at that output level in Figure 18-5.

The production possibilities of facility N are shown by inequality (18.4) and include both outputs. Since 0.03 of facility N are required for a unit of Y and 0.02 of it are required for a unit of X, (18.4) treated as an equation marks off possible combinations of outputs that the facility will allow from those it will not allow. If x were zero, thirty-three and one-third units of Y could be handled by the facility. If y were zero, fifty units of X could be handled by it per time period. Locating these two points at K and L, respectively, in Figure 18-5, the straight line joining them is the graphic representation of the equation.

Similarly, (18.5) treated as an equation separates the combinations of X and Y that facility S will permit from those it will not permit. If no X were produced, y could be fifty units per time period. If no Y were produced, x could be twenty-five units. The graphic representation of the equation is the line PT in Figure 18–5.

The area of feasible solutions, showing all combinations of X and Y that can be turned out per unit of time by the firm, is $OABCDE$. Facility M limits the firm to combinations equal to or smaller than those represented by AH; facility M and facility N limit it to combinations equal to or smaller than those represented by $ABL;$ facility M, facility N, and facility S further limit it to combinations equal to or smaller than those represented by $ABCT;$ facility N, facility S, and facility R limit it to combinations equal to or smaller than those represented by $BCD;$ facility S and facility R limit it to combinations equal to or smaller than those represented by $DE;$ and facility R limits it to combinations equal to or smaller than those represented by EJ.

The optimal solution to the firm's problem can be found graphically by moving to higher and higher isorent curves until the one just touched by the area of feasible solutions is reached. This will be isorent curve F_1G_1, which is just touched by point C in Figure 18–5. No other point either within or on the boundary of the area of feasible solutions touches an isorent curve as high as F_1G_1. Every point other than C on the isorent curve F_1G_1 lies outside the area of feasible solutions. The firm would produce and sell twenty-five units of Y receiving rent of $6 per unit. It would produce and sell twelve and one-half units of X receiving rent of $8 per unit. Thus the maximum total rent obtainable would be $250 per time period.

The facilities limitations are not all effective as constraints on the firm. At point C facility M is not used to capacity and therefore does not restrict the firm's output. Similarly, facility R is not used to capacity. To produce combination C, only facilities N and S are used to their full capacities. If more of these two facilities were available the firm could move to a higher isorent curve.

Algebraically the solution to the problem can be found by examining the "corners" of the area of feasible solutions. We need only to examine the corners since the number of processes involved in the problem will not exceed the number of effective constraints on the firm. Thus the points at which both X and Y are positive (that is, where two processes are used) and that would be possible optimal solutions must lie at corners formed by two constraints (that is, where two constraints would be effective). A possible optimal solution in which only X is produced would require but one effective constraint and thus would be the corner at the intersection of the X axis and the constraint that exercises the greatest restriction when used exclusively in the production of X. Similarly, the corner on the Y axis represents the only possible optimal solution if Y alone were produced. If the optimal solution were a zero output for both X and Y, the necessity of a corner solution at the origin is obvious.

Suppose now that we start with the corner at the origin and proceed clockwise around the area of feasible solutions, attempting to find the one at which total rent to the fixed facilities is maximum, that is, at which the objective equation (18.1) yields the maximum W. At O we find that W equals zero. To find the coordinates of corner A, we solve the facility M equation (18.2). At this corner x equals zero and y equals 30. Plugging these values for X and Y into equation (18.1) we find that W equals $180. The simultaneous solution of equations (18.2) and (18.4) for facilities M and N gives us corner B at which y equals 30 and x equals 5. Thus from equation (18.1), total rent is found to be $220. The simultaneous solution to equations (18.4) and (18.5) for facilities N and S is represented by corner C where y equals 25 and x equals 12½. Substituting these values in equation (18.1), total rent is $250. When equations (18.5) and (18.3) for facilities S and R are solved simultaneously for the coordinates of corner D, x equals 20 and y equals 10. Substituting these values in equation (18.1), total rent is $220. The solution to (18.3) provides the coordinates of corner E with x equal to 20 and y equal to zero. Substituting in (18.1) we find that total rent would be $160. Comparing the results obtained at the various corners shows that corner C provides maximum total rent. In problems where the number of outputs and constraints are too great for graphic analysis, this sort of algebraic examination of the "corners" of the area of feasible solutions can be used to find the one that provides the optimal solution.[4]

Different ratios of r_x to r_y may result in different optimal solutions to rent maximization. The slope of an isorent curve $(-r_x/r_y)$ could conceivably be small enough so that the area of feasible solutions touches the highest isorent curve at point B. Or it could be great enough for the highest possible isorent curve to be touched at point D. If $-r_x/r_y$ were equal to the slope of the line segment CD in Figure 18–5 — that is, if the highest attainable isorent curve were to coincide with the graphic representation of equation (18.5) — any combination of X and Y on line

---

[4] The method used here is called the complete description method. An alternative is provided by the simplex method. See Robert Dorfman, Paul A. Samuelson, and Robert M. Solow, *Linear Programming and Economic Analysis,* New York: McGraw-Hill Book Company, Inc., 1958, chap. 4.

segment CD would be an optimal solution to maximization of total rent. In this case the limitations imposed by facility S would be the only effective constraint on the firm.

The Dual Problem

Every linear programming problem has a counterpart problem called its *dual.* The original problem is referred to as the *primal* problem. If the primal problem requires maximization, the dual problem is one of minimization. Or if the primal is a minimization problem the dual is a maximization problem. An illustration of the relationship between a primal problem and its dual is provided in the theory of production and costs. Suppose that the primal problem were that of maximizing output with a given cost outlay. The dual would be that of minimizing costs for the given product output. Whether or not a particular problem to be programmed should be set up for solution in its primal or its dual form depends upon (1) which formulation yields more directly the desired information and (2) which formulation can be more easily solved.

In this section the dual of the primal problem of the proceding section will be formulated and solved. In the primal problem we sought the outputs of X and Y that would maximize total rent received by the firm, subject to capacity limitations of its fixed facilities M, N, R, and S. In the dual problem we seek to impute minimum values — sometimes called shadow prices — to the firm's fixed facilities just sufficient to absorb the firm's total rent.

The data available to us are those of the primal problem. Table 18-1 shows the amount of each fixed facility available (one unit of each) and the portion of each fixed facility required in the production of a unit of X and a unit of Y. The contribution per unit of product X to total rent is given as $8 while that per unit of product Y is given as $6. The objective equation of the dual problem can be stated as

$$v_m + v_n + v_r + v_s = V \qquad (18.6)$$

The term v_m denotes the value to be imputed to facility M while v_n, v_r, and v_s denote, respectively, the values to be imputed to facilities N, R, and S.* On the right side of the equation, V denotes the total valuation of the fixed facilities.

---

* In the present problem the coefficient of each of the variables on the left side of the equation will be one, since the entire capacity of each fixed facility is taken as being unity. If each fixed facility were to consist of some certain number of units, then the value per unit of each facility would have as its coefficient the number of units of the facility which are available.

The constraints placed on the assigning of minimum values to the fixed facilities are summed up in the following inequalities:

$$0.0v_m + 0.02v_n + 0.04v_s + 0.05v_r \geq 8 \tag{18.7}$$

and,
$$0.33v_m + 0.03v_n + 0.02v_s + 0.0v_r \geq 6 \tag{18.8}$$

in which $v_m \geq 0, v_n \geq 0, v_s \geq 0,$ and $v_r \geq 0$

Inequality (18.7) states that the values assigned to the various fixed facilities must be such that the values of productive capacity necessary for the production of one unit of X (see Table 18–1) when added together must not be less than the value of a unit of X. Inequality (18.8) states the same thing with respect to the production of Y. Together and treated as equations they state that the values assigned to each kind of productive capacity must be such that a dollar's worth of that productive capacity used in producing either X or Y must yield a dollar in rent.

We face the dilemma of having more unknowns than there are equations (treating (18.7) and (18.8) as equations) to solve for the unknowns. However, the linear programming principle cited earlier, together with conventional economic analysis, can serve as means of rescue. The linear programming principle tells us that the number of fixed facilities operating as effective constraints on the firm's output should not exceed the number of processes used. There are two processes used — one for producing X and one for producing Y. Consequently only two of the fixed facilities can be effective constraints on the firm's output and the other two must be underutilized.

Consider now an underutilized facility from the point of view of conventional economic analysis. A small increase — say, 1 percent — in such a facility would add nothing to the firm's output or total receipts. The marginal revenue product of such an increment would thus be zero, and so would its imputed value. Every other 1 percent of the facility would also have an imputed value of zero and so would the whole underutilized facility. Since we must have two underutilized facilities, two of the variables of (18.7) and (18.8) should have values of zero and the other two will take on positive values.

The problem now is to find which two of the variables — v_m, v_n, v_s, and v_r — have imputed values of zero and which two have positive values when the firm is minimizing total valuation of the fixed facilities. We can proceed by first assigning values of zero to any two of these, solving for the other two. Then we assign values of zero to another pair (one of the pair may be from the previous pair) and solve for the remaining paid. We proceed in this manner until every possible pair of the variables has been assigned zero values and the corresponding solutions in terms of the remaining variables have been obtained. Six solutions of this sort are possible. We shall examine them in turn.

TABLE 18–2

SOLUTION	IMPUTED VALUE IN DOLLARS				TOTAL VALUATION IN DOLLARS
	v_m	v_n	v_s	v_r	
(1)	0	0	300	−80	...
(2)	0	200	0	80	280
(3)	0	100	150	0	250
(4)	181.82	0	0	160	341.82
(5)	66.66	0	200	0	266.66
(6)	−181.82	400	0	0	...

Suppose that first of all that we let v_m and v_n take on values of zero. Equations (18.7) and (18.8) become

$$0.04v_s + 0.05v_r = 8 \tag{18.7a}$$

and

$$0.02v_s + 0.0\ v_r = 6 \tag{18.8a}$$

Solving equation (18.8a) for v_s we find that v_s equals $300. Substituting this value of v_s in equation (18.7a) we find that v_r equals −$80. This is recorded as solution (1) in Table 18–2.

Second, suppose we let v_m and v_s take on values of zero. Equations (18.7) and (18.8) become

$$0.02v_n + 0.05v_r = 8 \tag{18.7b}$$

and

$$0.03v_n + 0.0\ v_r = 6 \tag{18.8b}$$

Solving equation (18.8b) for v_n, we find that v_n is $200. Substituting in equation (18.7b), v_r is found to be $80. These values are recorded as solution (2) in Table 18–2.

Third, let v_m and v_r assume zero values. Equations (18.7) and (18.8) become

$$0.02v_n + 0.04v_s = 8 \tag{18.7c}$$

and

$$0.03v_n + 0.02v_s = 6 \tag{18.8c}$$

Solving these simultaneously we obtain v_n equal to $100 and v_s equal to $150. These are recorded as solution (3) in Table 18–2.

Fourth, let v_n and v_s be zero. Equations (18.7) and (18.8) become

$$0.05 \ v_r = 8 \tag{18.7d}$$

and

$$0.033v_m = 6 \tag{18.8d}$$

The solutions will be: v_r equals \$160 and v_m equals \$181.82. These are shown as solution (4) in Table 18–2.

Fifth, if v_n and v_r were zero, equations (18.7) and (18.8) would become

$$0.0 \ v_m + 0.04v_s = 8 \tag{18.7e}$$

and

$$0.033v_m + 0.02v_s = 6 \tag{18.8e}$$

Solving equation (18.7e) for v_s yields a value of \$200. Plugging this value for v_s into equation (18.8e), v_m becomes \$66.66. These are listed as solution (5) in Table 18–2.

Finally, when we let v_s and v_r take on values of zero, we will have exhausted the possibilities. In this case equations (18.7) and (18.8) become

$$0.0 \ v_m + 0.02v_n = 8 \tag{18.7f}$$

and

$$0.033v_m + 0.03v_n = 6 \tag{18.8f}$$

In equation (18.7f), v_n is equal to \$400. Substituting this value for v_n in equation (18.8f), we find that v_m is $-\$181.82$. These are shown as solution (6) in Table 18–2.

All six possible combinations of minimum values that may be assigned to the four facilities are shown in Table 18–2. Of the six possible solutions, two can be ruled out immediately. Solutions (1) and (6) yield negative values for one variable, thus violating the requirement that imputed values must be zero or larger. To find which of the remaining four solutions will minimize V of the objective equation (18.6) we can evaluate (18.6) using each of the four in turn. The results are listed in Table 18–2 in the last column. Thus of the four solutions it appears that solution (3) is the one we seek. Facilities M and R are assigned imputed values of zero. They are the ones that are not fully utilized. Facility N is assigned an imputed value of \$100. Facility S is assigned an imputed value of \$150. Thus the minimum possible valuation of the fully utilized fixed facilities is \$250 when the productive capacity of each of these is equally valuable in the production of either X or Y.

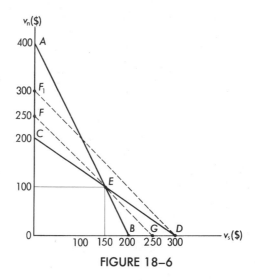

FIGURE 18–6

Alternatively, suppose we look at the problem geometrically. Since facilities M and R have imputed values of zero, the objective equation (18.6) becomes

$$v_n + v_s = V \tag{18.6a}$$

This equation yields a family of isovalue curves, each having a slope of -1. If V were \$300 then F_1D in Figure 18–6 would be the graphic representation of the objective equation. If V were \$250 then FG would be its graphic representation. For every different value assigned to V a different isovalue curve is established. All such curves are parallel to each other.

Equations (18.7c) and (18.8c) are plotted in Figure 18–6 as AB and CD, respectively. Curve AB shows the minimum possible combinations of values that could be assigned to facilities N and S such that a dollar's worth of productive capacity would yield a dollar in rent in the production of X. Curve CD shows the minimum possible combinations of values that could be assigned to facilities N and S such that a dollar's worth of productive capacity would yield a dollar in rent in the production of Y. Pairs of values represented by CE would undervalue the facilities in the production of X. Those represented by EB would undervalue the facilities in the production of Y. Thus the lines joining A, E, and D represent the minimum possible combinations of values of facilities N and S at which a dollar's worth of productive capacity would produce a dollar's worth of either X or Y. The area above and to the right of AED is the area of feasible solutions to the imputation problem.

The optimal solution is approached geometrically by locating first the lowest isovalue curve touched by the area of feasible solutions. This is curve FG. The pair of values of facilities N and S represented by point E is the optimal solution with v_n equal to $100 and v_s equal to $250. At no other point on, above, or to the right of AED will the total imputed value, as shown by an isovalue line through that point, be as low. At point E a dollar's worth of productive capacity will produce a dollar's worth of either X or Y or both. It is worth noting that the optimal solution to the dual problem, like that of the primal problem is a "corner" solution — the "corner" representing the simultaneous solution of two of the linear constraints on the firm.

A comparison of the dual solution with that of the primal problem shows that they provide the same information. In both we found that facilities M and R were underutilized and that only facilities N and S were utilized to capacity. We found that the minimum values that could be imputed to these two facilities total to an amount equal to the maximum rent that they can produce. Further, in the primal problem we found that maximum rent is obtained when twenty-five units of Y and twelve and one-half units of X are produced. Twenty-five units of Y, yielding $6 in rent per unit, yield a total rent of $150. Twelve and one-half units of X, yielding $8 in rent per unit, provide total rent of $100. From Table 18–1 we can determine that the production of twenty-five units of Y requires 75 percent of the capacity of facility N and 50 percent of the capacity of facility S. The production of twelve and one-half units of X requires 25 percent of the capacity of facility N and 50 percent of the capacity of facility S. From the dual problem, in which v_n and v_s were found to be $100 and $150, respectively, we find that the 75 percent of facility N used in producing Y is valued at $75 while the 50 percent of facility S used in producing Y is valued at $75, also. Thus, the total value imputed to that part of facilities N and S used in the production of Y is $150 — equal to the total rent that Y yields. Similarly, the 25 percent of facility N used in producing X is valued at $25 while the 50 percent of facility S used in its production is valued at $75. The total value of that part of the facilities used in the production of X is $100 — equal to the total rent yielded by product X.

SUMMARY

Linear programming is a technique for solving maximization and minimization problems subject to certain side conditions or constraints. The technique is based on certain assumptions. Decision making is accomplished subject to certain constraints on the decision-making agency;

input and output prices are assumed to be constant; and the firm's input-output, output-output, and input-input relationships are assumed to be linear.

The first problem considered was that of maximization of a firm's output (total revenue) subject to the constraint of a given cost outlay to be made by the firm. The production function of the firm was assumed to be linearly homogeneous and the firm was limited to a choice among four different processes in producing its product output. Isoquants and isocosts were established for the firm. The area of feasible solutions to the problem was established and then the optimal solution was found at the point where the isocost curve touched a corner of one of the firm's isoquants. Changes in cost outlay, given the prices of inputs, will not change which of the processes available is the optimal one but will affect only its level of use. Changes in the relative prices of inputs may result in changes in which of the processes available is the optimal one. If the constraints under which the firm maximizes output are quantity limitations on inputs, these rather than input prices determine the process or processes chosen. In general the number of processes required to carry on its activities will be equal to the number of constraints under which the firm operates.

The second problem was that of maximizing the firm's total rents where multiple outputs are produced and several limited facilities are used to produce them. The processes for producing each output are specified. These together with constraints, determine the area of feasible output solutions to the problem. Given the amount of rent yielded by each output isorent lines for the outputs can be established and the optimal solution of the problem is that at which the area of feasible solutions just touches the highest possible isorent line. This will ordinarily be at a corner of the area of feasible solutions. Not all input or facility quantity limitations need be effective constraints on the firm. The number of effective constraints will generally be equal to the number of processes used. Changes in relative rents yielded by each output may change the optimal solution and consequently, the input limitations which act as effective constraints.

Attention was then turned to the dual solution to a linear programming primal problem. For the primal linear programming problem summarized in the preceding paragraph the dual problem consists of imputing values to the inputs that serve as effective constraints on the firm. The imputed values of the total amounts available of such inputs must be such that their sum will not exceed the firm's total rent. This involves finding the combination of minimum valuations at which a dollar's worth of any one input yields a dollar in rent in any one of the products it is used to produce.

SUGGESTED READINGS

BAUMOL, WILLIAM J., "Activity Analysis in One Lesson," *American Economic Review,* vol. XLVIII (December 1958) pp. 837–873.

DORFMAN, ROBERT, "Mathematical or 'Linear' Programming: A Non-mathematical Exposition," *American Economic Review,* vol. XLIII (December 1953) pp. 797–825.

LIEBHAFSKY, H. H. *The Nature of Price Theory.* Homewood: The Dorsey Press, Inc., 1963, chap. 17.

WU, YUAN-LI and KWANG, CHING-WEN, "An Analytical Comparison of Marginal Analysis and Mathematical Programming in the Theory of the Firm," in Kenneth E. Boulding and W. Allen Spivey, eds., *Linear Programming and the Theory of the Firm.* New York: McGraw Hill Book Co., Inc., 1960, pp. 94–157.

Index